VW Transporter
Service and Repair Manual

Matthew Minter and John Mead

Models covered

VW Transporter with rear-mounted water-cooled petrol engines
1913 cc & 2109 cc

Van, Pick-up and Minibus (Caravelle)

Does not cover Diesel engines or Syncro models, nor features peculiar to specialist body or camper conversions
For models with air-cooled engines see manual No 0638

(3452 - 256 - 3AH1)

© Haynes Publishing 2004

ABCDE
FGHIJ
KLMNO
PQR
2

A book in the **Haynes Service and Repair Manual Series**

ISBN **978 0 85733 987 4**

British Library Cataloguing in Publication Data
A catalogue record for this book is available from the British Library.

Printed in Malaysia

Haynes Publishing
Sparkford, Yeovil, Somerset BA22 7JJ, England

Haynes North America, Inc
859 Lawrence Drive, Newbury Park, California 91320, USA

Printed using NORBRITE BOOK 48.8gsm (CODE: 40N6533) from NORPAC; procurement system certified under Sustainable Forestry Initiative standard. Paper produced is certified to the SFI Certified Fiber Sourcing Standard (CERT - 0094271)

Contents

LIVING WITH YOUR VW TRANSPORTER

Roadside Repairs

Weekly Checks

MAINTENANCE

Routine Maintenance and Servicing

Contents

The VW Transporter covered in this manual is the last of the rear-engined flat four models. The application of water cooling to this venerable engine design enabled it to serve for the best part of another decade. The water-cooled models are quieter and more powerful than their air-cooled forebears, but otherwise the two versions are very similar.

The engine and transmission are mounted at the rear of the vehicle, with drive to the rear wheels. Four-speed and five-speed manual transmissions and a three-speed automatic transmission are available. Clutch operation is hydraulic.

Body styles available as standard are Pick-up, Van and Minibus (Caravelle). Numerous specialist conversions, mostly to camper vans, are in existence. Optional extras include power steering, air conditioning and electric windows.

Maintenance is not particularly difficult, but the layout of some items will not be immediately familiar to the owner who has only had experience of conventional front-engined vehicles.

VW Caravelle Carat

Your VW Transporter manual

The aim of this manual is to help you get the best from your vehicle. It can do so in several ways. It can help you decide what work must be done (even should you choose to get it done by a garage), provide information on routine maintenance and servicing and give a logical course of action and diagnosis when random faults occur. However, it is hoped that you will use the manual by tackling the work yourself. On simpler jobs it may even be quicker than booking the vehicle into a garage and going there twice to leave and collect it. Perhaps most important, a lot of money can be saved by avoiding the costs the garage must charge to cover its labour and overheads.

The manual has drawings and descriptions to show the function of the various components so that their layout can be understood. Then the tasks are described and photographed in a step-by-step sequence so that even a novice can do the work.

References to the 'left' or 'right' of the vehicle are in the sense of a person in the driver's seat facing forwards.

The VW Transporter Team

Haynes manuals are produced by dedicated and enthusiastic people working in close co-operation. The team responsible for the creation of this book included:

Authors	**Matthew Minter** **John Mead**
Sub-editor	**Sophie Yar**
Editor & Page Make-up	**Steve Churchill**
Workshop manager	**Paul Buckland**
Photo Scans	**Steve Tanswell** **Paul Tanswell**
Cover illustration & Line Art	**Roger Healing**

We hope the book will help you to get the maximum enjoyment from your car. By carrying out routine maintenance as described you will ensure your car's reliability and preserve its resale value.

Acknowledgements

Thanks are due to Clive Davage of John Cornick Cars, Yeovil, for the loan of the vehicle seen in many of the photographs in this manual. Thanks are also due to Draper Tools Limited, who provided some of the workshop tools. Special thanks are due to all those people at Sparkford who helped in the production of this manual.

This manual is not a direct reproduction of the vehicle manufacturer's data, and its publication should not be taken as implying any technical approval by the vehicle manufacturers or importers.

We take great pride in the accuracy of information given in this manual, but vehicle manufacturers make alterations and design changes during the production run of a particular vehicle of which they do not inform us. No liability can be accepted by the authors or publishers for loss, damage or injury caused by any errors in, or omissions from the information given.

Working on your car can be dangerous. This page shows just some of the potential risks and hazards, with the aim of creating a safety-conscious attitude.

General hazards

Scalding

• Don't remove the radiator or expansion tank cap while the engine is hot.
• Engine oil, automatic transmission fluid or power steering fluid may also be dangerously hot if the engine has recently been running.

Burning

• Beware of burns from the exhaust system and from any part of the engine. Brake discs and drums can also be extremely hot immediately after use.

Crushing

• When working under or near a raised vehicle, always supplement the jack with axle stands, or use drive-on ramps. *Never venture under a car which is only supported by a jack.*

• Take care if loosening or tightening high-torque nuts when the vehicle is on stands. Initial loosening and final tightening should be done with the wheels on the ground.

Fire

• Fuel is highly flammable; fuel vapour is explosive.
• Don't let fuel spill onto a hot engine.
• Do not smoke or allow naked lights (including pilot lights) anywhere near a vehicle being worked on. Also beware of creating sparks (electrically or by use of tools).
• Fuel vapour is heavier than air, so don't work on the fuel system with the vehicle over an inspection pit.
• Another cause of fire is an electrical overload or short-circuit. Take care when repairing or modifying the vehicle wiring.
• Keep a fire extinguisher handy, of a type suitable for use on fuel and electrical fires.

Electric shock

• Ignition HT voltage can be dangerous, especially to people with heart problems or a pacemaker. Don't work on or near the ignition system with the engine running or the ignition switched on.

• Mains voltage is also dangerous. Make sure that any mains-operated equipment is correctly earthed. Mains power points should be protected by a residual current device (RCD) circuit breaker.

Fume or gas intoxication

• Exhaust fumes are poisonous; they often contain carbon monoxide, which is rapidly fatal if inhaled. Never run the engine in a confined space such as a garage with the doors shut.

• Fuel vapour is also poisonous, as are the vapours from some cleaning solvents and paint thinners.

Poisonous or irritant substances

• Avoid skin contact with battery acid and with any fuel, fluid or lubricant, especially antifreeze, brake hydraulic fluid and Diesel fuel. Don't syphon them by mouth. If such a substance is swallowed or gets into the eyes, seek medical advice.
• Prolonged contact with used engine oil can cause skin cancer. Wear gloves or use a barrier cream if necessary. Change out of oil-soaked clothes and do not keep oily rags in your pocket.
• Air conditioning refrigerant forms a poisonous gas if exposed to a naked flame (including a cigarette). It can also cause skin burns on contact.

Asbestos

• Asbestos dust can cause cancer if inhaled or swallowed. Asbestos may be found in gaskets and in brake and clutch linings. When dealing with such components it is safest to assume that they contain asbestos.

Special hazards

Hydrofluoric acid

• This extremely corrosive acid is formed when certain types of synthetic rubber, found in some O-rings, oil seals, fuel hoses etc, are exposed to temperatures above 400°C. The rubber changes into a charred or sticky substance containing the acid. *Once formed, the acid remains dangerous for years. If it gets onto the skin, it may be necessary to amputate the limb concerned.*
• When dealing with a vehicle which has suffered a fire, or with components salvaged from such a vehicle, wear protective gloves and discard them after use.

The battery

• Batteries contain sulphuric acid, which attacks clothing, eyes and skin. Take care when topping-up or carrying the battery.
• The hydrogen gas given off by the battery is highly explosive. Never cause a spark or allow a naked light nearby. Be careful when connecting and disconnecting battery chargers or jump leads.

Air bags

• Air bags can cause injury if they go off accidentally. Take care when removing the steering wheel and/or facia. Special storage instructions may apply.

Diesel injection equipment

• Diesel injection pumps supply fuel at very high pressure. Take care when working on the fuel injectors and fuel pipes.

⚠️ *Warning: Never expose the hands, face or any other part of the body to injector spray; the fuel can penetrate the skin with potentially fatal results.*

Remember...

DO

• Do use eye protection when using power tools, and when working under the vehicle.

• Do wear gloves or use barrier cream to protect your hands when necessary.

• Do get someone to check periodically that all is well when working alone on the vehicle.

• Do keep loose clothing and long hair well out of the way of moving mechanical parts.

• Do remove rings, wristwatch etc, before working on the vehicle – especially the electrical system.

• Do ensure that any lifting or jacking equipment has a safe working load rating adequate for the job.

DON'T

• Don't attempt to lift a heavy component which may be beyond your capability – get assistance.

• Don't rush to finish a job, or take unverified short cuts.

• Don't use ill-fitting tools which may slip and cause injury.

• Don't leave tools or parts lying around where someone can trip over them. Mop up oil and fuel spills at once.

• Don't allow children or pets to play in or near a vehicle being worked on.

The following pages are intended to help in dealing with common roadside emergencies and breakdowns. You will find more detailed fault finding information at the back of the manual, and repair information in the main chapters.

If your vehicle won't start and the starter motor doesn't turn

☐ If it's a model with automatic transmission, make sure the selector is in 'P' or 'N'.
☐ Look under the driver's seat and make sure that the battery terminals are clean and tight.
☐ Switch on the headlights and try to start the engine. If the headlights go very dim when you're trying to start, the battery is probably flat. Get out of trouble by jump starting (see next page) using a friend's car.

If your vehicle won't start even though the starter motor turns as normal

☐ Is there fuel in the tank?
☐ Is there moisture on electrical components in the engine compartment? Switch off the ignition, then wipe off any obvious dampness with a dry cloth. Spray a water-repellent aerosol product (WD-40 or equivalent) on ignition and fuel system electrical connectors like those shown in the photos. Pay special attention to the ignition coil wiring connector and HT leads. On fuel injection models, check the airflow meter wiring connector.

A Check that the spark plug HT leads are securely connected by pushing them onto the plugs.

B Check that the HT leads are securely connected to the distributor and to the ignition coil, and that the LT wiring connectors are secure.

C Check the security and condition of the battery terminals and leads.

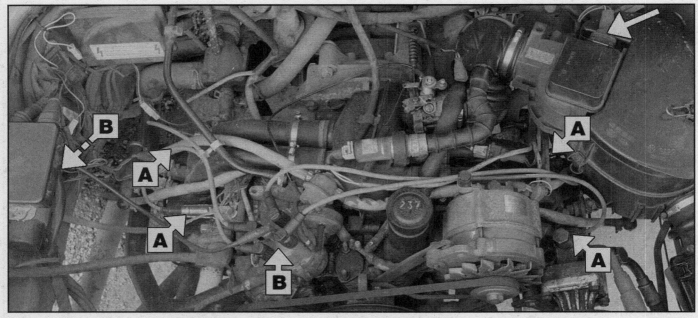

Check that electrical connections are secure (with the ignition switched off) and spray them with a water dispersant spray like WD40 if you suspect a problem due to damp. Check the HT leads at the spark plugs (A) and at the distributor and the ignition coil (B). On fuel injection models check the airflow meter wiring connector (plain arrow).

Jump starting

 HAYNES HiNT *Jump starting will get you out of trouble, but you must correct whatever made the battery go flat in the first place. There are three possibilities:*

1 *The battery has been drained by repeated attempts to start, or by leaving the lights on.*

2 *The charging system is not working properly (alternator drivebelt slack or broken, alternator wiring fault or alternator itself faulty).*

3 *The battery itself is at fault (electrolyte low, or battery worn out).*

When jump-starting a vehicle using a booster battery, observe the following precautions:

✔ Before connecting the booster battery, make sure that the ignition is switched off.

✔ Ensure that all electrical equipment (lights, heater, wipers, etc) is switched off.

✔ Take note of any special precautions printed on the battery case.

✔ Make sure that the booster battery is the same voltage as the discharged one in the vehicle.

✔ If the battery is being jump-started from the battery in another vehicle, the two vehicles MUST NOT TOUCH each other.

✔ Make sure that the transmission is in neutral (or PARK, in the case of automatic transmission).

1 Connect one end of the red jump lead to the positive (+) terminal of the flat battery

2 Connect the other end of the red lead to the positive (+) terminal of the booster battery.

3 Connect one end of the black jump lead to the negative (-) terminal of the booster battery

4 Connect the other end of the black jump lead to the bolt securing the far end of the battery earth lead on the vehicle to be started.

5 Make sure that the jump leads will not come into contact with the fan, drive-belts or other moving parts of the engine.

6 Start the engine using the booster battery and run it at idle speed. Switch on the lights, rear window demister and heater blower motor, then disconnect the jump leads in the reverse order of connection. Turn off the lights etc.

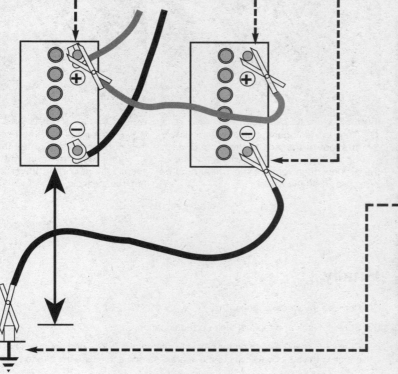

Wheel changing

Some of the details shown here will vary according to model. For instance, the location of the spare wheel. However, the basic principles apply to all models.

⚠️ **Warning: Do not change a wheel in a situation where you risk being hit by another vehicle. On busy roads, try to stop in a lay-by or a gateway. Be wary of passing traffic while changing the wheel - it is easy to become distracted by the job in hand.**

Preparation

- ☐ When a puncture occurs, stop as soon as it is safe to do so.
- ☐ Park on firm level ground, if possible, and well out of the way of other traffic.
- ☐ Use hazard warning lights if necessary.

- ☐ If you have one, use a warning triangle to alert other drivers of your presence.
- ☐ Apply the handbrake and engage first or reverse gear (or Park on models with automatic transmission).

- ☐ Chock the wheel diagonally opposite the one being removed – a couple of large stones will do for this.
- ☐ If the ground is soft, use a flat piece of wood to spread the load under the jack.

Changing the wheel

1 On some models the spare wheel is in the luggage compartment. Undo the central securing bolt to release it.

2 On other models the spare wheel is in a cradle underneath the front of the vehicle. Remove the bolt and pull the safety catch to release it. Keep clear of the cradle as it comes down: it is heavy.

3 Remove the wheel trim, when applicable, for access to the wheel nuts or bolts. Prise the trim off if necessary using a screwdriver or hook it off with the tool supplied.

4 Slacken the wheel nuts or bolts half a turn each using the wheelbrace. Engage the jack head in the jacking point nearest the wheel to be removed.

5 Turn the jack handle clockwise to lower the foot of the jack to the ground. Jack up the vehicle until the wheel is clear of the ground, then remove the wheel nuts or bolts and lift off the wheel.

6 Fit the new wheel and secure it with the nuts or bolts. Tighten the nuts or bolts until they are snug, but do not tighten them fully yet. Then lower the vehicle and remove the jack.

7 Carry out the final tightening of the wheel nuts in criss-cross sequence. The use of a torque wrench is strongly recommended. Refit the wheel trim, when applicable.

Finally...

- ☐ Remove the wheel chocks.
- ☐ Stow the jack and tools in their correct locations.
- ☐ Check the tyre pressure on the wheel just fitted. If it is low, or if you don't have a pressure gauge with you, drive slowly to the nearest garage and inflate the tyre to the right pressure.
- ☐ Have the damaged tyre or wheel repaired as soon as possible.

Identifying leaks

Puddles on the garage floor or drive, or obvious wetness under the bonnet or underneath the car, suggest a leak that needs investigating. It can sometimes be difficult to decide where the leak is coming from, especially if the engine bay is very dirty already. Leaking oil or fluid can also be blown rearwards by the passage of air under the car, giving a false impression of where the problem lies.

 Warning: Most automotive oils and fluids are poisonous. Wash them off skin, and change out of contaminated clothing, without delay.

 The smell of a fluid leaking from the car may provide a clue to what's leaking. Some fluids are distinctively coloured. It may help to clean the car carefully and to park it over some clean paper overnight as an aid to locating the source of the leak.

Remember that some leaks may only occur while the engine is running.

Sump oil

Engine oil may leak from the drain plug...

Oil from filter

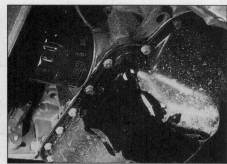

...or from the base of the oil filter.

Gearbox oil

Gearbox oil can leak from the seals at the inboard ends of the driveshafts.

Antifreeze

Leaking antifreeze often leaves a crystalline deposit like this.

Brake fluid

A leak occurring at a wheel is almost certainly brake fluid.

Power steering fluid

Power steering fluid may leak from the pipe connectors on the steering rack.

Towing

When all else fails, you may find yourself having to get a tow home – or of course you may be helping somebody else. Long-distance recovery should only be done by a garage or breakdown service. For shorter distances, DIY towing using another car is easy enough, but observe the following points:

☐ Use a proper tow-rope – they are not expensive. The vehicle being towed must display an 'ON TOW' sign in its rear window.

☐ Always turn the ignition key to the 'on' position when the vehicle is being towed, so that the steering lock is released, and that the direction indicator and brake lights will work.

☐ Only attach the tow-rope to the towing eyes provided.

☐ Before being towed, release the handbrake and select neutral on the transmission.

☐ Note that greater-than-usual pedal pressure will be required to operate the brakes, since the vacuum servo unit is only operational with the engine running.

☐ On models with power steering, greater-than-usual steering effort will also be required.

☐ The driver of the car being towed must keep the tow-rope taut at all times to avoid snatching.

☐ Make sure that both drivers know the route before setting off.

☐ Only drive at moderate speeds and keep the distance towed to a minimum. Drive smoothly and allow plenty of time for slowing down at junctions.

☐ On models with automatic transmission, special precautions apply. If in doubt, do not tow, or transmission damage may result.

Introduction

There are some very simple checks which need only take a few minutes to carry out, but which could save you a lot of inconvenience and expense.

These "Weekly checks" require no great skill or special tools, and the small amount of time they take to perform could prove to be very well spent, for example;

☐ Keeping an eye on tyre condition and pressures, will not only help to stop them wearing out prematurely, but could also save your life.

☐ Many breakdowns are caused by electrical problems. Battery-related faults are particularly common, and a quick check on a regular basis will often prevent the majority of these.

☐ If your vehicle develops a brake fluid leak, the first time you might know about it is when your brakes don't work properly. Checking the level regularly will give advance warning of this kind of problem.

☐ If the oil or coolant levels run low, the cost of repairing any engine damage will be far greater than fixing the leak, for example.

Engine bay check points

◀ **Carburettor model**

A *Engine oil level dipstick*

B *Engine oil filler cap*

C *Coolant top-up tank*

Engine oil level

Before you start
✔ Make sure that your vehicle is on level ground.
✔ Check the oil level before the vehicle is driven, or at least 5 minutes after the engine has been switched off.

 If the oil is checked immediately after driving the vehicle, some of the oil will remain in the upper engine components, resulting in an inaccurate reading on the dipstick!

The correct oil
Modern engines place great demands on their oil. It is very important that the correct oil for your car is used (See "Lubricants, fluids and tyre pressures").

Vehicle Care
● If you have to add oil frequently, you should check whether you have any oil leaks. Place some clean paper under the vehicle overnight, and check for stains in the morning. If there are no leaks, the engine may be burning oil.
● Always maintain the level between the upper and lower dipstick marks (see photo 3). If the level is too low severe engine damage may occur. Oil seal failure may result if the engine is overfilled by adding too much oil.

1 The dipstick is located more or less centrally at the bottom of the rear access hatch. Withdraw the dipstick.

2 Using a clean rag or paper towel remove all oil from the dipstick. Insert the clean dipstick into the tube as far as it will go, then withdraw it again.

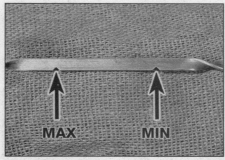

MAX   MIN

3 Note the oil level on the end of the dipstick, which should be between the hatched area on the dipstick. Approximately 1.0 litre of oil will raise the level from the lower mark to the upper mark.

4 Oil is added through the filler tube. Pull out the tube and unscrew the cap. Add the oil slowly, using a funnel if necessary, and checking the level on the dipstick often. Don't overfill (see "Vehicle Care" left).

Coolant level

 Warning: If the antifreeze concentration is too low, the internal components of the engine will rapidly become corroded and serious damage may result.

Vehicle Care
● The cooling system is sealed, so adding coolant should not be necessary on a regular basis. If frequent topping-up is required, it is likely there is a leak. Check the radiator, all hoses and joint faces for signs of staining or wetness, and rectify as necessary.

● It is important that antifreeze is used in the cooling system all year round, not just during the winter months, because it raises the boiling point of the coolant and protects the system against corrosion. Don't top-up with water alone except in an emergency, because the antifreeze will become diluted.

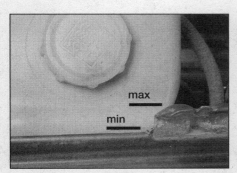

max
min

1 The coolant level varies with engine temperature. When cold, the coolant level should be between the "MAX" and "MIN" marks. When the engine is hot, the level may rise slightly above the "MAX" mark.

2 If topping up is necessary, unscrew the top-up tank cap. (It doesn't matter if the engine is hot - this tank is not under pressure so there is no risk of scalding.) Add a mixture of water and antifreeze to the top-up tank until the coolant level is up to the "MAX" mark. Refit the cap and tighten it securely.

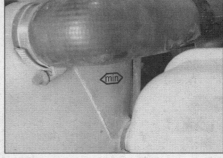

min

3 If the coolant level in the top-up tank was very low, or if the 'low coolant' warning light came on, check the level in the expansion tank. If it's below the "MIN" mark, **wait until the engine is cold**, then unscrew the expansion tank cap, fill it to the brim and refit the cap.

Brake/clutch fluid level

Warning:
● *Brake fluid can harm your eyes and damage painted surfaces, so use extreme caution when handling and pouring it.*
● *Do not use fluid that has been standing open for some time, as it absorbs moisture from the air, which can cause a dangerous loss of braking effectiveness.*

● *Make sure that your vehicle is on level ground.*
● *The fluid level in the reservoir will drop slightly as the brake pads wear down, but the fluid level must never be allowed to drop below the "MIN" mark.*

Safety First!

● If the reservoir requires repeated topping-up this is an indication of a fluid leak somewhere in the system, which should be investigated immediately.

● If a leak is suspected, the vehicle should not be driven until the braking system has been checked. Never take any risks where brakes are concerned.

1 The combined brake and clutch fluid reservoir is mounted under the instrument panel cover. Grip the front of the instrument panel cover and pull it upwards and towards you to release it.

2 The "MAX" and "MIN" marks are indicated on the side of the reservoir. The fluid level must be kept between the marks at all times.

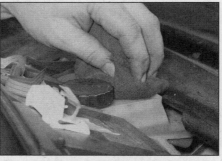
3 If topping-up is necessary, first wipe clean the area around the filler cap to prevent dirt entering the hydraulic system. Unscrew the reservoir cap.

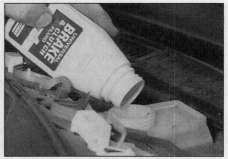
4 Carefully add fluid, taking care not to spill it onto the surrounding components. Use only the specified fluid; mixing different types can cause damage to the system. After topping-up to the correct level, securely refit the cap and wipe off any spilt fluid.

Power steering fluid level

Before you start:
✔ Park the vehicle on level ground.
✔ Set the steering wheel straight-ahead.
✔ The engine must be running.

If the level was much below the "MIN" mark, turn the steering wheel back and forth after topping-up. If the level falls, top up again, then turn the steering wheel again. Keep doing this until the level ceases to fall.

Safety First!
● The need for frequent topping-up indicates a leak, which should be investigated immediately.

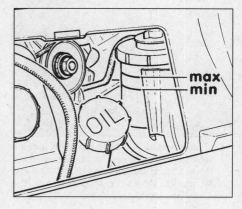

1 The power steering fluid reservoir is on the right-hand side of the engine compartment. If the fluid level is below the "MIN" mark, remove the cap and top up with the specified fluid, then refit the cap.

Battery

Caution: Before carrying out any work on the vehicle battery, read the precautions given in "Safety first" at the start of this manual.

✔ Make sure that the battery tray is in good condition, and that the clamp is tight. Corrosion on the tray, retaining clamp and the battery itself can be removed with a solution of water and baking soda. Thoroughly rinse all cleaned areas with water. Any metal parts damaged by corrosion should be covered with a zinc-based primer, then painted.

✔ Periodically (approximately every three months), check the charge condition of the battery as described in Chapter 5A.

✔ If the battery is flat, and you need to jump start your vehicle, see Roadside Repairs.

1 The battery is located under the right-hand front seat (the driver's seat on RHD models). Check that the battery itself is secure.

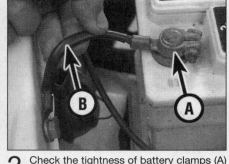

2 Check the tightness of battery clamps (A) to ensure good electrical connections. You should not be able to move them. Also check each cable (B) for cracks and frayed conductors.

Battery corrosion can be kept to a minimum by applying a layer of petroleum jelly to the clamps and terminals after they are reconnected.

3 If corrosion (white, fluffy deposits) is evident, remove the cables from the battery terminals, clean them with a small wire brush, then refit them. Automotive stores sell a tool for cleaning the battery post . . .

4 . . . as well as the battery cable clamps

Screen washer fluid level

Screenwash additives not only keep the winscreen clean during foul weather, they also prevent the washer system freezing in cold weather - which is when you are likely to need it most. Don't top up using plain water as the screenwash will become too diluted, and will freeze during cold weather. *On no account use coolant antifreeze in the washer system - this could discolour or damage paintwork.*

1 Fluid for the windscreen washer is stored in a plastic reservoir, the filler cap of which is located under the carpet in the left-hand front footwell. It also supplies the headlight washer, when fitted.

2 When topping-up the reservoir, add a screenwash additive in the quantities recommended on the bottle.

3 On models with a rear window washer, the reservoir is located on the right-hand side of the luggage area.

Tyre condition and pressure

It is very important that tyres are in good condition, and at the correct pressure - having a tyre failure at any speed is highly dangerous. Tyre wear is influenced by driving style - harsh braking and acceleration, or fast cornering, will all produce more rapid tyre wear. As a general rule, the front tyres wear out faster than the rears. Interchanging the tyres from front to rear ("rotating" the tyres) may result in more even wear. However, if this is completely effective, you may have the expense of replacing all four tyres at once! Remove any nails or stones embedded in the tread before they penetrate the tyre to cause deflation. If removal of a nail does reveal that the tyre has been punctured, refit the nail so that its point of penetration is marked. Then immediately change the wheel, and have the tyre repaired by a tyre dealer.

Regularly check the tyres for damage in the form of cuts or bulges, especially in the sidewalls. Periodically remove the wheels, and clean any dirt or mud from the inside and outside surfaces. Examine the wheel rims for signs of rusting, corrosion or other damage. Light alloy wheels are easily damaged by "kerbing" whilst parking; steel wheels may also become dented or buckled. A new wheel is very often the only way to overcome severe damage.

New tyres should be balanced when they are fitted, but it may become necessary to re-balance them as they wear, or if the balance weights fitted to the wheel rim should fall off. Unbalanced tyres will wear more quickly, as will the steering and suspension components. Wheel imbalance is normally signified by vibration, particularly at a certain speed (typically around 50 mph). If this vibration is felt only through the steering, then it is likely that just the front wheels need balancing. If, however, the vibration is felt through the whole car, the rear wheels could be out of balance. Wheel balancing should be carried out by a tyre dealer or garage.

1 *Tread Depth - visual check*
The original tyres have tread wear safety bands (B), which will appear when the tread depth reaches approximately 1.6 mm. The band positions are indicated by a triangular mark on the tyre sidewall (A).

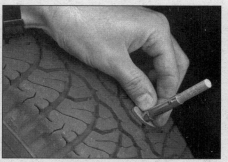

2 *Tread Depth - manual check*
Alternatively, tread wear can be monitored with a simple, inexpensive device known as a tread depth indicator gauge.

3 *Tyre Pressure Check*
Check the tyre pressures regularly with the tyres cold. Do not adjust the tyre pressures immediately after the vehicle has been used, or an inaccurate setting will result.

Tyre tread wear patterns

Shoulder Wear

Underinflation (wear on both sides)
Under-inflation will cause overheating of the tyre, because the tyre will flex too much, and the tread will not sit correctly on the road surface. This will cause a loss of grip and excessive wear, not to mention the danger of sudden tyre failure due to heat build-up.
Check and adjust pressures
Incorrect wheel camber (wear on one side)
Repair or renew suspension parts
Hard cornering
Reduce speed!

Centre Wear

Overinflation
Over-inflation will cause rapid wear of the centre part of the tyre tread, coupled with reduced grip, harsher ride, and the danger of shock damage occurring in the tyre casing.
Check and adjust pressures

If you sometimes have to inflate your car's tyres to the higher pressures specified for maximum load or sustained high speed, don't forget to reduce the pressures to normal afterwards.

Uneven Wear

Front tyres may wear unevenly as a result of wheel misalignment. Most tyre dealers and garages can check and adjust the wheel alignment (or "tracking") for a modest charge.
Incorrect camber or castor
Repair or renew suspension parts
Malfunctioning suspension
Repair or renew suspension parts
Unbalanced wheel
Balance tyres
Incorrect toe setting
Adjust front wheel alignment
Note: *The feathered edge of the tread which typifies toe wear is best checked by feel.*

Wiper blades

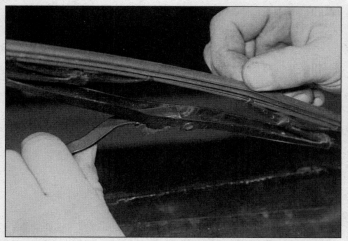 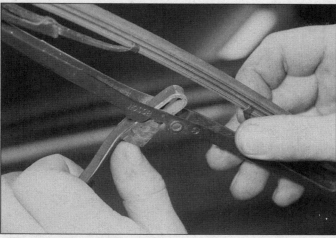

1 Check the condition of the wiper blades; if they are cracked or show any signs of deterioration, or if the glass swept area is smeared, renew them. Wiper blades should be renewed annually.

2 To remove a windscreen wiper blade, pull the arm fully away from the screen until it locks. Swivel the blade through 90°, press the locking tab with your fingers and slide the blade out of the arm's hooked end.

Lubricants and fluids

Engine oil grade . . . .   Multigrade engine oil to API SF or SG,
VW 501 01 or equivalent

Engine oil viscosity:

    Temperate climates (minimum temperature -15° C) . . .   SAE 15W/40 or 15W/50*

    Cold climates (minimum -20° C, maximum +15° C) . . .   SAE 10W/30 or 10W/40

    Very cold climates (always below -10° C) . . . .   SAE 5W/20 or 5W/30

20W/40 or 20W/50 can be used at temperatures above -10° C

Manual transmission oil . . . .   Gear oil, SAE 80, to API GL 4 or equivalent

Automatic transmission fluid . . . .   Dexron® type ATF

Automatic transmission final drive . . . .   Gear oil, SAE 90, to API GL 5 or equivalent

Power steering fluid . . . .   Dexron® type ATF

Brake and clutch hydraulic fluid . . . .   FMVSS DOT 4 or equivalent

Choosing your engine oil

Engines need oil, not only to lubricate moving parts and minimise wear, but also to maximise power output and to improve fuel economy.

HOW ENGINE OIL WORKS

• Beating friction

Without oil, the moving surfaces inside your engine will rub together, heat up and melt, quickly causing the engine to seize. Engine oil creates a film which separates these moving parts, preventing wear and heat build-up.

• Cooling hot-spots

Temperatures inside the engine can exceed 1000° C. The engine oil circulates and acts as a coolant, transferring heat from the hot-spots to the sump.

• Cleaning the engine internally

Good quality engine oils clean the inside of your engine, collecting and dispersing combustion deposits and controlling them until they are trapped by the oil filter or flushed out at oil change.

OIL CARE - FOLLOW THE CODE

To handle and dispose of used engine oil safely, always:

0800 66 33 66
www.oilbankline.org.uk

• *Avoid skin contact with used engine oil. Repeated or prolonged contact can be harmful.*
• *Dispose of used oil and empty packs in a responsible manner in an authorised disposal site. Call 0800 663366 to find the one nearest to you. Never tip oil down drains or onto the ground.*

Tyre pressures (cold)

	Front	Rear
175 R 14 C	2.8 bar (41 psi)	3.3 bar (48 psi)
185 R 14 C	2.6 bar (38 psi)	3.8 bar (55 psi)
185 SR 14 Reinforced	2.3 bar (33 psi)	2.9 bar (42 psi)
185 SR 14 C 6PR	2.7 bar (39 psi)	3.3 bar (48 psi)
205/70 R 14	2.1 bar (30 psi)	2.5 bar (36 psi)

Note: *Due to the great variety of tyre sizes and vehicle equipment, the above recommendations should be regarded only as a guide. Refer to the sticker on the left-hand front door pillar for vehicle-specific information, or consult a tyre specialist.*

Chapter 1
Routine maintenance and servicing

Contents

Degrees of difficulty

Easy, suitable for novice with little experience	**Fairly easy,** suitable for beginner with some experience	**Fairly difficult,** suitable for competent DIY mechanic	**Difficult,** suitable for experienced DIY mechanic	**Very difficult,** suitable for expert DIY or professional

Lubricants and fluids .... Refer to *"Weekly Checks"*

Capacities

Engine oil:
Drain and refill (including filter) .... 4.5 litres
Difference between MAX and MIN dipstick marks .... 1 litre approx
Cooling system .... 17.5 litres approx
Fuel tank .... 60 litres approx
Manual gearbox and final drive .... 3.5 litres
Automatic transmission fluid:
Drain and refill .... 3 litres approx
Difference between MAX and MIN dipstick marks:
Dipstick without tag .... 0.23 litre
Dipstick with tag .... 0.33 litre
Automatic transmission final drive .... 1.25 litres

Cooling system

Coolant mixture for protection to:	Antifreeze	Water
-25° C	40% (7 litres)	60% (10.5 litres)
-35° C	50% (8.75 litres)	50% (8.75 litres)

Fuel system

	Idle speed	Exhaust gas CO level at idle
Adjusting value (idle speed stabilisation disconnected when applicable):		
Engine code DF	750 ± 50 rpm	1.5 ± 0.5 %
Engine code DG	900 ± 50 rpm	1.5 ± 0.5 %
Engine code DJ	800 ± 50 rpm	2.0 ± 0.5 %
Engine code EY	850 ± 50 rpm	2.0 ± 1.0 %
Engine codes GW	880 ± 50 rpm	1.3 ± 0.5 %
Engine codes MV, SS	880 ± 50 rpm	0.7 ± 0.4 %

Fuel octane minimum requirement (refer to Chapter 4 for further details):
Engine codes DF and DG .... 91 RON
Engine code EY .... 83 RON
Engine codes GW and DJ .... 98 RON*
Engine codes MV and SS .... 91 RON unleaded
95 RON with timing adjustment - see Chapter 5B

Ignition system

Firing order 1-4-3-2
Location of No 1 cylinder .... Front right
Direction of distributor rotor arm rotation .... Clockwise (viewed from above)
Ignition timing .... See Chapter 5B

Spark plugs	Type	Electrode gap
1.9 litre:		
Engine codes DF and DG:		
Ignition coil with green sticker	Bosch WR 7 LT+	1.0 mm
Ignition coil with grey sticker	Bosch WR 7 D+	0.8 mm
Engine code EY	Bosch WR 7 CP	0.7 mm
Engine code GW	Bosch W 7 CC 0	0.7 mm
2.1 litre:		
Engine codes MV and SS	Bosch W 7 CC 0	0.7 mm
Engine code DJ:		
Ignition coil with green sticker	Bosch WR 7 LT+	1.0 mm
Ignition coil with grey sticker	Bosch WR 7 D+	0.8 mm

Braking system

Minimum front brake pad lining thickness .... 2.0 mm
Minimum rear brake shoe lining thickness .... 2.5 mm

Auxiliary drivebelts

Alternator/coolant pump drivebelt deflection:
New belt .... 10 mm approx
Used belt .... 15 mm approx
Air conditioning compressor/power steering pump drivebelt deflection:
New or used belt .... 10 to 15 mm

Torque wrench settings

	Nm	lbf ft
Engine oil drain plug	25	18
Wheel bolts	180	133
Spark plugs:		
1.9 litre engines	20	15
2.1 litre engines	25	18
Automatic transmission sump bolts	20	15

The maintenance intervals in this manual are provided with the assumption that you, not the dealer, will be carrying out the work. If you wish to keep your vehicle in peak condition at all times, you may decide to perform some of these procedures more often. We encourage frequent maintenance, because it enhances the efficiency, performance and resale value of your vehicle.

Maintenance intervals are specified both in mileage and in time. The interval observed should be whichever works out as more frequent - so vehicles which cover less than 10 000 miles a year should have the lubrication service every 6 months, the regular service every 12 months, and so on. This is necessary because some automotive fluids and components deteriorate with age as well as with use.

The 5000 mile/6-month lubrication service is only specified by VW as being necessary for early models (up to and including 1985). Our recommendation is that it should be carried out for all models in the interests of minimising engine wear. The intervals specified for certain other service operations have also been extended for later models; these are indicated in the service schedule.

If the vehicle is driven in dusty areas, used to tow a trailer, or driven frequently at slow speeds (idling in traffic) or on short journeys, more frequent maintenance intervals are recommended. If the vehicle is to be laid up for the winter, the engine oil and filter should be changed at the beginning of the lay-up period even if it is not otherwise due.

Maintenance is essential for ensuring safety and for getting the best in terms of performance and economy from your vehicle. Over the years, the need for periodic lubrication - oiling, greasing, and so on - has been drastically reduced, if not eliminated. This has unfortunately tended to lead some owners to think that because no action is required, components either no longer exist, or will last for ever. This is certainly not the case; it is essential to carry out regular visual examination comprehensively to spot any possible defects at an early stage before they develop into major expensive repairs.

Every 250 miles (400 km) or weekly

☐ Refer to "Weekly checks"

Lubrication service, every 5000 miles (7500 km) or 6 months - whichever comes sooner

Not specified at this interval, but recommended, for 1986 and later models

☐ Renew the engine oil and filter (Section 3).
☐ Check front brake pad thickness (Section 4).
☐ Check battery electrolyte level (Section 5).

Regular service, every 10 000 miles (15 000 km) or 12 months - whichever comes sooner

As well as the lubrication service, carry out the following

☐ Check for fluid leaks (Section 6).
☐ Check ignition timing (Section 7).
☐ Check idle speed and mixture (Section 8).
☐ Check exhaust system (Section 9).
☐ Check manual gearbox oil level (Section 10).
☐ Check automatic transmission fluid level (Section 11).
☐ Check steering components (Section 12).
☐ Check suspension and driveshaft rubber gaiters (Section 13).
☐ Check rear brake shoes for wear (Section 14).
☐ Check operation of footbrake and handbrake (Section 15).

Regular service, every 10 000 miles (15 000 km) or 12 months - whichever comes sooner (continued)

☐ Check auxiliary drivebelt(s) (Section 16).
☐ Lubricate hinges and locks (Section 17).
☐ Check HT leads and distributor cap (Section 18).
☐ Renew spark plugs (Section 19).*
☐ Check antifreeze concentration (Section 20).
☐ Check underbody sealant (Section 21).*

Specified at 20 000 miles/2 years for 1986 and later models

Extended service, every 20 000 miles (30 000 km) or 2 years - whichever comes sooner

As well as the lubrication and regular services, carry out the following:

☐ Renew air cleaner element (Section 22).
☐ Renew fuel filter (Section 23).
☐ Renew brake hydraulic fluid (Section 24).
☐ Renew coolant (Section 25).

Long-term service, every 30 000 miles (45 000 km) or 3 years - whichever comes sooner

As well as the lubrication service, carry out the following:

☐ Renew automatic transmission fluid (Section 26).*

Specified at 40 000 miles/4 years for 1986 and later models

Engine compartment seen through rear access hatch - carburettor engine in a pick-up

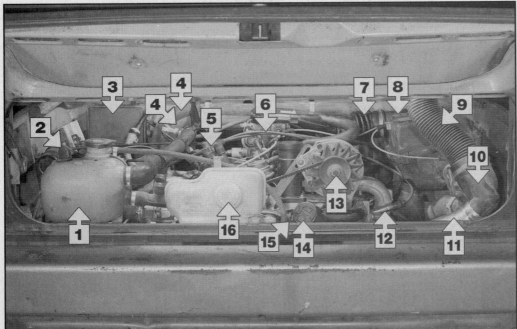

1 Cooling system expansion tank
2 Low coolant level sensor
3 Electrical junction box
4 Main coolant hoses
5 Distributor cap
6 Carburettor
7 Carburettor air intake trunking
8 Air cleaner housing
9 Cold air intake
10 Intake air temperature control unit
11 Hot air intake
12 No 2 spark plug cap
13 Alternator
14 Engine oil filler cap
15 Engine oil dipstick
16 Cooling system top-up tank cap

Engine compartment seen from above - carburettor engine in a pick-up

1 Engine oil filler
2 Engine oil dipstick
3 Cooling system top-up tank
4 Cooling system expansion tank
5 Main coolant hoses
6 No 4 spark plug cap
7 No 3 spark plug cap
8 Brake servo non-return valve
9 Coolant bleed valve
10 Carburettor
11 Idle cut-off valve
12 Carburettor air intake
13 Crankcase ventilation (breather) hose
14 Alternator
15 Alternator / coolant pump drivebelt
16 Breather housing
17 Fuel pump
18 Distributor cap
19 Inlet manifold heater thermoswitch
20 Distributor vacuum unit
21 Automatic choke vacuum unit

Engine compartment seen from above - fuel injected engine in a minibus

1 Ignition coil
2 Fuel injection relay box
3 Electrical junction box
4 Idle speed control valve
5 Throttle housing
6 Airflow meter
7 Air cleaner
8 Power steering pump
9 Alternator
10 Breather housing
11 Fuel pressure regulator
12 Distributor
13 Coolant pump
14 Expansion tank cap
15 No 4 spark plug cap
16 Fuel injectors

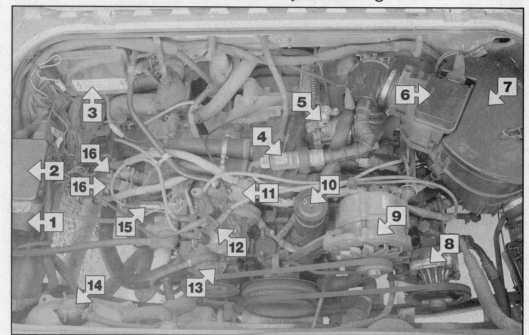

Front underside of a pick-up

1 Spare wheel carrier
   (pick-up models only)
2 Steering gear assembly
3 Radius rods
4 Shock absorber lower
   mountings
5 Anti-roll bar
6 Brake calipers

Typical rear underside

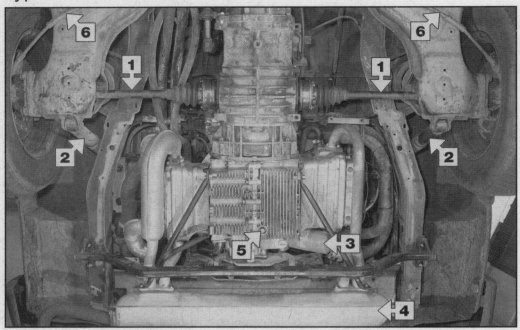

1 Driveshafts
2 Shock absorbers
3 Oil filter
4 Exhaust silencer
5 Engine oil drain plug
6 Handbrake cables

Maintenance procedures

1 Introduction

1 This Chapter is designed to help the home mechanic maintain his or her vehicle for safety, economy, long life and peak performance.
2 The Chapter contains a master maintenance schedule, followed by Sections dealing specifically with each task in the schedule. Visual checks, adjustments, component renewal and other helpful items are included. Refer to the accompanying illustrations of the engine compartment and the underside of the vehicle for the locations of the various components.
3 Servicing your vehicle according to the mileage/time maintenance schedule and the following Sections will provide a planned maintenance programme, which should result in a long and reliable service life. This is a comprehensive plan, so maintaining some items but not others at the specified intervals will not produce the same results.
4 As you service your vehicle, you will discover that many of the procedures can - and should - be grouped together, because of the particular procedure being performed, or because of the proximity of two otherwise-unrelated components to one another. For example, if the vehicle is raised for any reason, the exhaust can be inspected at the same time as the suspension and steering components.
5 The first step in this maintenance programme is to prepare yourself before the

actual work begins. Read through all the Sections relevant to the work to be carried out, then make a list and gather all the parts and tools required. If a problem is encountered which cannot be resolved by referring to the manual, seek advice from a VW dealer or other specialist.

2 Recovering from neglected maintenance

1 If, from the time the vehicle is new, the routine maintenance schedule is followed closely, frequent checks made of fluid levels and high-wear items, as recommended, the vehicle will be kept in relatively good running condition. The need for additional work will be minimised.
2 It is possible that there will be times when the engine is running poorly due to the lack of regular maintenance. This is even more likely if a used vehicle which has not received regular maintenance is purchased. In such cases, additional work may need to be carried out.
3 If engine wear is suspected, a compression test (refer to Chapter 2A) will provide valuable information regarding the overall performance of the main internal components. Such a test can be used as a basis to decide on the extent of the work to be carried out. If, for example, a compression test indicates serious internal engine wear, conventional maintenance as described in this Chapter will not greatly improve the performance of the engine. It may

also prove a waste of time and money, unless extensive overhaul work is carried out first.
4 The following series of operations are those most often required to improve the performance of a poorly running engine:

Primary operations

a) Clean and inspect the battery (See "Weekly Checks" and Section 5).
b) Check all the engine related fluids (See "Weekly Checks").
c) Check the condition and tension of the auxiliary drivebelt(s) (Section 16).
d) Renew the spark plugs (Section 19).
e) Inspect the distributor cap, rotor arm and HT leads (Section 18).
f) Check the condition of the air cleaner element, and renew if necessary (Section 22).
g) Renew the fuel filter (Section 23).
h) Check the condition of all hoses, and check for fluid leaks (Section 6).
i) Check the ignition timing and the idle speed and mixture settings (Sections 7 and 8).

5 If the above operations do not prove fully effective, carry out the following secondary operations:

Secondary operations

All items listed under "Primary operations", plus the following:
a) Check the charging system (Chapter 5A).
b) Check the ignition system (Chapter 5B).
c) Check the fuel system (Chapter 4).
d) Renew the distributor cap and rotor arm (Section 18).
e) Renew the ignition HT leads (Section 18).

3.6 Slackening the sump drain plug

3.9 Slackening the oil filter with a chain wrench

Lubrication service, every 5000 miles (7500 km) or 6 months

3 Engine oil and filter - renewal

1 Frequent oil changes are the best preventive maintenance the home mechanic can give the engine, because ageing oil becomes diluted and contaminated, which leads to premature engine wear.

2 Make sure that you have all the necessary tools and materials before you begin this procedure:

A 5-litre can of engine oil
A new oil filter
A new sump drain plug washer
A spanner to fit the sump drain plug
An oil filter removal tool
Disposable gloves
Plenty of rags or newspapers for mopping up spills

3 To avoid any possibility of scalding, and to protect yourself from possible skin irritants and other harmful contaminants in used engine oils, it is advisable to wear gloves when carrying out this work.

4 Engine oil is best drained warm, when it flows more freely and any contaminants are still in suspension, so take the vehicle for a short run before starting work.

5 Access to the underside of the engine is good when compared with most cars. If it is wished to raise the vehicle to improve access, do so without too much tilting, otherwise all the oil will not be able to drain out.

6 Remove the oil filler cap, then place the drain pan under the sump. Slacken the drain plug using a spanner (see illustration), then unscrew it the rest of the way by hand and allow the oil to drain into the container.

HAYNES HiNT *As the drain plug releases from the threads, move it away quickly so that the stream of oil running out of the sump goes into the drain pan and not up your sleeve!*

7 Remove the old washer from the drain plug. Wipe the drain plug clean and fit a new washer.

8 When the oil has finished draining, wipe clean around the drain plug hole, then refit and tighten the drain plug.

9 Move the drain pan under the oil filter. Slacken the oil filter by turning it anti-clockwise - it may be possible to do this by hand, but otherwise a chain or strap wrench will be needed (see illustration). Once the filter has started turning, unscrew it all the way by hand and remove it.

Caution: Be careful, the filter is full of oil!

10 Wipe clean around the filter seat on the crankcase. Smear a little clean engine oil on the sealing ring of the new filter, then screw it into place by hand (see illustrations). Unless

there are instructions to the contrary supplied with the new filter, tighten it by hand only - don't use any tools.

11 Pour about two-thirds of the specified quantity of new oil into the engine via the filler tube. Allow a couple of minutes for the oil to trickle down, then check the level on the dipstick. Keep checking and topping up until the level is up to the high mark on the dipstick. Don't overfill.

12 Start the engine. It will take a couple of seconds for the oil pressure warning light to go out while the new filter fills with oil; don't rev the engine until the light is out. Check that there are no leaks from around the drain plug or oil filter. Tighten a little further if necessary, but don't overtighten.

13 Switch off the engine. Wait a few minutes, then check the oil level and top up again to the high mark. (The level fell because the new filter absorbed some oil.)

14 Dispose of the old oil and filter safely (see *"General Repair Procedures"* at the end of the manual).

3.10A Smear a little clean oil on the sealing ring of the new filter. . .

3.10B . . . then screw it into position

4.2A Inspect the thickness of the brake pads through the hole in the front of the caliper

4.2B Friction lining thickness 'X' must be above the minimum specified (pad removed for clarity)

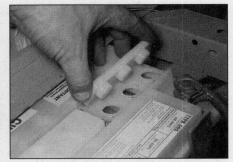

5.3A To top up the battery electrolyte, remove the cell covers . . .

4 Front brake pads - check

 Warning: Brake lining dust may contain asbestos. Refer to 'Safety First!' and to the warnings in Chapter 10.

1 Slacken the front wheel bolts. Chock the rear wheels, raise and support the front of the vehicle (see *"Jacking and vehicle support"*) and remove the front wheels.

2 Inspect the thickness of the brake pad friction linings through the hole in the front of the caliper **(see illustrations)**. The minimum lining thickness is given in the Specifications.

3 If one or more pads are worn down to the specified minimum, all four must be renewed as described in Chapter 10.

4 Also inspect the brake calipers for signs of fluid leaks, the brake pipes and hoses for deterioration and the brake discs for cracks, scores or other damage. Again, refer to Chapter 10 for more details.

5 Refit the wheels and hand-tighten the wheel bolts. Lower the vehicle to the ground and tighten the wheel bolts to the specified torque.

5 Battery electrolyte level - check

 Warning: The battery gives off an explosive mixture of gases. It also contains sulphuric acid. Refer to 'Safety First' and to the warnings in Chapter 5A.

1 This check is not needed if a so-called 'maintenance-free' battery is fitted. Look for instructions on top of the battery case.

2 If a conventional battery is fitted, check that the electrolyte (liquid) level is up to the minimum mark on the outside of the battery case. If there are no marks, or if the level cannot be seen from outside, remove the cell covers and check that the electrolyte is above the tops of the plates inside the battery. Check by shining a torch in through the cell cover holes - **do not** use a naked flame and **do not** stick your finger in to check the level.

3 If topping up is necessary, remove the cell covers if not already done and top up with distilled or de-ionised water **(see illustrations)**. Do not overfill. Tap water is best avoided because it can contain mineral salts which will damage the battery. Never add acid.

5.3B . . . and add distilled water

 HAYNES HINT *Water obtained when defrosting a fridge or freezer is suitable for topping-up the battery, provided it is still clean.*

4 If one or two cells repeatedly need topping-up while the others do not, the battery is probably on the way out. If all the cells repeatedly need topping-up, this may be a sign of overcharging. Refer to Chapter 5A or consult an auto electrician.

5 Refit the cell covers on completion and mop up any spillage.

Regular service, every 10 000 miles (15 000 km) or 12 months

6 Fluid leaks - check

Engine and transmission

1 Visually inspect the engine and transmission joint faces, gaskets and seals for any signs of water or oil leaks. Pay particular attention to the areas around the rocker covers, pushrod tubes, oil filter and crankcase joint faces. Remember that, over a period of time, some slight seepage from these areas is to be expected - what you are really looking for is any indication of a serious leak. Should a leak be found, renew the offending gasket or oil seal by referring to the appropriate Chapters in this manual.

2 Also check the security and condition of all the engine-related pipes and hoses. Ensure that all cable ties or securing clips are in place, and in good condition. Clips that are broken or missing can lead to chafing of the hoses, pipes or wiring, which could cause more serious problems in the future.

Cooling system

3 Carefully check the coolant hoses and pipes along their entire length. (This will involve getting under the vehicle and also removing the front grilles.). Renew any hose that is cracked, swollen or deteriorated. Cracks will show up better if the hose is squeezed. Pay close attention to the clips that secure the hoses to the cooling system components. Hose clips can pinch and puncture hoses, resulting in cooling system leaks. It is always beneficial to renew hose clips whenever possible.

4 Inspect all the cooling system components (radiator, joint faces, etc.) for leaks.

 HAYNES HINT *A leak in the cooling system will usually show up as white or rust coloured deposits on the area adjoining the leak.*

5 Where any problems are found on cooling system components, renew the component or gasket with reference to Chapter 3.

Fuel system

6 With the vehicle raised, inspect the petrol tank and filler neck for punctures, cracks and other damage. The connection between the filler neck and tank is especially critical.

6.9 Inspecting a brake flexible hose

Sometimes a rubber filler neck or connecting hose will leak due to loose retaining clamps or deteriorated rubber.

7 Carefully check all rubber hoses and metal fuel lines leading away from the petrol tank. Check for loose connections, deteriorated hoses, crimped lines, and other damage. Follow the lines to the rear of the vehicle, carefully inspecting them all the way. Renew damaged sections as necessary.

 HAYNES HiNT *The fabric-covered fuel hoses fitted to some models are particularly prone to deterioration. If they look or feel moist with fuel they must be renewed without delay.*

8 From within the engine compartment, check the security of all fuel hose attachments and unions, and inspect the fuel hoses and vacuum hoses for kinks, chafing and deterioration.

Clutch and brake pipes and hoses

9 Inspect the clutch and brake flexible hoses for splits, cracks or other damage (see illustration). Also inspect the rigid pipes for rust or impact damage.

Power steering

10 Where applicable, check the condition of the power steering fluid hoses and pipes.

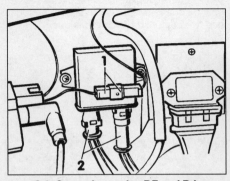

8.4 On engine codes DF and DJ, disconnect the electrical plugs (2) from the idle stabilizing unit and join them together. On engine code DJ, also disconnect the single connector (1)

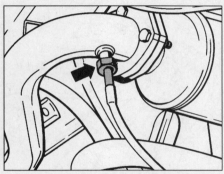

8.3 Exhaust gas analyser connection point (arrowed) on models with catalyst

7 Ignition timing - check

1 Refer to Chapter 5B. There is no reason for the ignition timing to be incorrect, but there is no point in trying to adjust the idle speed and mixture without checking the ignition timing first.

8 Idle speed and mixture - check

Caution: Some fuel system adjusting screws may be fitted with tamperproof caps. The purpose of such caps is to discourage, and to detect, adjustment by unqualified persons. In some territories (though not yet in the UK) it is illegal to have a vehicle on the road with broken or missing tamperproof caps.

⚠️ *Warning: Do not run the engine in a confined space (risk of carbon monoxide poisoning).*

1 Accurate checking of the idle speed and mixture requires a tachometer (rev counter) and an exhaust gas analyser (CO meter). In practice it is suggested that most owners content themselves with making small adjustments to the idle speed 'by ear', and if

necessary take the vehicle to a garage for an exhaust emission check. The check is part of the MoT in any case. If suitable equipment is available, proceed as follows.

2 Have the engine at normal operating temperature and make sure the ignition timing is correct. There must not be any leaks in the exhaust system. Any other work which may affect idle speed or mixture (eg spark plug or air cleaner element renewal) must also have been performed. The electric cooling fan must not be running during the checks, and the automatic choke (when applicable) must be fully released.

3 Connect up the tachometer and the exhaust gas analyser (engine stopped, ignition off) as instructed by their manufacturers. Note that on catalyst-equipped models the exhaust gas analyser needs to be connected at the take-off point on the left-hand exhaust pipe, using a threaded adaptor (see illustration).

Engine codes DF, EY (34 PICT carburettor)

4 On engine code DF only, disconnect the two electrical plugs at the idle stabilising unit and join them together (see illustration).
5 On all engines, disconnect the crankcase ventilation hose from the air inlet trunking on top of the carburettor. Leave the hose open.
6 Start the engine and allow it to idle. Check the idle speed on the tachometer against that given in the Specifications. If adjustment is necessary, turn the screw shown (see illustration).
7 Check the exhaust gas CO level against that given in the Specifications. If adjustment is necessary, turn the screw shown (see illustration).
8 Recheck the idle speed and readjust if necessary, then recheck the CO level.
9 On engine code DF only, reconnect the idle stabilising unit plugs and recheck the CO level; make a final adjustment if necessary.

Engine code DG (2E3 carburettor)

10 Proceed as just described for the 34 PICT carburettor, but note the locations of the adjustment screws (see illustration).

8.6 Adjusting the idle speed - 34 PICT carburettor

8.7 Adjusting the idle CO level (mixture) - 34 PICT carburettor

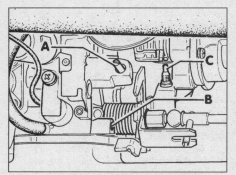

8.10 Idle adjustment points - 2E3 carburettor

A Idle speed
B CO level
C Fast idle screw (must not be on fast idle cam)

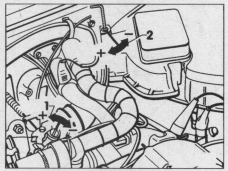

8.14 Idle adjustment points - Digijet

1 Idle speed
2 CO level

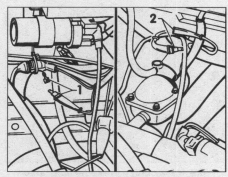

8.16 On catalyst-equipped models disconnect the Lambda sensor (1) and idle speed control valve (2)

Engine code DG (2E4 carburettor)

11 Idle speed is not adjustable on this carburettor. The CO adjustment screw is in the same place as on the 2E3 carburettor.

Engine codes GW, DJ (Digijet)

12 Disconnect and plug the distributor vacuum retard hose and the crankcase ventilation hose.
13 Disconnect the two electrical plugs at the idle stabilising unit and join them together. On the 2.1 litre engine (code DJ), also disconnect the single connector in front of the idle stabilising unit (see illustration 8.4).
14 Adjust the idle speed and CO level as described in paragraphs 6 to 8, noting the locations of the adjustment screws **(see illustration)**.

Engine codes MV, SS (Digifant with catalytic converter)

15 If an evaporative emission control charcoal canister is fitted, clamp the canister-to-air cleaner hose.
16 Disconnect the Lambda sensor and idle speed control valve connectors **(see illustration)**.
17 Adjust the idle speed and CO level as described in paragraphs 6 to 8. The

adjustment screws are located in the same place as for the Digijet system (see illustration 8.14).

All engines

18 Stop the engine and disconnect the test gear. Remake the original electrical and hose connections.
19 Restart the engine and allow it to idle. When applicable, operate accessories such as air conditioning, or turn the steering wheel on models with power steering, and check that a satisfactory idle speed is maintained.
20 Fit new tamperproof caps where required.

9 Exhaust system - check

1 With the engine off, check the security of the exhaust system. Perform a visual check to confirm that there are no obvious holes or other damage.
2 Start the engine and check underneath for leaks, which can often be heard. Holding a rag over the exhaust pipe will increase the pressure in the system and make any leaks more obvious. This job is made easier if you have access to a ramp.

3 Temporary repairs may be effected using proprietary exhaust repair kits. However, such measures are only short-term, and if parts of the system are badly corroded renewal is the only satisfactory long-term solution.

10 Manual gearbox oil level - check

1 If it is wished to raise the vehicle to improve access, do so in such a way that keeps it level, otherwise a false reading may result.
2 Wipe clean around the gearbox oil filler/level plug, then unscrew and remove the plug **(see illustrations)**.
3 Using your finger or a length of wire, check the level of oil relative to the plug hole. On 4-speed 091 gearboxes the oil level should be up to the bottom edge of the plug hole. On all other gearboxes the level should be approximately 15 mm below the bottom edge of the hole.
4 Top up if required via the filler/level plug hole, using the specified grade of gear oil **(see illustration)**.
5 Refit and tighten the filler/level plug.
6 If frequent topping-up is required, this can only be due to a leak, which should be found and fixed before it becomes serious.

10.2A Unscrew the gearbox filler/level plug . . .

10.2B . . . and remove it

10.4 Topping up the gearbox oil level

11 Automatic transmission fluid level - check

1 The engine and transmission must be at normal operating temperature (immediately after a short run) and the vehicle must be parked on level ground.

2 With the engine idling and 'P' selected, withdraw the automatic transmission dipstick. Wipe the dipstick with a clean lint-free cloth, re-insert it fully and withdraw it again, then read the level.

3 The fluid level must be between the MAX and MIN marks (see illustration). Only top up if it is below the MIN mark, and establish the reason for the low level. Topping-up is carried out via the dipstick tube, using clean ATF of the specified grade. Be very careful not to introduce dirt into the transmission; do not overfill.

4 If the level is too high, the reason for this must also be established. If it is simply overfilling, the excess should be siphoned or drained out. A more sinister reason for an excessively high level is the entry of coolant via the transmission fluid cooler; in this case expert advice should be sought without delay.

5 When the level is correct, re-insert the dipstick and switch off the engine.

12 Steering and suspension components - check

1 Raise the front of the vehicle and securely support it on axle stands (see "Jacking and vehicle support").

2 Visually inspect the balljoint dust covers and the steering rack-and-pinion gaiters for splits, chafing or deterioration (see illustrations). Any wear of these components will cause loss of lubricant, together with dirt and water entry, resulting in rapid deterioration of the balljoints or steering gear.

3 Check the condition and security of the pinion shaft flexible coupling (see illustration). The central part of the coupling is made of rubber which will eventually deteriorate.

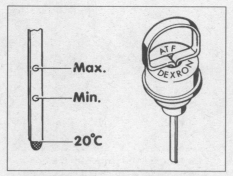

11.3 Automatic transmission dipstick markings. 20°C mark is only used when refilling

4 On vehicles with power steering, check the fluid hoses for chafing or deterioration, and the pipe and hose unions for fluid leaks. Also check for signs of fluid leakage under pressure from the steering gear rubber gaiters, which would indicate failed fluid seals within the steering gear.

5 Working on each front wheel in turn, grasp the wheel at the 9 o'clock and 3 o'clock positions and try to rock it. Very slight free play may be felt, but if the movement is appreciable, further investigation is necessary to determine the source. Continue rocking the wheel while an assistant depresses the footbrake. If the movement is now eliminated or significantly reduced, it is likely that the hub bearings are at fault. If the free play is still evident with the footbrake depressed, then there is wear in the steering track-rod balljoints. If the inner or outer balljoint is worn, the visual movement will be obvious.

6 Repeat the check in the previous paragraph, but this time grasp the wheel at the 12 o'clock and 6 o'clock positions. Movement which is eliminated by applying the footbrake is most likely due to worn or maladjusted hub bearings. Movement which persists with the footbrake applies will be due to worn suspension balljoints or bushes.

7 Using a large screwdriver or flat bar, check for wear in the suspension mounting bushes by levering between the relevant suspension component and its attachment point. Some movement is to be expected as the mountings are made of rubber, but excessive wear should be obvious. Also check the condition of any visible rubber bushes, looking for splits, cracks or contamination of the rubber (see illustration).

8 Check for any signs of fluid leakage around the shock absorber bodies. Should any fluid be noticed, the shock absorber is defective internally, and should be renewed. Also examine the shock absorber upper and lower mountings for any signs of wear.

9 Lower the vehicle to the ground and have an assistant turn the steering wheel back and forth about an eighth of a turn each way. There should be very little, if any, lost movement between the steering wheel and roadwheels. If this is not the case, closely observe the track-rod balljoints as previously described, but in addition, check the steering column universal joints for wear, and the rack-and-pinion steering gear itself.

12.2A Inspecting a suspension balljoint dust cover

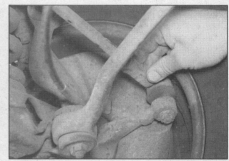

12.2B Inspecting a track rod end balljoint

12.2C Inspecting steering rack gaiters

12.3 Inspecting the steering pinion flexible coupling

12.7 A cracked suspension rubber bush

13.1 Inspecting a driveshaft gaiter

10 Again with the vehicle on the ground, the efficiency of the shock absorbers may be checked by bouncing the vehicle at each corner. The body will return to its normal position and stop after being depressed. If it rises and returns on a rebound, the shock absorber is probably suspect.

13 Driveshaft rubber gaiters - check

1 With the rear of the vehicle raised and securely supported on axle stands (see "*Jacking and vehicle support*"), slowly rotate the roadwheel. Inspect the condition of the inner constant velocity (CV) joint rubber gaiters, squeezing the gaiters to open out the folds **(see illustration)**. Check for signs of cracking, splits or deterioration of the rubber, which may allow the grease to escape, and lead to water and grit entry into the joint. Also check the security and condition of the retaining clips.
2 Repeat these checks on the outer CV joints. If any damage or deterioration is found, the gaiters should be renewed (see Chapter 8).

14 Rear brake shoes - check

1 Jack up the rear of the vehicle and support it securely on axle stands (see "*Jacking and vehicle support*").

16.2 Twist the drivebelt to view its underside

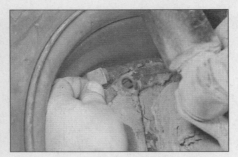
14.2 Remove the plug from the brake backplate for a quick check of lining thickness

2 For a quick check, the thickness of friction material remaining on one of the brake shoes can be observed through the hole in the brake backplate that is exposed by prising out the sealing grommet **(see illustration)**. If a rod of the same diameter as the specified minimum friction material thickness is placed against the shoe friction material, the amount of wear can be assessed. A torch or inspection light will probably be required to help observation.
3 If the friction material on any shoe is worn down to the specified minimum thickness or less, all four shoes must be renewed.
4 For a comprehensive check, the brake drum should be removed and cleaned. This will allow the wheel cylinders to be checked, and the condition of the brake drum itself to be fully examined (see Chapter 10).

15 Footbrake and handbrake operation - check

1 Check that the brake failure warning light on the instrument panel lights up with the ignition switched on and the handbrake applied, and goes out when the engine is started and the handbrake is released. If the bulb fails to illuminate, check the condition of the bulb: if satisfactory, there is a fault in the switch on the handbrake or in the wiring to the bulb. If the light does not go out when the engine is started, make sure that the handbrake is fully released. If the light remains illuminated there is a fault in one of the hydraulic circuits and the vehicle should not be driven until the fault is traced and rectified.

16.3 Check drivebelt tension by pressing firmly in the middle of the longest run

2 With the engine stopped, depress the brake pedal several times until it feels hard. Hold the brake pedal down and start the engine: the pedal should be felt to move downwards. If not, there is a fault in the vacuum servo unit - see Chapter 10.
3 Take the vehicle for a test drive. On a suitably clear piece of road, apply the brakes firmly and check that the vehicle pulls up in a straight line, without pulling to one side or juddering.
4 Check that the handbrake holds the vehicle on a slope.
5 If these checks show that attention is needed, refer to Chapter 10.

16 Auxiliary drivebelt(s) - check

1 One, two or three auxiliary drivebelts may be fitted according to model and equipment (power steering, air conditioning etc). The checking and adjustment procedures are similar in every case, although details of component fixings and access will differ. The belt shown here drives the alternator and coolant pump.
2 Inspect the drivebelt along its length for cracking, fraying or other obvious damage. Twist the belt to view its underside and turn the crankshaft if necessary to bring the whole run of the belt into view **(see illustration)**. Renew the belt if its condition is in doubt.

HAYNES HINT

Auxiliary drivebelt failure is one of the commonest causes of roadside breakdowns. Renew them before they are as badly worn as this one.

3 Check the belt tension by applying firm thumb pressure in the middle of the longest run **(see illustration)**. The belt should deflect by the amount given in the Specifications. A belt which is too loose will slip, squeal and wear rapidly; a belt which is too tight can cause premature wear of the components which it drives.
4 If adjustment is necessary, slacken the component fixings (in the case shown here, the alternator pivot and adjusting strap nuts and bolts). Move the component as necessary to tension the belt and hold it in this position

16.4 Hold the alternator in position and tighten the adjusting strap nut

17.1A Oil the door hinges . . .

17.1B . . . and the check straps

17.2 Apply a smear of grease to the door latches

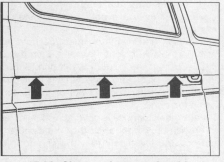

17.3A Clean and grease the side runner . . .

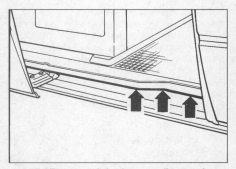

17.3B . . . and the lower roller track

while tightening the nuts and bolts **(see illustration)**. If using a lever against the component to provide the correct tension, do so with caution to avoid damage.

5 Recheck the tension and readjust if necessary. If a new belt has been fitted, check the tension again after a few miles.

5 Wipe off excess lubricant on completion so that it does not get onto passengers' clothes.

17 Hinges and locks - lubrication

1 Lightly oil the door hinges and check straps **(see illustrations)**.
2 Apply a smear of grease to the door latches **(see illustration)**.
3 On models with a sliding side door, clean the side runner and lower roller track with an oily rag, then apply a little grease **(see illustrations)**.
4 Wipe a little oil on the door key(s) and operate each door lock a couple of times to lubricate the lock internal components.
Caution: Do not attempt to oil the ignition switch/steering lock. If oil gets onto the switch contacts it will cause problems.

18 HT leads and distributor cap - check

1 Unclip and remove the distributor cap, and thoroughly clean it inside and out with a dry lint-free rag **(see illustrations)**. Examine the four HT lead segments inside the cap. If the segments appear badly burned or pitted, renew the cap. Make sure that the carbon brush in the centre of the cap is free to move and that it protrudes by approximately 3 mm from its holder.
2 With the distributor cap removed, lift off the rotor arm. Inspect it for cracks, burning or other damage **(see illustration)**. Renew the rotor arm if its condition is in doubt.

18.1A Unclip the distributor cap . . .

18.1B . . . remove it from the distributor . . .

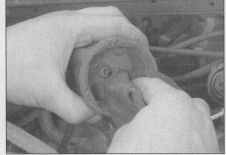

18.1C . . . and clean it inside and out

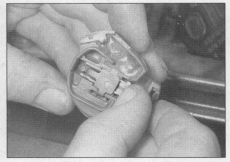

18.2 Inspect the rotor arm for cracks or burning

19.1 Disconnect the HT leads from the spark plugs

19.3A Unscrew the spark plugs . . .

11 Screw each spark plug into its hole in the cylinder head, being careful not to get the threads crossed. Tighten the spark plugs to the specified torque.

Use a short length of plastic hose slipped over the top of the spark plug to start it into its hole. If the threads are crossed, the hose will slip; remove the plug and try again.

3 Check the security and condition of all leads and wiring associated with the ignition system. Pay particular attention to the HT leads, which should be carefully inspected for any sign of corrosion inside their end fittings. If corrosion is evident, carefully scrape it away. Wipe clean the HT leads before refitting and inspect them for cracks or other damage; renew them if their condition is in doubt.

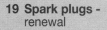

19 Spark plugs - renewal

1 Disconnect the HT leads from the spark plugs, marking the leads to identify them if there is any possibility of confusion **(see illustration)**.
2 Brush or blow away any dirt from around the spark plug recesses in the cylinder heads.
3 Using a spark plug spanner or a socket and a ratchet drive, unscrew each spark plug and remove it **(see illustrations)**.
4 The condition of the spark plugs will also tell much about the overall condition of the engine.
5 If the insulator nose of the spark plug is clean and white, with no deposits, this is indicative of a weak mixture, or too hot a plug.

(A hot plug transfers heat away from the electrode slowly – a cold plug transfers it away quickly.)
6 If the tip and insulator nose are covered with hard black-looking deposits, then this is indicative that the mixture is too rich. Should the plug be black and oily, then it is likely that the engine is fairly worn, as well as the mixture being too rich.
7 If the insulator nose is covered with light tan to greyish brown deposits, then the mixture is correct and it is likely that the engine is in good condition.
8 Do not attempt to clean the plugs with a wire brush, as this may leave conductive deposits on the insulator nose.
9 Check the electrode gap of each plug before fitting. (This does not apply to three-electrode plugs, whose gaps are present and should not be altered.) Slide a feeler blade or a wire gap gauge of the specified thickness between the plug electrodes: it should be a firm sliding fit. If adjustment is necessary, bend the side electrode as necessary, preferably using a proper spark plug gapping tool **(see illustration)**.
10 Smear the threads of each spark plug with a little copper-based anti-seize compound before refitting.

12 Reconnect the HT leads and run the engine to make sure all is well.

20 Antifreeze concentration - check

1 An antifreeze tester will be needed for this job. This is a device like a small battery hydrometer, containing various coloured balls which float or sink according to the concentration of antifreeze present.
2 With the engine cold, remove the cooling system filler cap. Dip the antifreeze tester into the coolant and withdraw a sample **(see illustration)**.

19.3B . . . and remove them. The three-electrode plugs shown here do not need to have their gaps checked

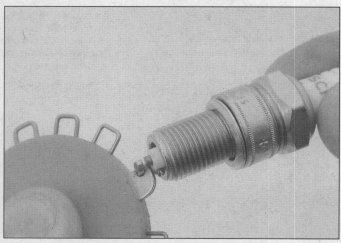

19.9 Checking a spark plug electrode gap

20.2 Checking antifreeze concentration with a hydrometer

3 Read the antifreeze concentration as instructed by the manufacturer of the tester. If the concentration is low, drain off some coolant (see Section 25) and top up via the expansion tank filler using neat antifreeze.

4 Refit the filler cap on completion.

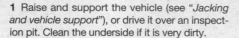

21 Underbody sealant - check

1 Raise and support the vehicle (see "*Jacking and vehicle support*"), or drive it over an inspection pit. Clean the underside if it is very dirty.

2 Thoroughly inspect the underside for any damage to the anti-corrosion coating and for consequent rust. Minor rusting may be treated with a suitable paint before re-applying underbody sealant. Rusting which has penetrated panels or attacked load-bearing members should be repaired by a specialist.

3 Apply fresh underbody sealant as necessary. Various proprietary preparations are available. Generally the non-hardening wax-based compounds are to be preferred to the old-fashioned bitumen paint.

4 Lower the vehicle to the ground on completion.

Extended service, every 20 000 miles (30 000 km) or 2 years

22 Air cleaner element - renewal

1 Various different types of air cleaner are fitted, depending on model and equipment. However, the renewal procedure is similar for all of them.

22.2 Release the spring clips around the air cleaner lid

2 Release the spring clips from around the air cleaner lid **(see illustration)**. Move the lid aside, being careful not to strain any vacuum or electrical connections; disconnect them if necessary.

3 Remove the old element. Clean out the housing and lid, being careful not to get any dust or dirt into the air intake.

4 Fit the new element, making sure it is the right way up **(see illustration)**.

5 Refit the lid and secure with the spring clips. Remake any disturbed electrical or vacuum connections.

23 Fuel filter - renewal

⚠ *Warning: Fuel will be spilt during this procedure. Take appropriate fire precautions, work in a well-ventilated area and have plenty of cloths ready to mop up spills.*

Carburettor models

1 Raise and support the rear of the vehicle (see "*Jacking and vehicle support*").

2 The fuel filter is located in the line between the fuel tank and the engine bay **(see illustration)**.

3 Clamp the hoses on each side of the fuel filter. Clean around the ends of the hoses, then release the hose clips and disconnect the hoses from the filter; be prepared for fuel spillage. Remove the old filter.

4 Fit the new filter, observing any arrows showing the direction of flow. Secure it with the hose clips, using new clips if necessary.

Fuel injection models

5 Depressurise the fuel injection system as described in Chapter 4B.

6 Raise and support the rear of the vehicle (see "*Jacking and vehicle support*").

7 The fuel filter is located in the line between the fuel tank and the engine bay, next to the fuel pump **(see illustration)**.

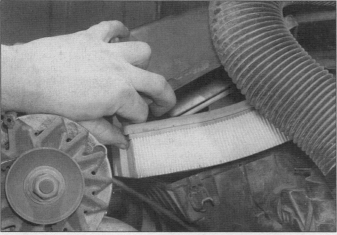

22.4 Fitting a new air cleaner element

23.2 Fuel filter location - carburettor models

23.7 Fuel filter (arrowed) - fuel injection models

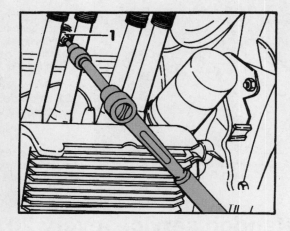

25.2A Removing a water jacket drain plug

8 Release the filter securing clamp. Clean around the unions, then release the hose connectors from the filter; be prepared for fuel spillage. Remove the old filter.
9 Fit the new filter, observing any arrows showing the direction of flow. Reconnect the hoses and tighten the securing clamp.

All models

10 Run the engine and check that there are no leaks from the new filter, then lower the vehicle to the ground.
11 Dispose of the old filter safely, bearing in mind it is full of fuel.

24 Brake hydraulic fluid - renewal

1 Hydraulic fluid absorbs moisture from the air. In time the concentration of water in the fluid becomes high enough to reduce the boiling point of the fluid to a dangerous level. Moisture in the fluid will also attack hydraulic system components. This is why periodic renewal is necessary.
2 The procedure is the same as that for bleeding the brake hydraulic system (Chapter 10), except that the system is bled at each

wheel until all the old fluid has been expelled and new fluid emerges.

> **HAYNES HiNT** *Old brake fluid is invariably much darker than new fluid, making it easy to distinguish between the two.*

25 Coolant - renewal

Note: *VW coolant type G11 lasts indefinitely. Provided you are sure that this type of coolant has been used and that the concentration is adequate, there is no need to renew it. Most other brands of antifreeze must be renewed every two years. Once the system has been drained, it is as well to flush it and to take the opportunity to renew any rubber hoses whose condition is in doubt. Proceed as follows.*

> ⚠️ **Warning: The engine must be cold before starting this procedure. Also, bear in mind that antifreeze is poisonous.** *Wash splashes off skin and paintwork immediately. Don't leave antifreeze lying around in open containers or in puddles on*

the floor - pets or children may drink it. They are attracted by its sweet smell.

Draining

1 Move the heater controls to 'hot'.
2 Place a large drain pan (capacity 20 litres or so) under the engine and remove the drain plug from the water jacket on each side. Remove the expansion tank and top-up tank caps and allow the coolant to drain **(see illustrations)**.

> **HAYNES HiNT** *If the water jacket drain plugs are rusted in place, drain the system by disconnecting the lowest coolant hose.*

3 Remove the radiator upper grille. Unscrew and remove the bleed screw from the right-hand side of the radiator **(see illustration)**.
4 When the coolant has finished draining, remove the drain pan. Dispose of the old coolant safely (not down the drain).

Flushing

5 Disconnect the two major coolant hoses from the thermostat housing and coolant pump. Insert a garden hose into one of the hoses and run water along the hose, through the radiator and back out of the other coolant hose. (Seal the garden hose to the coolant hose with rag wrapped around it in order to maintain sufficient pressure.) Allow the water to run until it emerges clear. Repeat the process in the opposite direction.
6 Similarly flush the engine water jackets by inserting the garden hose into the coolant pump connection and running water in so that it drains out of the water jacket drain holes. Also disconnect the heater hoses and flush the heater matrix if wished.

Filling and bleeding

7 Reconnect all coolant hoses. Refit and tighten the water jacket drain plugs. Make

25.2B Removing the expansion tank cap

25.3 Removing the radiator bleed screw

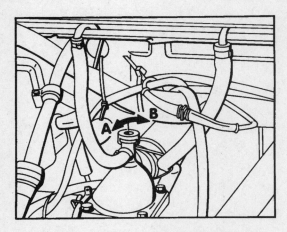

25.8 Coolant bleed valve in engine compartment

A Open   *B Closed*

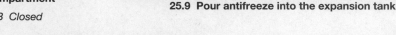

25.9 Pour antifreeze into the expansion tank

sure the radiator bleed screw is still out.

8 Open the bleed valve in the engine compartment **(see illustration)**. Do not force it, it is fragile.

9 Pour the specified quantity of neat antifreeze into the expansion tank **(see illustration)**. Follow it up with clean water until the expansion tank is full.

10 Run the engine at a fast idle (around 2000 rpm). With the help of an assistant, continue to top up the expansion tank until coolant free of air bubbles emerges from the radiator bleed screw hole, then refit and tighten the screw.

11 Fill the expansion tank to the brim and fit the cap. Stop the engine.

12 Chock the rear wheels. Raise and support the front of the vehicle so that it is at least 400 mm higher than the rear (see *"Jacking and vehicle support"*).

13 Start the engine and run it at a fast idle again. Unscrew the radiator bleed screw approximately 3 turns and remove the expansion tank cap.

14 When coolant free of air bubbles emerges from the radiator bleed screw, tighten the screw.

15 Top up the expansion tank again and refit the cap.

16 Stop the engine, then close the bleed valve in the engine compartment.

17 Run the engine up to normal operating temperature, then switch it off and allow it to cool. Inspect any disturbed hose connections for leaks.

18 Check the coolant level in the expansion tank and top up as necessary. If the level in the top-up tank is low, add neat antifreeze to bring it up to the mark, then refit the top-up tank cap.

Long-term service, every 30 000 miles (45 000 km) or 3 years

26 Automatic transmission fluid - renewal

Caution: Extreme cleanliness must be observed during the following procedure.

1 Raise and support the rear of the vehicle (see *"Jacking and vehicle support"*). Remove the transmission fluid dipstick.

2 Place a drain pan under the transmission. Unscrew the dipstick tube where it joins the transmission sump and allow the fluid to drain into the pan.

3 Unbolt and remove the transmission sump. Be prepared for fluid spillage.

4 Unbolt and remove the transmission fluid strainer **(see illustration)**.

5 Thoroughly clean the transmission sump and fluid strainer. Renew the strainer if it is damaged or very dirty.

6 Refit and secure the fluid strainer, then refit the sump, using a new gasket. Tighten the sump retaining bolts evenly to the specified torque.

7 Refit the dipstick tube to the sump, then lower the vehicle to the ground.

8 Pour 2.5 litres of transmission fluid in via the dipstick tube, using a clean funnel.

9 Run the engine. Apply the handbrake and footbrake, then select all gear positions a couple of times, starting and ending in 'P'.

10 With the engine still running, check the fluid level on the dipstick. Top up if necessary to bring the level up to the tip of the dipstick.

11 Take the vehicle for a short run (5 miles or so), then recheck the transmission fluid level as described in Section 11. Top up as necessary, being careful not to overfill.

12 Check that there are no leaks from the transmission sump.

13 Dispose of the old fluid safely (not down the drain).

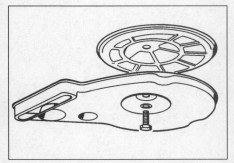

26.4 Automatic transmission fluid strainer components

Chapter 2 Part A:
Engine in-vehicle repair procedures

Contents

Degrees of difficulty

| **Easy,** suitable for novice with little experience | 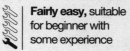 | **Fairly easy,** suitable for beginner with some experience | | **Fairly difficult,** suitable for competent DIY mechanic | | **Difficult,** suitable for experienced DIY mechanic | | **Very difficult,** suitable for expert DIY or professional | |

Specifications

1.9 litre engine - general

Type	Four-cylinder, horizontally opposed, overhead valve
Manufacturer's code letters:	
With 34 PICT carburettor	DF, EY
With 2E3 or 2E4 carburettor	DG
With fuel injection (Digijet)	GW
Bore	94 mm
Stroke	69 mm
Capacity	1913 cc
Compression ratio:	
DF, DG, GW	8.6 : 1
EY	7.5 : 1
Maximum power output:	
DF	44 kW @ 3700 rpm
DG	57 kW @ 4600 rpm
EY	41 kW @ 3700 rpm
GW	66 kW @ 4600 rpm
Maximum torque:	
DF	140 Nm @ 2200 rpm
DG	141 Nm @ 2600 rpm
EY	135 Nm @ 2200 rpm
GW	147 Nm @ 2800 rpm
Firing order	1–4–3–2
Location of No 1 cylinder	Front right

2.1 litre engine - general

Type	Four-cylinder, horizontally opposed, overhead valve
Manufacturer's code letters:	
With Digijet fuel injection	DJ
With Digifant fuel injection	MV, SS
Bore	94 mm
Stroke	76 mm
Capacity	2109 cc
Compression ratio:	
DJ	10.0 : 1
MV, SS	9.0 : 1
Maximum power output:	
DJ	82 kW @ 4800 rpm
MV	70 kW @ 4800 rpm
SS	68 kW @ 4500 rpm
Maximum torque:	
DJ	174 Nm @ 2800 rpm
MV	160 Nm @ 2800 rpm
SS	154 Nm @ 2800 rpm
Firing order	1–4–3–2
Location of No 1 cylinder	Front right

Compression pressures (all engines)

Engine code DJ:	
New	11 to 14 bar
Wear limit	8 bar
Engine codes DF, DG, GW, MV, SS:	
New	10 to 13 bar
Wear limit	8 bar
Engine code EY:	
New	8 to 10 bar
Wear limit	7 bar
Maximum difference between cylinders:	
Engine code EY	2 bar
All other engines	3 bar

Lubrication system (all engines)

Oil pump type	Twin gear
Oil pump gear axial clearance	0.1 mm
Oil filter type	Full-flow renewable cartridge
Oil pressure at 80°C and 2000 rpm	2.0 bar minimum
Warning light switch operating pressure:	
Single (low pressure) switch (all models)	0.30 ± 0.15 bar
Second (higher pressure) switch (when fitted)	0.90 ± 0.15 bar
Oil capacity	See Chapter 1 Specifications

Torque wrench settings (all engines)

	Nm	lbf ft
Rocker shaft to cylinder head	25	18
Oil cooler central securing nut	25	18
Oil pressure warning light switch:		
Single (low pressure) switch (on left-hand side of engine)	30	22
Second (high pressure) switch (when fitted, below oil pump)	25	18
Oil pump cover securing nuts	25	18
Oil pressure relief valve cap	20	15
Flywheel or driveplate to crankshaft	See Chapter 2B	
Crankshaft pulley bolt:		
Single-groove pulley	60	44
Three-groove pulley	315 to 350	232 to 258
Engine bearer bracket to crankcase	45	33
Engine bearer to engine mountings	45	33
Engine bearer to chassis rails	25	18
Engine mountings to bearer bracket	20	15
Oil drain plug	25	18

1 General information

The engine is of four-cylinder horizontally opposed ('flat four') configuration, mounted behind the transmission at the rear of the vehicle. Both the 1.9 and 2.1 litre engines are of the same basic layout apart from the different positions of certain ancillary components and other minor variations.

The crankcase is of split configuration with separate cylinder liners. The crankshaft is supported at the crankcase join in four main bearings. Crankshaft endfloat is controlled by shims fitted between the flywheel and No 1 crankshaft main bearing.

The connecting rods are attached to the crankshaft by split shell type big-end bearings and to the pistons by fully floating gudgeon pins. The aluminium alloy pistons are fitted with three piston rings, of which two are compression rings and one an oil control ring.

The camshaft is gear-driven from the crankshaft and operates the rocker arms via pushrods and hydraulic tappets. The inlet and exhaust valves operate in guides pressed into the cylinder head.

Engine lubrication is by a gear type oil pump driven by the camshaft. A full flow filter, oil strainer and pressure relief valve are included in the lubrication system. Some models have an oil cooler, mounted between the oil filter and the crankcase, which contains an oil-to-coolant heat exchanger.

The engine is water-cooled, the coolant circulating round passages in the cylinder heads and in jackets surrounding the cylinder liners. Procedures specific to the cooling system are covered in Chapter 3.

2 Major operations possible with the engine in the vehicle

The configuration of the engine and its location in the vehicle are such that very little major work can be done with the engine in place. In principle it is possible to remove a cylinder head with the engine in the vehicle, but this is not recommended because there is a high probability of disturbing the cylinder liner base seals in so doing. Operations with the engine installed should therefore be confined to those described in this part of Chapter 2.

Fortunately, engine removal is not as difficult a task as on some other vehicles and the power unit can be removed relatively easily. Removal and overhaul procedures are described in part B of Chapter 2.

3 Compression test – description and interpretation

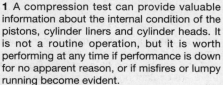

1 A compression test can provide valuable information about the internal condition of the pistons, cylinder liners and cylinder heads. It is not a routine operation, but it is worth performing at any time if performance is down for no apparent reason, or if misfires or lumpy running become evident.

2 A compression tester suitable for petrol engines will be needed. The type with an adaptor which screws into the spark plug holes is recommended. The services of an assistant will also be required.

3 The engine must be at normal operating temperature and the battery must be fully charged.

4 Remove the spark plugs (Chapter 5B) and disable the ignition system by unplugging the distributor LT connector.

5 Fit the compression tester adaptor to No 1 spark plug hole. Have an assistant depress the accelerator pedal fully and crank the engine (for at least four complete revolutions of the crankshaft) on the starter motor. Watch the reading on the compression tester: it should build up quickly. Record the highest reading obtained.

6 Repeat the test on the other three cylinders, recording the highest reading for each.

7 Compression test values are given in the Specifications. In terms of smooth running the difference between individual cylinders is more important than the absolute values obtained.

8 Low compression on the first stroke which builds up during successive strokes suggests worn pistons or piston rings. Low compression which does not build up significantly during subsequent strokes suggests leaking valves or a leaking joint between cylinder head and liner.

9 The traditional test of introducing 5 or 10 ml of engine oil via the plug hole and observing the effect on compression is liable to be inconclusive on this engine, since there is no guarantee that the oil will be evenly distributed around the piston rings. All that can safely be said is that if the introduction of oil temporarily improves a low compression reading, the problem is probably worn pistons and rings; but if the introduction of oil has no effect, this does not point conclusively to a top end problem.

10 If further diagnosis is required, a leak-down test should be performed by a suitably equipped garage. This test involves introducing compressed air via the spark plug hole and measuring the rate and the route of leakage.

11 On completion of the compression test, refit the spark plugs and reconnect the distributor.

4 Pushrod tubes – renewal

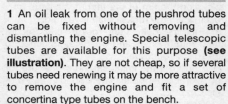

1 An oil leak from one of the pushrod tubes can be fixed without removing and dismantling the engine. Special telescopic tubes are available for this purpose (see illustration). They are not cheap, so if several tubes need renewing it may be more attractive to remove the engine and fit a set of concertina type tubes on the bench.

2 Raise and support the rear of the vehicle (see "Jacking and vehicle support").

3 Release the rocker cover on the side concerned by prising its spring clip free with a screwdriver (see illustration). Remove the cover; be prepared for some oil spillage.

4 Remove the two nuts and washers which secure the rocker shaft. Lift off the shaft and rockers (see illustration).

5 Remove the pushrod from the tube to be renewed.

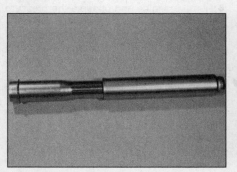

4.1 Telescopic pushrod tube for in-vehicle repair

4.3 Release the rocker cover clip (engine on bench for clarity)

4.4 Removing the rocker shaft assembly (engine on bench for clarity)

4.7 Secure the tube in the compressed position with sticky tape

4.8 Fitting the tube to the engine

4.12 Use a new rocker cover gasket if necessary

6 Remove the old pushrod tube, working it back and forth to collapse the concertina section. Do not worry if it gets bent or otherwise damaged, but be careful not to disturb the other tubes. Recover the old seals if they stayed on the head or block.

7 Compress the telescopic tube and secure it in the compressed position with sticky tape. Fit a new seal to each end of the tube **(see illustration)**.

8 Offer the tube into position, crankcase end first. Carefully remove the sticky tape, at the same time guiding the other end of the tube into its recess in the cylinder head **(see illustration)**.

9 Refit the pushrod, making sure that it enters the recess in the centre of the tappet. If it sticks on the rim of the tappet, damage may result when the rocker shaft is refitted.

10 Refit the rockers and rocker shaft. Secure them with the nuts and washers, tightened to the specified torque.

11 Carry out the initial setting procedure for the hydraulic tappets as described in part B of this Chapter.

12 Refit the rocker cover, using a new gasket if the old one was in poor condition **(see illustration)**.

13 Lower the vehicle. Check the engine oil level and top up if necessary (see "Weekly checks"), then run the engine and check that there are no leaks from the new pushrod tube.

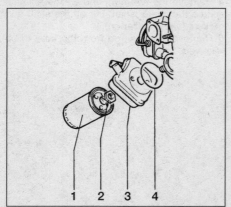

5.1 Oil cooler components

1 Oil filter	*3 Oil cooler*
2 Securing nut	*4 O-ring*

5 Oil cooler –
removal and refitting

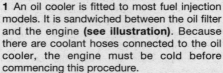

1 An oil cooler is fitted to most fuel injection models. It is sandwiched between the oil filter and the engine **(see illustration)**. Because there are coolant hoses connected to the oil cooler, the engine must be cold before commencing this procedure.

2 Remove the oil filter as described in Chapter 1.

3 Remove the cooling system expansion tank cap. Clamp the coolant hoses running to and from the oil cooler, or be prepared to plug them when they are disconnected.

4 Release the hose clips and disconnect the coolant hoses from the oil cooler.

5 Remove the nut in the middle of the oil cooler. Remove the oil cooler and recover the O-ring.

6 Use a new O-ring when refitting. Clean the oil cooler and block mating faces and coat them with a suitable sealant (VW type AMV 188 101 02 or equivalent), being careful not to get any sealant into the central area sealed by the O-ring.

7 With the O-ring and the oil cooler in place, refit the central nut and tighten it to the specified torque. Check that the oil cooler is not fouling any adjacent components.

8 Reconnect and secure the coolant hoses. Remove the hose clamps, if used.

9 Fit and tighten a new oil filter, applying a smear of clean oil to the filter sealing ring.

6.1 Oil pressure warning switch (arrowed) is screwed into side of crankcase

Hand-tighten only unless otherwise instructed by the filter manufacturer.

10 Check the oil and coolant levels and top up if necessary (see "Weekly checks").

11 Run the engine and check that there are no leaks, then carry out the coolant refilling procedure described in Chapter 1. Recheck the engine oil level on completion.

6 Oil pressure switches –
testing, removal and refitting

1 All models have at least one oil pressure switch, screwed into the left-hand side of the crankcase **(see illustration)**. This low pressure switch operates the oil pressure warning light on the instrument panel. Models with an audible warning of low oil pressure have a second, higher pressure switch mounted on the rear face of the engine below the oil pump.

2 It is not possible to test the switch itself without special test equipment, but a suspected false alarm can be verified as follows.

3 In the case of the higher pressure switch, it will first be necessary to unbolt and bend aside the exhaust cover plate.

4 Disconnect the lead from the switch and unscrew it from the engine; recover the O-ring.

5 Using a suitable adaptor, connect an oil pressure gauge to the switch hole.

6 Run the engine and observe the pressure on the gauge. If the oil pressure is above the switch operating pressure (see Specifications) and a warning of low oil pressure was being given, the switch is faulty and must be renewed.

7 Stop the engine and disconnect the oil pressure gauge.

8 Fit the switch, using a new O-ring if the old one was damaged, and tighten to the specified torque.

9 Reconnect the lead to the switch. Run the engine and check for correct operation.

10 Resecure the exhaust cover plate if it was disturbed.

7.2 Removing the crankshaft pulley bolt and washer

7.3A Removing the crankshaft pulley . . .

7.3B . . . and the Woodruff key

7 Oil pump – removal and refitting

Note: *The crankshaft pulley bolt is very tight and there is limited access with the engine in position; both these problems are worse on models with a three-groove pulley. A further possible problem is that the oil pump housing can be difficult to remove without a suitable puller. There is more room for improvisation with the engine on the bench, which is where the photographs in this Section were taken.*

1 Remove the auxiliary drivebelt(s) as described in Chapter 1.

2 Slacken the crankshaft pulley bolt. This bolt is very tight: stop the crankshaft turning by engaging a gear, or remove the starter motor and jam the flywheel ring gear with a large screwdriver. Remove the bolt and washer (see illustration).

3 Remove the crankshaft pulley. Recover the Woodruff key if it is loose (see illustrations).

4 Clean around the oil pump cover, then remove the four nuts which secure it. These are special nuts which must be renewed on reassembly.

5 Remove the oil pump cover (see illustration). Remove the two gears from the oil pump.

6 Remove the oil pump housing. It is a tight fit in the crankcase; if judicious levering will not free it, the use of a puller similar to that shown (see illustration) will be necessary. There is a threaded hole in the pump body to accept the puller spindle.

7 Clean off all traces of old gasket. Inspect the pump and cover as described in the next Section.

8 Commence refitting by putting a new base gasket over the studs on the crankcase (see illustration).

9 Fit the assembled oil pump, well lubricated, into its recess (see illustration).

10 Fit a new gasket to the outer face of the pump (see illustration).

11 Refit the cover plate and secure it with four new special nuts, sealing faces inward (see illustration). Tighten the nuts to the specified torque.

12 The remainder of refitting is a reversal of the removal procedure. Tighten the crankshaft pulley bolt to the specified torque.

13 Run the engine on completion and check that the oil pressure warning light goes out and that there are no leaks.

7.5 Removing the oil pump cover

7.6 Removing the oil pump housing with a puller

7.8 Fit a new base gasket . . .

7.9 . . . followed by the oil pump housing and gears . . .

7.10 . . . then a new outer face gasket . . .

7.11 . . . and finally the cover plate. The sealing faces of the nuts go towards the plate

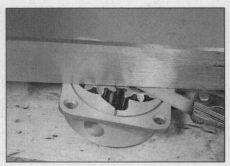

8.3 Checking the oil pump gear axial clearance

9.2A Remove the spring cap . . .

9.2B . . . followed by the spring . . .

8 Oil pump – inspection

1 Inspect the gears and pump housing visually for scoring or wear ridges. If any are present, renew the pump.

2 Inspect the inside surface of the pump cover plate. If it is scored, either have it refaced or renew it.

3 If the pump appears satisfactory, check the axial clearance of the gears using feeler gauges and a straight-edge **(see illustration)**. If the clearances are greater than the specified amount, renew the pump.

4 Thoroughly lubricate the gears before reassembling them into the body and housing. If a new pump is being fitted, observe any special instructions concerning initial lubrication or priming.

9 Oil pressure relief valve – removal, inspection and refitting

1 Raise and support the rear of the vehicle (see "*Jacking and vehicle support*").

2 Undo the large screw cap located on the bottom of the crankcase near the sump drain plug. Remove the cap and washer, followed by the spring and plunger **(see illustrations)**. Be prepared for oil spillage.

3 Inspect the components for obvious wear or damage and renew if necessary. The only sure check of the spring is to compare its length and strength against a new one. Make sure that the plunger moves freely in its bore.

4 Lubricate the plunger and refit it, followed by the spring, washer and screw cap. Tighten the screw cap to the specified torque.

5 Check the engine oil level and top up if necessary (see "*Weekly checks*"), then run the engine and check that the oil pressure warning light goes out and that there are no leaks.

6 Lower the vehicle to the ground.

10 Crankshaft oil seals – renewal

Front (flywheel end) seal

1 Remove the flywheel or driveplate as described in part B of this Chapter. Note that new bolts will be required for reassembly. Recover the shims.

2 Inspect the seal rubbing surface on the flywheel. If it is badly scored or grooved, refinishing or renewal may be necessary. Minor wear marks may be avoided by careful positioning of the new seal.

3 Prise out the old oil seal, being careful not to damage the seal housing in the crankcase.

4 Liberally grease the new seal and fit it into the housing, lips inwards **(see illustration)**.

5 Tap the seal home until it is flush with, or just below, the face of the crankcase **(see**

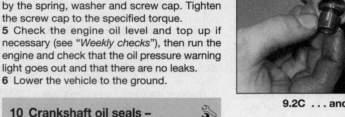

9.2C . . . and the plunger

illustration). If there are wear marks on the flywheel, position the new seal to avoid them.

6 Refit the flywheel or driveplate as described in part B of this Chapter, using a new O-ring between the flywheel and the crankshaft. Remember to use new bolts.

Rear (pulley end) seal

7 Remove the crankshaft pulley as described in Section 7.

8 Inspect the seal rubbing surface on the pulley. If it is badly scored or grooved, refinishing or renewal may be necessary. Minor wear marks may be avoided by careful positioning of the new seal.

9 Prise out the old oil seal, being careful not to damage the seal housing in the crankcase.

10 Liberally grease the new seal and fit it into the housing, lips inwards **(see illustration)**.

10.4 Fitting a new flywheel end oil seal

10.5 Flywheel end oil seal in position

10.10 Fitting a new pulley end oil seal

10.11 Tapping the seal home

11 Tap the seal home until it is flush with, or just below, the face of the crankcase (see illustration). If there are wear marks on the pulley, position the new seal to avoid them.
12 Refit the crankshaft pulley.

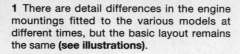

11 Engine mountings – removal and refitting

1 There are detail differences in the engine mountings fitted to the various models at different times, but the basic layout remains the same (see illustrations).

2 Before renewing a mounting, support the engine with a hoist or with a jack and a block of wood. Raise the engine sufficiently to take the load off the mountings without straining them (see "*Jacking and vehicle support*").
3 Unbolt the mounting from the engine bearer and bearer bracket. Raise the engine a little further if necessary and extract the mounting.
4 Fit the new mounting, lower the engine and tighten the nuts and bolts to the specified torque.

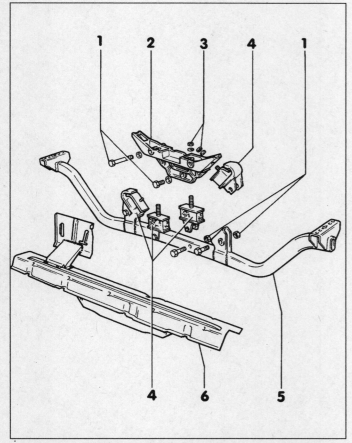

11.1A Engine bearer, bracket and mountings - early models

1	Bracket and mounting nuts and bolts	4	Mountings
2	Bearer bracket	5	Engine bearer
3	Mounting nuts	6	Exhaust cover plate

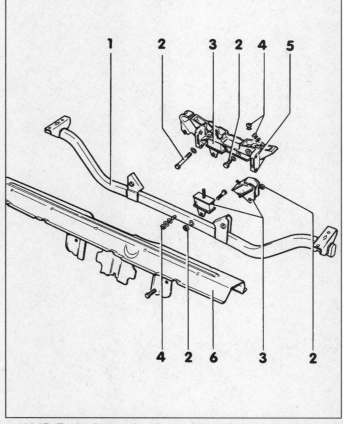

11.1B Engine bearer, bracket and mountings - later models

1	Engine bearer	4	Mounting nuts
2	Bracket and mounting nuts and bolts	5	Bearer bracket
3	Mountings	6	Exhaust cover plate

Chapter 2 Part B:
Engine removal and overhaul

Contents

Degrees of difficulty

Easy, suitable for novice with little experience	Fairly easy, suitable for beginner with some experience	Fairly difficult, suitable for competent DIY mechanic	Difficult, suitable for experienced DIY mechanic	Very difficult, suitable for expert DIY or professional

Specifications

For Specifications relating to operations possible with the engine in the vehicle, see Chapter 2A.

Crankshaft

Number of main bearings 4
Main bearing journal diameters - nominal:
  No 1 . . . . 60.00 mm
  Nos 2 and 3 . . . . 55.00 mm
  No 4 . . . . 40.00 mm
Main bearing journal diameters - actual:
  Nos 1, 2 and 3 (blue mark) . . . . 0.010 to 0.020 mm less than nominal
  Nos 1, 2 and 3 (red mark) . . . . 0.021 to 0.029 mm less than nominal
  No 4 . . . . 0.016 mm less than nominal
Crankpin journal diameter - nominal . . . . 55.00 mm
Crankpin journal diameter - actual . . . . 0.004 to 0.017 mm less than nominal
Maximum ovality of journals (suggested limit) . . . . 0.03 mm
Crankshaft endfloat:
  New . . . . 0.07 to 0.13 mm
  Wear limit . . . . 0.15 mm

Connecting rods

Type . . . . Forged steel
Maximum endfloat on journal . . . . 0.7 mm

Camshaft and bearings

Run-out . . . . 0.04 mm maximum
Camshaft endfloat . . . . 0.16 mm maximum
Gear backlash . . . . 0 to 0.5 mm

Cylinder liners

Type . . . . Single barrel cast iron
Cylinder bore diameter:
  Nominal . . . . 94 mm
  Actual:
    Blue . . . . 94.005 to 94.016 mm
    Pink . . . . 94.016 to 94.027 mm

Pistons and rings

Piston to cylinder bore clearance:
  New . . . . 0.03 to 0.06 mm
  Wear limit . . . . 0.2 mm
Piston ring to groove clearance:
  Upper ring:
    New . . . . 0.05 to 0.08 mm
    Wear limit . . . . 0.12 mm
  Middle ring:
    New . . . . 0.04 to 0.07 mm
    Wear limit . . . . 0.10 mm
  Oil control ring:
    New . . . . 0.02 to 0.05 mm
    Wear limit . . . . 0.10 mm
Piston ring end gaps:
  Upper and middle rings . . . . 0.30 to 0.90 mm
  Oil control ring . . . . 0.25 to 0.95 mm

Valves

Engine codes DF, EY

Head diameter:
  Inlet . . . . 35.5 mm
  Exhaust . . . . 30.0 mm
Stem diameter:
  Inlet . . . . 7.94 to 7.95 mm
  Exhaust . . . . 8.91 to 8.92 mm

Engine codes DG, DJ, MV, SS

Head diameter:
  Inlet . . . . 40.0 mm
  Exhaust . . . . 34.0 mm
Stem diameter:
  Inlet . . . . 7.96 to 7.97 mm
  Exhaust . . . . 8.91 to 8.92 mm

All engines

Maximum lateral rock in guide . . . . 1.2 mm
Valve seat width . . . . 1.4 to 2.5 mm
Valve seat angle . . . . 45°

Torque wrench settings

	Nm	lbf ft
Air conditioning compressor bracket to crankcase	35	26
Connecting rod big-end cap nuts:		
Rigid bolts (see text)	45	33
Stretch bolts* (see text):		
Stage 1	30	22
Stage 2	Tighten a further 180°	
Crankcase halves:		
M8 nut	20	15
M10 nuts - early models**	35	26
M10 nuts - later models**	45	33
Crankshaft pulley bolt:		
Single-groove pulley	60	44
Three-groove pulley	315 to 350	232 to 258
Cylinder head nuts:		
Stage 1	10	7
Stage 2	50	37
Engine bearer bracket to crankcase	45	33
Engine bearer to engine mountings	45	33
Engine bearer to chassis rails	25	18
Engine mountings to bearer bracket	20	15
Engine to transmission	30	22
Flywheel or driveplate to crankshaft*:		
Stage 1	60	44
Stage 2	Tighten a further 90°	
Inlet manifolds to cylinder heads	20	15
Oil cooler central securing nut	25	18
Oil drain plug	25	18

Torque wrench settings (continued)

	Nm	lbf ft
Oil filler tube nuts	20	15
Oil pressure warning light switch:		
Single (low pressure) switch (on left-hand side of engine)	30	22
Second (high pressure) switch (when fitted, below oil pump)	25	18
Oil pump cover securing nuts*	25	18
Oil pressure relief valve cap	20	15
Rocker shaft to cylinder head	25	18
Torque converter to driveplate	20	15
Transmission mountings	30	22

*Use new nuts or bolts

**Early models: engine numbers up to and including DF 035 607, DG 064 473, EY 000 352. Later models: engine numbers from DF 035 608, DG 064 474, EY 000 353, SP 000 001, and all DJ, MV and SS

---

1 Engine removal and overhaul – general information

Removal

Having decided that the engine must be removed for overhaul or major repair work, several preliminary steps should be taken.

Locating a suitable place to work is important. Adequate work space, along with storage space for the vehicle, will be needed. If a workshop or garage isn't available, at the very least, a flat, level, clean work surface made of concrete or asphalt is required.

Cleaning the engine compartment and engine/transmission before beginning the removal procedure will help keep tools clean and organised.

If this is the first time you have removed an engine, a helper should ideally be available. Advice and aid from someone more experienced would also be useful. There are some instances when one person cannot simultaneously perform all of the operations required when removing the engine from the vehicle.

Plan the operation ahead of time. Arrange for, or obtain, all of the tools and equipment you'll need prior to beginning the job. Some of the equipment necessary to perform engine removal safely and with relative ease, and which may have to be hired or borrowed, includes:

a) an engine hoist and/or a heavy-duty trolley jack
b) a strong pair or two of long-reach axle stands (see "Jacking and vehicle support")
c) some wooden blocks
d) an engine dolly (a low, wheeled platform capable of taking the weight of the engine/transmission, so that it can be moved easily when on the ground)

A complete set of spanners and sockets will obviously be needed, together with plenty of rags for mopping up spilled oil, coolant and fuel. If the hoist is to be hired, make sure that you arrange for it in advance, and perform all of the operations possible without it beforehand. This will save you money and time.

Plan for the vehicle to be out of use for quite a while. You will not necessarily know what replacement parts to order until after dismantling and inspection. An engine reconditioning specialist will be required to perform some of the work which the do-it-yourselfer can't accomplish without special equipment. These establishments often have a busy schedule, so it would be a good idea to consult them before removing the engine, to estimate the amount of time required to rebuild or repair components that may need work.

Always be extremely careful when removing and refitting the engine. Serious injury can result from careless actions. By planning ahead and taking your time, the job (although a major task) can be accomplished successfully.

Overhaul

It is not always easy to determine when, or if, an engine should be completely overhauled, as a number of factors must be considered. There is also the question of knowing where to stop. For example, if the cylinder liners are disturbed when removing the cylinder heads, they will have to be removed for their base seals to be renewed; this implies that the piston rings may as well be renewed, and so on. A full engine overhaul involves restoring all internal parts to the specification of a new engine.

High mileage is not necessarily an indication that an overhaul is needed, while low mileage doesn't preclude the need for an overhaul. Frequency of servicing is probably the most important consideration. An engine which has had regular and frequent oil and filter changes, as well as other required maintenance, will most likely give many thousands of miles of reliable service. Conversely, a neglected engine may require an overhaul very early in its life.

Excessive oil consumption is an indication that piston rings, valve seals and/or valve guides are in need of attention. Make sure that oil leaks aren't responsible before deciding that the rings and/or guides are worn. Perform a cylinder compression check (Part A of this Chapter) to determine the extent of the work required.

Loss of power, rough running, knocking or metallic engine noises, excessive valve train noise and high fuel consumption rates may also point to the need for an overhaul, especially if they're all present at the same time. If a full service doesn't remedy the situation, major mechanical work is the only solution.

 Always check first what replacement parts are available before planning any overhaul operation. VW dealers, or a good engine reconditioning specialist or automotive parts supplier, may be able to suggest alternatives which will enable you to overcome the lack of replacement parts.

The cylinder liners on these engines cannot be rebored; if they are significantly worn, new liners and pistons must be fitted. The main and big-end bearings are generally renewed. Regrinding of the crankshaft bearings is not recommended; in any case oversize bearings are not available as VW parts. Generally, the valves are serviced during engine overhaul, since they're usually in less-than-perfect condition at this point. While the engine is being overhauled, other components, such as the starter and alternator, can be renewed as well, or rebuilt if the necessary parts can be found. The end result should be an as-new engine that will give many trouble-free miles. **Note:** *Critical cooling system components such as the hoses, drivebelt, thermostat and water pump MUST be replaced with new parts when an engine is overhauled. The radiator should be checked carefully, to ensure that it isn't clogged or leaking (see Chapter 3). Also, as a general rule, the oil pump should be renewed when an engine is rebuilt.*

Before beginning the engine overhaul, read through the entire procedure to familiarise yourself with the scope and requirements of the job. Overhauling an engine isn't difficult, but it is time-consuming. Plan on the vehicle being off the road for a minimum of two weeks, especially if parts must be taken to an automotive machine shop for repair or reconditioning. Check on availability of parts, and make sure that any necessary special tools and equipment are obtained in advance. Most work can be done with typical hand tools, although a number of precision measuring tools are required, for inspecting parts to determine if they must be replaced. Often, an automotive machine shop will handle the inspection of parts, and will offer advice concerning reconditioning and replacement. **Note:** *Always wait until the engine has been completely dismantled, and*

3.3 Removing the engine oil filler tube

3.4 Dipstick tube securing clip

3.5 Disconnecting the brake servo vacuum hose

all components have been inspected, before deciding what service and repair operations must be performed by an automotive machine shop. The extent and cost of repairs will be the major factor to consider when determining whether to overhaul the original engine or buy a rebuilt one. As a general rule, time is the primary cost of an overhaul, so it doesn't pay to install worn or sub-standard parts.

As a final note, to ensure maximum life and minimum trouble from a rebuilt engine, everything must be assembled with care, in a spotlessly-clean environment.

2 Methods of engine removal

The engine is removed by lowering it out of the engine compartment and this may be done in unit with the transmission, or by leaving the transmission in the vehicle. The latter is recommended unless there is a good reason for removing the transmission at the same time. A sturdy hydraulic trolley jack or an engine crane will be needed whichever method is adopted.

Certain details of the removal operation will vary according to the version being worked on. The engine shown here is a carburettor model fitted to a Pick-up. Access and ancillary equipment differences are pointed out when known, but the reader should make his or her own notes of any particular points encountered during removal; they will be useful when the time comes for refitting.

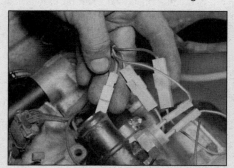

3.7 Identify the engine wiring connectors before disconnecting them

3 Engine alone – removal and refitting

> ⚠️ **Warning: Several safety hazards will be encountered during this procedure. In particular, fuel may be spilt. Take appropriate fire precautions and work in a well-ventilated area. For further details refer to 'Safety first!' at the beginning of the manual.**

1 Disconnect the battery negative terminal.
2 Although not essential at this stage, it is recommended to drain the cooling system (Chapter 1). This will save some mess later on.
3 Remove the engine oil filler tube **(see illustration)**.
4 Remove the dipstick and the dipstick tube. The tube pulls out after releasing any securing clips **(see illustration)**.
5 Disconnect the brake servo vacuum hose from the left-hand side of the inlet manifold **(see illustration)**.
6 Disconnect the HT leads from the spark plugs and the ignition coil, then remove the distributor cap.
7 Disconnect the electrical wiring on the left-hand side of the engine **(see illustration)**, making notes for assistance when refitting. This will vary considerably according to model.
8 Disconnect the distributor LT connector.
9 Unbolt the earth strap from the left-hand side of the crankcase.

3.20 Removing an engine splash shield

10 Remove the air inlet trunking from the carburettor or inlet manifold. Also disconnect the vacuum pipe(s) from the air intake temperature control system, when applicable.
11 Disconnect the fuel supply and return hoses. Be prepared for fuel spillage, especially on fuel injection models where the hoses may be under pressure - wrap rags around the unions when disconnecting. Clamp or plug the hoses.
12 Disconnect the accelerator cable from the carburettor or throttle housing.
13 Disconnect the two main coolant hoses from the left-hand side of the engine. Be prepared for coolant spillage.
14 Disconnect the minor coolant hoses from around the engine. These are numerous and will vary according to model. Also unclip and remove the coolant overflow (top-up) tank.
15 Disconnect the alternator wiring and move it aside.
16 On models with power steering, unbolt the steering pump and move it aside. Do likewise with the air conditioning compressor, when fitted.

> ⚠️ **Warning: Do not disconnect the refrigerant lines from the compressor.**

17 On models with automatic transmission, unbolt the torque converter from the driveplate as described in Chapter 7B. Also remove the transmission fluid dipstick and dipstick tube grommet.
18 Remove the upper two engine-to-transmission nuts and bolts.
19 Have a look around to see if there is anything else to disconnect from above, then raise and securely support the rear of the vehicle. It needs to be high enough to allow the engine to be withdrawn from underneath.
20 Remove any splash shields from underneath if they are going to get in the way **(see illustration)**.
21 Disconnect the hot air intake hoses from the shroud around the right-hand side exhaust pipe.
22 Slacken, but do not remove, the transmission front mounting nut and bolt **(see illustration)**.
23 If not already done, drain the engine oil. It is easier to do it now than when the engine is on the bench. Refit the drain plug on completion.

3.22 Slackening the transmission mounting

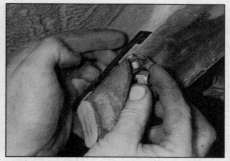

3.27A Remove the engine bearer nuts . . .

3.27B . . . recover the washers . . .

24 Disconnect the starter motor wiring and move it aside.

25 On models with automatic transmission, disconnect the throttle linkage rod from the kickdown lever.

26 Attach the lifting or support gear to the engine. If a hoist is being used, attach slings or chains to the inlet manifold; if a trolley jack is being used, it will be necessary to make up a suitable cradle. Take the weight of the engine.

27 Undo the two nuts and bolts on each side securing the engine bearer to the chassis rails. Recover the washers and reinforcement plates **(see illustrations)**.

28 Lower the engine and transmission assembly approximately 80 mm, being careful not to strain the clutch flexible hose (when applicable).

29 Support the transmission with a trolley jack or axle stands (see "*Jacking and vehicle support*").

30 Remove the two remaining engine-to-transmission nuts and bolts.

31 Check that all cables, pipes and attachments in the engine compartment are clear and then carefully ease the engine rearwards off the transmission. On vehicles with automatic transmission, ensure that the torque converter remains on the transmission.

32 Continue lowering the engine and then withdraw it from under the rear of the vehicle **(see illustration)**.

33 Refitting the engine is the reverse sequence to removal, but bear in mind the following points:

a) *On vehicles with manual transmission, lubricate the transmission input shaft sparingly with molybdenum disulphide grease*

b) *On vehicles with automatic transmission check that the torque converter is properly seated as described in Chapter 7B before the engine is fitted*

c) *Note the directional arrows on the engine bearer (see illustration). They point to the front of the vehicle*

d) *Adjust the accelerator linkage as described in Chapter 4*

e) *Tighten all nuts and bolts to the specified torque where applicable*

f) *Fill and bleed the cooling system as described in Chapter 1*

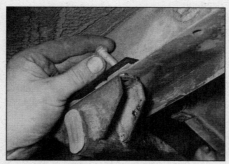

3.27C . . . remove the bolts . . .

3.27D . . . and recover the reinforcement plates

4 Engine and transmission – removal and refitting

1 Refer to the previous Section and carry out the operations described in paragraphs 1 to 24 with the exception of paragraphs 17 and 18.

2 Undo the socket-headed bolts securing the driveshaft inner constant velocity joints to the differential drive flanges. Move the driveshafts clear and tie them up so they do not hang unsupported.

3 Detach the clutch hydraulic pipe support bracket from the side of the transmission and undo the two clutch slave cylinder retaining nuts and bolts. Move the cylinder, with hydraulic pipe and hose still attached, to one side.

4 On vehicles with automatic transmission remove the throttle rod, accelerator cable and

selector cable from the gearbox lever. Also remove the selector lever from the side of the transmission. Remove the two bolts and move the selector cable and support bracket to one side.

5 On vehicles with manual transmission, disconnect the gearshift rod from the transmission linkage.

6 On all vehicles, undo the bolt and remove the earth strap from the mounting bracket.

7 Disconnect the two reversing light wires from the switch.

8 Using a trolley jack in conjunction with a crane or other suitable equipment, take the weight of the engine and transmission assembly.

9 Undo the nut and remove the long bolt securing the transmission bracket to the rubber mounting.

10 Undo the two bolts each side securing the engine bearer to the chassis rails.

3.32 Lowering the engine out of the vehicle

3.33 Arrow on engine bearer points to front

7.3 Removing the distributor driveshaft

11 Check that all cables, pipes and attachments are well clear then slowly lower the engine and transmission assembly to the ground. Withdraw the unit from under the rear of the vehicle.

12 Refitting is the reverse sequence to removal, referring to the points listed at the end of the previous Section.

5 Engine and transmission – separation and attachment

1 If the engine is to be separated from the transmission after removal as a complete assembly, proceed as follows according to transmission type.

Manual transmission

2 This is simply a matter of undoing the two upper and two lower retaining nuts and bolts and withdrawing the transmission from the engine. Do not allow the weight of the engine to hand on the transmission input shaft.

3 Before refitting, lightly lubricate the input shaft splines with molybdenum disulphide grease.

4 Refit the two units and secure with the nuts tightened to the specified torque.

 Renew the clutch components while the engine is out, unless you're sure that they are in perfect condition.

Automatic transmission

5 Remove the plug at the top of the crankcase, turn the engine as necessary until each torque converter retaining bolt is accessible through the plug hole and remove the three bolts.

6 Undo the four nuts securing the transmission to the engine and separate the two units. Make sure that the torque converter remains on the transmission.

7 Refitting is the reverse sequence to removal, but check that the torque converter is properly seated as described in Chapter 7B before fitting and tighten the nuts and bolts to the specified torque.

6 Engine dismantling for overhaul – general information

If the engine has been removed for major overhaul or if individual components have been removed for repair or renewal, observe the following general hints on dismantling and reassembly.

Drain the oil into a suitable container (if not already done) and then thoroughly clean the exterior of the engine using a degreasing solvent or paraffin. Clean away as much of the external dirt and grease as possible before dismantling.

As parts are removed, clean them in a bath of paraffin or other suitable solvent. However, do not immerse parts with internal oilways in paraffin as it is difficult to remove, usually requiring a high pressure hose. Clean oilways with nylon pipe cleaners.

Avoid working with the engine or any of the components directly on a concrete floor, as grit presents a real source of trouble.

Wherever possible work should be carried out with the engine or individual components on a strong bench. If the work must be done on the floor, cover it with a board or sheets of newspaper.

Have plenty of clean, lint-free rags available and also some containers or trays to hold small items. This will help during reassembly and also prevent possible losses.

Always obtain a complete set of new gaskets and oil seals if the engine is being completely dismantled, or all those necessary for the individual component or assembly being worked on. Keep the old gaskets with a view to using them as a pattern to make a replacement if a new one is not available.

When possible refit nuts, bolts and washers in their locations after removal as this helps to protect the threads and avoids confusion or loss. Note that certain fasteners (eg flywheel bolts) must be renewed as a matter of course - this is indicated in the text.

During reassembly thoroughly lubricate all the components, where this is applicable, with engine oil, but avoid contaminating the gaskets and joint mating faces.

7 Engine ancillary components – removal

1 Before major dismantling begins, the externally mounted ancillary components should be removed as follows.

2 Remove the clutch assembly, alternator, mechanical fuel pump, distributor, thermostat housing and coolant pump by referring to the appropriate Chapters of this manual.

3 Remove the distributor driveshaft using a puller with an expanding end, or a thin rod with some sticky tape wrapped round the end to make it a tight fit in the hole in the middle of the shaft **(see illustration)**.

4 Note the location of the various wiring looms, label each lead, then disconnect and remove all the engine wiring.

5 Remove the inlet manifold and carburettor or fuel injection equipment.

6 Remove the exhaust assembly, being careful not to damage the studs or strip the threads in the cylinder heads. These fastenings can be very stubborn. If threads are stripped, make a note to have them repaired by the fitting of thread inserts.

7 Prevent the crankshaft from turning by jamming the flywheel ring gear. Slacken the crankshaft pulley bolt, then remove the bolt and pulley. This bolt is very tight.

8 Remove the remaining coolant distribution pipes and hoses, making notes or marks to assist when refitting.

9 When applicable, unbolt and remove the breather housing from the top of the crankcase.

8 Cylinder heads, pistons and liners – removal

1 Spring back the retaining clamp and lift off the rocker cover **(see illustration)**.

2 Undo the rocker shaft support retaining nuts and remove the rocker shaft assembly **(see illustration)**.

3 Lift out the pushrods, keeping them in order **(see illustration)**.

8.1 Removing a rocker cover

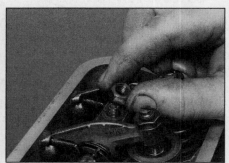

8.2 Removing a rocker shaft retaining nut

8.3 Lift out the pushrods

8.9 Using the special VW tool to withdraw a gudgeon pin

4 Slacken the cylinder head nuts in the reverse order to that shown in illustration 16.19C. Remove the nuts and withdraw the head from the studs and cylinder liners. Recover the metal sealing rings. (If the head sticks to the liners, the head and liners may be withdrawn as an assembly; in this case be careful that the pistons are not damaged as they emerge. Separate the liners from the head on the bench, if necessary after soaking them in a suitable solvent.)

5 Remove the pushrod tubes with their seals. The tappets may now be removed; keep them in order if they are to be re-used.

6 Note the rubber sealing rings at the top of each liner and remove them. Also remove the gasket from around the lip of the water jacket.

9.4 Removing the flywheel

Jam the flywheel using a piece of scrap metal shaped like this and secured to one of the crankcase studs.

7 Mark the cylinders and their corresponding liners 1 to 4 as applicable if they are to be re-used, then carefully withdraw each liner. Recover the sealing ring from the base of each liner.

8 If it is not intended to separate the crankcase halves, stuff rags into the opening so that circlips cannot spring inside during the following operations.

9 Working through the hole in the pulley end of the water jacket, extract the circlip from the gudgeon pin nearest the hole. Withdraw the gudgeon pin. There is a special VW tool (No 3091) with an expanding end for this (see illustration), but unless the pin is very tight a stout piece of wire with a hook bent on the end can be used instead.

10 Remove the piston, making a mark if necessary to show which cylinder it belongs to and which way round it is fitted. Original equipment pistons have an arrow pointing towards the flywheel.

11 Repeat the operation on the piston at the flywheel end. This one is easier to get at.

12 Repeat the above procedures for the remaining cylinder head.

9 Crankcase, crankshaft and camshaft – dismantling

1 Refer to part A of this Chapter and remove the crankshaft pulley and the oil pump.

9.7 Removing a camshaft bearing shell. This flanged one goes at the distributor end

2 Unscrew the oil pressure relief valve and take out the spring and plunger.

3 Jam the flywheel ring gear, undo the retaining bolts securing the flywheel or driveplate to the crankshaft (see *Tool tip*). New bolts will be needed for reassembly.

4 Withdraw the flywheel or driveplate, noting the O-ring seal on the inner face (see illustration). Be careful, the flywheel is heavy. The shims controlling crankshaft endfloat are located behind the oil seal and can be taken out when the casings are separated.

5 Undo the nuts which hold the crankcase halves together. Work methodically, using wooden blocks to support the crankcase, as there are studs sticking out in all directions.

6 Tap the halves apart with a wooden or plastic mallet, but do not tap too hard. If it will not come apart look for more studs or bolts. When all of these are out it does come easily. **Do not** push the faces apart with a wedge. Tap the right-hand half and lift it off the left-hand half, leaving the crankshaft and camshaft in the lower half.

7 Put the right-hand half of the crankcase safely away and turn to the left-hand half. Lift out the camshaft and remove the shell bearings from both halves of the crankcase, noting which way they came out (see illustration).

8 With the camshaft removed, remove the oil seal and shims from the end of the crankshaft, followed by the crankshaft itself (see illustration).

9.8 Removing the crankshaft

9.9 Identification marks on big-end bearing cap and rod

9.10A Remove the connecting rod nuts . . .

9.10B . . . and lift off the cap

9.12A Remove the circlip . . .

9.12B . . . and pull the gears off the crankshaft

9.13 Remove the No 3 main bearing

9 Mark the big-end bearing caps, or make a note of the significance of the existing marks **(see illustration)** so that they can be refitted in the same place and the same way round.
10 Remove the nuts from the connecting rod bolts and ease the cap from the rod **(see illustrations)**. Remove the rod from the shaft and replace the cap on the connecting rod. Keep the bearing shells with their respective rods.
11 Lift off the oil thrower and slide off No 4 main bearing from the pulley end of the crankshaft.
12 Extract the circlip, then draw off the crankshaft gear and the distributor drivegear together using a puller **(see illustrations)**. Recover the Woodruff key and put it somewhere safe.
13 Remove No 3 main bearing **(see illustration)**.
14 Remove the No 1 main bearing from the flywheel end of the crankshaft. On later

models with thin-walled main bearings also remove the thrust washer.
15 Finally, on the right-hand half take out the oil pick-up pipe and strainer, which is secured by a single screw **(see illustration)**.

10 Crankcase, crankshaft and camshaft – inspection

1 All the parts should now be cleaned again and oiled lightly.
2 Examine the two halves of the crankcase. Look for cracks, burrs, loose studs and any sign of rotating parts fouling the crankcase. If all is well set the two halves on one side.
3 Next examine the crankshaft. If it can be run between centres the main bearing surfaces must be checked to ensure the shaft is straight.

4 All bearing surfaces of the crankshaft must be checked for scoring or signs of overheating. Measure them accurately with a micrometer, checking the diameter against that specified and also checking for ovality **(see illustration)**.

HAYNES HiNT

A quick check of crankshaft journal condition can be made by rubbing a copper coin along it. If the journal is rough enough to take copper off the coin, it probably needs reworking.

5 The connecting rods should be examined for twist and bending. Unless special tools are available this is beyond the scope of the home mechanic and should be entrusted to a machine shop. Unless something drastic has occurred the rods will not be distorted. If there has been a seizure or sudden stop then take the rods along for checking. If rods are renewed they must be matched for weight. This again is a job for the specialist.

9.15 Removing the oil pick-up pipe securing screw

10.4 Measure the crankshaft journals with a micrometer

6 Assuming that the rods and crankshaft are in good order, next examine the big-end shells. With the shells fitted correctly and the caps torqued to the right amount, the roundness or ovality of the bearing may be measured with an inside micrometer. Unless the bearings are nearly new, it is a false economy not to fit new big-end shells. If for some reason the old shells are to be re-used, they must go back to their original locations.

7 Regrinding of the crankshaft is not recommended by VW. This is not to say that it is impossible, but a machine shop carrying out the work will have to source the appropriate bearing shells. Satisfy yourself of the competence of the workshop and make sure the shaft is assembled and runs freely when returned to you.

8 A reasonable test for a new big-end when assembled is that the rod should fall slowly under its own weight from just off top dead centre. If it doesn't it is too tight, but it must descend slowly or the clearances are too great.

9 Examine the main bearings. As with the big-end bearings, unless they are in perfect condition they too should be renewed as a matter of course. Note that there are two standard sizes of bearing; the size fitted to a particular crankshaft is identified by a blue or red paint spot in one of the positions shown **(see illustration)**. There are also differences between early (thick-walled) and later (thin-walled) bearings.

10 Check the needle roller bearing in the flywheel end of the crankshaft. Only remove it if it is to be renewed. Use a puller with an expanding end. Alternatively, screw in something like a heavy-duty masonry fitting with an expanding sleeve and use a slide hammer to pull the bearing out. Fit the new bearing with the lettering facing outwards.

11 Endfloat of the connecting rods and of the crankshaft should be checked during reassembly.

12 The camshaft must show no signs of wear or overheating on the bearing and cam surfaces. The gear must be firmly riveted to the shaft. If either of these do not seem right the shaft must be renewed. Note that various sizes of camshaft gear are supplied in order to achieve the correct backlash. Standard size

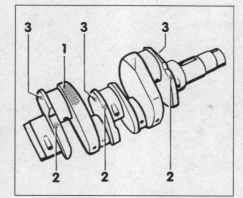
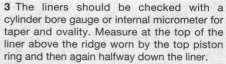

10.9 Significance of crankshaft colour coding

1 *Green mark identifies 2.1 litre version*
2 *Blue or red spot for bearing identification*
3 *Alternative locations for blue or red spots*

gears are marked '0'; oversize or undersize gears are marked '+1', '-2' etc. It is unlikely that the DIY mechanic will have access to a selection of camshafts for trial purposes, so fit a camshaft with the same size gear as the one being removed unless there is a good reason for supposing that it was incorrect.

13 The camshaft bearing shells must now be checked. They are all different so make sure the right partners go together. Check them for obvious wear or damage. Again, if there is the least doubt, renew the whole lot.

---

11 Cylinder liners, pistons and rings – inspection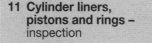

1 Inspect the pistons, piston rings and cylinder liners for obvious signs of scoring, burning, wear ridges or other damage.

2 Remove the rings from the pistons, identifying them if they are to be re-used. The compression rings are brittle and will snap if spread too far. Special piston ring pliers are available, or a couple of old feeler blades can be slid underneath each ring as it is expanded and the ring then slid off.

Caution: Be careful not to scratch the pistons!

---

3 The liners should be checked with a cylinder bore gauge or internal micrometer for taper and ovality. Measure at the top of the liner above the ridge worn by the top piston ring and then again halfway down the liner.

4 New pistons may be fitted to existing liners providing the liner is in a satisfactory condition. If the liners are worn, new pistons and liners should be obtained. Pistons and liners are available in two standard sizes and if one assembly is being replaced the new assembly must be of the same size group as the other three pistons and liners.

5 Pistons should be checked for ovality using a micrometer and the rings should be checked for excessive clearance in their grooves.

6 Piston ring gaps may be checked by placing each ring squarely in the liner and measuring the gap with feeler blades **(see illustration)**. If the gap is excessive the rings must be renewed.

7 If new rings are to be fitted to existing pistons, clean out the grooves in the pistons using a broken piece of old piston ring. Protect your fingers - piston rings are sharp! The new top compression rings should be of 'ridge dodger' pattern, having a small step machined into their top face. If such rings cannot be obtained then any wear ridges at the tops of the liners must be removed using a ridge reamer, otherwise the new rings may hit the ridge and break.

---

12 Cylinder head and valve gear – inspection and bleeding of tappets

Inspection

1 Remove each valve from its location by compressing the spring caps and lifting out the collets. Withdraw the springs and cap, then remove the valve from its guide **(see illustrations)**. Remove all the valves in this way and keep them in order after removal.

2 Check the condition of the cylinder head visually after removing all traces of carbon from the combustion chambers and ports. Small cracks (less than 0.5 mm wide) between the valve seats or around the spark plug hole

---

11.6 Checking a piston ring end gap

12.1A Compress the valve spring to release the collets

12.1B Removing a valve from its guide

12.5A Remove the spring clip . . .

12.5B . . . and slide the components off the rocker shaft

may be ignored. The valve seats should be free from severe pitting or any other sign of damage. The seats may be recut with special equipment, but if they are damaged beyond reclamation, a new head will be required.

3 The condition of the valve guides can be checked by 'rocking' the valve in the guide. If the movement is excessive, check the valve stem diameter with a micrometer. If the valve is not worn, new guides will be needed and this work must be left to a VW specialist or machine shop.

4 If the valves appear satisfactory after removing all carbon, they may be lapped into their seats using coarse and fine grinding paste. Refacing of valves is not permitted.

5 Check the rockers and rocker shaft for signs of wear or excessive play of the rockers on the shafts. The components can be removed from the shaft after taking off the spring clip at the end **(see illustrations)**. Keep the components in order and make sure all oilways are clear.

6 Check the valve springs for damaged or broken coils. It is advisable to renew the springs at time of overhaul in any case. Also check the pushrods for straightness.

7 Check the hydraulic tappets externally for signs of wear or scuff marks. If they were excessively noisy under all engine conditions they should be renewed. If the plungers 'give' when pressed down firmly with the thumb, there is air in the pressure chamber and the tappet must be dismantled for bleeding. This

will also be necessary if new tappets are being fitted.

Bleeding hydraulic tappets

8 To bleed the tappet, dismantle it by removing the circlip and lifting out the components in the order shown **(see illustration)**.

9 Fill the tappet with clean engine oil up to the level of the hole in its side **(see illustration)**.

10 Insert the plunger spring followed by the plunger and valve assembly **(see illustrations)**.

11 Using a thin rod inserted through the hole in the plunger, depress the spring-loaded ball to allow the trapped air to escape **(see illustration)**.

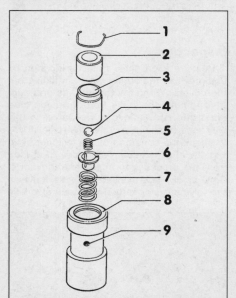

12.8 Hydraulic tappet components

1 Circlip
2 Pushrod socket
3 Plunger
4 Valve ball
5 Valve spring
6 Valve retainer
7 Spring
8 Tappet body
9 Hole

12.9 Fill the tappet with clean oil

12.10A Fit the spring . . .

12.10B . . . followed by the plunger and valve assembly

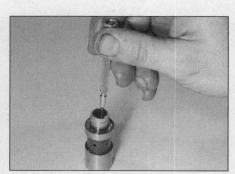

12.11 Depress the ball to let the air out

12.12 Fit the pushrod socket

12.13A Press the plunger down in a vice . . .

12.13B . . . until the circlip can be fitted

12 Remove the rod and fit the pushrod socket **(see illustration)**.

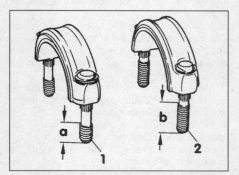

13.2 Identification of big-end cap bolts

1 Rigid bolt - can be re-used
2 Stretch bolt - must be renewed
a = 13 mm approx
b = 22 mm approx

13 The pushrod socket must now be pushed down using a blunt instrument (ideally an old pushrod cut in half, though a bolt will do) so that the circlip can be fitted. The force needed to push down the pushrod socket is quite high. Put the tappet on its side in a vice, with the drilling in the side uppermost, and compress it a little at a time until the circlip can be fitted **(see illustrations)**.

14 After bleeding the tappets, store them vertically and submerged in a bath of clean engine oil until they are needed for refitting.

13 Engine reassembly – general information

1 To ensure maximum life with minimum trouble from a rebuilt engine, not only must everything be correctly assembled, but it must also be spotlessly clean. All oilways must be clear, and locking washers and

spring washers must be fitted where indicated. Oil all bearings and other working surfaces thoroughly with engine oil during assembly.

2 Before assembly begins, renew any bolts or studs which have damaged threads. New flywheel or driveplate bolts and new oil pump cover nuts will be needed in any case. Connecting rod big-end cap bolts must be renewed if they are of the 'stretch' type; rigid bolts can be re-used **(see illustration)**.

3 Gather together a torque wrench, oil can, clean rags and a set of engine gaskets and oil seals, together with a new oil filter.

14 Crankcase, crankshaft and camshaft – reassembly

1 Place the crankshaft on a clean surface. Inject oil into the oilways and lubricate the bearing surfaces **(see illustration)**.

2 Lubricate the No 3 main bearing and fit it onto the crankshaft **(see illustration)**. On early models with thick-walled bearings the blind hole must be next to the crankshaft web. On later models with thin-walled bearings the locating lugs go on the right-hand side and the oil drillings face downwards (imagining the engine to be in its fitted position).

3 Refit the crankshaft Woodruff key if it was removed. Heat the camshaft drive pinion in water or with a hot air gun to 80°C and slide it into position, the chamfer edge of the bore leading; tap it home with a suitable tube and then fit the spacer **(see illustrations)**.

14.1 Crankshaft ready for reassembly

14.2 Lubricate the bearings before fitting

14.3A Fit the gear with the chamfer inwards . . .

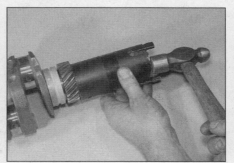

14.3B . . . and tap it home with a hammer and a tube . . .

14.3C . . . followed by the spacer

14.4A Fit the distributor drive pinion . . .

14.4B . . . and tap it home with a soft metal drift

14.5 Fitting a big-end bearing shell to its cap

4 Now heat the distributor drive pinion to 80°C and slide it on. Tap it home with a soft metal drift if necessary and then fit the circlip **(see illustrations)**.

5 Position the big-end shells in the connecting rods and caps and then place each rod and cap assembly adjacent to its big-end journal on the crankshaft **(see illustration)**. The numbers on the ends of the cap and rod must be together and the same, and the forged marks on the rods must be uppermost when in their normal running position.

6 Lubricate the bearing shells. Reassemble the caps and rods and progressively tighten the nuts to the specified torque **(see illustrations)**. Remember to use new bolts if they are of the 'stretch' type.

7 Measure the endfloat of each connecting rod using feeler blades and ensure that it is as specified **(see illustration)**.

8 Fit the locating dowels in place in the crankcase journals, then assemble the No 2 main bearing shells to both halves of the crankcase **(see illustrations)**.

9 On early models with thick-walled bearings, slide No 1 (flywheel end) main bearing onto the crankshaft with the dowel hole towards the flywheel, followed by No 4 (pulley end) main bearing, oil groove towards the pulley **(see illustrations)**.

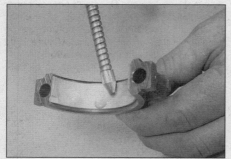

14.6A Lubricate the bearing shells

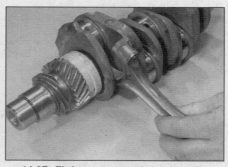

14.6B Fitting a connecting rod to the crankshaft

14.6C Tightening a connecting rod cap nut

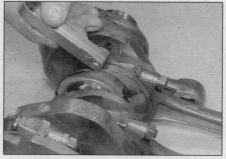

14.7 Measuring connecting rod endfloat

14.8A Fit the locating dowels . . .

14.8B . . . and the No 2 main bearing shells

14.9A Fit the No 1 main bearing with the dowel hole towards the flywheel . . .

14.9B . . . and the No 4 main bearing with the oil groove towards the pulley

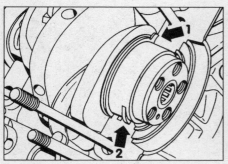

14.10 No 1 main bearing and thrust washer arrangement - later models

1 *Thrust washer lug*
2 *Oil drillings in bearing*

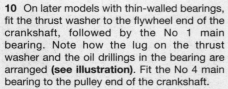

10 On later models with thin-walled bearings, fit the thrust washer to the flywheel end of the crankshaft, followed by the No 1 main bearing. Note how the lug on the thrust washer and the oil drillings in the bearing are arranged **(see illustration)**. Fit the No 4 main bearing to the pulley end of the crankshaft.
11 Fit the camshaft bearings to the crankcase, try the camshaft in position and remove it. Note that the flanged thrust bearing goes at the distributor end.
12 Oil the bearing surfaces of the crankshaft and camshaft. Lift the crankshaft by the 2nd and 4th cylinder con rods and lower it into the crankcase, feeding Nos 1 and 3 con rods through the holes in the crankcase. Check that Nos 1, 3 and 4 mains have located properly, with the dowels in place, and that No 2 main bearing shell is in place.
13 Rotate the crankshaft so that the two punch marks on the side of the drivegear are horizontal and install the camshaft so that the pip mark on the camshaft gear fits between the two marks on the drivegear **(see illustration)**. Check all the bearing shells again.
14 Fit the sealing plug for the end of the camshaft into position, applying sealing compound (VW AMV 188 001 02 or equivalent) to the plug and its recess **(see illustrations)**.
15 Now turn to the other half of the casing. Install the oil suction pipe and the strainer, using a new sealing ring. Insert and tighten the retaining screw.

14.13 Correct alignment of camshaft timing marks (arrowed)

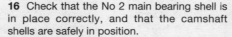

16 Check that the No 2 main bearing shell is in place correctly, and that the camshaft shells are safely in position.
17 Wipe carefully round the two mating surfaces of the crankcase and coat the one in which the crankshaft is installed with the same jointing compound as was used for the camshaft sealing plug. Use this sparingly.
18 Oil the bearing surfaces, and holding the crankcase by the studs lower it carefully into position over the crankshaft and camshaft, feeding the connecting rods through the cylinder openings as the case is lowered.
19 Fit the nuts and washers to the crankcase studs, coating them with sealing compound. Tighten all the nuts slightly, working in a diagonal sequence.
20 Temporarily fit a couple of flywheel bolts to the crankcase and use a lever between the bolts to turn the crankshaft through 360° to make sure that nothing is fouling. Some stiffness is to be expected if new components have been fitted, but there must be no tight spots or binding.
21 Tighten the crankcase nuts progressively to the specified torque. Begin with the M8 (smaller) nut located by the tappet bores, followed by the M10 (larger) nuts, then finally the remaining M8 nuts **(see illustrations)**. Note that the tightening torque specified for the M10 nuts is different for early and later models.
22 Check the rotation of the crankshaft again. If it is binding undo the nuts, split the case and search for the reason. It will probably be a bearing not seating properly.

14.14A Apply sealant to the plug recess . . .

14.14B . . . then fit the sealing plug itself

23 It is now necessary to determine crankshaft endfloat, which is adjusted by changing the thickness of the shim pack between the crankshaft and the flywheel or driveplate. Details differ slightly according to whether thick-walled or thin-walled main bearings are fitted. Proceed as follows.

Early models (thick-walled bearings)

24 Fit the flywheel with two shims behind it **(see illustration)**. Do not fit the oil seal or the O-ring yet. Insert the flywheel bolts and tighten them moderately.
25 Set up a dial gauge to bear on the face of the flywheel **(see illustration)**. Lever the flywheel back and forth and observe the change in the dial gauge reading: this is the endfloat. Make a note of this measurement.

14.21A Tightening the crankcase nuts. Start with the M8 nut (arrowed) by the tappet bores

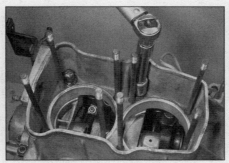

14.21B Tightening the crankcase nuts inside the water jacket

14.24 Fit two shims before measuring crankshaft endfloat

14.25 Measuring crankshaft endfloat with a dial gauge

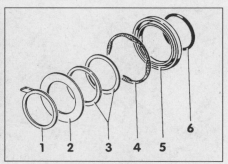

14.27 Endfloat shims and associated components - later models

1 *Thrust washer*   4 *Retainer*
2 *Large shim*   5 *Seal*
3 *Selective shims* 6 *O-ring*

14.32 Angle-tightening the flywheel bolts

26 Subtract 0.10 mm from the endfloat reading just obtained and this will give the thickness of the third shim required. Shims of various thicknesses are available; they have their thickness engraved on them, but it is best to check with a micrometer. Unless major repairs have been done, the reinstallation of the old shims will usually meet the requirement.

Later models (thin-walled bearings)

27 Lubricate the thrust washer and fit it with its locating tag towards the main bearing. Fit the large shim washer **(see illustration)**.
28 Fit the flywheel, without any other shims or seals. Insert the flywheel bolts and tighten them moderately.
29 Measure and note the crankshaft endfloat as described for earlier models.
30 Subtract 0.10 mm from the endfloat reading just obtained and this will give the combined thickness of the two shims required. Shims of various thicknesses are available; they have their thickness engraved on them, but it is best to check with a micrometer. Unless major repairs have been done, the reinstallation of the old shims will usually meet the requirement.

All models

31 Remove the flywheel, fit the shim pack, fit the O-ring to the flywheel and a new oil seal in the crankcase. Tap the seal fully into its location (see part A of this Chapter).
32 Fit the flywheel and secure it with new bolts. Jam the flywheel and tighten each bolt

14.35 Fitting the oil thrower to the pulley end of the crankshaft

to the Stage 1 specified torque, then tighten through the angle specified for Stage 2 **(see illustration)**.
33 Refit the oil pressure relief valve components and screw home the plug. Also refit the oil pressure switch(es).
34 Fit the oil pump as described in part A of this Chapter, remembering to use new cover plate nuts.
35 Fit the oil thrower to the pulley end of the crankshaft **(see illustration)**.
36 Fit a new oil seal to the pulley end of the crankshaft, referring if necessary to part A of this Chapter. Refit the crankshaft pulley, the pulley bolt and washer. Jam the flywheel and tighten the pulley bolt to the specified torque **(see illustration)**.

14.36 Tightening the crankshaft pulley bolt

15 Cylinder heads – reassembly

1 The clean cylinder heads should now be assembled with the valves. The valves have been serviced, either machined or ground in and are ready for fitting. If old components are being re-used they should go back to their original locations.
2 Lubricate the valve stem and insert the valve into the guide. Slip the springs over the stem, fit the spring cap, compress the springs with a valve spring compressor and fit the collets in place **(see illustrations and *Haynes Hint*)**.

15.2A Fit the inner valve spring . . .

15.2B . . . and the outer spring . . .

15.2C . . . fit the spring cap . . .

15.2D . . . compress the springs and
fit the collets

3 When the valve components are
assembled, carefully release the compressor,
then tap the valve stem sharply using a
hammer and a soft metal drift **(see
illustration)**. This will show whether the
collets are properly seated.
4 Repeat the operations on the other cylinder
head.

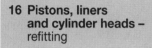

**16 Pistons, liners
and cylinder heads –
refitting**

Pistons and liners

1 Bleed the hydraulic tappets as described in
Section 12, if this has not already been done,
then lubricate and insert each tappet into its
original bore **(see illustrations)**.

*If the collets are difficult hold them on
the end of a screwdriver with a blob of
grease and poke them into place that
way.*

2 If new piston rings are to be fitted, do so
now, observing any 'TOP' markings and
following any particular instructions supplied
with the rings **(see illustrations)**. Space the
ring gaps 180° apart and away from the
gudgeon pin holes, so that the gaps will be at
top and bottom of the piston in the installed
position.
3 Lay out the pistons and liners so that it is
clear which one goes where. Fit a gudgeon
pin circlip to the front (flywheel end) of each
piston **(see illustration)**.
4 Start with a piston and liner which will go at
the flywheel end. Lubricate the piston and fit a
piston ring compressor to it. Introduce the
piston to its liner, making sure that both are

15.3 Settle the valve components by
tapping the stem like this

the right way round (arrow on piston crown
points towards flywheel, cast lugs at tops of
liners face each other). Push the piston into the
liner so that the rings are inside the barrel but
the gudgeon pin hole is still free, then release
the ring compressor **(see illustrations)**.
5 Fit a new base seal to the cylinder liner **(see
illustration)**. Do not mix up the top seals and
the base seals: the base seals are thick and
black, while the top seals are thin and green.
6 Turn the crankshaft to bring the connecting
rod belonging to the piston as far out of the
crankcase as possible.
7 Stuff some clean rag into the crankcase to
catch any errant circlips during the following
operations.
8 Lubricate the gudgeon pin and push it part
way into its piston, then lower the piston/liner
assembly over the connecting rod. Move the
rod back and forth until the gudgeon pin can

16.1A Oil the tappets . . .

16.1B . . . and insert them into their bores

16.2A Fit the oil control ring expander . . .

16.2B . . . followed by the oil control ring
rail . . .

16.2C . . . and the compression rings. Note
'TOP' marking

16.3 Fitting a gudgeon pin circlip

16.4A Introducing a piston to its cylinder liner

16.4B Piston rings are inside the barrel but the gudgeon pin hole is still free

16.5 Fitting a liner base seal

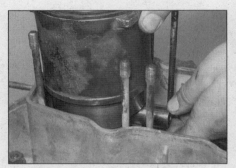

16.8 Push the gudgeon pin through the connecting rod small end

16.9 Fitting the other circlip. Note rag to stop it falling into crankcase

16.11 Gudgeon pin has to be fitted through the hole in the water jacket

16.13 Fitting a new liner top seal

be pushed through the small end **(see illustration)**.

9 Push the gudgeon pin fully home, then fit the other circlip **(see illustration)**.

10 Push the liner home into its location in the crankcase.

11 Repeat the operations on the other piston on this side of the engine, but this time working through the hole in the water jacket when it comes to fitting the gudgeon pin and circlip **(see illustration)**.

12 Remove the rag and repeat the whole sequence on the other side of the engine.

Cylinder heads

13 Working on one side of the engine at a time, fit a new top seal (thin, green) to each liner **(see illustration)**.

14 Prepare the pushrod tubes by carefully stretching each one until the length measured between the outer ends of the corrugated sections is approximately 194 mm **(see illustration)**. Be careful when doing this: the

corrugations will crack if handled roughly, and the damage may not be evident until oil starts to leak out after start-up.

15 Fit new seals to both ends of each pushrod tube, then fit the tubes to their locations in the crankcase **(see illustrations)**.

16 Fit a new rubber gasket to the rim of the water jacket. Apply a thin bead of sealant (VW D 000 400 01 or equivalent) to the mating face of the gasket **(see illustrations)**. Once the sealant has been applied, the cylinder head must be fitted and tightened down within 45 minutes. Do not apply excessive amounts of sealant, for fear of blocking coolant passages.

17 Lightly grease the new metal sealing rings and fit them into the cylinder head **(see illustration)**.

18 Lower the cylinder head over the studs, being careful that the metal sealing rings do not

16.14 Stretch the pushrod tubes so that the distance between arrows is approximately 194 mm

16.15A Fit new seals to the pushrod tubes . . .

16.15B . . . then fit them to the crankcase

16.16A Fit a new water jacket gasket . . .

16.16B . . . and apply a bead of sealant

16.17 Apply a smear of grease to the head sealing rings to stop them falling out

16.18 Fitting a cylinder head

16.19A Apply sealant to the contact surfaces of the cylinder head nuts . . .

16.19B . . . then tighten them in stages to the specified torque

fall out and making sure that the pushrod tubes engage in their sockets (see illustration).

19 Coat the contact surfaces of the cylinder head nuts with sealant (VW AKD 456 000 02 or equivalent). Fit the nuts and tighten them in stages, and in the order shown, to the specified torque (see illustrations).

20 Lubricate the pushrods and refit the pushrods to their original locations, making sure that each one enters the recess in the centre of its tappet.

21 Fit the rocker gear onto its studs, engaging the tops of the pushrods in the cups while so doing. Fit the washers and retaining nuts and tighten the nuts to the specified torque (see illustration).

22 Repeat the operations on the other side of the engine.

16.19C Cylinder head nut tightening sequence

16.21 Tightening the rocker shaft nuts

as it turns under the meshing action of the skew gears, it adopts the final fitted position shown (see illustration). The smaller

segment, or offset, faces towards the coolant pump. Several attempts may be necessary before the correct position is achieved.

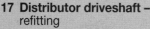

17 Distributor driveshaft – refitting

1 Turn the engine in the normal direction of rotation until No 1 piston approaches TDC on compression. Check this by viewing the inlet valve rocker arm for No 1 cylinder; it must just have finished closing as the notch on the crankshaft pulley approaches the upper join in the crankcase halves. Align the marks so that No 1 piston is at TDC.

2 Position the thrust washer(s) over the end of the driveshaft and retain them with a little grease (see illustration).

3 Insert the driveshaft into its location so that

17.2 Fitting the distributor driveshaft. Note thrust washers (arrowed) secured with grease

17.3 Correct alignment of distributor driveshaft - slot in shaft must line up with threaded hole as indicated by dotted line

4 With the driveshaft in place, slide the preload spring into the centre of the driveshaft **(see illustration)**.

18 Engine ancillary components – refitting

1 Refit the breather housing (when applicable) to the top of the crankcase, using a new O-ring. Note the earth wire connection at the base of the breather **(see illustrations)**.
2 Refit the various coolant distribution pipes and hoses, using new seals and gaskets as appropriate.
3 Refit the exhaust system, referring if necessary to Chapter 4.
4 Refit the inlet manifold and carburettor or fuel injection equipment, again referring if necessary to Chapter 4.
5 The fitting of the remaining ancillary components and the remainder of reassembly now follows a reverse of the sequence described in Section 7. Always use new gaskets and seals when appropriate. Refer to the various Chapters concerned for details of the fitting and adjustment of the components where necessary.

18.1A Fit a new O-ring to the base of the breather . . .

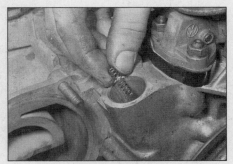

17.4 Fitting the distributor preload spring

19 Hydraulic tappets – initial setting

1 An initial basic setting for the hydraulic tappets must be carried out whenever the rocker shaft assembly has been removed or a tappet renewed. After this initial setting has been carried out, no further adjustment is required in service.
2 Position the engine so that No 1 piston is at TDC on compression with the distributor rotor arm pointing to the notch in the distributor body rim.
3 Slacken the rocker arm locknuts for No 1 cylinder. Back off the adjusting screws until they are clear of the valve stems, then screw them back in until they make light contact with no clearance. From this position tighten the screws two further turns, then tighten the lock nuts without allowing the screws to move **(see illustration)**.
4 Rotate the crankshaft half a turn so that No 4 cylinder is at TDC on compression and repeat the adjustment on the rocker arms for that cylinder. Repeat this procedure for cylinders 3 and 2.
5 After carrying out this setting, refit the rocker covers using new gaskets.
6 When the engine is started the tappets will initially be noisy and it may be some time (even after driving several miles) before all the noise disappears completely. This is quite normal and is no cause for alarm.

7 Note that it is also normal for the tappets to be noisy for a little while after the first start of the day, and when idling after a high-speed run. Fitting new tappets will not necessarily improve things. Experimenting with the make and grade of engine oil may minimise these symptoms; consult a VW specialist if further advice is required.

20 Initial start-up after overhaul – general information

With the engine refitted and ready to start, recheck the fluid levels (see "*Weekly checks*"), make sure that the battery is fully charged and have a good look around to make sure that no tools or rags have been left in the engine compartment.

Disable the ignition system by unplugging the distributor LT connector, then crank the engine on the starter motor until the oil pressure warning light goes out. This will also serve to prime the fuel system.

Reconnect the distributor and start the engine. Do not race it, but allow it to run at a fast idle. Look all around and under the engine to check that no serious leaks are evident. Make sure that the oil pressure warning light stays out.

Be prepared for some odd smells and smoke from parts getting hot and burning off oil deposits.

Bleed the cooling system as described in Chapter 1 while the engine is warming up.

When the engine has warmed up, check the ignition timing and adjust the idle speed if necessary.

Switch the engine off and allow it to cool, then recheck the fluid levels and carry out a close inspection for leaks. If all is well, take the vehicle for a test drive.

If new pistons, rings or crankshaft bearings have been fitted, the engine must be run-in for the first 500 miles (800 km) or so. Do not exceed 60 mph (100 kph), operate the engine at full throttle or allow it to labour in any gear.

Change the engine oil and oil filter at the end of the running-in period (see Chapter 1).

18.1B . . . then fit the breather to the crankcase

18.1C Don't forget the earth wire connection

19.3 Basic adjustment of hydraulic tappets

Chapter 3
Cooling, heating and air conditioning systems

Contents

Degrees of difficulty

| Easy, suitable for novice with little experience | | Fairly easy, suitable for beginner with some experience | | Fairly difficult, suitable for competent DIY mechanic | | Difficult, suitable for experienced DIY mechanic | | Very difficult, suitable for expert DIY or professional | |

Specifications

General
Cooling system type .... Pressurised, pumped circulation, front-mounted radiator, electric cooling fan
Coolant capacity .... See Chapter 1 Specifications
Pressure cap rating .... 0.90 to 1.15 bar

Thermostat
Starts to open .... 85° C
Fully open .... 105° C
Stroke .... 8 mm

Cooling fan thermoswitch
Carburettor engines:
First speed cuts in at .... 93° to 98° C
First speed cuts out at .... 88° to 93° C
Second speed (when applicable) cuts in at .... 99° to 105° C
Second speed (when applicable) cuts out at .... 91° to 97° C
Fuel injection engines:
First speed cuts in at .... 89° to 94° C
First speed cuts out at .... 81° C
Second speed cuts in at .... 95° to 100° C
Second speed cuts out at .... 87° C

Torque wrench settings	Nm	lbf ft
Coolant pump to engine	20	15
Coolant pump flange bolts (later models)	20	15
Coolant pump pulley bolts	20	15
Thermostat housing to coolant pump (early models)	20	15
Thermostat housing cover bolts (early models)	7	5
Thermostat housing cover bolts (later models)	10	7
Temperature sensor to thermostat housing	10	7
Radiator mounting bolts	15	11
Fan thermoswitch to radiator	25	18

1 General information and precautions

General information

The primary function of the cooling system is to dissipate heat produced by the engine. The system is designed to allow the engine to warm up as quickly as possible after a cold start and to maintain the optimum operating temperature after warm-up. It also provides heat for the interior heater when required. The system operates as follows.

Coolant (a mixture of water and antifreeze) is circulated round the engine water jackets by a belt-driven pump. The coolant also passes through channels in the inlet manifold in order to keep the manifold warm and promote fuel vaporisation.

When the engine is cold, a thermostat confines the coolant circulation to the engine, manifold and the heater radiator. When the coolant temperature is high enough, the thermostat opens, allowing coolant to flow to the radiator at the front of the vehicle. The coolant flows from top to bottom of the radiator and is cooled by the airflow created by the vehicle's forward motion, after which it returns to the engine. On models with automatic transmission, coolant also passes through a heat exchanger mounted on the transmission; a similar heat exchanger is used to cool the engine oil on fuel injection models. There is a multitude of distribution pipes and hoses (see illustrations).

If the coolant temperature in the radiator exceeds a certain value, a thermoswitch mounted in the side of the radiator switches on an electric cooling fan to increase the airflow to the radiator. Depending on model and specification, a single-speed or two-speed fan may be fitted.

An expansion tank accommodates the increase in volume which occurs when the coolant heats up. The expansion tank proper vents into an overflow or 'top-up' tank which is not pressurised.

Apart from the top-up tank just mentioned, the cooling system is sealed and pressurised. If there is a regular need for topping-up, this can only be due to a leak, which should be investigated and fixed before it becomes serious.

An air conditioning system is available on some models. This is described in Section 13.

Special notes

The cooling system is more complicated, and perhaps more demanding, than that found on many cars. The main reason for this is the fact that the engine and the radiator are as far removed from each other as they could possibly be horizontally, but that they are not much different in height. Follow the filling and bleeding procedure in Chapter 1 carefully after each intervention in the cooling system.

A secondary complication comes from the fact that the water cooling system has necessarily been designed around the old air-cooled engine, with the result reflecting the fact that it is easier and cheaper to add external pipework than to remake engine

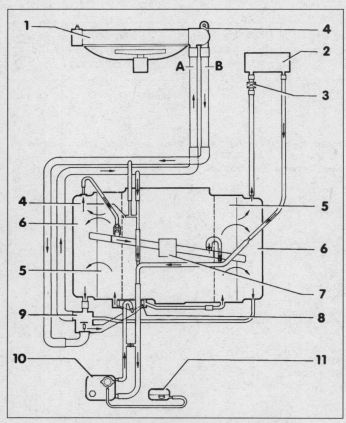

1.3A Cooling system pipe and hose connections - early models with manual transmission

1 Radiator	5 Cylinder water jacket	9 Thermostat
2 Heater	6 Cylinder head	10 Expansion tank
3 Heater valve	7 Inlet manifold	11 Overflow ('top-up') tank
4 Bleed screw	8 Coolant pump	

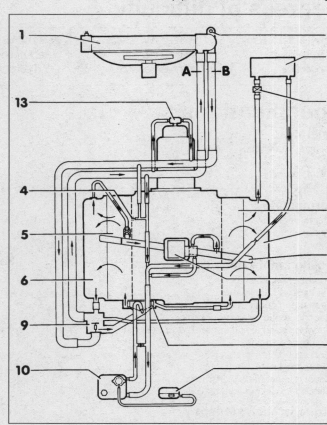

1.3B Cooling system pipe and hose connections - early models with automatic transmission

1 Radiator	6 Cylinder head	11 Overflow ('top-up') tank
2 Heater	7 Inlet manifold	12 Carburettor
3 Heater valve	8 Coolant pump	13 Automatic transmission fluid cooler
4 Bleed screw	9 Thermostat	
5 Cylinder water jacket	10 Expansion tank	

castings. The two main rubber hoses in the engine bay are of an astonishing length and are correspondingly expensive to renew. This should perhaps be accepted as the price paid for retaining the pleasures of the flat four.

Caution: It is extremely important that the correct concentration of antifreeze be maintained in the cooling system at all times. If the antifreeze is diluted by repeated addition of plain water, there is a risk of corrosion occurring in the engine water jackets. This corrosion can weaken the cylinder head retaining studs which can in turn lead to catastrophic engine failure.

Precautions

 Warning: Do not remove the expansion tank cap or disturb any part of the system while the engine is hot, as there is a risk of scalding. If the cap must be removed before the system has cooled completely, cover the cap with a thick rag and release it slowly, waiting for any hissing to stop before removing it completely.

 Warning: Do not allow antifreeze to come into contact with skin or with painted surfaces. Wash off spillages immediately with plenty of water. Never leave antifreeze lying around in open containers or in puddles on the driveway or garage floor. Children and pets are attracted by its sweet smell. Antifreeze is poisonous if swallowed.

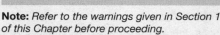 *Warning: If the radiator is hot, the electric cooling fan may start even if the engine is not running.*

Note: *Refer to Section 13 for precautions to be taken when working on models with air conditioning.*

2 Cooling system hoses - renewal

Note: *Refer to the warnings given in Section 1 of this Chapter before proceeding.*

1 If the checks described in Chapter 1 reveal a faulty hose, it must be renewed as follows.

2.3 **Disconnecting a main coolant hose**

2 First drain the cooling system (see Chapter 1). If the coolant is not due for renewal, it may be re-used if it is collected in a clean container.

3 To disconnect a hose, release its retaining clips, then move them along the hose, clear of the relevant inlet/outlet union **(see illustration)**. The hose clips fitted as original equipment are released by squeezing their tangs together with pliers. Carefully work the hose free. While the hoses can be removed with relative ease when new or hot, **do not** attempt to disconnect any part of the system while it is still hot.

4 To renew the stub hose which connects the thermostat housing to the left-hand cylinder head it will be necessary to remove the thermostat housing.

5 Note that some of the coolant unions are fragile, in particular the plastic bleed valve located in the engine bay; do not use excessive force when attempting to remove the hoses. If a hose proves to be difficult to remove, try to release it by rotating the hose ends before attempting to free it.

 HAYNES HiNT *If all else fails, cut the hose with a sharp knife, then slit it so that it can be peeled off in two pieces. Although this may prove expensive if the hose is otherwise undamaged, it is usually cheaper to renew the hose than the component to which it is attached.*

6 When fitting a hose, first slide the clips onto the hose, then work the hose into position. Renew the hose clips if there is any doubt about the condition of the old ones. If the hose is stiff, use a little soapy water as a lubricant, or soften the hose by soaking it in hot water.

7 Work the hose into position, checking that it is correctly routed, then slide each clip along the hose until it passes over the flared end of the relevant inlet/outlet union, before securing it in position with the retaining clip.

8 Refill the cooling system (see Chapter 1).

9 Check thoroughly for leaks as soon as possible after disturbing any part of the cooling system.

3 Radiator - removal and refitting

Note 1: *Refer to the warnings given in Section 1 of this Chapter before proceeding.*

Note 2: *On models with air conditioning, the condenser is attached to the radiator, from which it can be separated after lowering the radiator. Do not disconnect the refrigerant lines from the condenser - see Section 13.*

1 Disconnect the battery negative lead.

2 Raise and support the front of the vehicle (see "*Jacking and vehicle support*").

3 Remove the spare wheel and the spare wheel carrier. The carrier supports are secured by hairpin clips which can be prised out with a screwdriver **(see illustration)**.

4 Remove the undertray from below the radiator. This is secured by two self-tapping screws **(see illustration)**.

5 Place a container under the right-hand side of the radiator. Disconnect the hoses from the base of the radiator and catch the coolant in the container **(see illustration)**.

6 Remove the front grille panels. The upper grille is secured by three or five fasteners which must be turned through 90° to release them. The lower grille is secured by five screws.

7 Disconnect the wiring harness from the cooling fan and from the fan thermoswitch. Free the harness from any cable ties **(see illustrations)**.

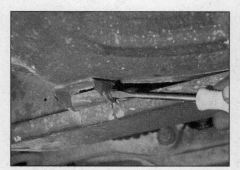
3.3 **Removing a hairpin clip from one of the spare wheel carrier supports**

3.4 **Removing a radiator undertray screw**

3.5 **Coolant hose connections at base of radiator**

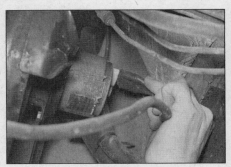

3.7A Disconnect the wiring from the radiator cooling fan . . .

3.7B . . . and from the thermoswitch

3.8 Radiator mounting bracket

8 With the aid of an assistant, support the radiator and unbolt the two lower brackets **(see illustration)**. Lower the radiator and remove it.
Caution: Be careful! the radiator is quite heavy and its fins are sharp.
9 Recover the rubber mounting bushes from the lugs on the radiator **(see illustration)**.
10 Refitting is a reversal of the removal procedure. Do not refit the upper grille panel until the cooling system has been refilled and bled as described in Chapter 1.

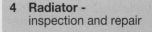

4 Radiator -
inspection and repair

1 If the radiator has been removed due to suspected blockage, flush it with copious quantities of clean water, first in one direction and then in the other. Shaking the radiator gently during flushing may help to loosen stubborn deposits. The use of chemical descaling compounds is only recommended as a last resort.
2 Clean dirt and debris from the radiator fins, using an air line (in which case, wear eye protection) or a soft brush.
Caution: Be careful, as the fins are sharp and easily damaged.
3 If necessary, a radiator specialist can perform a flow test on the radiator, to establish whether an internal blockage exists.

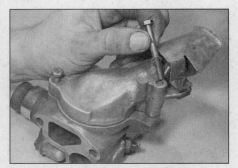

5.4 Removing the thermostat housing cover bolts (early type shown) - housing has been removed and turned over in order to show the bolts

If there is a blockage it may be possible to clear it mechanically ('rodding out'), but in bad cases the heat exchanger itself will have to be renewed ('recoring'). Both these operations should be carried out by a specialist, who will normally provide a guarantee of some kind.
4 Leaks from the radiator can usually be recognised by characteristic green or white stains. Refer to a specialist for permanent repair. Do not attempt to weld or solder a leaking radiator, as damage may result.
5 In an emergency, minor leaks from the radiator can sometimes be cured using a suitable radiator sealant in accordance with the manufacturer's instructions without removing the radiator. However, these products are unlikely to provide a long-term solution.
6 If the radiator is to be sent for repair or renewed, remove the cooling fan switch.

5 Thermostat -
removal, testing
and refitting

Note: *Refer to the warnings given in Section 1 of this Chapter before proceeding.*

Removal

1 Disconnect the battery negative lead.
2 Drain the cooling system (see Chapter 1). If the coolant is not due for renewal, it may be re-used if it is collected in a clean container.
3 Disconnect the wiring from the coolant temperature sensor(s).
4 On early models (built up to July 1985), remove the two bolts which secure the thermostat housing lower cover **(see illustration)**. Access is not very easy with the engine in the vehicle; if problems are experienced, it may be easier to remove the thermostat housing complete (see Section 9).
5 On later models, the thermostat housing is located above the engine **(see illustration)**. Remove the bolts securing the top cover.
6 On all models, move the cover away, being careful not to strain the coolant hoses. Remove the thermostat, noting which way round it is fitted **(see illustration)**. Recover the O-ring.

3.9 Recover the rubber mountings from the lugs

Testing

7 A rough test of the thermostat may be made by suspending it with a piece of string in a container full of water. Heat the water to bring it to the boil - the thermostat must open by the time the water boils. If not, renew it. (Note however that the fully-open temperature on some models is in excess of the boiling point of water.)
8 If a thermometer is available, the precise opening temperature of the thermostat may be determined, and compared with the figures given in the Specifications. The opening temperature is also marked on the thermostat. A thermostat which fails to close as the water cools must also be renewed.

Refitting

9 Fit the thermostat into its housing and install a new O-ring **(see illustration)**.
10 Refit and secure the thermostat housing cover.
11 Reconnect the wiring to the coolant temperature sensor(s).
12 Refill and bleed the cooling system as described in Chapter 1.

6 Cooling fan and
thermoswitch -
testing

1 If problems are experienced with overheating (especially in traffic) and the cooling fan appears not to be working, first check the fuse (see Chapter 12). If the fuse is intact, test the system as follows.

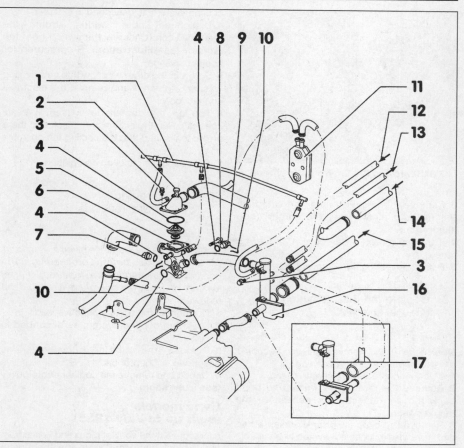

5.5 Thermostat housing and associated fittings - later models

1 Distribution pipe
2 Bleed screw
3 Bolt
4 O-ring
5 Thermostat
6 Thermostat housing
7 Coolant temperature sensor (fuel injection)
8 Bolt
9 Coolant temperature gauge sensor
10 Spring clip
11 Automatic transmission fluid cooler
12 From heater
13 To heater
14 From radiator
15 To radiator
16 Distribution pipe (to October 1986)
17 Distribution pipe (later models)

2 Remove the lower grille panel and bend back the air deflector for access to the thermoswitch.

Single-speed fan

3 Disconnect the wiring from the thermoswitch and join the wire terminals together with a paper clip or a similar piece of wire. (Don't let the bare wire touch vehicle metal, otherwise the fuse will blow.)

4 Switch on the ignition. If the fan now runs where it did not before, the thermoswitch is almost certainly faulty and should be renewed (Section 8).

Two-speed fan

5 The procedure is the same, but only two out of the three wires should be joined at once. Of the three possible pairings, one will produce no result, one should cause the fan to run at low speed and one at high speed.

All models

6 If the fan does not run during the above test and the fuse and wiring are OK, the fan motor is defective and should be removed as described in the next Section.

7 Remake the original wiring connections and refit the grille panel on completion.

7 Cooling fan - removal and refitting

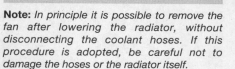

Note: *In principle it is possible to remove the fan after lowering the radiator, without disconnecting the coolant hoses. If this procedure is adopted, be careful not to damage the hoses or the radiator itself.*

1 Remove the radiator as described in Section 3, without actually disconnecting the hoses if wished (see Note above).

2 Unbolt the fan shroud from the radiator and remove it complete with fan **(see illustration)**.

5.6 Removing the thermostat (early type shown)

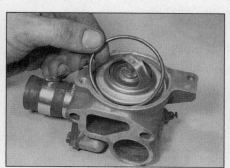

5.9 Use a new O-ring when refitting the thermostat

7.2 Removing the fan and shroud from the radiator

7.3 Removing the fan from the shroud

3 Remove the securing nuts and withdraw the fan and motor from the shroud **(see illustration)**.
4 If the fan motor is defective it should be renewed.
5 Refit by reversing the removal operations.

8 Cooling fan thermoswitch - removal and refitting

Note: *Refer to the warnings given in Section 1 of this Chapter before proceeding.*
1 Disconnect the battery negative lead.
2 Remove the lower grille panel and bend back the air deflector for access to the thermoswitch.
3 Remove the expansion tank pressure cap and have the replacement switch or a suitable bung to hand. If this is not possible, drain the

cooling system as described in Chapter 1.
4 Disconnect the wiring from the thermoswitch. Unscrew the switch from the radiator **(see illustration)**. Be prepared for coolant spillage.
5 Screw in the new switch, with a new sealing washer. Tighten it and remake the electrical connections.
6 Top up the coolant level (see *"Weekly checks"*). Run the engine and check that there are no leaks, and that the cooling fan operates correctly.
7 Refit the grille panel on completion.

9 Coolant pump - removal and refitting

Note: *Refer to the warnings given in Section 1 of this Chapter before proceeding. The coolant pump cannot be repaired; if it is leaking or noisy in operation it should be renewed.*
1 Disconnect the battery negative lead.
2 Drain the cooling system as described in Chapter 1.
3 Remove the auxiliary drivebelt(s) as described in Chapter 5A.
4 Unbolt and remove the coolant pump pulley **(see illustration)**.

Early models (built up to July 1985)

5 Disconnect the coolant pipes and hoses from the coolant pump and from the thermostat

8.4 Unscrew the thermoswitch from the radiator

housing. In the case of the stub hose which joins the thermostat housing to the left-hand cylinder head, just slacken the hose clips **(see illustration)**.
6 Disconnect the wiring from the temperature sensor(s) on the thermostat housing.
7 Unbolt the thermostat housing from the coolant pump and remove it, at the same time freeing the stub hose **(see illustrations)**. Take the opportunity to renew this hose if its condition is at all doubtful.
8 Unbolt the coolant pump from the engine and remove it **(see illustration)**. Depending on equipment, it may be necessary to remove one of the coolant distribution pipes if this blocks removal of the pump.
9 Commence refitting by fitting a new O-ring to the groove in the pump flange **(see illustration)**.
10 Offer the pump to the engine and tighten its fastenings to the specified torque.

9.4 Removing the coolant pump pulley

9.5 Slacken the clips on the stub hose (early models)

9.7A Unbolting the thermostat housing from the coolant pump (early models)

9.7B Separating the thermostat housing from the coolant pump (early models)

9.8 Removing the coolant pump

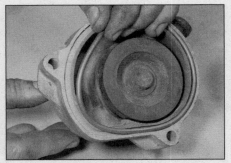

9.9 Fit a new O-ring to the coolant pump flange

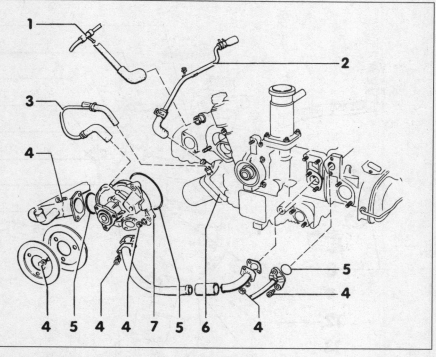

9.13 Coolant pump and associated fittings
- later models

1 Distribution pipe
2 From oil cooler
3 To oil cooler
4 Flange bolt
5 O-ring
6 Oil cooler (when fitted)
7 Coolant pump

11 Refit the thermostat housing to the pump, using a new gasket on the pump face and a new O-ring on the distribution pipe. Tighten the bolts to the specified torque.
12 The remainder of refitting is a reversal of the removal procedure. Use new gaskets and O-rings as a matter of course, and renew hoses and hose clips as necessary.

Later models

13 Proceed as described above, but ignoring references to the thermostat housing, which is located remotely on these engines **(see illustration)**.

10 Cooling system sensors - general information

1 All models are fitted with a coolant level sensor in the expansion tank. To remove the sensor, disconnect the wiring plug and unscrew it **(see illustration)**.
2 The temperature gauge sensor is located on the thermostat housing. On models with fuel injection a second sensor, which provides information to the electronic control unit, is also fitted.
3 On models with an inlet manifold heater, the thermoswitch which controls the heater is found in the adjacent coolant distribution pipe **(see illustration)**. For further details of this system refer to Chapter 4A.
4 The cooling fan thermoswitch has already been dealt with in Sections 6 and 8.
5 In all cases, renewal of a defective or suspect sensor is carried out with the system cold and after removing the expansion tank pressure cap. Provided the new sensor or a suitable bung is to hand, there is no need to drain the cooling system, but it should be topped up and bled afterwards if significant quantities of coolant were lost (see *Weekly checks* and Chapter 1).

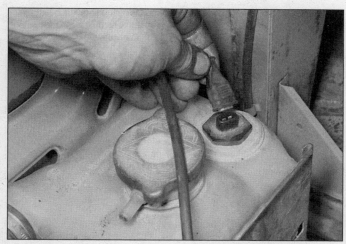

10.1 Disconnecting the wiring plug from the coolant level sensor

10.3 Removing the inlet manifold heater thermoswitch

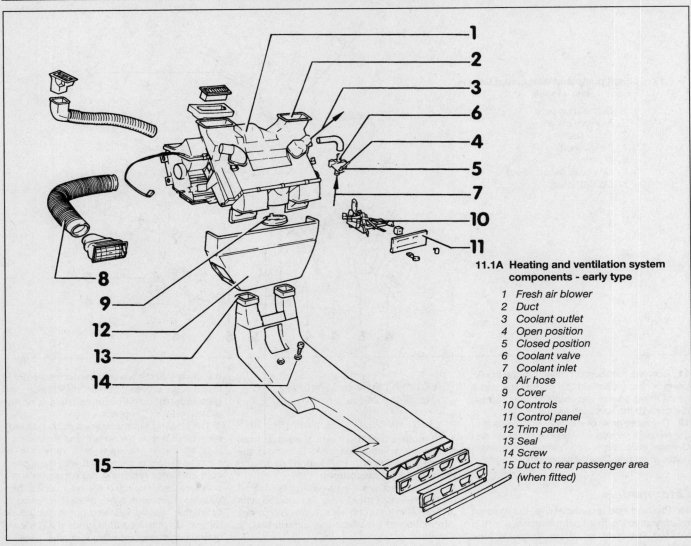

11.1A Heating and ventilation system components - early type

1 Fresh air blower
2 Duct
3 Coolant outlet
4 Open position
5 Closed position
6 Coolant valve
7 Coolant inlet
8 Air hose
9 Cover
10 Controls
11 Control panel
12 Trim panel
13 Seal
14 Screw
15 Duct to rear passenger area (when fitted)

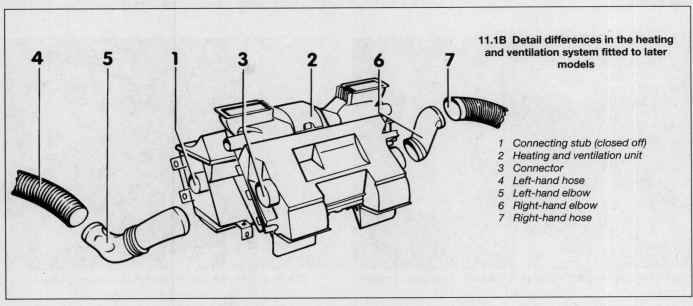

11.1B Detail differences in the heating and ventilation system fitted to later models

1 Connecting stub (closed off)
2 Heating and ventilation unit
3 Connector
4 Left-hand hose
5 Left-hand elbow
6 Right-hand elbow
7 Right-hand hose

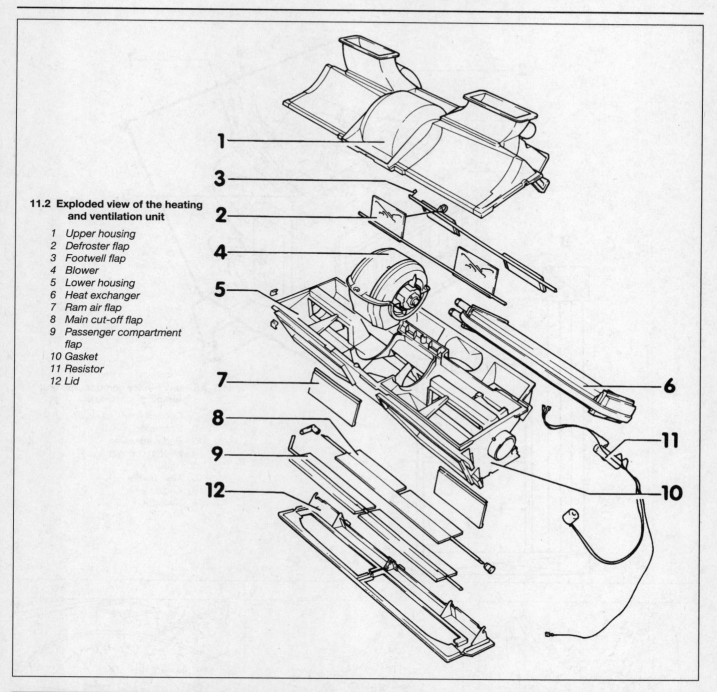

11.2 Exploded view of the heating and ventilation unit

1 Upper housing
2 Defroster flap
3 Footwell flap
4 Blower
5 Lower housing
6 Heat exchanger
7 Ram air flap
8 Main cut-off flap
9 Passenger compartment flap
10 Gasket
11 Resistor
12 Lid

11 Heating and ventilation system - general information

1 The heating and ventilation system fitted as standard is of conventional pattern **(see illustrations)**. The heater housing in the cab contains air ducts, flaps, a blower motor and a heat exchanger. The various controls enable the driver or passenger to admit fresh air, to control the temperature by altering the flow of hot coolant through the heat exchanger and to direct the resulting mixture towards the windscreen, the footwell and (on some models) the rear passenger area. The blower allows the airflow to be increased when that provided by the forward motion of the vehicle is insufficient.
2 Full access to the heater assembly requires removal of the facia as described in Chapter 11. After this the unit can be removed and dismantled if necessary for the renewal of individual components **(see illustration)**. Separation of the flap housings requires the opening of the retaining tabs with a knife or chisel; spring clips are available for reassembly. Remember to bleed and top up the cooling system on completion if the connections to the heater radiator were broken (see "Weekly checks" and Chapter 1).
3 An auxiliary coolant-fed heater for the passenger area was fitted to some models **(see illustration)**. Petrol-fired auxiliary heating was also available; the petrol-fired system should **not** be interfered with by unqualified persons, since the consequences of malfunction could be serious.
4 For models fitted with air conditioning, see also Section 13.

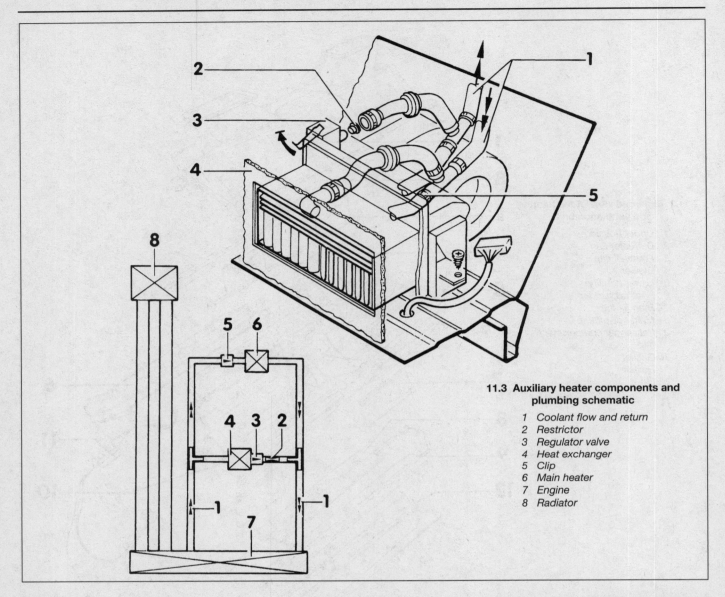

11.3 Auxiliary heater components and plumbing schematic

1 Coolant flow and return
2 Restrictor
3 Regulator valve
4 Heat exchanger
5 Clip
6 Main heater
7 Engine
8 Radiator

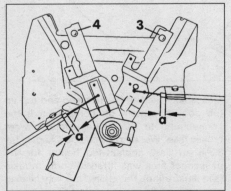

**12.2 Heater control cable attachments -
lower levers**

3 Main cut-off flap lever
4 Passenger compartment flap lever
a = 3 mm approx

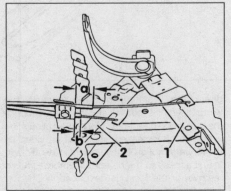

**12.3 Heater control cable attachments -
upper levers**

1 Distribution (screen / footwell) flap
2 Temperature control
   a = 30 mm   b = 20 mm

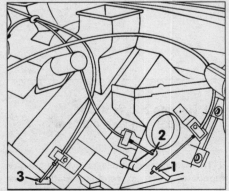

**12.4 Heater control cable attachments to
heater housing**

1 Passenger compartment flap
2 Main cut-off flap
3 Screen / footwell flap

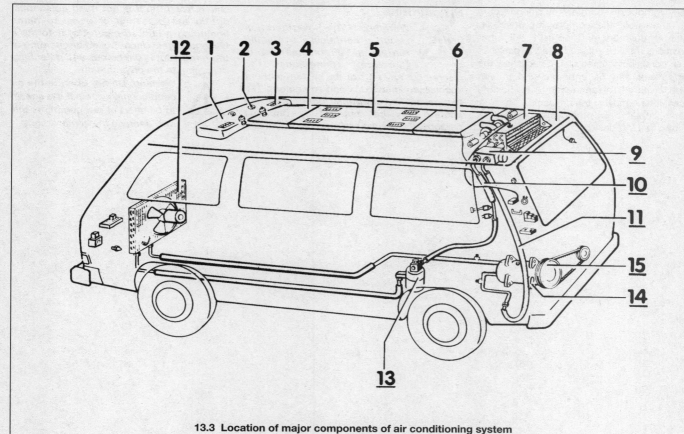

13.3 Location of major components of air conditioning system

1	Windscreen duct	6	Rear duct	11	Refrigerant hose
2	Air outlet	7	Evaporator assembly	12	Condenser
3	Air outlet	8	Water drain hose	13	Receiver/dryer
4	Front duct	9	Expansion valve	14	Compressor
5	Centre duct	10	Refrigerant hose	15	Compressor clutch

12 Heater control cables - adjustment

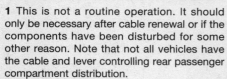

1 This is not a routine operation. It should only be necessary after cable renewal or if the components have been disturbed for some other reason. Note that not all vehicles have the cable and lever controlling rear passenger compartment distribution.

2 The passenger compartment control cable (when fitted) is identified with two green marks. The main cut-off flap cable has a green and yellow mark. They are attached to the levers as shown **(see illustration)**.

3 The screen/footwell distribution control cable is identified with a red mark and the temperature control cable with two blue and yellow marks. They are connected as shown **(see illustration)**.

4 With the cables connected as shown, operate the heater controls and check the movement of the flaps and levers on the side of the heater housing and on the control valve **(see illustration)**.

13 Air conditioning system - general information and precautions

General information

An air conditioning system is available on certain models. It enables the temperature of incoming air to be lowered, and dehumidifies the air, which makes for rapid demisting and increased comfort.

The cooling side of the system works in the same way as a domestic refrigerator.

Refrigerant gas is drawn into a belt-driven compressor and passes into a condenser mounted in front of the radiator, where it loses heat and becomes liquid. The liquid passes through an expansion valve to an evaporator, where it changes from liquid under high pressure to gas under low pressure. This change is accompanied by a drop in temperature, which cools the evaporator. The refrigerant returns to the compressor and the cycle begins again.

Air blown through the evaporator passes to air distribution ducts in the roof, where it can be directed to achieve the desired temperature in the passenger compartment **(see illustration)**.

The heating side of the system works in the same way as on models without air conditioning (see Section 11).

The only operation which can be carried out

easily without discharging the refrigerant is the renewal of the compressor drivebelt, which is covered in Chapter 1. All other operations must be referred to a VW dealer or an air conditioning specialist. If necessary the compressor can be unbolted and moved aside, without disconnecting its flexible hoses, after removing the drivebelt.

Any problems with the system should be referred to a VW dealer.

Precautions

 Warning: The refrigeration circuit contains a liquid refrigerant (Freon) and it is therefore dangerous to disconnect any part of the system without specialised knowledge and equipment. The refrigerant is potentially dangerous and should only be handled by qualified persons. If it is splashed onto the skin it can cause frostbite. It is not itself poisonous, but in the presence of a naked flame (including a lighted cigarette) it forms a poisonous gas. Uncontrolled discharging of the refrigerant is dangerous and potentially damaging to the environment.

 Warning: Do not operate the air conditioning system if it is known to be short of refrigerant, as this may damage the compressor.

Chapter 4 Part A:
Fuel and exhaust systems - carburettor models

Contents

Degrees of difficulty

Easy, suitable for novice with little experience		**Fairly easy,** suitable for beginner with some experience		**Fairly difficult,** suitable for competent DIY mechanic		**Difficult,** suitable for experienced DIY mechanic		**Very difficult,** suitable for expert DIY or professional	

Specifications

System type
All models .... Mechanical fuel pump, single or twin barrel downdraught carburettor

Fuel pump
Type .... Mechanical, driven by camshaft
Delivery pressure .... 0.2 to 0.3 bar (2.9 to 4.3 lbf/in^2)

Carburettor
Type:
   Engine codes DF and EY .... Solex 34 PICT-5
   Engine codes DG and SP .... Pierburg 2E3 or 2E4

Carburettor specification - Solex 34 PICT-5	**Engine code DF**	**Engine code EY (when different)**
Venturi diameter	26 mm	
Main jet	127.5	132.5
Air correction jet	60Z	
Pilot jet	50	55
Pilot air jet	140	
Auxiliary fuel jet	45	
Auxiliary air jet	90	
Accelerator pump injection quantity	1.30 ± 0.15 ml/stroke	
Float needle valve	1.5 mm	
Float weight	11.0 ± 0.5 g	
Float needle valve washer thickness	0.5 mm	
Choke flap gap	2.8 ± 0.2 mm	
Fast idle speed	1900 ± 100 rpm	
Idle speed	See Chapter 1 Specifications	
Exhaust gas CO content	See Chapter 1 Specifications	

Carburettor specification - Pierburg 2E3 and 2E4

	Primary	Secondary
2E3 - models up to October 1985 (engine code DG only):		
Venturi diameter	22 mm	26 mm
Main jet	102.5	110
Air correction jet	50	45
Pilot fuel jet	45	-
Pilot air jet	110	-
Full load enrichment	-	1.1 mm
Accelerator pump injector:		
Manual transmission	0.45 mm	-
Automatic transmission	0.30 mm	-
Accelerator pump injection quantity:		
Manual transmission	1.35 ± 0.20 ml/stroke	
Automatic transmission	1.00 ± 0.20 ml/stroke	
Choke flap gap	3.3 ± 0.2 mm	
Fast idle speed	2000 ± 200 rpm	
Idle speed	See Chapter 1 Specifications	
Exhaust gas CO content	See Chapter 1 Specifications	
2E3 and 2E4 - models from November 1985 (engine codes DG and SP) - as above except:		
Pilot air jet	125	
Full load enrichment	0.5 mm	
Choke flap gap	2.5 ± 0.2 mm	
Fast idle speed (2E4)	3600 ± 200 rpm	

Fuel tank capacity
60 litres (13 gallons) approx

Fuel octane rating
All carburettor models .... 91 RON minimum (see Section 2)

Torque wrench settings

	Nm	lbf ft
Fuel tank retaining bolts	25	18
Exhaust system M8 retaining bolts	20	15

1 General information and precautions

The fuel system on carburettor models consists of a fuel tank, mechanical fuel pump and a single or twin barrel downdraught carburettor. The air cleaner is of the disposable paper element type with automatic air temperature control.

A number of different types of exhaust systems are used according to engine size, year of manufacture and operating territory.

Fuel injection equipment and associated systems are described in Part B of this Chapter.

 Warning: Many of the procedures in this Chapter entail the removal of fuel pipes and connections which may result in some fuel spillage. Before carrying out any operation on the fuel system refer to the precautions given in Safety First! at the beginning of this manual and follow them implicitly. Petrol is a highly dangerous and volatile liquid and the precautions necessary when handling it cannot be overstressed.

2 Unleaded petrol – general information

Note: *The information in this Section is correct at the time of writing and applies to fuel available in the UK. Seek advice from a VW dealer if in doubt. If travelling abroad, especially outside the EC, seek advice from a* motoring organisation on fuel quality and grades available.

All carburettor models covered by this manual can use 95 octane unleaded fuel without any adjustment to the ignition timing. 98 octane fuel (so-called 'super unleaded') can also be used, but there is no advantage in doing so.

For models built before January 1984 it is recommended that one tankful of leaded (4-star) fuel be used after every four tankfuls of unleaded. Failure to observe this recommendation may lead to rapid wear of the valves and valve seats.

In the event that leaded fuel becomes unavailable, the early models just mentioned will have to use a proprietary fuel additive to compensate for the absence of lead. Alternatively it may be possible to have new valves and hardened valve seats fitted, after which unleaded fuel can be used continuously. Consult an engine reconditioning specialist.

3 Air cleaner and inlet trunking – removal and refitting

1 Removal of the air cleaner element is described in Chapter 1.
2 To remove the air cleaner assembly, identify the location of each vacuum pipe, then disconnect the pipes from the air cleaner housing **(see illustrations)**.

3.2A Disconnect the vacuum pipes from the temperature regulator . . .

3.2B . . . and from the vacuum unit

3.4A Disconnect the crankcase ventilation hose

3.4B Remove the nut . . .

3.4C . . . and lift off the inlet trunking

3 Detach the inlet and outlet hoses, withdraw the unit from the fresh air intake and remove it from the engine.
4 Removal of the inlet trunking from the top of the carburettor is carried out after disconnecting the crankcase ventilation hose and removing the securing nut(s) **(see illustrations)**.
5 Refitting is the reverse sequence to removal.

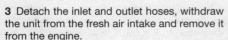

4 Air intake temperature control – testing

1 The operation of the air temperature control system may be tested as follows.
2 With the air cleaner installed, and the engine idling at normal operating temperature, detach the vacuum pipes from the temperature regulator on the air cleaner and

join them together **(see illustration 3.2A)**.
3 Disconnect the vacuum pipe from the vacuum unit. If the system is operating correctly, the flap valve in the vacuum unit will be heard to close as the pipe is detached. If this is not the case the temperature regulator may be at fault, or there may be a loss of vacuum due to a leaking or damaged vacuum pipe.

5 Fuel pump – removal, testing and refitting

 Warning: Refer to Section 1 before starting work.

1 The fuel pump is situated on top of the crankcase, next to the distributor. The pump

is of sealed construction and cannot be dismantled.
2 To remove the pump, first disconnect the battery negative terminal.
3 Note the location of the fuel pipes and mark them to avoid confusion. Disconnect the pipes from the pump and plug their ends to prevent fuel spillage **(see illustration)**.
4 Remove the two securing nuts and washers **(see illustration)**.
5 Withdraw the pump from its location and recover the insulating block and gaskets **(see illustration)**. The pump pushrod may also be withdrawn if necessary at this stage.
6 To test the pump operation, refit the fuel inlet pipe to the pump inlet and hold a wad of rag near the outlet. Depress the pump lever using a rod or small bolt. If the pump is satisfactory, a strong jet of fuel should be ejected from the outlet when the lever is released. If this is not the case, make sure that fuel will flow from the tank when the pipe is held below tank level. If so the pump is faulty and should be renewed.
7 Before refitting, clean away all traces of old gasket on all mating faces. Pack the insulating block with grease **(see illustration)**.
8 Refit the insulating block, with a new gasket on each side. Also refit the pushrod if it was removed, with the conical end towards the camshaft **(see illustrations)**.
9 Refit the pump and secure it with the washers and nuts.
10 Refit the fuel pipes to the locations noted during removal.

5.3 Disconnect the fuel pipes from the pump

5.4 Remove the fuel pump securing nuts

5.5 Removing the fuel pump

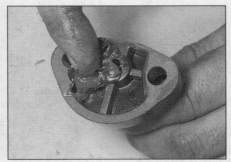

5.7 Pack the fuel pump insulating block with grease

5.8A Fit a new gasket . . .

5.8B . . . then the insulating block . . .

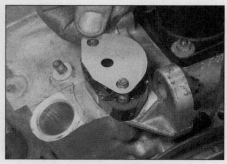

5.8C . . . another new gasket . . .

5.8D . . . and the pushrod, conical end downwards

6 Fuel tank – removal, servicing and refitting

Warning: Refer to Section 1 before starting work.

1 Disconnect the battery negative terminal.

2 A drain plug is not provided. It is recommended that the tank be emptied by siphoning or hand pumping the fuel out before removal. Store the fuel in a suitable sealed container.

3 Having emptied the tank, jack up the front of the vehicle and support it securely on axle stands (see "Jacking and vehicle support").

4 Slacken the clamp securing the filler pipe to the filler neck elbow, detach the vent hose and remove the filler pipe **(see illustration)**. Be prepared for any fuel remaining in the tank to drain out.

5 Disconnect the fuel feed and return pipes from the tank and plug their ends and the tank outlets.

6 Support the tank on a jack with interposed block of wood.

7 Undo the bolts securing the tank support brackets to the underbody at one end and slip the other ends out of the locating channels.

8 Accurately mark the location of all accessible breather pipes and disconnect them **(see illustration)**. The number and location of the pipes varies according to model and export territory.

9 Slowly lower the tank and disconnect the remaining breather pipes and the fuel gauge sender unit wires.

10 With everything disconnected, finish lowering the tank and remove it from under the vehicle.

11 The expansion tanks can be removed if necessary by undoing the retaining nuts and removing them from under the wheel arches.

12 If the tank is contaminated with sediment or water, remove the sender unit, as described in Section 7, and swill the tank out with clean fuel. If the tank is damaged, or leaks, it should be repaired by a specialist or, alternatively, renewed. **Do not** under any circumstances solder or weld the tank. Proprietary sealing compounds are available for repairing small leaks, but make sure that

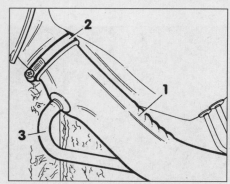

6.4 Fuel tank filler pipe (1), clamp (2) and vent pipe (3)

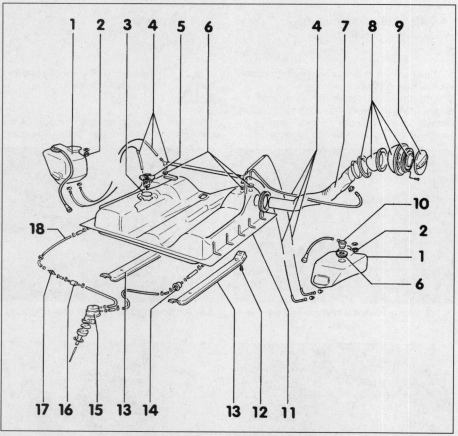

6.8 Typical fuel tank installation

1 Expansion tanks	7 Filler pipe	13 Rail
2 Nut	8 Filler elbow	14 Filter
3 Seal	9 Filler cap	15 Fuel pump
4 Breather pipes	10 Valve	16 Carburettor connections
5 Fuel gauge sender	11 Tank	17 Restrictor
6 Gasket	12 Nut	18 Return line

the compound chosen is suitable for use in contact with petrol.

13 Refitting the tank is the reverse sequence to removal.

7 Fuel gauge sender unit – removal and refitting

1 Refer to Section 6 and remove the fuel tank.
2 Note the angle at which the electrical connection on the sender unit adopts with relation to the tank, and mark the tank accordingly **(see illustration)**.
3 Engage a screwdriver, flat bar or other suitable tool with the lugs of the locking ring and turn the ring anti-clockwise to release it.
4 Withdraw the locking ring, seal and sender unit.
5 Refitting is the reverse sequence to removal, but always use a new seal and position the sender unit as noted during removal.

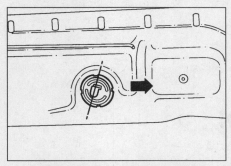

7.2 Correct fitted angle of fuel gauge sender unit. Arrow points to front of vehicle

8 Accelerator cable (manual transmission vehicles) – adjustment

1 Before adjusting the cable, check the condition of the accelerator pedal pushrod,

lever and the cable itself and ensure that there is no wear in the bushes and linkage **(see illustration)**. If necessary renew any worn parts and lubricate the pedal linkage with multi-purpose grease.
2 Have an assistant depress the accelerator pedal fully (engine switched off) and hold it in the full throttle position.
3 With the pedal fully depressed, the throttle lever at the carburettor should be just in contact with its stop (not under tension) or no more than 1 mm from it.
4 If the clearance is not as specified, slacken the cable at the clamping pin or tensioning pin and reposition the linkage as necessary.

9 Accelerator linkage (automatic transmission) – checking and adjustment

1 Before carrying out any checks or adjustment, visually inspect the accelerator linkage components for wear, excessive free

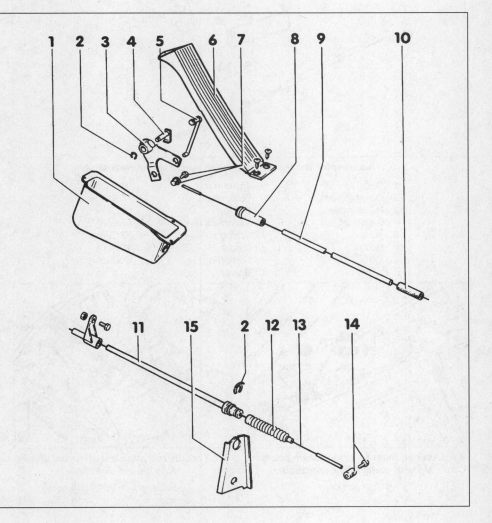

8.1 Accelerator linkage - models with manual transmission

1 Cover
2 Circlip
3 Lever
4 Pin
5 Pushrod
6 Pedal
7 Pins
8 Grommet
9 Tube
10 Hose
11 Sleeve
12 Bellows
13 Cable
14 Clamping pin
15 Bracket

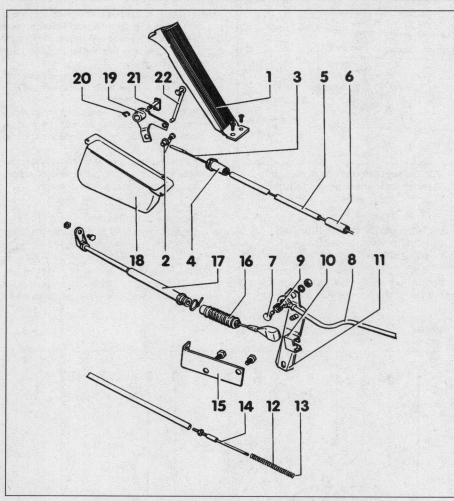

9.1 Accelerator linkage - models with automatic transmission

1 Pedal	8 Throttle rod	16 Bellows
2 Clamping pin	9 Bush	17 Sleeve
3 Pedal cable	10 Clamp	18 Cover
4 Grommet	11 Kickdown lever	19 Lever
5 Tube	12 Spring	20 Circlip
6 Hose	13 Circlip	21 Pin
7 Pin	14 End fitting	22 Pushrod
	15 Bracket	

play or deterioration of the protective rubber boots **(see illustration)**. Renew any worn parts and lubricate the pedal linkage with multi-purpose grease.

2 To check the linkage adjustment, have an assistant depress the accelerator pedal to the full throttle position so that the throttle lever is against its stop on the carburettor. Hold the pedal in this position.

3 Check that the gearbox lever on the side of the transmission is not in the kick-down position.

4 Now depress the accelerator pedal fully to the floor. Check that the override spring on the end of the adjusting rod is in tension and that the gearbox lever is against its stop in the kick-down position **(see illustration)**. If this is not the case adjust the linkage as follows.

5 Slacken the adjusting rod locknut, extract the circlip and remove the override spring.

6 Start the engine, allow it to reach normal operating temperature and let it idle.

7 If necessary adjust the engine idling speed as described in Chapter 1.

8 Switch the engine off and pull the throttle rod as far as it will go, by hand, to the throttle fully closed position **(see illustration)**.

9 Using a screwdriver, turn the adjusting rod as necessary so that its shoulder just contacts the pivot bush in the linkage or throttle lever.

10 Refit the override spring, start the engine and check that the adjustments have not altered the idling speed. Turn the adjusting rod as necessary to return the speed to the specified setting. Now tighten the adjusting rod locknut and switch off the engine.

11 Depress the accelerator pedal fully to the floor and hold it in this position.

12 Check that the gearbox lever is in the kickdown position. Now release the pedal and check that the gearbox lever returns to the idle position out of kickdown. If necessary remove the cover below the accelerator pedal and adjust the cable position at the clamping bolt **(see illustration)**.

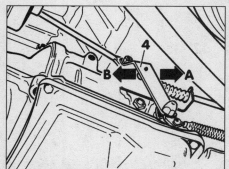

9.4 Lever (4) must be in kickdown position (A) with pedal fully depressed

B Idle position

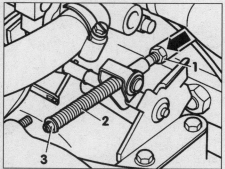

9.8 Throttle rod adjustment. Arrow shows fully closed direction

1 Locknut 3 Adjusting
2 Spring   rod

9.12 Adjust the accelerator cable at the clamping bolt (arrowed)

10.2A Exploded view of carburettor top cover components (34 PICT)

1 Fuel return	8 Screw
2 Restrictor	9 Choke pull-down
3 Screw	unit
4 Fuel inlet	10 Gasket
5 Choke spindle	11 Needle valve
6 Gasket	12 Washer
7 Choke cover	

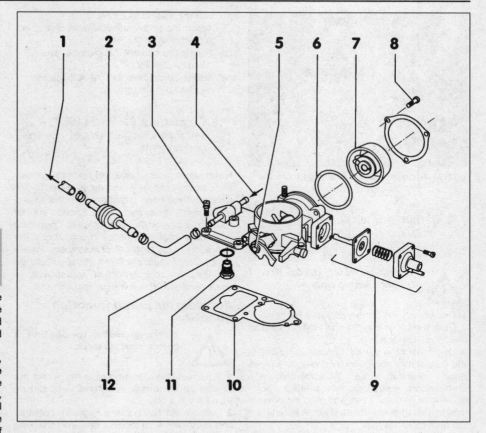

10 Carburettor (Solex 34 PICT) – description

1 The Solex 34 PICT carburettor is of the fixed-jet, single-barrel downdraught type incorporating a mechanically operated accelerator pump, automatic choke for cold start enrichment and a throttle damper.
2 The unit consists of two main assemblies, namely the main body and top cover **(see illustrations)**. The main body incorporates the float chamber, throttle barrel venturi, accelerator pump, the various jets and internal drillings and the throttle valve and linkage assembly. It also carries the bypass cut-off valve, which interrupts the idle mixture circuit when the engine is switched off. The top cover houses the fuel inlet needle valve and the automatic choke.
3 The carburettor is of simple design and layout and all adjustment and settings can be carried out using instruments readily available to the home mechanic.

10.2B Exploded view of carburettor main body components (34 PICT)

1 Plug	11 Delay valve
2 Main jet	12 Throttle damper
3 Seal	13 Plug
4 CO adjusting	14 Auxiliary fuel jet
screw	15 Injection tube
5 Pin	16 Fast idle speed
6 Float	adjusting screw
7 Air correction jet	17 Bypass cut-off
and tube	valve
8 Pilot jet	18 Idle speed
9 Valve	adjusting screw
10 Accelerator pump	
adjusting screw	

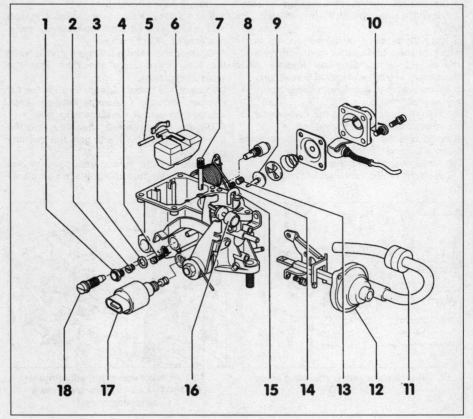

11.3 Disconnecting a fuel pipe from the carburettor

11 Carburettor (all types) – removal and refitting

Warning: Refer to Section 1 before starting work.

1 Disconnect the battery negative terminal.
2 Remove the air cleaner and inlet trunking as described in Section 3.
3 Disconnect the fuel inlet and return pipes at the carburettor top cover and plug the pipes after removal **(see illustration)**. On carburettors with a coolant-heated choke housing, also disconnect and plug the coolant hoses, taking precautions against scalding if the coolant is still hot.
4 Disconnect the electrical lead at the automatic choke and at the bypass cut-off valve.
5 Note the position of the various vacuum pipes at their carburettor connections and disconnect them. Similarly identify and disconnect any other electrical connectors.
6 Disconnect the accelerator cable from the carburettor linkage.
7 Undo the nuts securing the carburettor to the manifold and withdraw the unit.
8 Refitting is the reverse sequence to removal bearing in mind the following points:
a) *Use a new gasket between the carburettor and inlet manifold and ensure that the mating faces are clean*
b) *Adjust the accelerator cable as described in Section 8 or 9*
c) *Top up the coolant if applicable (see "Weekly checks")*
d) *Adjust the carburettor idle settings as described in Chapter 1*

12 Carburettor (Solex 34 PICT) – setting and adjustment of components

Note: *Under normal operating conditions only the carburettor idle adjustments described in Chapter 1 will need attention. The checks and adjustments described in this Section are not routine operations and should only be necessary after carburettor overhaul or if the operation of the carburettor is suspect. Where tamperproof seals are fitted, these should be renewed on completion of adjustment; in some territories this is a legal requirement.*

Accelerator pump injection quantity

Warning: Refer to Section 1 before starting work.

1 To check the injection quantity warm the engine up to normal operating temperature then switch it off.
2 Disconnect the battery negative terminal and remove the air cleaner and inlet trunking as described in Section 3.
3 Place a suitable tube over the injection tube and have a graduated measuring glass available to collect the fuel.
4 Operate the throttle linkage by hand to fill the tube then direct the tube into the measuring glass.
5 Operate the throttle linkage through five full strokes, allowing 3 seconds between each stroke, then remove the measuring glass.
6 Divide the injected quantity in the measuring glass by five to give the quantity per stroke.
7 If this is not in accordance with the specified value turn the adjusting screw as necessary **(see illustration)**. Check also that the injected fuel strikes the collar in the discharge arm and carefully bend the injection tube if necessary.
8 Refit the air cleaner and reconnect the battery.

Choke valve gap

9 This adjustment may be carried out with the carburettor in position on the engine or removed.
10 Mark the relationship of the automatic choke body to the housing on the carburettor top cover.
11 Undo the screws, lift off the retaining ring and remove the automatic choke body and gasket.
12 Push the vacuum diaphragm pullrod towards the vacuum unit as far as it will go using a screwdriver.
13 Hold the choke flap operating arm against the pullrod, then turn the vacuum unit adjusting screw as necessary until a twist drill of diameter equal to the specified choke flap gap will just fit between the choke flap and the throttle barrel wall **(see illustration)**.
14 After adjustment, refit the automatic choke ensuring that the peg on the choke flap operating arm engages with the loop in the choke body. Align the marks made during removal before tightening the retaining ring screws.

Fast idle speed

15 Warm the engine up until normal operating temperature is obtained, then switch off. Connect a tachometer to the engine.
16 Position the throttle valve adjusting screw on the third step of the fast idle cam, then start the engine again without touching the accelerator. Check that the engine speed is in accordance with the value specified for fast idle.
17 If necessary remove the tamperproof cap and turn the screw until the specified fast idle speed is obtained **(see illustration)**. Stop the engine and disconnect the tachometer.

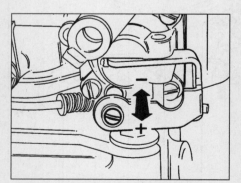

12.7 Accelerator pump adjusting screw (34 PICT)

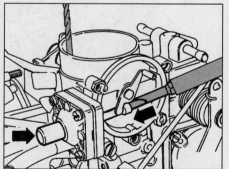

12.13 Choke valve gap adjustment (34 PICT). Left-hand arrow shows adjusting screw

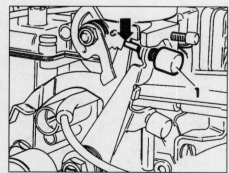

12.17 Fast idle adjustment (34 PICT). Arrow shows screw on third step of cam

1 Adjusting screw

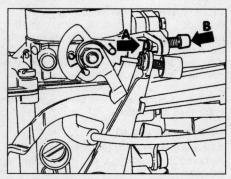

12.19 Throttle damper adjustment (34 PICT)

A Press lever
   against screw

B Adjusting
   screw

Throttle damper adjustment

18 Warm the engine up until normal operating temperature is obtained, then allow the engine to idle.

19 Press the lever on the linkage against the adjusting screw on the top cover **(see illustration)** and check that the engine speed increases to approximately 1300 rpm. If necessary turn the adjusting screw to achieve the specified speed after removing the tamperproof cap.

20 Increase the engine speed to approximately 3000 rpm so that the throttle damper lever is pulled against the adjusting screw.

21 Release the throttle valve lever. The damper lever should slowly lift the adjusting screw and the throttle valve should close fully after approximately 3 seconds.

13 Carburettor (Pierburg 2E3 and 2E4) – description

1 The Pierburg 2E3 carburettor is a fixed-jet twin-barrel downdraught instrument with an automatic choke. It has a mechanically-operated accelerator pump. Opening of the secondary barrel throttle plate is controlled by vacuum.

2 The unit consists of two main assemblies, namely the main body and top cover **(see illustrations)**. The main body incorporates the float chamber, throttle barrel venturi, accelerator pump, part load enrichment device, the various jets and internal drillings and the throttle valves and linkage assemblies. It also carries the bypass cut-off valve, which interrupts the idle mixture circuit when the engine is switched off. The top cover houses the fuel inlet needle valve and the automatic choke.

3 The 2E4 carburettor is a development of the 2E3 fitted to some later models with automatic transmission, power steering and/or air conditioning. The main difference is

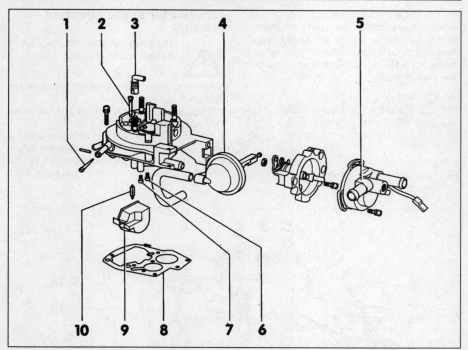

13.2A Exploded view of carburettor top cover components (2E3 / 2E4)

1 Strainer	4 Choke pull-down unit	8 Gasket
2 Pilot jet	5 Choke cover	9 Float
3 Breather pipe	6 Secondary main jet	10 Needle valve
	7 Primary main jet	

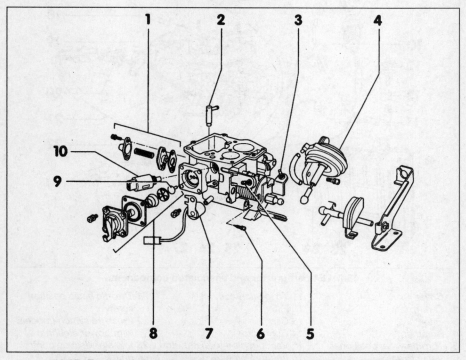

13.2B Exploded view of carburettor main body components (2E3 / 2E4)

1 Part load enrichment valve	4 Vacuum unit (2E3 only)	7 Part load duct heater
2 Injection tube	5 Idle speed adjustment (2E3 only)	8 Accelerator pump
3 Fast idle adjusting screw	6 CO adjusting screw	9 Valve
		10 Bypass cut-off valve

that the idle speed is monitored electronically, an electrical throttle valve positioner being used to maintain a steady idle speed despite changing load requirements. The external connections to this carburettor are as shown (see illustration).

14 Carburettor (Pierburg 2E3 and 2E4) – setting and adjustment of components

1 Refer to the introductory note at the beginning of Section 12 before proceeding.

Accelerator pump injection quantity

⚠ **Warning: Refer to Section 1 before starting work.**

2 Remove the carburettor. Make sure the float chamber is full of fuel.
3 Place a graduated measuring glass under the base of the carburettor.
4 Turn the fast idle cam and hold it so that it is not in contact with the fast idle adjusting screw.
5 Operate the throttle linkage through five full strokes, allowing 3 seconds between each

stroke, then remove the measuring glass.
6 Divide the injected quantity in the measuring glass by five to give the quantity per stroke.
7 If this is not in accordance with the specified value, slacken the clamping screw and turn the cam as necessary. Check also that the injected fuel strikes the recess in the barrel (see illustrations).

Choke valve gap

8 This adjustment may be carried out with the carburettor in position on the engine or removed.

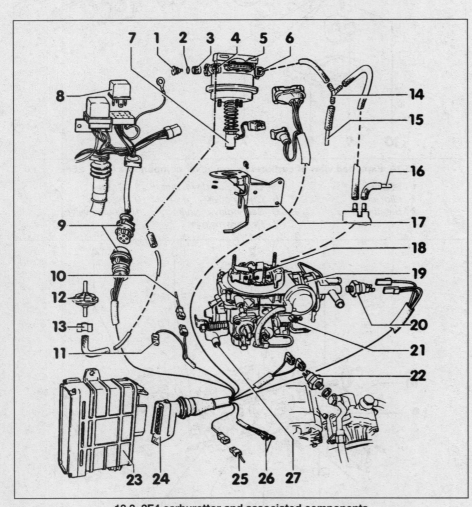

13.3 2E4 carburettor and associated components

1 Cover
2 O-ring
3 Filter
4 Breather
5 Throttle valve positioner
6 Vacuum valve
7 Throttle valve switch
8 Relay
9 Connector
10 To ignition control unit
11 To ignition coil
12 Filter
13 Clip
14 Connector
15 Vacuum pipe to distributor
16 Vacuum pipe to temperature regulator
17 Bracket
18 Choke valve
19 Fast idle cam
20 Thermal switch
21 Throttle basic position screw
22 Pressure switch (models with power steering)
23 Idle stabilisation control unit
24 Connector
25 To air conditioning compressor
26 Earth wire
27 Adjustment screw

14.7A Accelerator pump adjustment (2E3 / 2E4)

1 Clamping screw   A Increase delivery
2 Cam   B Reduce delivery

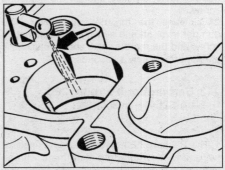

14.7B Correct alignment of accelerator pump spray (arrowed)

14.11 Choke valve gap adjustment (2E3 / 2E4) - fast idle screw (2) must be on highest step of cam (1)

9 Mark the relationship of the automatic choke body to the housing on the carburettor top cover.

10 Undo the screws and remove the automatic choke body and gasket.

11 Open the throttle and position the fast idle adjusting screw on the highest step of the cam **(see illustration)**.

12 Push the vacuum diaphragm pullrod towards the vacuum unit as far as it will go using a screwdriver.

13 Hold the pullrod in this position, then turn the vacuum unit adjusting screw as necessary until a twist drill of diameter equal to the specified choke flap gap will just fit between the choke flap and the throttle barrel wall **(see illustration)**.

14 After adjustment, refit the automatic choke body, ensuring that the peg on the choke flap operating arm engages with the loop in the choke body. Align the marks made during removal before tightening the screws.

Fast idle speed

15 Warm the engine up until normal operating temperature is obtained, then switch off. Connect a tachometer to the engine.

16 With the engine running, position the throttle valve adjusting screw on the second step (2E3) or the highest step (2E4) of the fast idle cam. Check that the engine speed is in accordance with the value specified for fast idle.

17 If necessary turn the screw until the specified fast idle speed is obtained. Stop the engine and disconnect the tachometer.

Choke pull-down vacuum unit

18 Remove the air inlet trunking. Start the engine and allow it to idle.

19 Feel the resistance offered by the choke valve when it is closed by hand. It should be easy to close it until the gap remaining is of the order of 3 mm; further closing should be quite difficult.

20 If there is no resistance to full closing of the choke valve, the pull-down unit is

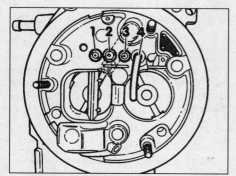

15.7A Jet identification (2E3 / 2E4) - top half

1 Pilot jet
2 Primary air correction jet
3 Secondary air correction jet
4 Full throttle enrichment tube

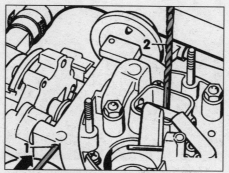

14.13 Choke valve gap adjustment (2E3 / 2E4)

1 Adjusting screw   2 Twist drill

defective or there is a leak in its vacuum supply. Special test equipment is required to diagnose the problem and reference should be made to a VW dealer or other specialist.

Other tests

21 It is not possible to test the secondary throttle vacuum unit or the throttle valve positioner (2E4) without special test equipment. Setting of the basic throttle valve position or intervention in the idling speed stabilisation system is likewise a specialist job. Consult a VW dealer or carburettor specialist if it is felt that adjustments of this nature are required.

15 Carburettor (all types) – overhaul

1 Major carburettor overhaul is not a routine operation and should only be carried out when components are obviously worn. Removing the top cover, cleaning out the sediment from the float chamber and clearing the jets with compressed air is usually sufficient to keep a carburettor operating efficiently. When a unit has covered a high mileage, it will probably be more economical to replace it with a new or exchange carburettor rather than to renew individual components. The following instructions are of a general nature and are intended to assist the experienced mechanic.

2 With the carburettor removed from the engine and cleaned externally, begin dismantling as follows.

3 Undo the retaining screws and separate the top cover from the main body. Recover the gasket.

4 Remove the accelerator pump and the vacuum unit housings and carefully inspect the diaphragms for signs of cracks or deterioration.

5 Place a finger over the fuel return outlet and blow through the fuel feed outlet. Check that as the needle valve is raised it shuts off the flow and opens again as soon as it is released.

6 Check the operation of the bypass cut-off valve by applying 12 volts to its terminal. When voltage is applied it should be heard and felt to operate. If the valve is defective it will have been difficult or impossible to adjust the idle speed satisfactorily. Renew the valve if necessary.

7 Identify and unscrew the various jets **(see illustrations)**. Blow through them and the carburettor drillings with compressed air.

8 It is recommended that the automatic choke, throttle linkage and the various tamperproofed adjusting screws be left undisturbed.

9 Thoroughly clean the float chamber, removing all sediment, then obtain a carburettor repair kit consisting of new diaphragms, gaskets and washers if these parts are required.

10 Reassemble the carburettor using the reverse sequence to removal, but carry out the appropriate checks and adjustments described in Section 12 or 14 as work proceeds.

16 Emission control systems – general

The only emission control equipment fitted to carburettor models is the crankcase ventilation system.

A closed circuit is used, whereby engine crankcase emissions are recirculated to the air cleaner. From an oil separator on the crankcase a breather hose directs fumes to the air cleaner, where they are mixed with the intake air and later burned in the engine.

Note that a side-effect of this system is a possible raising of exhaust gas CO levels at idle. This can occur if the main pattern of vehicle use consists of short journeys. Fuel condenses into the oil when the engine is cold and the fuel vapour is subsequently drawn into the intake air, enriching the idle mixture excessively. The condition can be cured by taking the vehicle for a long fast run, or (temporarily) by changing the engine oil.

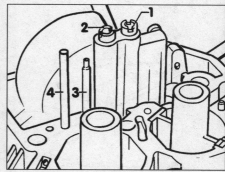

15.7B Jet identification (2E3 / 2E4) - bottom half

1 Primary main jet
2 Secondary main jet
3 Full throttle enrichment tube
4 Transition tube

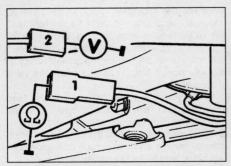

17.2 Inlet manifold preheater testing

1 Resistance of element
2 Supply voltage

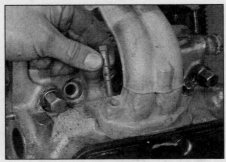

17.6A Removing an inlet manifold bolt

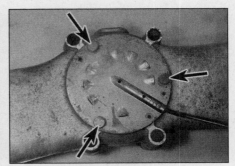

17.6B Inlet manifold heater securing screws (arrowed) - manifold removed for clarity

17 Inlet manifold heater – testing, removal and refitting

1 All carburettor models are fitted with an inlet manifold heater, which is intended to improve fuel economy and promote smooth running during the warm-up period. The heater is an electrical element located in the base of the manifold underneath the carburettor. It is controlled by a thermal switch located in a nearby coolant pipe (early models) or in the thermostat housing (later models). The switch breaks the heater circuit when coolant temperature reaches around 60° C.

Testing

2 If it is suspected that the heater is not working, first check that voltage is present at its supply terminal (ignition on, engine cold) (see illustration). If not, either the thermal switch is defective or there is some other fault in the circuit.

3 If voltage is present, check the resistance of the heater element. The specified value is 0.25 to 0.50 ohms; a digital multi-meter will be needed to distinguish this sort of resistance from a short-circuit. A high or infinite resistance reading (open-circuit) indicates that the heater is defective.

Removal and refitting

4 Remove the carburettor as described earlier in this Chapter.

5 Unbolt the coolant distribution pipe from the inlet manifold (early models only).

6 Unbolt the inlet manifold from the cylinder heads. Lift up the manifold and remove the three screws which secure the heater (see illustrations).

7 Support the manifold on wooden blocks and drive the heater out, using a wooden or plastic hammer.

8 When fitting the new heater, lubricate its rubber sealing ring with a little neat antifreeze.

9 The remainder of refitting is a reversal of the removal procedure. Use new gaskets at the cylinder heads.

18 Exhaust system – removal and refitting

1 Numerous exhaust systems have been fitted according to engine size, operating territory and year of manufacture. The basic division is between early and later types (see illustrations).

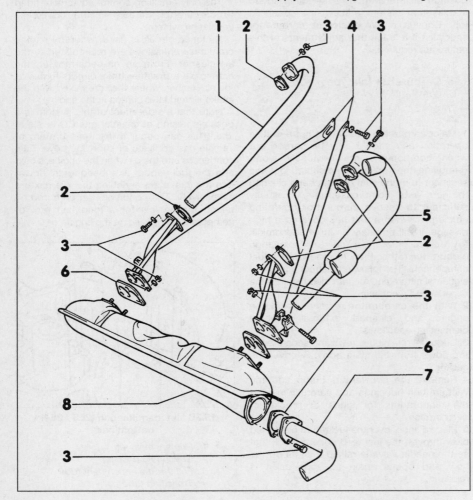

18.1A Exhaust system components - early models

1 Pipe	5 Right-hand pipe
2 Gaskets	and heat
3 Nuts	exchanger
4 Brackets	6 Gasket
	7 Tail pipe
	8 Silencer

18.1B Exhaust system components - later models

A To silencer	8 Bracket
B To silencer	9 Rear pipe
bracket	10 Bracket
1 Bracket	11 Heat shield
2 Gasket	(option)
3 Front pipe	12 Pipe
4 Strut	13 Washers
5 Gasket	14 Spacer
6 Manifold	15 Pipe (alternative
7 Seal	to 12)

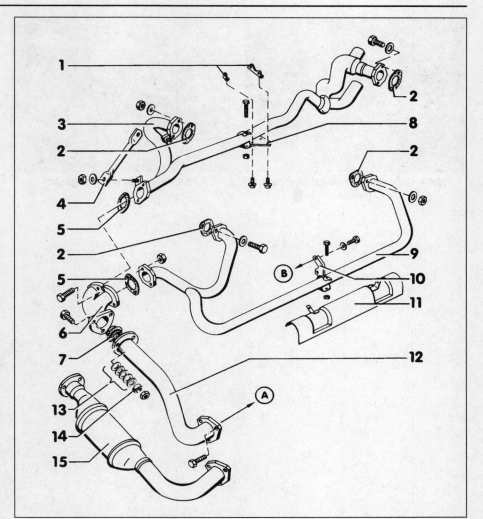

2 Removal and refitting of the system components is not always an easy task. Although the systems consist chiefly of bolt-together sections, corrosion and lack of accessibility are common problems. Be particularly careful when removing the exhaust pipes from the cylinder heads: it is easy to strip the threads in the heads.
3 A visible inspection and reference to the illustrations will show how the systems come apart and in what sequence. Before starting work, liberally soak all nuts and bolts in penetrating oil, leave it to stand for a while and then soak them again. If it is safe to do so, cut off really stubborn fastenings or pipes - new ones will be needed in any case if the corrosion is that bad.
4 Renew all gaskets when refitting the system and ensure that mating faces are clean, with all traces of old gasket removed **(see illustrations overleaf)**. The use of a copper-based anti-seize compound on nuts, bolts and sliding joints will make dismantling easier next time round.

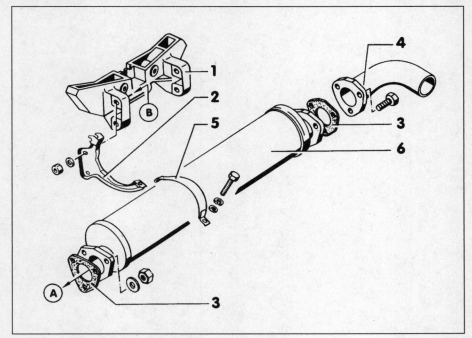

18.1C Silencer components - later models

A To exhaust pipe
B Rear pipe support point
1 Bracket
2 Bracket
3 Gaskets
4 Tail pipe
5 Strap
6 Silencer

18.4A Cylinder head-to-exhaust pipe gasket

18.4A Exhaust silencer gasket

18.4C Assembling the right-hand side exhaust pipes

Chapter 4 Part B:
Fuel and exhaust systems - fuel injection models

Contents

Degrees of difficulty

| Easy, suitable for novice with little experience | Fairly easy, suitable for beginner with some experience | Fairly difficult, suitable for competent DIY mechanic | Difficult, suitable for experienced DIY mechanic 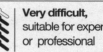 | Very difficult, suitable for expert DIY or professional |

Specifications

System type
Engine codes GW, DJ .... Digijet
Engine codes MV, SS .... Digifant

Fuel pump
Delivery rate (minimum) .... 500 ml in 30 seconds
Regulated pressure .... See text

Idle speed control valve
Resistance .... 2 to 10 ohms
Current draw .... 430 ± 20 mA

Sensor test data
Coolant temperature sensor resistance:
    At 50° C .... 800 ohms approx
    At 75° C .... 350 ohms approx
    At 100° C .... 200 ohms approx
Intake air temperature sensor resistance:
    At 0° C .... 5500 ohms approx
    At 20° C .... 2500 ohms approx
    At 45° C .... 1000 ohms approx
Power steering pressure sensor resistance (engine running):
    Steering straight-ahead .... Infinity (open-circuit)
    Steering on full lock .... 1.5 ohms or less

Fuel tank capacity .... 60 litres (13 gallons) approx

Fuel octane rating
Engine codes GW, DJ .... 98 RON minimum, leaded or unleaded, or 95 octane with ignition timing adjustment (also see Section 2)
Engine codes MV, SS .... 91 RON minimum, unleaded only (also see Section 2)

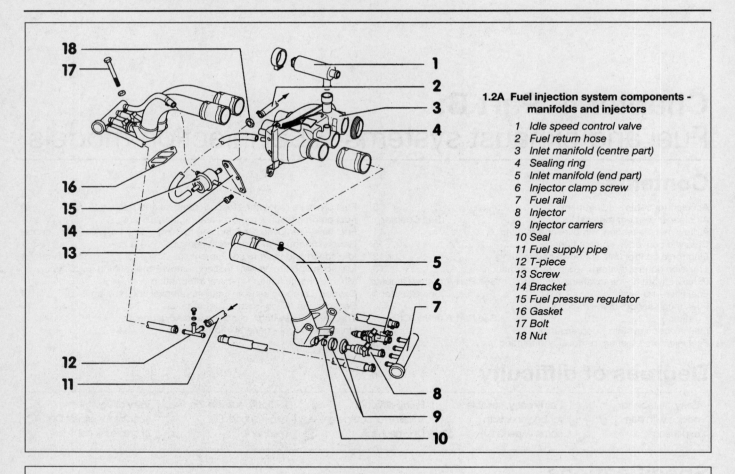

1.2A Fuel injection system components - manifolds and injectors

1 Idle speed control valve
2 Fuel return hose
3 Inlet manifold (centre part)
4 Sealing ring
5 Inlet manifold (end part)
6 Injector clamp screw
7 Fuel rail
8 Injector
9 Injector carriers
10 Seal
11 Fuel supply pipe
12 T-piece
13 Screw
14 Bracket
15 Fuel pressure regulator
16 Gasket
17 Bolt
18 Nut

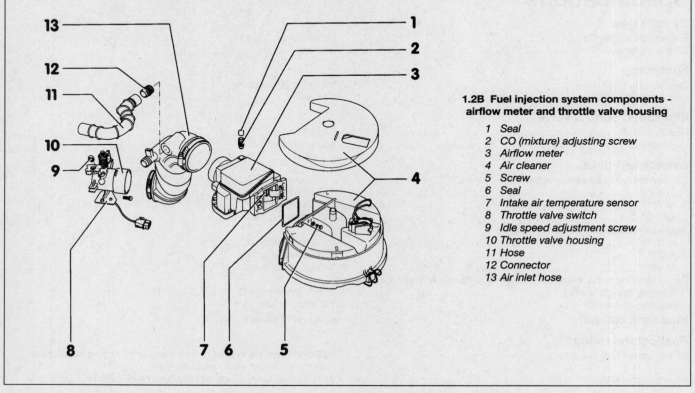

1.2B Fuel injection system components - airflow meter and throttle valve housing

1 Seal
2 CO (mixture) adjusting screw
3 Airflow meter
4 Air cleaner
5 Screw
6 Seal
7 Intake air temperature sensor
8 Throttle valve switch
9 Idle speed adjustment screw
10 Throttle valve housing
11 Hose
12 Connector
13 Air inlet hose

1 General information and precautions

The electronic fuel injection system fitted to some 1.9 litre and all 2.1 litre models is known as Digijet or Digifant, the latter being a development of the former. The main difference between the two systems is that Digijet controls fuel injection only, whilst Digifant is an integrated engine management system which controls both the fuel injection and the ignition systems. Models with Digifant have a catalytic converter in the exhaust system.

The main components of the system are an electrically-operated fuel pump, an electronic control (computer) unit and the necessary sensors, fuel injectors, fuel lines and manifolds **(see illustrations)**.

The quantity of fuel delivered is dependent upon the volume of air being drawn into the engine. This in turn is affected by temperature and engine operating load. The Digifant system monitors the oxygen content of the exhaust gas by means of an oxygen (Lambda) sensor and also controls ignition timing.

Peripheral components (air cleaner, fuel tank, exhaust system etc) are similar to those used on carburettor models. For information on such items refer to Part A of this Chapter.

The fuel injection system is normally very reliable. Procedures in this Chapter are limited to those which can be undertaken by the DIY mechanic with commonly-available equipment. The reader who wishes to know more about the principles of operation of such systems is recommended to consult the *Haynes Automotive Engine Management and Fuel Injection Systems Manual* (book No 3344), obtainable from stockists of Haynes manuals.

Precautions

The electronic control unit is electrically fragile. Disconnect both battery terminals if battery charging or electric welding is to be carried out. Be careful not to subject the electrical system to voltage surges (for instance when boost starting a vehicle with a flat battery). Only connect or disconnect test equipment with the ignition switched off.

When working on or near ignition-related components, take appropriate precautions against electric shock - see Chapter 5B.

Observe scrupulous cleanliness when working on the fuel injection system. Clean around fuel unions before disconnecting them, and plug or cap open unions. Only use clean lint-free cloths for cleaning components, and do not unpack new components until they are needed.

 Warning: Some procedures in this Chapter entail the removal of fuel pipes and connections which may result in some fuel spillage. Others involve the deliberate release of quantities of fuel for test purposes. Before carrying out any operation on the fuel system refer to the precautions given in Safety First! at the beginning of this manual and follow them implicitly. Petrol is a highly dangerous and volatile liquid and the precautions necessary when handling it cannot be overstressed.

2 Unleaded petrol – general information

Note: *The information in this Section is correct at the time of writing and applies to fuel available in the UK. Seek advice from a VW dealer if in doubt. If travelling abroad, especially outside the EC, seek advice from a motoring organisation on fuel quality and grades available.*

1 All fuel injection models covered by this manual can use unleaded fuel continuously without damage. Models with a catalytic converter **must** use unleaded, otherwise the catalyst will be poisoned.

2 Engines with codes GW (1.9 litre) and DJ (2.1 litre) can run on 98 octane unleaded fuel (so-called 'super unleaded') without adjustment to the ignition timing. If they are to use 95 octane fuel, the ignition timing must be retarded slightly - see Chapter 5B.

3 All other engines can use 91 octane fuel (if available) or 95 octane without adjustment; 98 octane can be used if wished, but there is no advantage in doing so.

3 Fuel injection system – depressurising

1 It is necessary to depressurise the fuel injection system before disconnecting fuel lines or unions on the high pressure side of the system. This minimises the risk of fuel spillage.

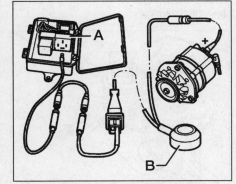

4.3 Connections for fuel pump delivery test

A *Relay socket*
B *Switch*

2 On Digijet models, disconnect the earth lead from the fuel pump underneath the vehicle.

3 On Digifant models, remove the fuel pump relay from its socket (see Section 10). (This will not work on Digijet models because the same relay energises the pump and the injectors. If the injectors are not energised the pressure will not be released.)

4 On all models, try to start the engine by cranking it on the starter motor. It may run briefly and then stop. The fuel system is now depressurised.

5 Reconnect the fuel pump earth lead or refit the relay on completion.

4 Fuel pump – testing, removal and refitting

Note: *Refer to the warning at the end of Section 1 before starting this procedure.*

Testing

Simple test

1 A simple test may be carried out by getting under the vehicle and feeling the fuel pump while an assistant switches on the ignition. When the ignition is switched on, the pump should run and be felt to vibrate for a second or so and then stop.

2 If the pump does not run, check for voltage at the pump electrical connector when the ignition is first switched on. If there is no voltage, the fuel pump relay or the relay circuit is at fault. If voltage is present but the pump does not run, the pump itself is faulty and must be renewed.

Delivery test

3 To check the delivery of the pump, first disconnect the battery earth lead. Remove the fuel pump relay and connect a jumper lead and switch between the alternator output (+) terminal and terminal 87 of the relay socket **(see illustration)**. Reconnect the battery earth lead but do not close the switch on the jumper lead yet.

4 Disconnect and cap the return hose from the fuel pressure regulator. Be prepared for fuel spillage.

5 Connect a short length of flexible fuel hose to the return connection on the fuel pressure regulator and lead it into a clean measuring jug **(see illustration)**.

6 Close the switch on the jumper lead: the fuel pump will run. Measure the quantity of fuel delivered in exactly 30 seconds and compare it with the minimum given in the Specifications. Low delivery can be caused by a blocked fuel pipe, a blocked fuel filter or a defective pump.

7 Remake the original hose connections and either return the fuel to the tank or (if it is dirty) dispose of it safely.

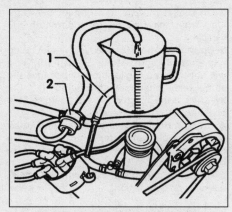

4.5 Testing fuel pump delivery

1 Fuel return hose   2 Pressure regulator

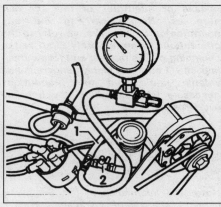

4.8 Testing fuel pump pressure

1 Fuel supply line   2 T-piece

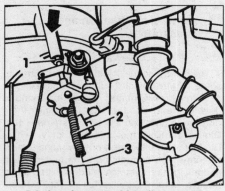

**5.3 Accelerator cable adjustment -
models with automatic transmission**

| *1 Locknut* | *3 Adjusting* |
| *2 Spring* | *rod* |

Pressure test

8 Disconnect the fuel supply line from the T-piece. Connect a suitable pressure gauge (range 0 to 3 bar approx) to the fuel supply line as shown **(see illustration)**.
9 Run the fuel pump as described for the delivery test until a pressure of 2.5 bar is established. Stop the pump and observe the gauge reading. Pressure must be maintained above 1.5 bar for at least 10 minutes. If the pressure falls faster than this, either there is a leak or the non-return valve inside the fuel pump is faulty.

Removal and refitting

10 Depressurise the fuel system as described in Section 3, then disconnect the battery earth lead.
11 Working under the vehicle, clamp or prepare to plug the hoses leading to and from the pump.
12 Disconnect the pump electrical leads and slacken the fuel unions. Unbolt the pump from its cradle, disconnect the fuel pipes and remove it. Be prepared for fuel spillage.
13 Refit by reversing the removal operations. Check for correct operation and the absence of leaks on completion.

6.4 Throttle valve switch adjustment

1 Ohmmeter connected to terminals	*2 Securing screw*
	3 Adjustment screw
	a Feeler blade

5 Accelerator cable – adjustment

Manual transmission

1 Refer to Part A of this Chapter, Section 8, substituting references to the throttle valve housing for those to the carburettor.

Automatic transmission

2 Refer to Part A of this Chapter, Section 9, substituting references to the throttle valve housing for those to the carburettor.
3 The adjustment points on the throttle valve housing are as shown **(see illustration)**.

6 Throttle valve switch – checking and adjustment

1 Correct adjustment of the throttle valve switch is important for smooth running. Surging, stalling and erratic idling can all be caused by a maladjusted switch.
2 Unplug the connector from the throttle valve switch. Connect an ohmmeter across the switch terminals.

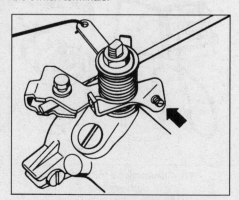

**6.5 Throttle valve basic setting screw
(arrowed) - do not adjust**

3 Open and close the throttle and observe the ohmmeter reading. There should be a reading of 1.5 ohms or less at idle and at full throttle positions, and an infinite (open-circuit) reading at all other positions.
4 To adjust, insert a feeler blade of thickness 0.05 to 0.10 mm between the throttle valve lever and the idle stop **(see illustration)**.
5 Slacken the switch securing screw and turn the adjusting screw until the switch just opens (infinite resistance). **Do not** attempt to adjust the throttle valve basic setting screw **(see illustration)**.
6 Tighten the screws, remove the feeler blade and recheck the operation of the switch.

7 Idle speed control valve – testing, removal and refitting

Testing

1 Start the engine and allow it to idle. Feel the idle speed control valve **(see illustration)**. It should be felt to vibrate.
2 If the valve does not vibrate, stop the engine and unplug the electrical connector from the valve. Measure the resistance across the valve terminals: it must be as specified.

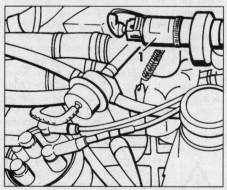

7.1 Idle speed control valve (1)

3 If the resistance is not as specified, the valve must be renewed. If the resistance is correct but the valve does not operate, there is a problem in the idle speed control unit or in its wiring.

Removal and refitting

4 Unplug the electrical connector from the valve. Disconnect the air hose from the valve and remove it from the inlet manifold.
5 Refit by reversing the removal operations. Check for correct operation on completion.

8 Fuel injectors –
testing, removal and refitting

Note: *Refer to the warning at the end of Section 1 before starting this procedure.*

Testing

1 Remove the injector clamping screw and withdraw the pair of injectors from the inlet manifold on the side concerned, leaving the electrical and fuel connections undisturbed.
2 Unplug the electrical connectors from the injectors on the other side of the engine.
3 Direct the injectors under test into a tray or other receptacle. Have an assistant crank the engine on the starter motor for a few seconds and observe the spray from the injectors **(see illustration)**.
4 Each injector should produce a cone-shaped spray of fuel; if not, renew it.
5 Unplug the electrical connectors from the injectors under test. Switch on the ignition for 5 seconds to pressurise the fuel system, then switch it off again. Observe the tips of the injectors: fuel must not leak from them. The maximum leakage tolerated is 2 drops per minute. A leaking injector must be renewed.
6 Refit the injectors and remake the original connections, ensuring that the injector sealing rings are in good condition.

Removal and refitting

7 Proceed as just described, but also release the clamps and disconnect the injectors from the fuel rail. Be prepared for fuel to spray out when this is done, or depressurise the fuel system as described in Section 3.

9 Fuel pressure regulator –
testing, removal and refitting

Note: *Refer to the warning at the end of Section 1 before starting this procedure.*

Testing

1 Check that the fuel pump delivery is correct (Section 4).
2 Connect a suitable pressure gauge (range 0 to 3 bar approx) into the T-piece on the fuel rail as shown **(see illustration)**.
3 Start the engine and allow it to idle. Read the pressure on the gauge: it must be around 2 bar.

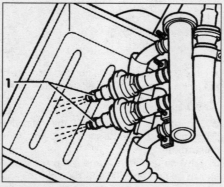

8.3 Testing the fuel injectors. Renew seals (1) if necessary

4 Disconnect the vacuum hose from the pressure regulator **(see illustration)**. The fuel pressure must increase to around 2.5 bar.
5 Switch off the ignition and observe the gauge. The pressure must stay above 1.5 bar for at least 10 minutes.
6 If the pressure drops too rapidly, repeat the previous test but also clamp the fuel return hose when the ignition is switched off. If the pressure does not now drop, the pressure regulator is defective. If the pressure still drops, the fault is elsewhere (leakage or defective pump non-return valve).
7 Remake the original connections on completion.

Removal and refitting

8 Depressurise the fuel system (Section 3) or prepare for fuel spray from disconnected lines.
9 Clean around the fuel unions on the pressure regulator and disconnect them. Also disconnect the vacuum hose.
10 Unscrew the nut which holds the pressure regulator to its bracket and remove the pressure regulator.
11 Refit by reversing the removal operations. Check for correct operation and the absence of leaks on completion.

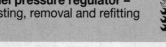

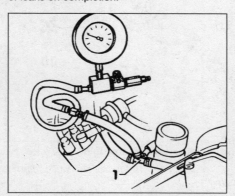

9.2 Testing the fuel pressure regulator - pressure gauge connection

1 T-piece

10 Sensors and relays –
general information

1 This Section explains the location and function of the various sensors and relays associated with the fuel injection system **(see illustration overleaf)**. Without special test equipment, testing is normally limited to substitution of a known good unit. When applicable, resistance or other basic test values are given in the Specifications. Not all the components described here are fitted to all models.

Sensors

Coolant temperature

2 The sensor is located in the thermostat housing, where it is secured by a hairpin clip. It provides the ECU with coolant temperature information, on the basis of which additional fuel is delivered to a cold engine.

Power steering pressure

3 The sensor is screwed into the steering pump outlet union. It informs the ECU when the power steering is loaded, enabling a correction to the idle speed to be made if necessary.

Oxygen (Lambda) sensor

4 See Section 14.

Relays

Idle speed stabilisation unit

5 Strictly speaking this is a control unit rather than a relay. It is located in front of the right-hand tail light cluster. The unit receives signals indicating engine speed and load, on the basis of which it opens or closes the idle speed control valve.

Fuel pump relay

6 This relay is located in a plastic box on the wall of the engine compartment. On Digijet systems it energises the fuel pump and also provides the injector operating voltage. On Digifant systems it supplies the fuel pump only.

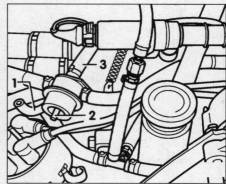

9.4 Testing the fuel pressure regulator - disconnect vacuum hose (1)

2 Vacuum hose connector
3 Fuel return hose

7 On all systems, when the ignition is switched on the relay must be heard or felt to operate.

Current supply relay

8 This is located in the same box as the fuel pump relay. On Digijet systems it supplies the idle speed stabilisation unit and the power steering pressure sensor. On Digifant systems it also supplies the fuel injectors, the oxygen sensor heating and the fuel pump relay.

9 On all systems, when the ignition is switched on the relay must be heard or felt to operate.

11 Airflow meter – testing, removal and refitting

1 Unplug the wiring connector and disconnect the air inlet hose from the airflow meter.

Testing

2 Connect an ohmmeter to the following terminals and observe the readings **(see illustration)**.

3 Between terminals 3 and 4 the resistance should be between 500 and 1000 ohms.

4 Between terminals 2 and 3 the resistance should vary as the airflow meter flap is moved back and forth.

5 Between terminals 1 and 4 the resistance should correspond to that given in the Specifications for the intake air temperature sensor.

6 If the resistances are not as specified, the airflow meter must be renewed. If it is the temperature sensor which is defective, seek advice as to whether this can be renewed separately.

7 Remake the original connections on completion.

Removal and refitting

8 Remove the securing screws and lift the airflow meter away from the air cleaner. Be careful, it is fragile.

9 Refit by reversing the removal operations.

12 Electronic control unit – removal and refitting

Note: *Complete testing of the electronic control unit (ECU) is not possible without special equipment. For verifying the correct operation of the oxygen sensor associated function, when applicable, see Section 14. The ECU is normally very reliable and in case of malfunction it should be the last component to suspect.*

1 Disconnect the battery earth lead.

Digijet system

2 Remove the left-hand tail light cluster for access to the control unit.

3 Unplug the connector from the control unit and remove it.

4 Refit by reversing the removal operations.

Digifant system

5 Proceed as just described for the Digijet system, but note that the Digifant control unit is located under the rear bench seat (on models so equipped) or in the corresponding position in the load space. On pick-up models it is in the locker below the load platform.

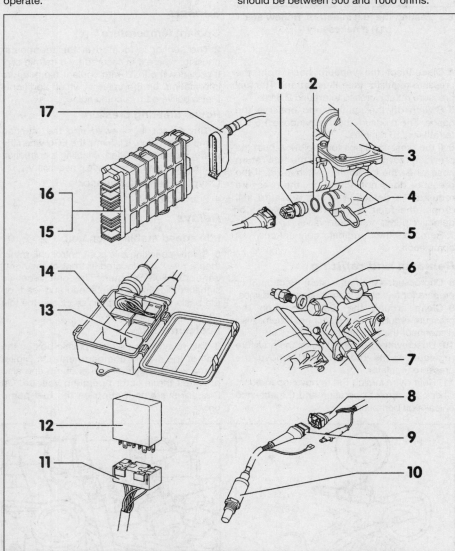

10.1 Fuel injection system sensors, relays and control units

1 Coolant temperature sensor	6 Seal	12 Idle speed stabilisation unit
2 O-ring	7 Steering pump	13 Fuel pump relay
3 Thermostat housing	8 Connector	14 Current supply relay
4 Hairpin clip	9 Connector	15 Digijet control unit
5 Power steering pressure sensor	10 Oxygen (Lambda) sensor (Digifant only)	16 Digifant control unit
	11 Socket	17 Connector

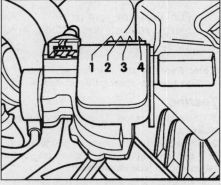

11.2 Airflow meter test points. For 1, 2, 3 and 4 see text

13 Emission control systems – general information

Note: *Four types of emission control systems may be used in part or in whole according to vehicle operating territory and date of manufacture. These are a crankcase ventilation system, a catalytic converter, an evaporative emission control system and a mixture charge limiter.*

Crankcase ventilation system

1 A closed circuit is used whereby engine crankcase emissions are recirculated to the air cleaner. From an oil separator on the crankcase a breather hose directs fumes to the air cleaner where they are mixed with the intake air and later burned in the engine.

Exhaust emission control system

2 On Digifant models, a catalytic converter is incorporated in the exhaust system to convert carbon monoxide and hydrocarbons into carbon dioxide and water. The catalytic converter is located in the exhaust system between manifold and silencer and the exhaust gases pass through it before being released into the atmosphere.
3 An oxygen (Lambda) sensor mounted in the exhaust manifold monitors the oxygen content of the exhaust gas and relays this information to the Digifant control unit. The control unit then alters the fuel injection time accordingly so that the engine always receives an accurately metered air/fuel mixture. Combustion is thus at its most efficient and exhaust gas pollutants are at their lowest level.

Evaporative emission control system

4 The fuel system, tank and fuel lines are effectively sealed from the atmosphere to prevent the escape of hydrocarbon vapours. Fuel tank venting is through expansion tanks which allow expansion and contraction of the fuel without allowing any escape of vapour.
5 A charcoal filter is used in the tank vent lines to remove hydrocarbons from the fuel vapours. Fresh air entering the filter cleans the charcoal and routes the hydrocarbons back to the engine where they are burned during normal combustion.

Mixture charge limiter

6 See Section 16.

14 Oxygen (Lambda) sensor – testing, removal and refitting

Note: *Special oxygen sensor testers are available. If such an instrument is being used, follow the maker's instructions. The procedure in this Section does not actually test the sensor itself, but observes the effect (or lack of effect) which the sensor has on the exhaust gas CO level. It will not distinguish between a defective sensor and a bad connection in the wiring to the sensor.*

Testing

1 Adjust the idle speed and mixture as described in Chapter 1. Leave the tachometer and CO meter connected and allow the engine to idle.
2 Artificially enrich the fuel mixture by disconnecting and plugging the vacuum hose from the fuel pressure regulator. Watch what happens to the CO level. It should rise briefly, then return to its previous value. If it does not, either the oxygen sensor or the ECU is faulty. Find out which as follows.
3 Disconnect the oxygen sensor-to-control unit wiring plug **(see illustration)**. Earth the ECU side of the connector: the CO level must rise. Apply 12 volts to the ECU side of the connector: the CO level must fall.
4 If the CO level did not change during either test, it is probably the ECU which is at fault. If the CO level did not change during the first test (paragraph 2) but did change during the second test (paragraph 3), the ECU is OK and it is probably the oxygen sensor which is at fault. In either event, perform a thorough check of the wiring before renewing either component.

Removal and refitting

5 Disconnect the sensor wiring plugs and free the wiring from any cable ties.
6 Unscrew the oxygen sensor from the catalytic converter and remove it.
7 Refit by reversing the removal operations. Apply a little anti-seize compound to the sensor threads, but be careful not to get any onto the business end or into the slots of the sensor.

15 Catalytic converter – precautions

The catalytic converter is a reliable and simple device which forms part of the exhaust system. It needs no maintenance in itself, but there are some facts of which an owner should be aware if the converter is to function properly for its full service life.

a) DO NOT use leaded petrol in a vehicle equipped with a catalytic converter - the lead will poison the precious metals, reducing their converting efficiency and will eventually destroy the converter.
b) Always keep the ignition and fuel systems well-maintained.
c) If the engine develops a misfire, do not drive the vehicle at all (or at least as little as possible) until the fault is cured.
d) DO NOT push- or tow-start the vehicle - this will soak the catalytic converter in unburned fuel, causing it to overheat when the engine does start.
e) DO NOT switch off the ignition at high engine speeds.
f) DO NOT use fuel or engine oil additives - these may contain substances harmful to the catalytic converter.
g) DO NOT continue to use the vehicle if the engine burns oil to the extent of leaving a visible trail of blue smoke.
h) Remember that the catalytic converter operates at very high temperatures. DO NOT, therefore, park in dry undergrowth, over long grass or piles of dead leaves after a long run.
i) Remember that the inside of the catalytic converter is FRAGILE - do not drop it or strike it with tools during servicing work.
j) In some cases a sulphurous smell (like that of rotten eggs) may be noticed from the exhaust. This is common to many catalytic converter-equipped vehicles. Sometimes changing the brand of fuel used will reduce the smell.
k) The catalytic converter on a well-maintained and well-driven vehicle should last for between 50 000 and 100 000 miles. When the converter is no longer effective it must be renewed.

16 Mixture charge limiter – general information

1 The mixture charge limiter system is fitted to engine code SS only. Its function is to limit exhaust emissions under certain operating conditions at high engine speeds (above 4500 rpm).
2 The system consists of an additional throttle valve, a vacuum actuator for this valve, a control unit and associated hoses, check valves and control valves **(see illustration overleaf)**.
3 Testing of the system is not possible without special equipment. If malfunction is suspected, check the integrity of all electrical and vacuum connections. If no fault is evident, consult a VW dealer or other specialist.

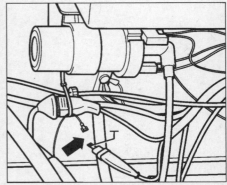

14.3 Disconnect the oxygen sensor-to-control unit wiring plug (arrowed)

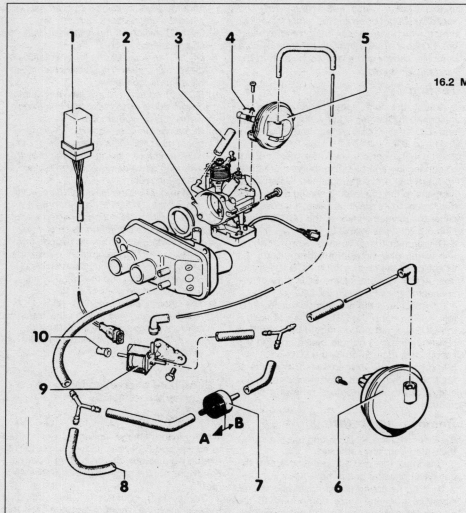

16.2 Mixture charge limiter system components

1 Control unit
2 Throttle valve housing
3 To charcoal canister (when fitted)
4 Clip
5 Vacuum actuator
6 Vacuum tank
7 Non-return valve (A - flow; B - no flow)
8 To fuel pressure regulator
9 Control valve
10 Vent cap

Chapter 5 Part A:
Starting and charging systems

Contents

Degrees of difficulty

Easy, suitable for novice with little experience	**Fairly easy,** suitable for beginner with some experience	**Fairly difficult,** suitable for competent DIY mechanic 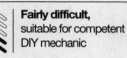	**Difficult,** suitable for experienced DIY mechanic	**Very difficult,** suitable for expert DIY or professional

Specifications

Battery
Type	Low-maintenance, or maintenance-free 'sealed for life'
Capacity	45, 54 or 63 amp hr

Alternator
Type	Bosch
Maximum output	45 or 65 amps
Brush length:	
New	13 mm (0.5 in)
Minimum	5 mm (0.2 in)
Drivebelt deflection	Approximately 15 mm (0.6 in) under moderate pressure midway between pulleys

Starter motor
Type	Bosch pre-engaged
Minimum brush length	11.5 mm (0.45 in)

Torque wrench settings	**Nm**	**lbf ft**
Alternator pulley nut	35	26
Alternator mountings	30	22
Alternator tensioning bracket	20	15

1 General information and precautions

General information

The engine electrical system consists mainly of the charging and starting systems. Because of their engine-related functions, these components are covered separately from the body electrical devices such as the lights, instruments, etc (which are covered in Chapter 12). Refer to Chapter 5B for information on the ignition system.

The electrical system is of the 12-volt negative earth type. The battery is of the low maintenance or "maintenance-free" (sealed for life) type and is charged by the alternator, which is belt-driven from the crankshaft pulley.

The starter motor is of the pre-engaged type, incorporating an integral solenoid.

Precautions

Further details of the various systems are given in the relevant Sections of this Chapter. While some repair procedures are given, the usual course of action is to renew the component concerned. The owner whose interest extends beyond component renewal should obtain a copy of the *"Automotive Electrical & Electronic Systems Manual"*, available from the publishers of this manual.

It is necessary to take extra care when working on the electrical system to avoid damage to semi-conductor devices (diodes and transistors), and to avoid the risk of personal injury. In addition to the precautions given in *"Safety first!"* at the beginning of this manual, observe the following when working on the system:

Always remove rings, watches, etc before working on the electrical system. Even with the battery disconnected, capacitive discharge could occur if a component's live terminal is earthed through a metal object. This could cause a shock or a burn.

Do not reverse the battery connections. Components such as the alternator, electronic control units, or any other components having semi-conductor circuitry could be irreparably damaged.

If the engine is being started using jump leads and a slave battery, connect the batteries positive-to-positive and negative-to-negative (see "Booster battery (jump) starting"). This also applies when connecting a battery charger.

Never disconnect the battery terminals, the alternator, any electrical wiring or any test instruments when the engine is running.

Do not allow the engine to turn the alternator when the alternator is not connected.

Never "test" for alternator output by 'flashing' the output lead to earth.

Never use an ohmmeter of the type incorporating a hand-cranked generator for circuit or continuity testing.

Always ensure that the battery negative(earth) lead is disconnected when working on the electrical system.

Before using electric-arc welding equipment on the car, disconnect the battery, alternator and (if applicable) components such as the electronic control units to protect them from the risk of damage.

If a radio/cassette unit equipped with a built-in security code is fitted, the anti-theft system will activate if the battery is disconnected. Even if the power source is immediately reconnected, the unit will not function until the correct security code has been entered. Therefore, do not disconnect the battery if you do not know the correct security code. Refer to the manufacturer's instructions if necessary.

2 Battery – removal and refitting

⚠️ *Warning: Refer to the precautions in Section 1 before starting work.*

1 The battery is located in the driver's cab, beneath the front right-hand side seat.
2 To gain access to the battery, move the seat fully forward or, if swivel seats are fitted, turn the seat through 180°.
3 Lift up the battery box lid, slacken the negative (–) terminal clamp nut or bolt and lift the terminal off the battery post **(see illustration)**.
4 Slacken the positive (+) terminal clamp nut or bolt and lift the terminal off the battery post.
5 Remove the battery retaining clamp and withdraw the battery from its location. Be careful, it is heavy. Keep it upright: remember it contains sulphuric acid.
6 Before refitting, apply a smear of petroleum jelly to the battery terminals to prevent corrosion.
7 Refitting the battery is the reverse sequence to removal. Do not overtighten the terminal clamps.

2.3 Battery negative terminal

3 Battery – charging

⚠️ *Warning: Refer to the precautions in Section 1 before starting work.*

1 In normal use the battery should remain adequately charged from the alternator. A regular need for charging from an external source suggests a problem with the battery or charging system (see Section 7). However, charging will be necessary if the battery has been accidentally discharged by leaving the lights or other electrical equipment switched on. Charging will also sometimes temporarily revive a failing battery.
2 Charging is also useful if the vehicle is laid up for long periods. In this case a 'top-up' charge every month or 6 weeks is suggested.
3 The charging rate should be approximately 10% of the battery capacity, i.e. for a 45 amp hour battery, the charge rate should be 4.5 amps. In all cases however the charging rate should not exceed 6 amps. Most domestic battery chargers fall within this limit.
4 If the battery is not removed from the vehicle for charging, disconnect both leads from it. Wherever charging is taking place, ensure adequate ventilation.
5 The leads of the battery charger and the terminals of the battery must be connected positive to positive and negative to negative. Ensure that the charger is switched off before connecting or disconnecting the charger leads.
6 On batteries where provision is made for topping up, ensure that the electrolyte level is between the MIN and MAX marks on the battery case and top up with distilled water if necessary. Unscrew the vent caps before charging. Check the electrolyte level again when charging is complete.
7 Rapid or 'boost' charging should only be carried out by a VW agent or auto electrician. It is necessary to monitor the charge rate and electrolyte temperature when charging at a high rate, and certain maintenance free type batteries are not suited to this process. If in any doubt about the suitability of charging equipment, consult a specialist.

4 Alternator drivebelt – removal and refitting

⚠️ *Warning: Refer to the precautions in Section 1 before starting work.*

1 Disconnect the battery negative terminal.
2 Slacken the alternator mounting and tensioning bracket nuts and bolts. Move the alternator towards the engine and slip the drivebelt off the pulleys **(see illustration)**.

4.2 Removing the alternator drivebelt (engine removed for clarity)

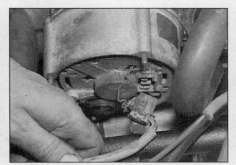

6.2 Disconnect the wiring from the rear of the alternator

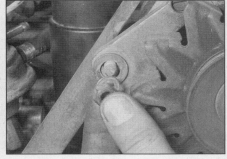

6.3A Remove the tensioning bracket nut and washer . . .

3 Fit the new drivebelt and tension it as described in Chapter 1.

4 Reconnect the battery. If a new drivebelt has been fitted, recheck the tension after 500 miles or so.

5 Alternator – general description

Vehicles covered by this manual are equipped with Bosch alternators. All are virtually identical in construction but have different outputs. The alternator generates alternating current (ac) which is rectified by diodes into direct current (dc) as this is the current needed for charging the battery.

The alternator is of the rotating field, ventilated design and consists principally of a laminated stator (on which is wound the output winding), a rotor carrying the field winding, and a diode rectifier. A voltage regulator/brush carrier is separately mounted at the rear. The alternator generates its current in the stator windings and the rotor carries the field. The field brushes therefore are only required to carry a light current and as they run on plain slip rings they have a relatively long life. This design makes the alternator a reliable machine requiring little servicing.

The rotor is belt-driven from the crankshaft through a pulley keyed to the rotor shaft.

6 Alternator – removal and refitting

 Warning: Refer to the precautions in Section 1 before starting work.

1 Remove the alternator drivebelt as described in Section 4.

2 Disconnect the wiring from the rear of the alternator **(see illustration)**.

3 Remove the alternator tensioning bracket nut and bolt **(see illustrations)**.

4 Remove the alternator mounting nut and bolt and lift the alternator from the engine **(see illustration)**.

5 Refitting is a reversal of the removal procedure. Adjust the drivebelt tension on completion as described in Chapter 1.

7 Charging system – fault tracing and rectification

 Warning: Refer to the precautions in Section 1 before starting work.

1 If the ignition warning light fails to illuminate when the ignition is switched on, first check the alternator wiring connections for security.

If satisfactory, check that the warning light bulb or LED has not blown, and that the bulbholder is secure in its location in the instrument panel (Chapter 12). If the light still fails to illuminate, check the continuity of the warning light feed wire from the alternator to the bulbholder. If all is satisfactory, the alternator is probably at fault and should be renewed or taken to an auto-electrician for testing and repair.

2 If the ignition warning light illuminates when the engine is running, stop the engine and check that the drivebelt is correctly tensioned (see Chapter 1) and that the alternator connections are secure. If all is so far satisfactory, have the alternator and voltage regulator checked by an auto-electrician **(see illustrations)**.

3 If the alternator output is suspect even though the warning light functions correctly, the regulated voltage may be checked as follows.

4 Connect a voltmeter across the battery terminals and start the engine.

5 Increase the engine speed until the voltmeter reading remains steady. The reading should be approximately 13 volts - no less than 12 volts and no more than 14 volts.

6 Switch on as many electrical accessories (eg, the headlights, heated rear window and heater blower) as possible, and check that the alternator maintains the regulated voltage at around 13 volts.

6.3B . . . and the tensioning bracket bolt

6.4 Removing the alternator mounting bolt

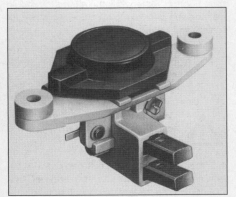

7.2A Alternator voltage regulator and brushbox assembly

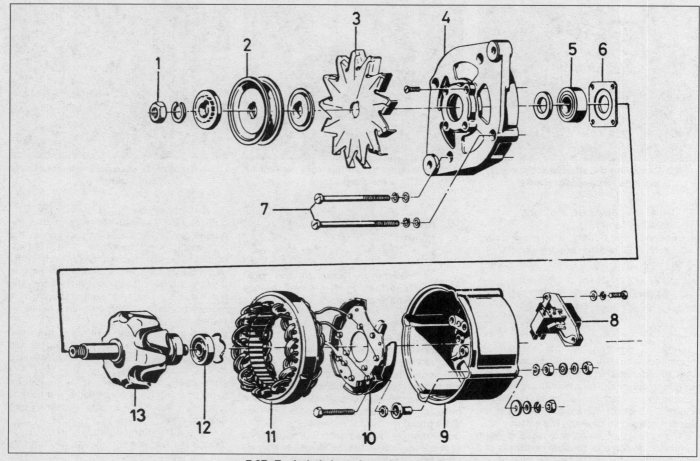

7.2B Exploded view of a typical alternator

1 Pulley nut	4 Drive end housing	8 Brush holder/regulator	12 Bearing
2 Pulley	5 Bearing	9 Slip ring end housing	13 Rotor
3 Fan	6 Bearing retainer	10 Endplate	
	7 Through-bolts	11 Stator	

7 If the regulated voltage is not as stated, the fault may be due to worn brushes, weak brush springs, a faulty voltage regulator, a faulty diode, a severed phase winding or worn or damaged slip rings. For renewal of the brushes and voltage regulator, refer to the next Section. Otherwise, the alternator should be renewed or taken to an auto-electrician for testing and repair.

8 Alternator brushes – inspection and renewal

⚠ **Warning: Refer to the precautions in Section 1 before starting work.**

1 If this operation is being carried out with the alternator in position on the engine, first disconnect the battery negative terminal.
2 Undo and remove the two screws, spring and plain washers which secure the voltage regulator to the alternator. Lift away the voltage regulator complete with brushes.
3 Check that the carbon brushes are able to slide smoothly in their guides without any sign of binding.
4 Measure the length of the brushes. If they have worn below the specified limit, they must be renewed.
5 At this stage it is recommended to consult an auto electrician. If new brushes are available separately, have some fitted. This operation requires some skill in soldering and is not recommended to the amateur. It is good practice to renew the brush springs at the same time.
6 If new brushes are not available separately, it will be necessary to renew the voltage regulator and brush carrier assembly complete. This should be done in any case if the operation of the voltage regulator was suspect.
7 Refitting the voltage regulator and brush carrier is the reverse sequence to removal.

9 Starter motor – general description

When the starter switch is operated, current flows from the battery to the solenoid which is mounted on the starter body. The plunger in the solenoid moves inwards, so causing a centrally pivoted lever to push the drive pinion into mesh with the starter ring gear. When the solenoid plunger reaches the end of its travel, it closes an internal contact and full starting current flows to the starter field coils. The armature is then able to rotate the crankshaft, so starting the engine.

A freewheel clutch is fitted to the starter drive pinion so that as soon as the engine fires and starts to operate on its own it does not drive the starter motor.

When the starter switch is released, the solenoid is de-energised and a spring moves the plunger back to its rest position. This operates the pivoted lever to withdraw the drive pinion from engagement with the starter ring.

10 Starter motor – testing

Warning: Refer to the precautions in Section 1 before starting work.

1 If the starter motor fails to turn the engine when the switch is operated, there are five possible causes:

a) *The battery is discharged*
b) *The electrical connections between the switch, solenoid, battery and starter motor are somewhere failing to pass the necessary current from the battery through the starter to earth*
c) *The solenoid switch is faulty*
d) *The starter motor is mechanically or electrically defective*
e) *The starter motor pinion and/or flywheel ring gear is badly worn and in need of replacement*

2 To check the battery, switch on the headlights. If they dim after a few seconds the battery is in a discharged state. If the lights glow brightly, operate the starter switch and see what happens to the lights. If they dim then you know that power is reaching the starter motor but failing to turn it. If the starter turns slowly when switched on, proceed to the next check.

3 If, when the starter switch is operated the light stays bright, then insufficient power is reaching the motor. Remove the battery connections, the starter/solenoid power connections and the engine/transmission earth strap and thoroughly clean them and refit them. (Disconnect the battery earth lead first, and reconnect it last.) Corroded connections are the most frequent cause of electrical system malfunctions.

4 When the above checks and cleaning tasks have been carried out but without success, you will possibly have heard a clicking noise each time the starter switch was operated. This was the solenoid switch operating, but it does not necessarily follow that the main contacts were closing properly. (If no clicking has been heard from the solenoid, it is certainly defective). The solenoid contact can be checked by putting a voltmeter or bulb between the main cable connection on the starter side of the solenoid and earth. When the switch is operated, there should be a reading or a lighted bulb. If there is no reading or lighted bulb, the solenoid unit is faulty and should be renewed.

5 If the starter motor operates but does not turn the engine, first check the security of its mounting bolts and of the engine-to-transmission nuts. If these are satisfactory, it is probable that the starter pinion and/or flywheel ring gear are badly worn, in which case the starter motor will have been noisy in operation.

11.5A Starter motor lower securing nut (arrowed)

6 Finally, if it is established that the solenoid is not faulty and 12 volts are getting to the starter, then the motor itself is faulty and should be removed for inspection.

11 Starter motor – removal and refitting

Warning: Refer to the precautions in Section 1 before starting work.

1 Jack up the rear of the vehicle and support it on axle stands (see "*Jacking and vehicle support*").
2 Disconnect the battery negative terminal.
3 Although not essential, it will improve access if the right-hand driveshaft is disconnected from the transmission (see Chapter 8).
4 Working under the rear right-hand side of the vehicle, make a note of the wiring connections at the solenoid and disconnect them. If the wiring harness is secured to the starter motor or solenoid body with a clip or retaining band, release it and move the wiring harness aside.
5 Undo the two nuts and bolts securing the starter motor to the clutch housing and withdraw the starter motor from its location **(see illustrations)**. Access to the upper bolt is easier from above.
6 Refitting is the reverse sequence to removal.

12 Starter motor renovation – general

Such is the inherent reliability and strength of the starter motor that it is very unlikely that a motor will need dismantling until it is totally worn out and in need of replacement as a whole.

If, however, the motor has not seen much service and a solenoid or brush fault is suspected, then it may be worth while to remove the motor from the engine and dismantle it as described in the following Sections. Seek advice on the availability and cost of spare parts before proceeding.

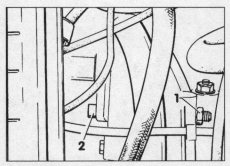

11.5B Starter motor upper securing nut (1) and bolt (2)

13 Starter solenoid – removal and refitting

1 With the starter motor removed from the engine and on a clean bench, undo the retaining nut and washer at the rear of the solenoid and slip the starter electrical feed wire off the solenoid stud.
2 Undo the two screws securing the solenoid to the starter drive end housing.
3 Disengage the solenoid shaft from the pinion carriage actuating arm and withdraw the solenoid **(see illustration)**.
4 Refitting is the reverse sequence to removal.

14 Starter motor brushes – inspection and renewal

1 With the starter removed from the engine and on a clean bench, begin by removing the armature end cap which is secured by two small screws on the end of the motor. Remove the armature retaining clip, washers and the rubber sealing ring which were exposed. Undo and remove the two long bolts which hold the motor assembly together. The end cover can now be removed to reveal the brushes and mounting plate **(see illustrations)**.
2 Take the brushes from the holder and slip the holder off the armature shaft. Retrieve the

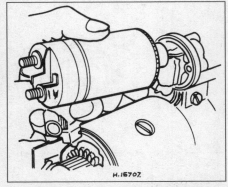

13.3 Releasing the solenoid from the actuating arm

14.1A Remove the armature end cap . . .

14.1B . . . followed by the retaining clip, washers and sealing ring

14.1C Undo and remove the two long through bolts. . .

14.1D . . . and lift off the end cover

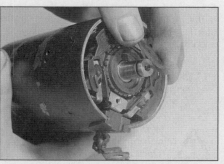

14.1E Commutator and field coil bushes

14.5 Brush holder with brushes ready for refitting

spacer washers (when fitted) from between the brush plate and the armature block.

3 Inspect the brushes; if they are worn down to less than the minimum length given in Specifications, they should be renewed. The old brushes must be destroyed by crushing and new brushes soldered in place. The DIY mechanic is advised to take the brush plate and yoke to an auto electrician to have new brushes fitted.

4 Wipe the starter motor armature and commutator with a non-fluffy rag wetted with petrol.

5 Reassemble the brushes into the holder **(see illustration)** and refit the holder over the armature shaft, remembering to fit the two washers between the holder and armature, where fitted.

6 Refit the motor end cover and secure with two long bolts.

7 Refit the armature shaft end cap after fitting the rubber sealing ring, washer and shaft clip.

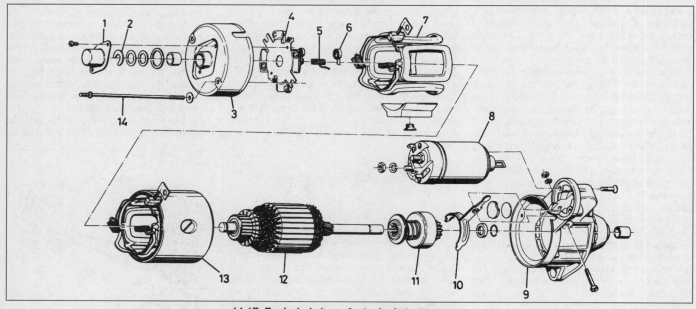

14.1F Exploded view of a typical starter motor

1 End cap	4 Brush holder	7 Field coils
2 Armature retaining clip	5 Brush	8 Solenoid
3 Commutator end cover	6 Brush spring	9 Drive end housing

10 Actuating arm	12 Armature	
11 Pinion and clutch assembly	13 Yoke	
	14 Through-bolt	

Chapter 5 Part B:
Ignition system

Contents

Degrees of difficulty

Easy, suitable for novice with little experience		**Fairly easy,** suitable for beginner with some experience		**Fairly difficult,** suitable for competent DIY mechanic		**Difficult,** suitable for experienced DIY mechanic		**Very difficult,** suitable for expert DIY or professional	

Specifications

General

Type:

All 1.9 litre engines, and 2.1 litre code DJ . . . . TCI-H, breakerless, mechanical advance and retard

2.1 litre engines codes MV, SR and SS . . . . Digifant (integral with fuel injection system), electronic advance and retard

Firing order . . . . 1 – 4 – 3 – 2

(No 1 cylinder on right-hand side of engine nearest the flywheel)

Distributor

Type . . . . Bosch

Direction of rotation . . . . Clockwise (viewed from cap)

Ignition timing

1.9 litre engines:

Code EY . . . . 5° ± 1° BTDC at 850 ± 50 rpm, vacuum disconnected

Code DF . . . . 5° ± 1° ATDC at 750 ± 50 rpm, vacuum connected

Codes DG and SP . . . . 5° ± 1° BTDC at 900 ± 50 rpm, vacuum disconnected

Code GW, for 98 octane fuel . . . . 10° ± 1° BTDC at 880 ± 50 rpm, vacuum disconnected

Code GW, for 95 octane fuel . . . . 5° ± 1° BTDC at 880 ± 50 rpm, vacuum disconnected

2.1 litre engines:

Code DJ, for 98 octane fuel . . . . 10° ± 1° BTDC at 800 ± 50 rpm, vacuum disconnected

Code DJ, for 95 octane fuel . . . . 5° - 1° BTDC at 800 ± 50 rpm, vacuum disconnected

Codes MV, SR and SS . . . . 5° ± 1° BTDC at 2000 to 2500 rpm (no vacuum on this system)

Ignition coil

Make . . . . Bosch

Primary resistance (typical) . . . . 0.5 to 0.8 ohms

Secondary resistance:

Coil with green sticker . . . . 2.4 to 3.5 k ohms

Coil with grey sticker . . . . 6.9 to 8.5 k ohms

1 General description

TCI-H system

The ignition system is divided into two circuits, low tension and high tension. The high tension (HT or secondary) circuit consists of the high tension coil windings, the heavy ignition lead from the centre of the coil to the distributor cap, the rotor arm, spark plugs and spark plug leads. The low tension (LT or primary) circuit consists of the battery, ignition switch, low tension or primary coil windings and a vane and pick-up unit operating in conjunction with an electronic control unit. The vane and pick-up unit are located in the distributor and carry out the same function as the contact breaker points and condenser used on conventional systems **(see illustration)**.

The vane is a four-toothed wheel (one tooth for each cylinder) which is fitted to the distributor shaft. The pick-up unit is fitted to the distributor baseplate and consists essentially of a coil and a permanent magnet.

The control unit is located in the engine compartment. It contains an amplifier module that is used to boost the voltage induced by the pick-up coil. When the ignition switch is on, the ignition primary circuit is energised. When the distributor vane teeth approach the magnetic coil assembly, a voltage is induced which signals the control unit to turn off the coil primary circuit. A timing circuit in the amplifier module turns on the coil current again after the coil magnetic field has collapsed.

When switched on, current flows from the battery through the ignition switch, through the coil primary winding, through the amplifier module and then to ground (earth). When the current is off, the magnetic field in the ignition coil collapses, inducing a high voltage in the coil secondary windings. This is conducted to the distributor cap where the rotor arm directs it to the appropriate spark plug. This process is repeated for each power stroke of the engine.

The distributor is fitted with devices to control the actual point of ignition according to the engine speed and load. As the engine speed increases, two centrifugal weights within the distributor body, and connected to the vane armature, move outwards. This alters the position of the vane in relation to the distributor shaft and advances the spark accordingly. A vacuum advance and retard unit is attached externally to the distributor body and connected by a pullrod to the baseplate. Variations in inlet manifold vacuum cause a diaphragm within the unit to deflect thus moving the pullrod. The baseplate and pick-up unit move under the action of the pullrod thus advancing or retarding the spark according to engine load.

An idle stabilizing unit, consisting of an additional electronic module and located in the engine compartment adjacent to the control unit, maintains a stable engine idling speed. The unit advances or retards the spark as necessary when the engine is idling so that a near constant idling speed is obtained under all conditions of engine load.

Digifant system

The Digifant system is very similar to the TCI-H system just described, but it has a more powerful control unit which is shared with the fuel injection system. Changes in ignition timing with speed and load are controlled electronically, without the need for centrifugal or vacuum devices attached to the distributor.

The Digifant control unit is located under the rear bench seat (on models so equipped) or in the corresponding position in the load space. On pick-up models it is in the locker below the load platform.

Information on the fuel-related parts of the Digifant system will be found in Chapter 4B.

2 Electronic ignition system – precautions

⚠ *Warning: When working on the electronic ignition system the following precautions must be strictly observed to prevent damage to the electronic components and to avoid the risk of personal injury.*

1 The voltages produced are considerably higher than those produced by a conventional system. Extreme care must be taken if work is being done with the ignition switched on, particularly by persons fitted with a cardiac pacemaker.

2 The ignition must be switched off before any ignition wiring, including HT leads or test equipment wiring, is disconnected or connected.

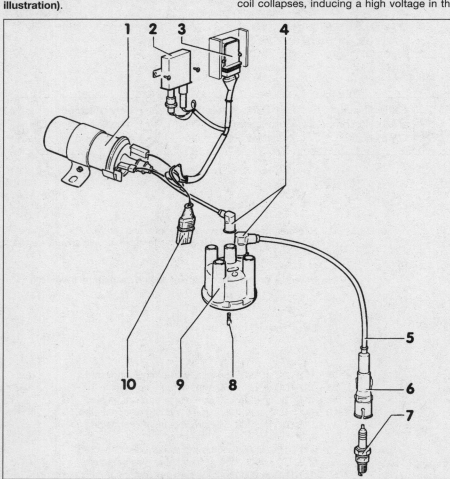

1.1 TCI-H ignition system components

1 Coil	6 Spark plug connector
2 Idle stabilising unit	7 Spark plug
3 Control unit	8 Carbon brush
4 HT lead connectors	9 Distributor cap
5 HT lead	10 Connector

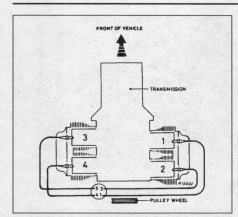

3.1 Cylinder numbering sequence and HT lead arrangement

3 If, for any reason, the engine is to be cranked on the starter without starting, remove the HT lead from the centre of the distributor cap and earth it (TCI-H system) or unplug the distributor LT connector (Digifant system).

4 If the engine is to be steam cleaned, de-greased, or washed in any way, the ignition must be switched off.

5 The battery must be completely discon-nected (both leads removed) before any electric welding or spot welding on the vehicle takes place.

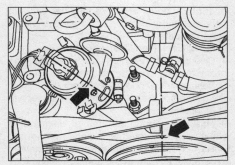

3.5 Correct position of ignition timing mark and distributor rotor arm (arrowed) - No 1 cylinder firing

6 Where there is a known or suspected defect in the ignition system, the wiring plug at the control unit must be disconnected if the vehicle is to be towed with the ignition on.

7 Do not connect a condenser to the negative terminal (1) of the ignition coil.

8 Never substitute the standard fitting 1 k ohm rotor arm (marked R 1) with a different type.

9 For the purposes of radio suppression, only 1 k ohm spark plug HT leads with 1 k ohm to 5 k ohm spark plug connectors may be used.

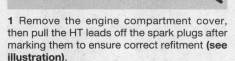

3 Distributor – removal and refitting

1 Remove the engine compartment cover, then pull the HT leads off the spark plugs after marking them to ensure correct refitment (see illustration).

2 Spring back the distributor cap retaining clips, lift off the cap and place it to one side (see illustration).

3 Remove the spark plug from No 1 cylinder (on the right-hand side of the engine nearest the flywheel).

4 Place a finger over the plug hole and turn the engine, using a spanner on the crankshaft pulley bolt, until compression can be felt building up in the cylinder.

5 When compression can be felt in No 1 cylinder, continue turning the engine until the ignition timing mark on the crankshaft pulley is uppermost and aligned with the join in the crankcase halves (see illustration).

6 With the engine in this position the distributor rotor arm should be pointing towards the No 1 cylinder HT lead segment in the cap and should also be pointing towards the notch in the rim of the distributor body. Make alignment marks if necessary.

7 If applicable, disconnect the advance and retard pipes from the distributor vacuum unit, making a note of which side of the unit the respective pipes are fitted (see illustration).

8 Disconnect the control unit wiring plug from the socket on the distributor body.

3.2 Removing the distributor cap

9 Undo the nut and remove the washer securing the distributor clamp to the stud on the crankcase then withdraw the distributor upwards and out of its location (see illustration).

10 Before refitting the distributor, check that the engine has not been inadvertently turned whilst the distributor was removed. If it has, return it to the original position as described in paragraphs 4 and 5.

11 Position the rotor arm so that it is pointing to the notch in the rim of the distributor body and then insert the distributor into its location. Turn the rotor arm very slightly as necessary so that the boss at the base of the distributor engages with the driveshaft. Position the clamp over the retaining stud and push the distributor fully home. Refit the washer and retaining nut and tighten the nut.

12 When applicable, reconnect the vacuum and retard pipes to the vacuum unit. Reconnect the control unit wiring plug to the distributor socket.

13 Check that the rotor arm is still pointing to the notch on the rim of the distributor body. If not, slacken the distributor clamp pinch-bolt and turn the distributor body as necessary. Now tighten the pinch-bolt.

14 Refit the spark plug, distributor cap and HT leads. If removed, refit the protective grille over the crankshaft pulley and the timing scale.

15 Refer to Section 5 and adjust the ignition timing.

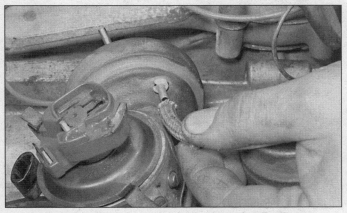

3.7 Disconnecting a vacuum pipe from the distributor

3.9 Removing the distributor securing nut

4.2A Begin dismantling the distributor by removing the rotor arm . . .

4.2B . . . followed by the protective plastic cover

4.3A Extract the retaining circlip (arrowed) . . .

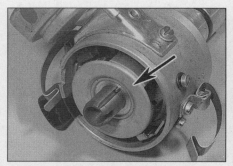

4.3B . . . then carefully withdraw the vane (arrowed) using two screwdrivers if necessary

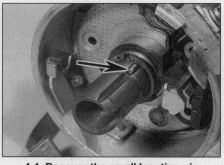

4.4 Recover the small locating pin (arrowed) . . .

4.5 . . . then extract the second circlip

4 Distributor – dismantling, inspection and reassembly

TCI-H system

1 Remove the distributor from the engine as described in Section 3, then prepare a clean uncluttered working area.

2 Begin dismantling by lifting off the rotor arm followed by the protective plastic cover (see illustrations).

3 Using circlip pliers, extract the vane retaining circlip (see illustration). Carefully prise the vane off the distributor shaft using two thin screwdrivers positioned opposite each other under the vane centre boss (see illustration).

4 Recover the small locating pin from the groove in the distributor shaft (see illustration).

5 Again using circlip pliers extract the second circlip on the distributor shaft (see illustration).

6 Undo the screws around the side of the distributor body which secure the vacuum unit, distributor cap clips and the baseplate. Note the different lengths of the screws and their locations (see illustration).

7 Disengage the vacuum unit pullrod from the baseplate peg and withdraw the unit.

8 Release the wiring socket from the side of the distributor body then lift out the baseplate (see illustration).

9 This is the practical limit of dismantling which may be undertaken since none of the parts below the baseplate can be renewed separately. Lay out all the components in their

4.6 Remove the screws around the side of the distributor body (arrowed) and withdraw the vacuum unit

4.8 Release the wiring socket and lift out the baseplate assembly

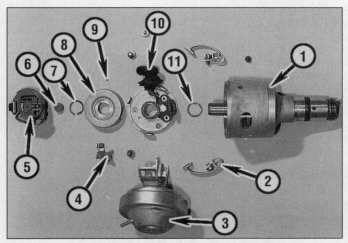

4.9 TCI-H Distributor component parts

1 *Distributor body*	7 *Circlip*
2 *Distributor cap clip*	8 *Vane*
3 *Vacuum unit*	9 *Locating pin*
4 *Baseplate support*	10 *Baseplate and*
5 *Rotor arm*	*pick-up unit*
6 *Felt pad*	11 *Circlip*

4.13 Lubricate both centrifugal advance weight pivot and contact areas (A) and the distributor shaft (B) before reassembly

order of removal, taking particular note of the location and number of any shim washers which may be fitted to control shaft endfloat **(see illustration)**. Carry out a careful inspection of the other components as follows.

10 Examine the rotor arm for cracks and ensure that it is a snug fit on the distributor shaft. Any slight burning on the end of the metal portion of the arm may be removed with a fine file. If the rotor arm is badly burned, cracked, or a loose fit on the shaft, it should be renewed.

11 Hold the drive boss at the base of the distributor with one hand and turn the upper part of the distributor shaft clockwise with the other. Firm spring resistance should be felt with no slackness or binding apparent. Check that the centrifugal advance weights move freely and return under the tension of the springs. Any faults noticed during this inspection will necessitate renewal of the complete distributor as component parts are not available separately.

4.18 If necessary renew the O-ring at the base of the distributor

12 The vacuum unit may be checked for correct operation by sucking the vacuum pipe connections whilst observing the action of the pullrod. If no movement of the rod is apparent when suction is applied, it is likely that the diaphragm in the vacuum unit is punctured necessitating renewal of this unit.

13 Begin reassembly by applying a few drops of engine oil to the centrifugal advance weight pivots and to the centre of the distributor shaft **(see illustration)**.

14 Locate the baseplate in position and secure it to the distributor body with the retaining screws.

15 Engage the vacuum unit pullrod with the baseplate peg then refit the vacuum unit retaining screws and the distributor cap clips. Tighten all the screws securely.

16 Refit the lower circlip to the distributor shaft. Place the small locating pin in its groove then carefully push the vane down into contact with the circlip. Secure this assembly with the remaining circlip.

17 Refit the protective plastic cover, followed by the rotor arm.

18 Renew the O-ring seal at the base of the distributor if necessary **(see illustration)**.

19 The distributor can now be refitted as described in Section 3.

Digifant system

20 The distributor used with the Digifant system is very similar to the TCI-H unit just described, but with the following differences **(see illustration)**:

a) *There are no centrifugal or vacuum advance components*

b) *The shaft is removed from the distributor body after extracting the pin which secures the driving dog to the base of the shaft*

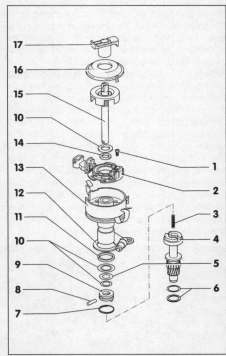

4.20 Exploded view of Digifant system distributor

1 *Screw*	9 *Driving dog*
2 *Baseplate and*	10 *Shim(s)*
pick-up unit	11 *Seal*
3 *Spring*	12 *Clamp*
4 *Driveshaft*	13 *Body*
5 *Plastic washer*	14 *Plastic washer*
6 *Thrust washers*	15 *Shaft*
7 *Spring*	16 *Cover*
8 *Pin*	17 *Rotor arm*

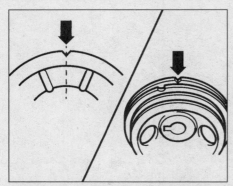

5.2 Ignition timing mark (arrowed). The pulley on the right also has a TDC mark; the one on the left does not

5 Ignition timing – adjustment

1 For prolonged engine life, efficient running, performance and economy it is essential for the fuel/air mixture in the combustion chambers to be ignited by the spark plugs at precisely the right moment in relation to engine speed and load. For this to occur the ignition timing must be set accurately and should be checked at the intervals given in Chapter 1 or whenever the position of the distributor has been altered. To check and adjust the ignition timing it is necessary to use a stroboscopic timing light, whereby the timing is checked with the engine running at idling speed.

2 The timing marks consist of two notches on the crankshaft pulley, one denoting TDC and the other the ignition timing (firing) point for the engine concerned. The ignition timing mark is the V-shaped notch in the rim of the pulley nearest the crankcase. The TDC mark is the U-shaped notch in the rim of the pulley further from the crankcase. The engine is at TDC or at the firing point when the appropriate notch is uppermost and in alignment with the join in the crankcase halves **(see illustration)**.

3 Start the engine, allow it to reach normal operating temperature and then switch it off.
4 Connect a stroboscopic timing light to the HT lead of No 1 cylinder (right-hand side of the engine nearest the flywheel) and make any other electrical connections necessary according to timing light type by following the manufacturer's instructions. Connect a tachometer to the engine, following the manufacturer's instructions for this instrument also.

TCI-H system

1.9 litre engine code DF and 2.1 litre engine code DJ

5 Disconnect the two electrical plugs at the idle stabilizing unit and join them together **(see illustration)**. On the 2.1 litre engine (code DJ), also disconnect the single connector in front of the idle stabilizing unit.

1.9 litre engine codes DG and SP and 2.1 litre engine code DJ

6 Disconnect the vacuum hose(s) from the distributor.

All TCI-H engines

7 Start the engine again and allow it to idle. Check that the engine is idling at the specified speed for ignition timing and if necessary adjust the idling speed as described in Chapter 1.
8 Refer to the Specifications for the correct ignition timing setting and then point the timing light at the timing marks **(see illustration)**. The notches in the crankshaft pulley will appear stationary. If the timing is correct, the ignition timing mark will be aligned with the join in the crankcase halves.

> **HAYNES HiNT**
> *If adjusting the 1.9 litre engine code GW or the 2.1 litre engine code DJ for unleaded fuel, make a pulley mark halfway between the original timing mark (10° BTDC) and the TDC mark.*

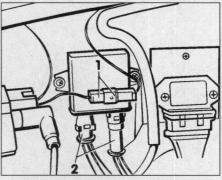

5.5 On engine codes DF and DJ, disconnect the electrical plugs (2) from the idle stabilizing unit and join them together. On engine code DJ, also disconnect the single connector (1)

9 If the marks are not aligned, slacken the distributor clamp pinch-bolt and then slowly turn the distributor body in whichever direction is necessary to align the marks. Hold the distributor in this position and tighten the pinch-bolt **(see illustration)**.
Caution: Be careful not to get caught up in the auxiliary drivebelt(s). Stop the engine if necessary before making any adjustment.
10 Open the throttle slightly and note the movement of the timing marks. If the centrifugal advance mechanism in the distributor is working correctly, the marks should appear to move away from each other as the engine speed increases. Disconnecting or reconnecting the distributor vacuum pipe(s) should also cause the marks to move. If the marks do not move after disconnecting or reconnecting the vacuum pipe(s) then either the vacuum unit is faulty, or the throttle valve basic setting or throttle linkage adjustments are incorrect (see Chapter 4A).
11 After adjustment, reset the engine idling speed if necessary and then switch off the engine. Disconnect the instruments and remake the original vacuum and electrical connections.

5.8 Point the timing light at the timing marks

5.9 Tightening the distributor clamp pinch-bolt

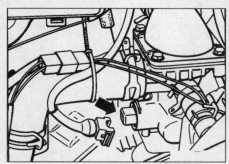

5.12 Before checking the timing on the Digifant system, disconnect the temperature sensor (arrowed) with the engine running

Digifant system

12 Start the engine and run it at a speed of 2000 to 2500 rpm. Disconnect the blue connector from the coolant temperature sensor **(see illustration)**. **Note:** *If the engine stalls, reconnect the temperature sensor before restarting it, otherwise the electronic control unit will register a fault.*

13 Maintain the engine speed as specified and point the timing light at the timing marks. If the timing is correct, the ignition timing mark will be aligned with the join in the crankcase halves.

14 If the marks are not aligned, slacken the distributor clamp pinch-bolt and then slowly turn the distributor body in whichever direction is necessary to align the marks. Hold the distributor in this position and tighten the pinch-bolt.

Caution: Be careful not to get caught up in the auxiliary drivebelt(s). Stop the engine if necessary before making any adjustment.

15 No further tests on this system are possible without dedicated test equipment.

16 After adjustment, disconnect the instruments and reconnect the coolant temperature sensor.

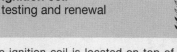

6 Ignition coil –
   testing and renewal

1 The ignition coil is located on top of the engine cowling, adjacent to the distributor. Periodically the electrical connections should be checked for security and the coil wiped clean to prevent high tension (HT) voltage loss through arcing.

2 If the operation of the coil is suspect, the resistance of the primary and secondary windings may be checked with an ohmmeter. To do this disconnect the leads at the coil terminals after first marking them to ensure correct refitment **(see illustration)**.

3 Using the ohmmeter, measure the coil primary resistance between the two LT terminals (1 and 15). Now measure the secondary resistance between the negative LT terminal (1) and the HT terminal in the centre of the coil (4). Compare the values obtained with those given in the Specifications. If the primary or secondary resistance is outside the specified tolerance, the coil must be renewed.

4 To renew the coil, disconnect the leads (if this has not already been done to test the unit), slacken the clamp bolt and slide the coil out of its bracket. Refitting is the reverse of the removal procedure.

6.2 Disconnecting the coil HT lead

7 TDC sensor –
   general

All models covered by this manual incorporate a TDC sensor which is used for ignition system checking purposes in conjunction with VW test equipment.

Without a suitable ignition tester it is unlikely that this device will be of use to the home mechanic, but it is useful to know its location and purpose.

The sensor is situated on the upper face of the crankcase and consists of a lead with a plug on one end. When connected to the tester, the sensor at the other end of the lead monitors the exact position of the crankshaft by detecting the position of two metal studs in the flywheel.

Removal and refitting of the sensor can only be carried out with the engine dismantled and is removed by pushing out of the crankcase towards the flywheel side. Refitting is the reverse of this procedure.

Chapter 6
Clutch

Contents

Degrees of difficulty

| **Easy,** suitable for novice with little experience | | **Fairly easy,** suitable for beginner with some experience | | **Fairly difficult,** suitable for competent DIY mechanic | | **Difficult,** suitable for experienced DIY mechanic | | **Very difficult,** suitable for expert DIY or professional | |

Specifications

General

Type	Single dry plate, diaphragm spring, hydraulically operated
Clutch disc diameter	215 mm (8.46 in) or 228 mm (8.97 in), according to model
Clutch pedal free play	Approximately 0.5 mm (0.02 in)

Torque wrench settings

	Nm	lbf ft
Clutch cover assembly to flywheel	25	18
Master cylinder to bracket	25	18
Slave cylinder to bracket	25	18
Slave cylinder bracket to gearbox	45	33
Release shaft bush retaining bolt	15	11

---

1 General description

All manual transmission models are equipped with a single dry plate diaphragm spring clutch. The unit consists of a steel cover which is bolted to the flywheel and contains the pressure plate and diaphragm spring.

The clutch disc is free to slide along the splined gearbox input shaft and is held in position between the flywheel and the pressure plate by the pressure of the diaphragm spring. Friction lining material is riveted to the clutch disc, which has a spring cushioned hub to absorb transmission shocks and help ensure a smooth take-up of the drive.

The clutch is operated hydraulically by a master and slave cylinder. The clutch release mechanism consists of a release shaft and

release bearing which are mounted in the clutch housing on the end of the gearbox **(see illustration)**.

The clutch assembly is self-adjusting, and requires no maintenance other than periodically checking the hydraulic fluid level in the master cylinder reservoir. The clutch hydraulic fluid is supplied by the brake master cylinder reservoir and reference should be made to *"Weekly checks"* for level checking procedures.

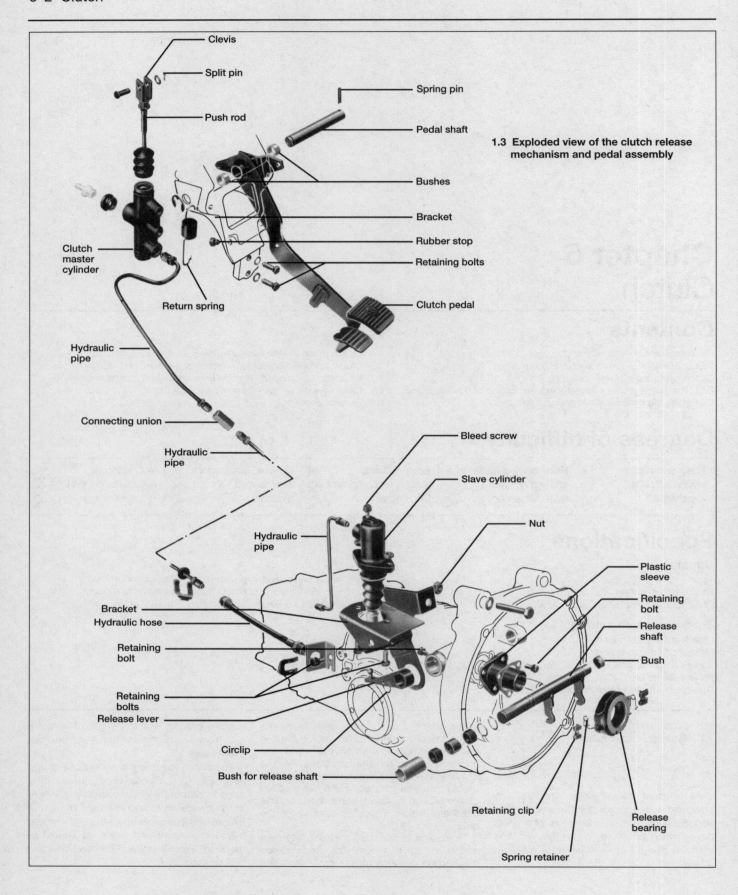

Clevis

Split pin

Push rod

Spring pin

Pedal shaft

1.3 Exploded view of the clutch release
mechanism and pedal assembly

Bushes

Bracket

Rubber stop

Retaining bolts

Clutch
master
cylinder

Return spring

Clutch pedal

Hydraulic
pipe

Connecting union

Bleed screw

Hydraulic
pipe

Slave cylinder

Nut

Plastic
sleeve

Retaining
bolt

Release
shaft

Bush

Bracket

Hydraulic hose

Retaining
bolt

Hydraulic
pipe

Retaining
bolts

Release lever

Circlip

Bush for release shaft

Retaining clip

Spring retainer

Release
bearing

2 Clutch hydraulic system – bleeding

⚠️ *Warning: Brake fluid can harm your eyes and damage painted surfaces, so use extreme caution when handling and pouring it. Wash spillages off skin or paintwork immediately with plenty of cold water. Do not use fluid that has been standing open for some time, as it absorbs moisture from the air which can cause corrosion of clutch and brake hydraulic system components. For preference, only use new fluid from a freshly opened container.*

1 On vehicles equipped with a hydraulically operated clutch, air will have been introduced into the system if any of the hydraulic components have been removed or disconnected. For the clutch to function correctly all air must be removed from the system. This process is known as bleeding.

2 To bleed the system, first gather together a clean glass jar, a suitable length of rubber or plastic tubing, which is a tight fit over the bleed screw on the clutch slave cylinder, and a container of the specified hydraulic fluid. The help of an assistant will also be required. If a one-man do-it-yourself bleeding kit as used for bleeding the brake hydraulic system is available, this can be used quite satisfactorily for the clutch also. Full information on the use of these kits will be found in Chapter 10.

3 Jack up the rear of the vehicle and support it on axle stands (see *"Jacking and vehicle support"*).

4 From inside the car remove the instrument panel cover and if necessary top up the fluid level in the brake master cylinder reservoir until it is up to the MAX mark. (The clutch and brake hydraulic systems are both supplied from a common reservoir). Keep the reservoir topped up during subsequent operations.

5 From under the rear of the vehicle wipe clean the area around the bleed screw on the slave cylinder and remove the rubber dust cover.

6 Connect one end of the bleed tube to the bleed screw, and insert the other end of the tube in the jar containing sufficient clean hydraulic fluid to keep the end of the tube submerged.

7 Unscrew the bleed screw half a turn, and have an assistant fully depress the clutch pedal. As the pedal reaches the end of the downstroke close the bleed nipple. With the bleed nipple closed, release the clutch pedal. Repeat this procedure until the fluid entering the jar is free of air bubbles. Make sure that the fluid level in the reservoir does not drop to the level of the cylinder outlet, otherwise air will be drawn into the system.

8 Check the operation of the clutch pedal. It may take a few further strokes for the pressure to build up and then it should feel normal. Any sponginess would indicate air still present in the system.

9 On completion remove the bleed tube and refit the dust cover. Top up the master cylinder reservoir if necessary and refit the cap and instrument panel cover. Fluid expelled from the hydraulic system should now be discarded as it will be contaminated with moisture, air and dirt, making it unsuitable for further use.

10 Finally lower the vehicle to the ground and check the operation of the clutch.

3 Clutch assembly – removal and refitting

⚠️ *Warning: Dust created by clutch wear and deposited on clutch components may contain asbestos, which is a health hazard. DO NOT blow it out with compressed air or inhale any of it. DO NOT use petrol or petroleum-based solvents to clean off the dust. Use brake system cleaner or methylated spirit to flush the dust into a suitable receptacle. After the clutch components have been wiped clean with rags, dispose of the contaminated rags and cleaner in a sealed, marked container.*

1 To gain access to the clutch assembly it is first necessary to remove the gearbox as described in Chapter 7A.

2 Before removing the clutch assembly from the flywheel, inspect the clutch cover in the area of the retaining bolts for any aligning marks that may be visible. If no markings are present, scribe a line between the clutch cover and flywheel to ensure correct reassembly should the original components be refitted.

3 Remove the clutch assembly by unscrewing the six retaining bolts in a diagonal sequence half a turn at a time to prevent distortion of the cover flange.

4 With the bolts removed, lift the clutch assembly off the flywheel locating dowels. Be prepared to catch the clutch disc which will fall out at this stage – it is not attached to the cover assembly or flywheel.

5 It is important that no oil or grease is allowed to come into contact with the clutch disc friction linings, or the pressure plate and flywheel faces. It is advisable to handle the parts with clean hands and to wipe off the pressure plate and flywheel faces with a clean dry rag before inspection or refitting commences.

6 To refit the clutch, place the clutch disc against the flywheel with the extended boss in the centre of the hub facing away from the flywheel. The disc is normally marked 'SCHWUNGRAD' or 'FLYWHEEL SIDE'.

7 Place the cover assembly in position over the dowels and (if applicable) with the previously made alignment marks in line (see illustration). Secure the cover with the six retaining bolts and tighten them finger tight so that the clutch disc is gripped but can still be moved.

8 The clutch disc must now be centralised so that when the engine and gearbox are mated, the gearbox input shaft splines will pass through the splines in the centre of the hub. If centralisation is not carried out accurately, it will be difficult or impossible to refit the gearbox.

9 Centralisation can be carried out by inserting a round bar or long screwdriver through the hole in the centre of the hub, so that the end of the bar rests in the small hole in the crankshaft containing the input shaft spigot bearing. Moving the bar sideways or up and down will move the clutch disc in whichever way is necessary to achieve centralisation.

10 Centralisation is easily judged by removing the bar and viewing the clutch disc hub in relation to the crankshaft spigot bearing and the hole in the centre of the diaphragm spring. When the hub appears exactly in the centre all is correct. Alternatively if an old input shaft or universal clutch aligning tool (see illustration) can be obtained, this will eliminate all the guesswork, obviating the need for visual alignment.

11 Tighten the cover retaining bolts fully in a diagonal sequence to ensure the cover plate is pulled down evenly without distortion of the flange. Tighten the bolts to the torque setting given in the Specifications.

12 The gearbox can now be refitted to the vehicle as described in Chapter 7A. Make sure that the gearbox input shaft splines are clean and apply a light smear of copper-based anti-seize compound to them.

3.7 Refitting the clutch disc and cover assembly

3.10 Using a universal clutch aligning tool to centralise the clutch disc

5.2 Clutch release bearing spring retainers (A) and retaining clips (B)

5.4 Clutch slave cylinder and mounting bracket assembly

A Slave cylinder
B Slave cylinder retaining nuts
C Mounting bracket retaining bolt
D Release lever

4 Clutch assembly – inspection

Note: *Refer to the warning at the beginning of the previous Section.*

1 With the clutch disc and pressure plate removed from the flywheel, clean off all traces of dust using a damp cloth. Seal the cloth in a plastic bag for disposal.

2 Examine the clutch disc friction linings for wear and loose rivets, and the disc for rim distortion, cracks, broken hub springs and worn splines. The surface of the friction linings may be highly glazed, but as long as the clutch material pattern can be clearly seen, this is satisfactory. If the friction material is less than 1 mm (0.04 in) above the rivet heads, or if the linings are black in appearance (indicating oil contamination), the disc must be renewed. If oil contamination is evident, usually from a leaking crankshaft oil seal or gearbox input shaft seal, the leak must be rectified before refitting the clutch assembly.

3 Check the machined faces of the flywheel and pressure plate. If either is grooved or heavily scored, it should be machined until smooth, or preferably, renewed.

4 If the pressure plate is cracked or split, or if the diaphragm spring is damaged or its pressure suspect, a new unit must be fitted.

5 Also, check the release bearing for smoothness of operation. There should be no harshness or slackness in it. It should spin reasonably freely, bearing in mind it has been pre-packed with grease.

Caution: When considering renewing clutch components individually, bear in mind that new parts (or parts from different manufacturers) do not always bed into old ones satisfactorily. A clutch pressure plate or disc renewed separately may sometimes cause judder or snatch. The clutch pressure plate, disc and release bearing should be renewed together, as a complete assembly, wherever possible.

5 Clutch release mechanism – removal, overhaul and refitting

Note: *The clutch release mechanism is contained within the clutch housing and it is necessary to remove the gearbox as described in Chapter 7A to gain access to these components.*

1 With the gearbox on the bench, check the release bearing for smoothness of operation. There should be no harshness or slackness in it and it should spin reasonably freely, bearing in mind it has been pre-packed with grease. If a definite roughness can be felt the bearing should be renewed. It is not possible to dismantle the release bearing for cleaning or for packing with fresh grease. In case of doubt, renew the bearing.

2 To remove the bearing, carefully prise off the spring retainers and the retaining clips, then lift the bearing off the release shaft and guide sleeve **(see illustration)**.

3 Check the release shaft for play in the support bushes. If play is evident it is likely to be at the end nearest to the release lever. If the bushes are worn the release shaft should be removed and the bushes renewed as follows.

4 Undo and remove the two slave cylinder retaining nuts and bolts and lift off the cylinder. Undo and remove the large nut and bolt securing the slave cylinder mounting bracket to the gearbox casing. Extract the circlip, slide off the release lever and then remove the mounting bracket **(see illustration)**.

5 Undo and remove the bolt which locates the release shaft bushes in the casing **(see illustration)**.

6 From inside the clutch housing withdraw the release shaft inner circlip from its groove **(see illustration)** and slide it, together with the washer, towards the centre of the shaft.

7 Slide the release shaft to the left to release one end from its bush, then withdraw the shaft from the clutch housing. The bushes and the two concertina type grease seals can now be removed also.

8 The release mechanism is now completely dismantled. All the parts should be cleaned and then carefully inspected for wear. Pay particular attention to the bushes and grease seals and renew any parts that are worn **(see**

5.5 Removing the locating bolt for the release shaft bushes

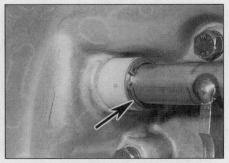

5.6 Release shaft inner retaining circlip (arrowed)

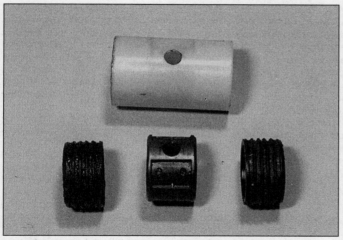

5.8 Release shaft support bushes and grease seals

5.9 Refitting the release shaft . . .

illustration). Note that the bush that supports the other end of the release shaft is still in position in the gearbox casing. Special tools are required to remove and refit this bush and the work should be left to a VW dealer. This bush however is not subject to the same loads and wear is uncommon.

9 Lubricate the components with multi-purpose grease and begin reassembly by placing the release shaft in position. Make sure that the inner circlip and washer are in place on the shaft before you do this **(see illustration)**.

10 Now slide on the large bush **(see illustration)**, followed by the inner grease seal, small bush and then the outer grease seal. Make sure that the holes in the bushes face towards the locating bolt hole and are correctly aligned to accept the bolt. Refit the bolt and tighten it fully.

11 Slide the release shaft inner circlip and washer towards the end of the shaft and locate the circlip into its groove.

12 Refitting the remainder of the release mechanism is the reverse sequence to removal. When refitting the release bearing smear a trace of molybdenum disulphide grease on the guide sleeve, contact fingers and the bearing thrust face. Ensure also that the spring retainers and retaining clips are correctly located and secure.

5.10 . . . and large support bush

13 Note that the release bearing is self-centering. A new bearing may appear to have its thrust ring offset relative to the bearing housing, but this will correct itself automatically in use.

14 Check that the mechanism operates smoothly and then refit the gearbox using the procedure described in Chapter 7A.

6 Clutch master cylinder – removal and refitting

Note: *Refer to the warning at the beginning of Section 2.*
Note: *The clutch master cylinder is located inside the cab at the base of the clutch and brake pedal mounting bracket. Hydraulic fluid for the unit is supplied from the brake master cylinder reservoir.*

1 To remove the master cylinder first cover the floor beneath the pedals with some old rags. Some hydraulic fluid will be spilled during the removal sequence – this is unavoidable.

2 Carefully pull the hydraulic fluid supply hose off the outlet on the cylinder and quickly plug the hose with an old bolt or a rod of suitable diameter.

3 Unscrew the hydraulic pipe union at the base of the cylinder and carefully ease out the pipe.

4 Finally undo and remove the two master cylinder retaining bolts and lift out the cylinder. Note that as the cylinder is removed the pushrod and clevis will stay behind as they are still attached to the clutch pedal.

5 Refitting is the reverse sequence to removal. Bleed the clutch hydraulic system after refitting the master cylinder using the procedure described in Section 2.

6 Check the free play between the pushrod and master cylinder piston after refitting is completed and adjust the pushrod if the free play is more than 0.5 mm (0.02 in). Adjustment is carried out by slackening the locknut and turning the pushrod in the desired direction to increase or decrease the free play.

7 Clutch master cylinder – dismantling, inspection and reassembly

Note: *Refer to the warning at the beginning of Section 2.*

1 Before dismantling the master cylinder, prepare a clean uncluttered working area on the bench.

2 Remove the dust cover from the master cylinder and then extract the piston retaining circlip and washer.

3 Tap the end of the cylinder on a block of wood until the piston emerges from the end of the cylinder bore.

4 Withdraw the piston from the cylinder together with the return spring **(see illustration)**. Carefully remove the spring from the piston and recover the spring retainer.

5 Lay the parts out in the order of removal **(see illustration)** and then carefully remove the main and secondary cup seals from the piston, noting which way round they are fitted.

6 Wash the components in clean hydraulic fluid and then wipe dry with a lint-free cloth.

7 Examine the cylinder bore and piston carefully for signs of scoring, pitting, rust or wear ridges. If these are apparent renew the complete master cylinder. If the condition of the components appears satisfactory a new set of rubber seals must be obtained. Never

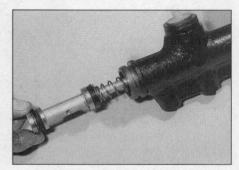

7.4 Withdrawing the clutch master cylinder piston and spring assembly

re-use old seals as they will have deteriorated with age even though this may not be evident during visual inspection.

8 Begin reassembly by thoroughly lubricating the internal components and the cylinder bore in clean hydraulic fluid.

9 Using fingers only, place the main and secondary cup seals in position with the lip of the seals facing towards the spring.

10 Place the spring retainer and spring in position over the piston and carefully insert this assembly into the cylinder bore. Take care not to allow the lips of the seals to roll over as they are inserted.

11 Push the piston assembly fully into the cylinder bore and then refit the washer and retaining circlip. Smear the inside of the dust cover with rubber grease and place it in position over the end of the cylinder.

12 The assembled master cylinder can now be refitted as described in Section 6.

8 Clutch slave cylinder – removal and refitting

Note: *Refer to the warning at the beginning of Section 2.*

1 Jack up the rear of the vehicle and support it on axle stands (see "*Jacking and vehicle support*").

2 Using a brake hose clamp or a pair of self-locking grips with their jaws suitably protected, clamp the hydraulic fluid flexible hose located on the left-hand side of the gearbox. This will prevent loss of fluid when the hydraulic pipe union at the slave cylinder is disconnected.

3 Wipe the area around the hydraulic pipe union on the side of the slave cylinder and then unscrew the union nut. Carefully pull the pipe clear of the cylinder.

4 Undo and remove the two nuts and bolts securing the slave cylinder to the mounting bracket and lift away the cylinder.

5 Refitting is the reverse sequence to removal, bearing in mind the following points:

a) *Lubricate the clutch release lever with multi-purpose grease*

b) *Place the slave cylinder retaining bolt nearest the engine in position in the bracket before fitting the cylinder*

c) *Bleed the clutch hydraulic system as described in Section 2 after fitting*

9 Clutch slave cylinder – dismantling, inspection and reassembly

Note: *Refer to the warning at the beginning of Section 2.*

1 With the slave cylinder on the bench, wipe the exterior with a clean rag until it is free from dirt.

2 Release the small wire retaining ring securing the rubber dust cover to the pushrod and withdraw the pushrod.

3 Now release the large wire retaining ring securing the rubber dust cover to the cylinder and withdraw the dust cover.

4 Extract the circlip and then tap the cylinder on a block of wood until the piston emerges from the cylinder bore. Lift out the piston followed by the return spring.

5 Remove the dust cover from the bleed screw and then undo and remove the screw.

6 Thoroughly clean all the parts in clean hydraulic fluid and wipe dry with a lint-free cloth.

7 Lay out all the components in the order of removal ready for inspection **(see illustration)**.

8 Carefully examine the piston and cylinder bore for signs of scoring, pitting, rust or wear ridges and if apparent renew the complete cylinder assembly. If these parts are in a satisfactory condition a new set of rubber seals must be obtained. Never re-use old seals as they will have deteriorated with age even though this may not be evident during visual inspection.

9 Begin reassembly by thoroughly lubricating the internal components and the cylinder bore in clean hydraulic fluid.

10 Using fingers only, remove the old seal from the piston and carefully ease on the new one. The lip of the seal must be toward the spring end of the piston.

11 Insert the spring and then the piston into the cylinder bore, taking care not to allow the lip of the seal to roll over as it is inserted.

12 Push the piston fully into the cylinder bore and then refit the retaining circlip.

13 Smear the inside of the rubber dust cover with rubber grease and then place it in position over the end of the cylinder. Secure with the large wire retaining ring.

14 Insert the pushrod into the dust cover and ease the end of the cover into the machined groove in the pushrod. Secure the dust cover to the pushrod with the small wire retaining ring.

15 Finally refit the bleed screw and dust cover.

16 The assembled slave cylinder can now be refitted as described in Section 8.

10 Clutch pedal – removal and refitting

The clutch pedal is removed in conjunction with the brake pedal. Full information will be found in Chapter 10.

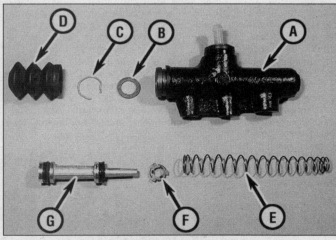

7.5 Component parts of the clutch master cylinder

A   Master cylinder body
B   Washer
C   Circlip
D   Rubber dust cover
E   Return spring
F   Spring retainer
G   Piston assembly

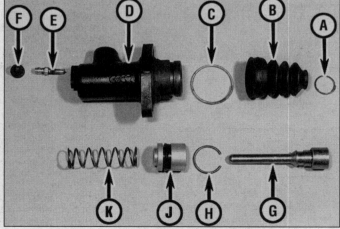

9.7 Component parts of the clutch slave cylinder

A   Wire retaining ring (small)
B   Rubber dust cover
C   Wire retaining ring (large)
D   Slave cylinder body
E   Bleed screw
F   Dust cover
G   Pushrod
H   Circlip
J   Piston and seal
K   Return spring

Chapter 7 Part A:
Manual transmission

Contents

Degrees of difficulty

Easy, suitable for novice with little experience	**Fairly easy,** suitable for beginner with some experience	**Fairly difficult,** suitable for competent DIY mechanic	**Difficult,** suitable for experienced DIY mechanic	**Very difficult,** suitable for expert DIY or professional

Specifications

Type . . . . Four or five forward speeds (all synchromesh) and reverse.
Final drive integral with main gearbox

Identification code
4-speed 091/1
5-speed 094

Gearbox ratios (typical)
4-speed:
   1st . . . . 3.78 : 1
   2nd . . . . 2.06 : 1
   3rd . . . . 1.26 : 1
   4th . . . . 0.85 : 1
   Reverse . . . . 3.67 : 1
5-speed:
   1st . . . . 4.11 : 1
   2nd . . . . 2.33 : 1
   3rd . . . . 1.48 : 1
   4th . . . . 1.02 : 1
   5th . . . . 0.76 : 1
   Reverse . . . . 3.67 : 1

Final drive ratios (typical)
4-speed . . . . 4.57 : 1 or 4.86 : 1
5-speed . . . . 4.86 : 1

Adjustment data
Gearshift linkage adjustment dimension:
  4-speed . . . . 23 mm (0.91 in)
  5-speed . . . . 3 mm (0.12 in)

Torque wrench settings	**Nm**	**lbf ft**
Clutch housing to engine	30	22
Driveshaft to differential flange	45	33
Transmission front mounting bracket to body	25	18
Reversing light switch	30	22
Drain and filler plugs	20	15
Gearshift lever to gearshift shaft	25	18
Gearshift linkage clamp bolt	25	18
Gear lever to front shift rod	10	7
Gear lever plate to mounting plate	10	7

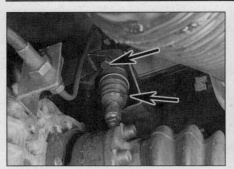

2.3 Clutch slave cylinder retaining bolts (arrowed) . . .

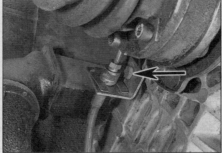

2.4 . . . and hose support bracket retaining bolt (arrowed)

1 General description

The manual transmission fitted to vehicles covered by this manual has four or five forward gears and one reverse gear. All forward gears are engaged through synchromesh units to obtain smooth, silent gear changes.

The transmission consists of four main housings bolted together to form the complete assembly. The clutch housing contains the clutch release mechanism and, when the transmission is attached to the engine, houses the flywheel and clutch assembly. The gearbox housing contains the final drive (differential) and is located between the clutch and geartrain housings. The input shaft, pinion shaft, gears and selector

mechanism are located within the geartrain housing which has the gearshift housing bolted to its front face in the form of an end cover. This last unit contains the gear selector shaft and attachment for the external gear selector linkage.

Gear selection is by a floor-mounted lever, connected by a remote control housing and a series of rods to the mechanism at the gearshift housing.

2 Transmission – removal and refitting

Note: *On some models it may be necessary to release the throttle cable support (with cable) from the top engine/transmission bolt before the transmission can be removed.*

1 As the majority of the work is carried out from below, drive the vehicle over a pit, raise it on ramps or a hoist, or securely support it at the rear on axle stands (see "*Jacking and vehicle support*").

2 Disconnect the battery negative terminal.

3 Undo the two nuts and bolts securing the clutch slave cylinder to the support bracket on the clutch housing **(see illustration)**.

4 Undo the bolt securing the flexible hose support bracket to the gearbox housing **(see illustration)**. Lift the slave cylinder out of its location and tie it up out of the way with the hydraulic fluid pipe still connected.

5 Remove the nut which secures the lever to the gearshift shaft. Unbolt the support plate and remove the rear shift rod and associated components, then move the rod to one side.

6 Make a note of the wiring connections at the rear of the starter motor solenoid and disconnect them **(see illustration)**.

7 Using an Allen key, undo and remove the socket headed bolts securing both driveshaft inner constant velocity joints to the differential drive flanges. Recover the washers from under the bolt heads and tie the driveshafts up using string or wire. Do not let the driveshafts hang unsupported.

8 Remove the two engine-to-transmission upper nuts. Depending on model, it may be necessary to remove the air cleaner for access. Undo the two nuts from within the engine compartment while the bolts are held from below **(see illustration)**.

9 Disconnect the two wires at the reversing light switch **(see illustration)**.

10 Position a jack with an interposed block of wood beneath the engine and raise the jack until the engine is just supported.

11 Position a second jack beneath the transmission in the same way.

12 Undo the two nuts at the base of the clutch housing securing the transmission to the engine studs.

13 When fitted, undo the nut and bolt securing the earth braid to the transmission mounting bracket **(see illustration)**.

14 Undo the four bolts securing the transmission front mounting bracket to the vehicle underbody, lower the two jacks until the transmission is clear at the front, then withdraw the unit from the engine. Be careful, the transmission is heavy.

15 Refitting the transmission is the reverse sequence to removal, bearing in mind the following points:

a) *Apply a trace of molybdenum disulphide grease to the input shaft splines before refitting the transmission*

b) *Ensure that the transmission is fully secured to the engine before finally tightening the transmission mounting bracket bolts*

c) *Refill the transmission with the specified lubricant*

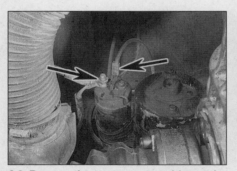

2.6 Remove the starter motor wiring at the terminals arrowed

2.8 Engine-to-transmission upper retaining nuts (arrowed)

2.9 Disconnect the reversing light switch wires

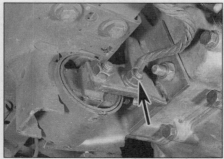

2.13 Disconnect the earth braid for the transmission mounting bracket (arrowed)

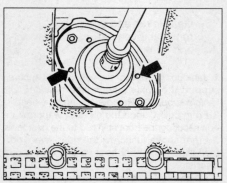

4.3 Gear lever plate alignment holes (arrowed) - early models

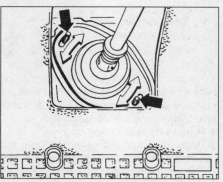

4.4 On later models, twist the plate until the slots touch the studs (black arrows)

4.6 Pinch-bolt (arrowed) securing the shift rods together

3 Transmission overhaul – general

Repair and overhaul of the transmission is considerably involved and cannot be carried out successfully without extensive garage equipment and preferably access to certain VW special tools. Although the transmission can, with some improvisation, be dismantled into its major assemblies, problems arise if dismantling is carried further, particularly if new parts are required. Preloads, running clearances and adjustments are carried out during manufacture using special jigs. Although the parts can be marked during dismantling and refitted in their original positions when reassembling, this is only possible if the same parts are being used. If new parts are needed the special jigs will also be required to assemble the parts correctly and this can only be done by a VW agent or other specialist suitably equipped to carry out the work. Also there is a cost consideration: the new parts, plus the labour charges to carry out the setting up, may exceed the price of an exchange or good second-hand transmission.

If the transmission develops a fault or is suspect in any way, first check that the oil level is correct and that the correct grade of oil is in use. If the fault is in the transmission itself, an accurate diagnosis whilst the transmission is still in the vehicle is strongly advised, even if it is necessary to seek professional help for this. A VW dealer or transmission specialist can then advise whether repair is economically viable.

HAYNES HiNT *Difficulties in engaging gears can be due to wear or maladjustment of the gearshift linkage or to a clutch fault, and noise or vibration apparently coming from the transmission can be caused by worn driveshaft joints.*

4 Gearshift linkage – adjustment

1 Jack up the front of the vehicle and securely support it on axle stands (see *"Jacking and vehicle support"*). Remove the spare wheel.
2 Slide up the rubber boot around the gear lever.
3 On early models (up to June 1988), check that the two holes in the gear lever plate are aligned with the two holes directly below in the mounting plate **(see illustration)**. If not, slacken the two retaining nuts or bolts, align the two plates, then tighten the nuts or bolts.
4 On later models there are no alignment holes. Slacken the retaining nuts and twist the plate in either direction until the slots in the plate are touching the mounting studs **(see illustration)**. Tighten the nuts.

5 Move the gear lever to the neutral position. Check that the gearbox is in fact in neutral.
6 From under the vehicle slacken the clamp pinch-bolt securing the shift rods together **(see illustration)**.
7 Set the lever on the gearbox to the vertical position **(see illustration)**.

4-speed

8 Refer to the Specifications for the gearshift linkage adjustment dimension. Make up a gauge using any suitable material equal in width to this dimension.
9 Position the metal tag or "stop finger" at the base of the gear lever centrally along the length of the stop plate in the housing. Place the gauge between the stop finger and stop plate, then tighten the clamp pinch-bolt **(see illustration)**. Remove the gauge.

5-speed

10 With the lever on the gearbox in the vertical position, push the gearshift shaft into the gearbox until it is possible to feel spring pressure.
11 Refer to the Specifications for the gearshift linkage adjustment dimension. Make up a gauge using any suitable material equal in width to this dimension, bent through 90° at the end.
12 With the help of an assistant, move the gear lever into the 1st/reverse plane, then move it back and forth until the gauge will just fit between the reverse gear stop and the lug on the shift rod **(see illustration)**.

4.7 Shift lever on gearbox must be vertical

4.9 Place the gauge in the gap 'a' (4-speed models)

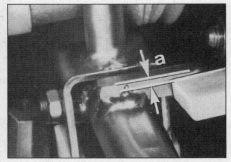

4.12 Place the gauge in the gap 'a' (5-speed models)

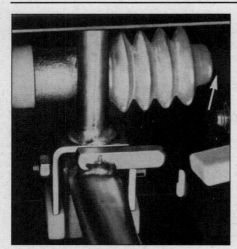

4.13 Plastic bellows must just touch the housing (arrowed)

13 Allow the gear lever to move to the left into the 2nd/3rd plane, then press it slightly to the right so that the plastic bellows just touch the shift linkage housing **(see illustration)**. Hold the lever in this position and tighten the clamp pinch-bolt.

All models

14 Check the engagement of all the gears. When first gear is engaged, there must be a gap of at least 15 mm between the base of the gear level and the heater housing **(see illustration)**; if not, slacken the mounting plate nuts or bolts and reposition the gear lever within the limits of the slotted mounting holes.
15 Refit the spare wheel and lower the vehicle to the ground.

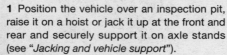

5 Gearshift linkage – removal, overhaul and refitting

1 Position the vehicle over an inspection pit, raise it on a hoist or jack it up at the front and rear and securely support it on axle stands (see "Jacking and vehicle support").
2 Remove the spare wheel.
3 Undo the nut and withdraw the bolt securing the front shift rod to the gear lever.
4 Slacken the clamp pinch-bolt securing the centre and rear shift rods together.
5 Lower the linkage at the front, then withdraw the front and centre shift rods from the rear shift rod and centre support bush.
6 At the transmission end, remove the nut which secures the lever to the gearshift shaft. Unbolt the support plate and remove the rear shift rod and associated components.
7 Examine the condition of the support bushes, the rubber boot(s) and the shift rods **(see illustration opposite)**. Renew any parts that show signs of wear or damage.
8 Lubricate all the bushes, joints and friction surfaces with the special VW lubricant.
9 Refitting the linkage is the reverse sequence to removal. On models with rubber boots on either side of the rear mounting bush, adjust the position of the front boot as shown **(see illustration)** by moving the clip along the shift rod.
10 On all models, carry out the adjustment procedure described in the previous Section before tightening the clamp pinch-bolt.

6 Gear lever and housing – removal, overhaul and refitting

1 Jack up the front of the vehicle and securely support it on axle stands (see "Jacking and vehicle support"). Remove the spare wheel.
2 From below undo the nut and withdraw the bolt securing the front shift rod to the gear lever.
3 From above, unscrew the gear lever knob, then slide the rubber boot up and off the gear lever.
4 Undo the two nuts or bolts which secure the lever plate to the mounting plate and lift out the gear lever assembly.
5 Slacken the grub screw then withdraw the bush and spring upwards off the gear lever. The lever can now be slid down and out of the bearing assembly.
6 If further dismantling is necessary, push the rubber guide out of the lever plate, spread the two shells and withdraw the upper ball half, spring and lower ball half.
7 Inspect all the parts before assembly. On 5-speed models, pay attention to the condition of the reverse gear catch components. Coat all moving and sliding surfaces with special VW lubricant.
8 Locate the two shells in the rubber guide, noting that the guide is installed in the lever plate with its shoulder upwards.
9 Spread the shells and insert the lower ball half followed by the spring and upper ball half. Now fit this assembly into the lever plate.
10 The remainder of reassembly and refitting is the reverse of the dismantling and removal procedures.

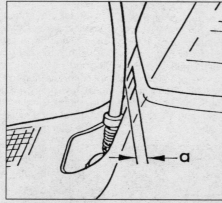

4.14 With first gear engaged, gap 'a' must be at least 15 mm

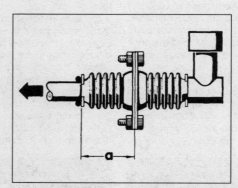

5.9 Adjustment of rear mounting bush boot (when fitted). Arrow points to front of vehicle

a   60 mm

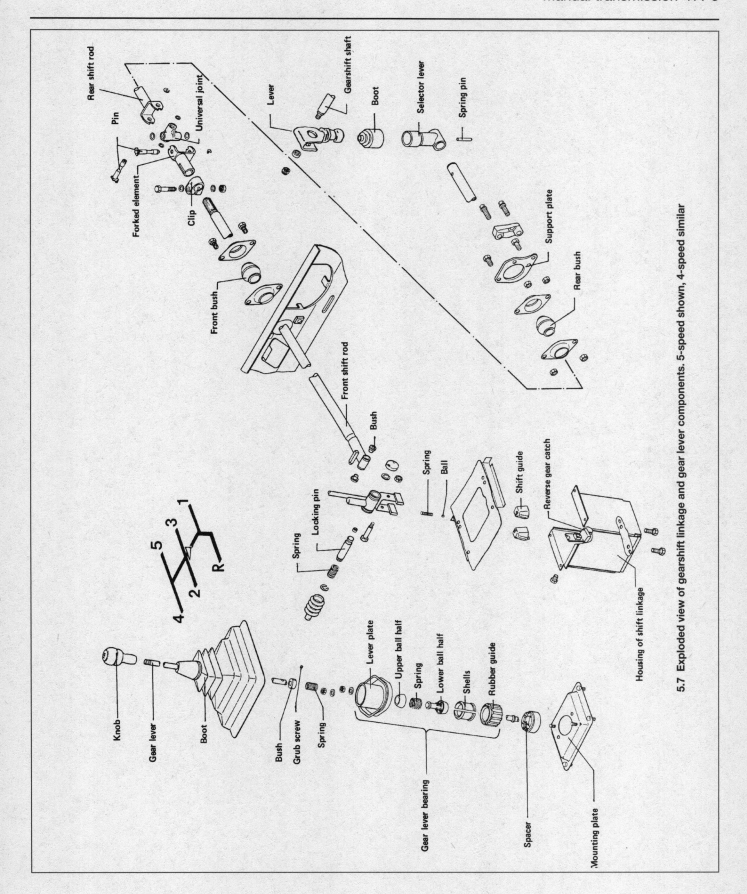

5.7 Exploded view of gearshift linkage and gear lever components. 5-speed shown, 4-speed similar

Notes

Chapter 7 Part B:
Automatic transmission

Contents

Degrees of difficulty

Easy, suitable for novice with little experience		Fairly easy, suitable for beginner with some experience		Fairly difficult, suitable for competent DIY mechanic		Difficult, suitable for experienced DIY mechanic		Very difficult, suitable for expert DIY or professional	

Specifications

Type .... Three element torque converter, hydraulically controlled epicyclic geartrain and integral final drive assembly

Identification .... Manufacturer's type 090

Gear ratios (typical)

Final drive	4.09 : 1 or 3.74 : 1
First gear	2.71 : 1
Second gear	1.50 : 1
Third gear	1.00 : 1
Reverse gear	2.43 : 1

Lubricant capacity

Automatic transmission:

Refill after fluid change	3.0 litres (5.3 pints) approx
Total capacity – dry unit	6.0 litres (10.6 pints) approx
Final drive	1.25 litres (2.2 pints)

Torque wrench settings

	Nm	lbf ft
Transmission drain plug	30	22
Oil pan to transmission	20	15
Oil cooler to transmission	40	30
Driveshaft to drive flange	45	33
Drive flange to differential	25	18
Torque converter to driveplate	30	22
Transmission to final drive housing	30	22
Engine to transmission	55	41
Front mounting to transmission	55	41
Front mounting to body	40	30

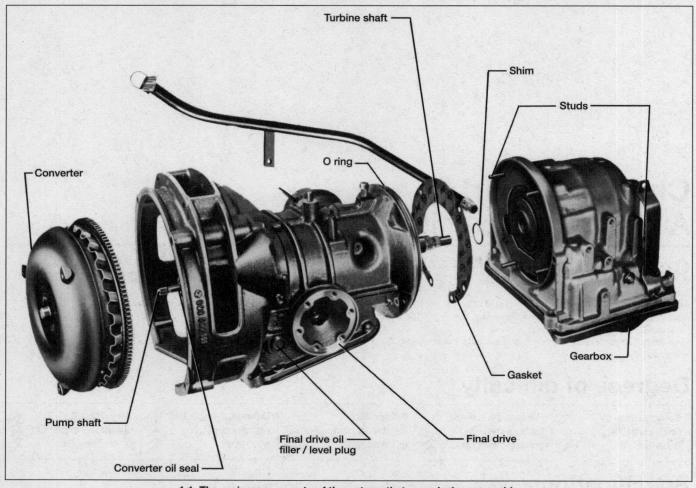

1.1 The main components of the automatic transmission assembly

1 General description

The automatic transmission fitted as an optional extra consists of three main assemblies, namely the torque converter, which takes the place of the conventional clutch, the epicyclic geartrain, and the final drive. These assemblies are housed within two castings which are bolted together and then attached to the engine casing at the rear **(see illustration)**.

In view of the complexity of the automatic transmission and the need for special tools and equipment when carrying out overhaul work or repairs, the following Sections are therefore confined to supplying general information and any service information or instruction that can be used by the owner. In the event of a fault developing on the transmission or a major adjustment being necessary, this work should be left to a VW agent or transmission specialist who will have the necessary tools and equipment for diagnosis and rectification.

2 Automatic transmission – removal and refitting

Note: *The automatic transmission may be removed together with the engine as described in Chapter 2B, or separately, leaving the engine in the vehicle as described in this Section. If the transmission is being*

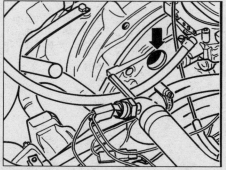

2.4 Torque converter retaining bolt access hole in the crankcase

removed for repair or overhaul make sure that any suspected faults are referred to a VW dealer before the unit is removed. With this type of transmission the fault must be confirmed using specialist test equipment and this can only be done with the transmission installed in the vehicle.

1 Disconnect the battery earth terminal.

2 If necessary, remove the air cleaner assembly for improved access.

3 Withdraw the grommet from the upper left-hand side of the crankcase to provide access to the torque converter retaining bolts.

4 Turn the crankshaft until one of the three torque converter retaining bolts becomes accessible through the hole previously covered by the grommet. Undo and remove the bolt, then turn the crankshaft and remove the remaining two converter bolts **(see illustration)**.

5 Undo and remove the two upper bolts securing the engine to the transmission casing.

6 Remove the transmission dipstick from the filler tube.

7 Jack up the rear of the vehicle and support it on axle stands (see *"Jacking and vehicle support"*) positioned under the rear suspension crossmember.

8 Undo and remove the six socket headed bolts each side that secure the driveshaft inner joints to the transmission drive flanges. Move the joints away from the drive flanges and tie the driveshafts up out of the way.

9 Disconnect the leads from the starter motor.

10 Undo and remove the bolt securing the dipstick/filler tube support bracket to the transmission casing.

11 Undo and remove the nut and spring washer securing the throttle operating rod to the lever on the side of the transmission casing **(see illustration)**.

12 Using a wide-bladed screwdriver, carefully prise the accelerator cable socket off the transmission lever. Free the cable from its bracket and move it aside.

13 Extract the circlip securing the selector cable to the transmission selector lever and slide off the cable.

14 Clamp the coolant hoses leading to and from the transmission fluid cooler, then disconnect the hoses. Be prepared for some coolant spillage.

15 Undo and remove the bolt securing the earth strap to the transmission casing and lift away the strap **(see illustration)**.

16 Undo and remove the two bolts which secure the selector cable support bracket to the transmission casing. Place the cable and bracket to one side.

17 Position a suitable jack beneath the transmission and just take the weight of the unit. Make sure that a block of wood is placed between the jack and transmission to protect the casing and spread the load.

18 Undo and remove the four bolts securing the transmission mounting bracket to the body crossmember.

19 Support the engine using a second jack and interposed block of wood, then undo and remove the two lower transmission casing-to-engine retaining nuts.

20 The transmission can now be drawn away from the engine, and, as soon as it is clear of the two lower studs, lowered to the ground. Whilst doing this make sure that the torque converter stays in place on the transmission and does not fall out. As soon as it is convenient, secure it in position using a length of wire inserted through the openings in the side of the casing. Note also that it may be necessary to lower the two jacks slightly to provide clearance between the transmission and crossmember. If so, check that nothing is fouling or being strained in the engine compartment or under the vehicle as the jacks are lowered.

21 With the transmission lowered to the ground, slide it out from under the vehicle.

22 Refitting the automatic transmission is the reverse sequence to removal, bearing in mind the following points:

a) Ensure that the torque converter is in position on the transmission and properly seated as described in Section 3 before refitting the transmission

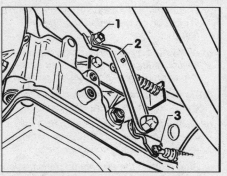

2.11 Control connections on right-hand side of transmission casing

1 Throttle operating rod retaining nut
2 Accelerator cable ball socket
3 Selector cable circlip

b) Observe the correct torque wrench settings on all retaining nuts and bolts where applicable
c) After refitting, fill the transmission with the specified fluid (see Chapter 1)
d) Check the coolant level and top up if necessary (see "Weekly checks")
e) Adjust the gear selector mechanism if necessary as described later in this Chapter

3 Torque converter – removal and refitting

1 Begin by removing the transmission assembly from the vehicle as described in the previous Section.

2 Release the retaining wire used to hold the converter in place during removal of the transmission and slide the unit off the pump driveshaft and one-way clutch splines. Have some rags handy to catch any fluid that may be spilled as the converter is removed. After removal place it flat on the bench with the starter ring gear uppermost.

3 It is not possible to overhaul the torque converter as it is welded together and cannot be separated. If tests have shown the unit to be faulty a factory exchange torque converter should be obtained. The one item which can be renewed is the bush in the centre of the hub. However, special tools are required to do this and if the bush is worn the job of renewal should be left to a VW dealer.

4 If the automatic transmission fluid is dirty due to wear of the clutch linings, or if the transmission is being overhauled or renewed, the fluid in the torque converter should be syphoned off as follows.

5 Obtain a length of small bore plastic tube and a plastic bottle with a sealed top. (Windscreen washer tube and an old washer bottle are ideal). Affix one end of the tube to the bottle either by cutting a hole in the top, inserting the tube and then sealing the hole, or

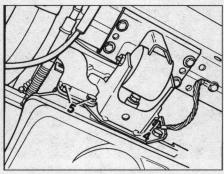

2.15 Attachments at front of transmission casing

4 Earth strap
5 Selector cable support bracket retaining bolts

by attaching the tube to the union or valve in the bottle top if that type is being used. Place the other end of the tube in the torque converter hub so it touches the bottom. Squeeze the bottle then release it to start the syphon. As soon as the fluid starts to flow unscrew the top slightly to relieve pressure in the bottle **(see illustration)**. **Note:** The fluid in the torque converter can only be completely drained by syphoning. There are obviously other ways of starting a syphon than the one described but do not under any circumstances start it by sucking on the tube, because automatic transmission fluid is poisonous.

6 To refit the torque converter to the transmission, position it squarely over the pump driveshaft and one-way clutch support and turn it back and forth slightly to engage the splines. Make sure that the torque converter is properly seated, otherwise there is a risk of damaging the driveplate and the torque converter itself when refitting the transmission.

7 Retain the unit in position with a suitable length of wire until the transmission is refitted to the vehicle.

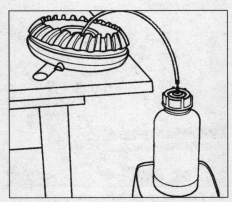

3.5 Draining the torque converter by means of a syphon

5.3 Removing the final drive flange retaining bolt

4 Final drive – removal and refitting

1 First remove the automatic transmission assembly from the vehicle as described in Section 2, and the torque converter as described in the previous Section.

2 It is now possible to remove the final drive housing from the main gearbox, leaving the transmission separated into its three main assemblies. These can then be renewed individually or taken to a VW dealer for repair or overhaul.

3 Make sure that the casings are thoroughly cleaned off externally using paraffin or a suitable solvent and a plentiful supply of clean rags.

4 Undo and remove the four nuts and washers securing the final drive and main gearbox casings together and carefully separate the two units. Recover the gasket from the main gearbox and the axial play adjusting shim from the pinion shaft. Note that the thickness of this shim is critical and must be recalculated if any of the components in the main gearbox or final drive are dismantled or renewed. Calculation of the shim thickness is rather involved and it is advisable to take the two assemblies to a VW dealer for determination of the thickness required.

5 Refitting the final drive is the reverse sequence to removal bearing in mind the following points:

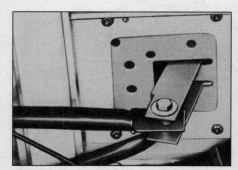

6.6 Selector rod to lever retaining nut, bolt and washers

a) Ensure that the axial play adjusting shim is in position on the pinion shaft before fitting

b) Always use a new gasket between the final drive and main gearbox and a new O-ring on the final drive casing periphery

c) Tighten all retaining nuts and bolts to the specified torque where applicable

d) Ensure that the pump driveshaft is fully inserted in the pump driveplate before refitting the torque converter

e) After refitting the assembled transmission in the vehicle top up or refill the final drive with the specified type and quantity of gear oil (see Chapter 1)

5 Final drive flange oil seal – removal and refitting (transmission in vehicle)
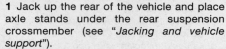

1 Jack up the rear of the vehicle and place axle stands under the rear suspension crossmember (see "Jacking and vehicle support").

2 Undo and remove the six socket headed bolts securing the driveshaft inner joint to the final drive flange.

3 Undo and remove the socket headed retaining bolt in the centre of the final drive flange. To prevent the flange from turning, refit two of the driveshaft retaining bolts and lever against them with a screwdriver or suitable bar **(see illustration)**.

4 Place a tray or bowl beneath the drive flange to catch any oil that may spill out and then withdraw the drive flange. If it is tight, ease it out using two screwdrivers as levers.

5 The oil seal can now be removed using a suitable hooked tool or screwdriver to lever it out.

6 Fill the space between the lips of a new seal with multi-purpose grease and fit the seal to the housing. Tap the seal fully into position using a block of wood.

7 The remainder of the refitting is the reverse sequence to removal. Top up the final drive with the specified type of gear oil after refitting (see Chapter 1).

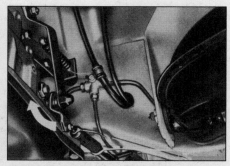

6.7 Adjust selector mechanism with gear lever in 'P' and transmission selector lever moved fully rearward in direction of arrow

6 Gear selector mechanism – adjustment

⚠ Warning: Take precautions against accidental movement of the vehicle during this procedure.

1 Adjustment of the gear selector mechanism is catered for by the provision of an elongated slot at the forward end of the selector rod. Adjustment is carried out as follows.

2 With the selector lever in the 'P' position, start the engine and allow it to idle.

3 Chock the rear wheels and make sure that the handbrake is fully applied. Slowly move the selector lever to the 'R' position. As you do this note the change in engine speed and the point at which the transmission can be felt to take up the drive. Now move the lever to 'N' again noting the change in engine speed and the point when the drive can be felt releasing.

4 If the adjustment of the mechanism is correct the drive take-up should be just before the selector lever engages with the gate detent in the 'R' position. The drive should release just after the lever is moved out of 'R' towards 'N'.

5 If this is not the case, move the selector lever to 'P' and switch off the engine.

6 From under the front of the vehicle undo and remove the nut, bolt and washers securing the selector rod to the gear selector lever **(see illustration)**.

7 Move the operating lever on the right-hand side of the transmission fully rearward into the 'P' position **(see illustration)**.

8 Now push the selector rod towards the rear and whilst holding it in this position, refit and tighten the nut, bolt and washers securing the rod to the selector lever.

9 Carry out the checks described in paragraphs 2 and 3 again and if necessary make small adjustments to the position of the selector rod.

10 Finally check that the engine will only start when the selector lever is in the 'P' or 'N' position. This condition is achieved by the correct positioning of a contact plate located inside the gear lever console. If adjustment is required, remove the console as described in Section 7, and then reposition the contact plate as necessary.

7 Gear selector mechanism – removal and refitting

Selector rod and cable

1 Jack up the rear of the vehicle and support it on axle stands placed under the rear suspension crossmember (see "Jacking and vehicle support").

2 Using a small screwdriver, carefully prise off the small circlip securing the selector cable to the transmission selector lever on the right-hand side of the transmission casing. Slide the cable off the lever pin and recover the sealing ring.

3 Undo and remove the two bolts securing the selector cable bracket to the transmission casing, noting the position of the spacer on the outer bolt.

4 Undo and remove the two nuts and bolts securing the intermediate support bracket to the body crossmember **(see illustration)**.

5 At the front of the vehicle undo and remove the nut, bolt and washers securing the selector rod to the gear selector lever.

6 Withdraw the rod and cable assembly rearwards through the body crossmember and remove it from under the vehicle.

7 If it is wished to separate the rod from the cable, slide back the rubber boot and using a parallel pin punch tap out the spring pin that retains the two parts together.

8 Reassembling the rod and cable and refitting the assembly to the vehicle is the reverse sequence to removal. Adjust the selector mechanism as described in Section 6 after refitting.

Gear selector lever and console

9 Undo and remove the small grub screw securing the handle to the gear lever and lift off the handle **(see illustration overleaf)**.

10 Using a small screwdriver carefully prise up the gear selector cover and remove it from the housing.

11 Undo and remove the four screws securing the console to the floor and lift it up over the gear lever. Disconnect the wiring for the illumination bulbs.

12 From under the front of the vehicle undo and remove the nut, bolt and washers securing the selector rod to the lever and the four nuts securing the lever bracket to the floor.

13 The lever and bracket assembly can now be removed from inside the vehicle after disconnecting the contact plate wiring.

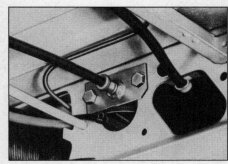

7.4 Selector cable intermediate support bracket

14 Refitting is the reverse sequence to removal. Adjust the selector mechanism as described in Section 6 after refitting.

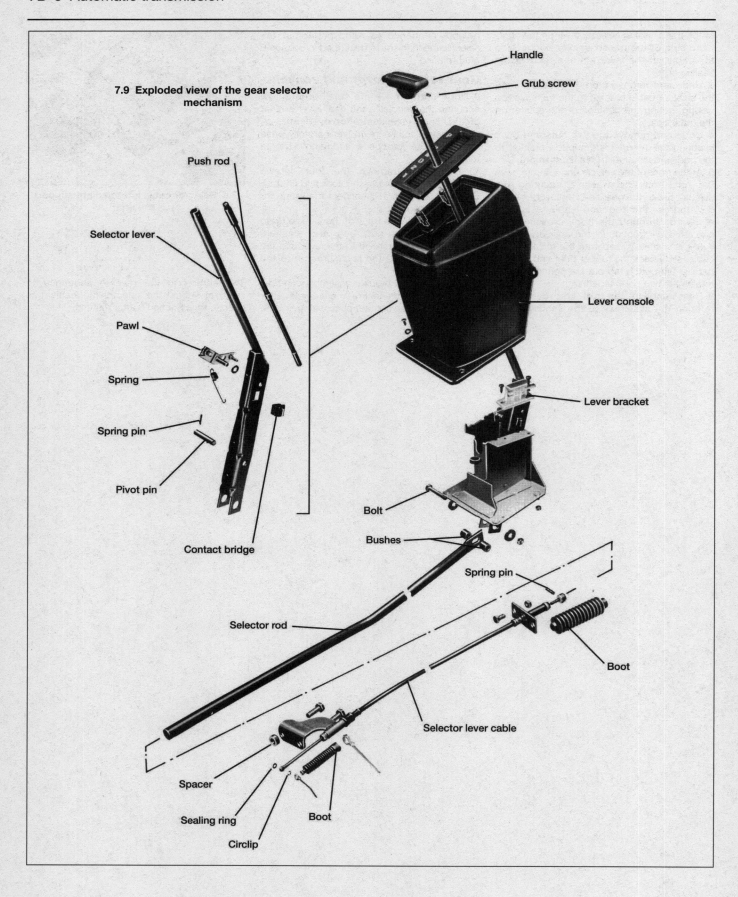

7.9 Exploded view of the gear selector mechanism

Handle

Grub screw

Push rod

Selector lever

Lever console

Pawl

Lever bracket

Spring

Spring pin

Bolt

Pivot pin

Bushes

Spring pin

Contact bridge

Selector rod

Boot

Selector lever cable

Spacer

Sealing ring

Boot

Circlip

Chapter 8
Rear suspension and driveshafts

Contents

Degrees of difficulty

Easy, suitable for novice with little experience	Fairly easy, suitable for beginner with some experience	Fairly difficult, suitable for competent DIY mechanic	Difficult, suitable for experienced DIY mechanic	Very difficult, suitable for expert DIY or professional

Specifications

Rear suspension

Type	Independent by trailing arms, coil springs and telescopic shock absorbers
Camber angle	- 30' ± 30'
Maximum permissible difference between sides	30'
Toe setting (per wheel)	0° ± 10'

Driveshafts

Type	Solid shaft with inboard and outboard homokinetic constant velocity joints

Driveshaft length

Manual gearbox	547.8 mm (21.5 in)
Automatic transmission:	
Left-hand shaft	531.0 mm (20.9 in)
Right-hand shaft	579.3 mm (22.8 in)

Torque wrench settings

	Nm	lbf ft
Trailing arm to mounting bracket	100	74
Shock absorber to trailing arm and body	90	66
Wheel bearing housing to trailing arm	140	103
Driveshaft to differential and wheel shaft	45	33
Wheel hub to wheel shaft (castellated nut) - see text:		
Old pattern - nut with 6 split pin slots	350	258
New pattern - nut with 10 split pin slots	500	369
Brake shoe pivot assembly to wheel bearing housing	65	48
Brake wheel cylinder to wheel bearing housing	20	15
Roadwheel to hub	175	129

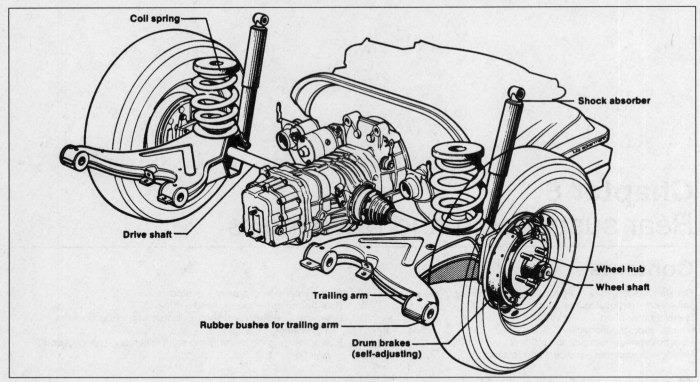

Coil spring

Shock absorber

Drive shaft

Wheel hub

Wheel shaft

Trailing arm

Rubber bushes for trailing arm

Drum brakes
(self-adjusting)

1.1 General layout of the rear suspension

1 General description

The independent rear suspension is by trailing arms, coil springs and telescopic shock absorbers **(see illustration)**. Drive is taken from the differential to the rear wheels by two solid steel driveshafts incorporating a constant velocity joint at each end.

The trailing arms are secured to brackets on the vehicle underbody by bolts which pass through rubber bushes in the arm. The brackets incorporate elongated horizontal and vertical slots to provide for adjustment of rear wheel alignment and camber angle.

The driveshaft constant velocity joints are bolted to the differential drive flanges at their inner ends and to the wheel shaft flanges at their outer ends. The wheel shafts are supported in roller and ball bearings contained within a housing bolted to the trailing arm. The wheel shafts are splined to accept the rear hubs to which the brake drum and roadwheel are attached.

No maintenance is required on the rear suspension assembly other than a periodic visual inspection for damage or deterioration of the constant velocity joint rubber boots.

2 Driveshaft –
removal and refitting

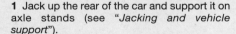

1 Jack up the rear of the car and support it on axle stands (see *"Jacking and vehicle support"*).
2 Using an Allen key of the appropriate size, undo and remove the socket headed bolts securing the inner constant velocity joint to the differential drive flange **(see illustration)**. Recover the tab washers fitted behind each pair of bolts.
3 The bolts securing the outer joint to the wheel shaft are rather inaccessible as the joint is housed within a recess in the trailing arm. If an ordinary key is cut in half a metric socket of

the appropriate size can be placed over the key and the bolts removed using an extension bar and ratchet **(see illustration)**. When all the retaining bolts have been removed together with the tab washers, lift the driveshaft away.
4 Refitting is a direct reversal of the removal procedure. Tighten the socket headed retaining bolts to the specified torque given in the Specifications.

3 Constant velocity joint –
dismantling, inspection and reassembly

1 Remove the driveshaft from the car as described in the previous Section.

2.2 Removing the inner constant velocity joint to differential drive flange retaining bolts

2.3 The outer constant velocity joint retaining bolts are inaccessible requiring the use of an extension bar and ratchet

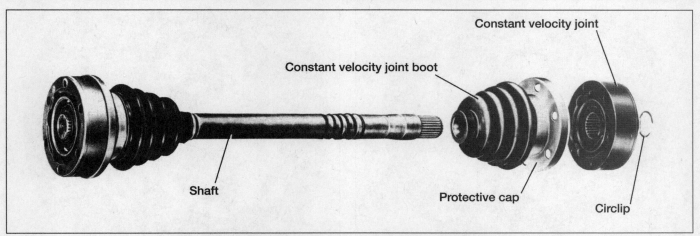

3.2a Driveshaft and constant velocity joint assemblies

2 Secure the driveshaft in a vice and then extract the circlip from the end of the shaft **(see illustrations)**.

3 Using a suitable drift tap the protective cap off the joint and then slide the cap and rubber boot towards the centre of the driveshaft **(see illustration)**.

4 Support the joint across the vice jaws with the driveshaft hanging down. Using a large drift, drive the shaft downwards and out of the joint. The rubber boot and protective cap can now be removed from the driveshaft.

5 With the joint removed from the driveshaft pivot the ball hub and ball cage assembly through approximately 90° and then push it out of the joint outer member **(see illustration)**.

6 Remove the six balls from the cage, tilt the ball hub and position it so that the two grooves in the ball track are aligned with the cage edge and then separate the two parts **(see illustration)**.

7 Wash all the components in paraffin and wipe dry with a lint-free cloth.

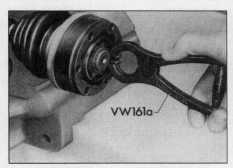

3.2b Removing circlip from end of driveshaft

8 Carefully examine the six steel balls, the ball hub, ball cage and the outer member for wear ridges, pitting or scoring. Make sure that the tracks in which the balls run are not grooved or damaged and that the slots in the ball cage are not appreciably wider than the balls. The balls themselves must be quite spherical with no sign of ridging or pitting. Also check the rubber boot for cracks, splits or deterioration.

3.3 Using a drift to tap off joint protective cap

Caution: It is advisable to renew the rubber boot whenever a joint is dismantled, as a matter of course. If a rubber boot fails in service, water and grit will enter the joint causing rapid wear of the internal components.

9 If inspection shows any of the joint parts to be worn or damaged a complete new assembly must be obtained. The balls, ball hub, ball cage

3.5 Removing ball hub and ball cage assembly from constant velocity joint outer member

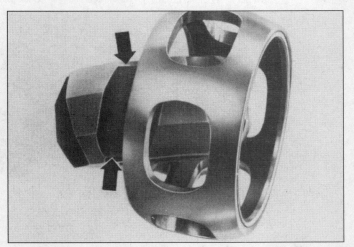

3.6 With the two grooves in the ball hub (arrowed) aligned with the ball cage edge the two parts can be separated

3.13 Ensure that wide track in outer member (a) and narrow track in ball hub (b) will be together when the hub is moved in direction of arrow

3.14 Final assembly of ball hub and cage assembly to outer member. Arrows indicate correct position of hub to allow balls to enter their tracks

and outer member all belong to a tolerance group which is selected during manufacture. For this reason new parts are not available separately, only as a completely assembled constant velocity joint. The exception to this is the rubber boots which may be obtained individually.

10 If the joint components are in a satisfactory condition the unit should be reassembled as follows.

11 First obtain a 90g tube of VW type G-6 grease from your VW dealer. Do not use any other type of grease in the joint.

12 Align the two grooves in the ball hub track with the edge of the ball cage and insert the hub into the cage. Now press the six balls into the cage slots and ball hub tracks.

13 When the joint is assembled the chamfer on the inside diameter of the ball hub splines must be towards the larger diameter side of the outer member. Bearing this in mind place

the hub, cage and ball assembly into the outer member as shown **(see illustration)**. Make sure that a wide ball track in the outer member and a narrow track in the ball hub will be on the same side when the hub is swung into its fitted position.

14 Pivot the ball hub and cage into the outer member ensuring that the balls all enter their tracks correctly. It may be necessary to pivot the ball hub out of the cage slightly to achieve this **(see illustration)**.

15 Firmly press the edge of the ball cage towards the outer member until the whole assembly swings fully into position.

16 Check that the ball hub can be moved in and out by hand over the full range of axial movement.

17 With the joint fully assembled press 90g of the special grease equally into both sides of the joint (45g each side).

18 Position the new rubber boot on the driveshaft and then refit the joint. Press or drive the joint fully onto the driveshaft splines until it contacts the register. Now refit the circlip to its groove, making sure that it is fully seated. Tap it home with a suitable tube if necessary.

19 Slide up the rubber boot and position the protective cap over the joint. Carefully tap the periphery of the cap until it is fully in place.

20 The driveshaft can now be refitted to the car as described in Section 2.

4 Rear wheel bearing housing and shaft assembly – removal and refitting

1 Remove the hub cap and extract the split pin from the wheel shaft castellated retaining nut **(see illustration)**.

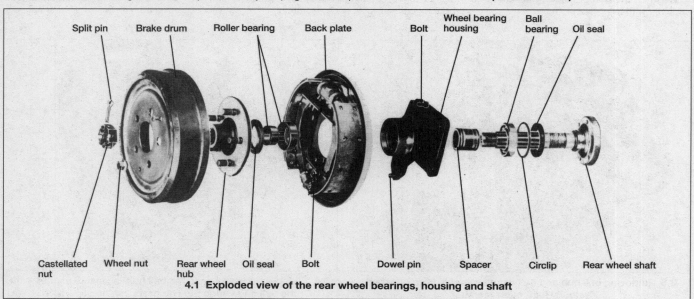

4.1 Exploded view of the rear wheel bearings, housing and shaft

Split pin Brake drum Roller bearing Back plate Bolt Wheel bearing housing Ball bearing Oil seal

Castellated nut Wheel nut Rear wheel hub Oil seal Bolt Dowel pin Spacer Circlip Rear wheel shaft

2 With the handbrake firmly applied, slacken the wheel shaft nut using a socket and long bar. This nut will be extremely tight. If the nut being removed has six split pin slots, a new pattern nut with ten slots should be obtained for use when refitting.

3 Jack up the rear of the vehicle and support it on axle stands (see "*Jacking and vehicle support*"). Remove the appropriate rear roadwheel.

4 Remove the driveshaft as described in Section 2.

5 Refer to Chapter 10 and remove the rear brake shoes. On models with ABS, also remove the rear wheel speed sensor.

6 Unscrew the wheel shaft castellated retaining nut and then using a universal puller, draw off the rear wheel hub.

7 Using a brake hose clamp or self-locking grips with their jaws suitably protected, clamp the flexible hydraulic brake hose located at the front of the suspension trailing arm. This will prevent loss of hydraulic fluid during subsequent operations.

8 Unscrew the brake hydraulic pipe union at the rear of the wheel cylinder. Carefully ease the pipe out of the cylinder and protect its end against dirt ingress.

9 Withdraw the handbrake cable from its location in the brake backplate.

10 From the front of the backplate undo and remove the two bolts securing the brake shoe pivot assembly and backplate to the wheel bearing housing. Lift off the pivot assembly. It may be necessary to ease it away using a screwdriver as it is located by a dowel pin which is often tight.

11 From the rear of the backplate undo and remove the single bolt securing the wheel cylinder and backplate to the wheel bearing housing. Undo and remove the wheel cylinder bleed screw and then lift off the cylinder.

12 The brake backplate can now be removed from the wheel bearing housing. Again note the dowel pin.

13 Finally undo and remove the four bolts and washers securing the wheel bearing housing to the trailing arm and lift away the assembly.

14 Refitting is the reverse sequence to removal, bearing in mind the following points:

a) *Tighten all retaining nuts and bolts to the specified torque where applicable*

b) *It will be necessary to bleed the brake hydraulic system after refitting the brake shoes and drum. Full information will be found in Chapter 10*

c) *When refitting the wheel shaft retaining nut, note the different tightening torques for old and new pattern nuts. VW state that the old pattern nut should be replaced by a new pattern nut. Tighten the nut to the specified torque and then continue until the split pin holes are aligned. Use a new split pin and make sure that the vehicle is standing on its wheels when tightening the nut*

5.2 Using a press and special tool to remove wheel shaft from bearing housing

5 Rear wheel bearings and shaft – dismantling, inspection and reassembly

1 Remove the rear wheel bearing housing and shaft assembly from the vehicle as described in the previous Section.

2 With the bearing housing supported in a vice, drive out the wheel shaft using a soft metal drift or preferably use a press **(see illustration)**.

3 Using a large screwdriver, lever out the oil seals on both sides of the bearing housing **(see illustration)**. It will be necessary to obtain new oil seals before reassembling as the old ones will be damaged during removal.

4 From the wheel side of the housing lift out the roller bearing inner race, then slide out the spacer (or ABS sensor wheel) located between the bearings.

5 Now turn the housing over and knock out the roller bearing outer race with a soft metal drift.

6 Extract the circlip from behind the ball bearing and then remove this bearing in the same way.

7 Thoroughly wash all the parts in paraffin and dry them with a lint free cloth.

8 Examine the rollers and inner race of the roller bearing for signs of pitting, scoring or wear ridges. Spin both the bearings and check for roughness, remembering that they are dry. If in doubt repack them with fresh

5.3 Removal of the bearing housing oil seals with a screwdriver

multi-purpose grease and spin them again. Renew the bearings if they are suspect, together with the oil seals.

9 Begin reassembly by packing both the bearings with multipurpose grease.

10 Place the ball bearing in position in the housing and drive it in using a tube of suitable diameter against the outer race. Make sure the bearing is kept square during fitting and drive it in until it contacts the register in the housing.

11 Refit the bearing retaining circlip and the inner oil seal. Use a block of wood when tapping in the seal and make sure that the open side of the seal is toward the centre of the housing.

12 Pack the space between the bearings in the centre of the housing with grease and place the bearing spacer (or ABS trigger wheel) in position.

13 Drift in the roller bearing outer race using the same procedure as for the ball bearing. Insert the roller bearing inner race followed by the oil seal. Tap in the seal until it is flush with the housing.

14 Place the flange of the wheel shaft face down on the bench and lay the assembled bearing housing over the shaft. Make sure that the shaft enters the ball bearing inner race and bearing spacer squarely.

15 Using a tube of suitable diameter in contact with the roller bearing inner race, drive or press the bearing housing onto the wheel shaft as far as it will go. As you do this make sure that the bearing inner races do not tip slightly and jam on the shaft otherwise they may crack.

16 After reassembly check that the shaft turns freely and smoothly in the bearings and then refit the housing to the vehicle as described in the previous Section.

6 Rear shock absorber – removal and refitting

1 Jack up the rear of the vehicle and support it on axle stands (see "*Jacking and vehicle support*").

2 Place a jack beneath the appropriate suspension trailing arm and raise the arm slightly.

3 Undo and remove the nut and bolt securing the shock absorber to the trailing arm and the bolt securing it to the bracket on the vehicle underbody **(see illustrations)**. Ease the shock absorber out of its locations and lift it away.

4 With the unit removed hold it in an upright position and fully extend and compress it several times. The shock absorber should operate with a smooth even pressure, free from dead areas, over the whole stroke. If not the shock absorber must be renewed. It must also be renewed if there is any damage or deterioration of the chrome on the piston rod or if there is evidence of excessive fluid loss.

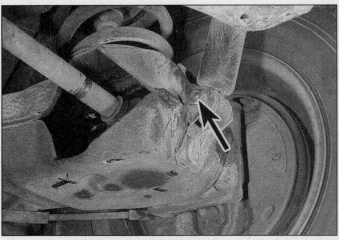

6.3A Shock absorber to trailing arm (arrowed) . . .

6.3B . . . and vehicle underbody mountings

There are quite a number of different types of shock absorbers available for Transporter models and their derivatives and care must be taken to ensure that compatible types are fitted.

Caution: Shock absorbers may be renewed individually if one becomes defective early in its service life. It is advisable to renew them in pairs if they have been in service for more than 30 000 miles (48 000 km).

5 The shock absorber rubber bush and steel sleeve can be renewed separately. The bush and sleeve can be removed by pressing them out in a vice using tubes of suitable diameter **(see illustration)**. When refitting make sure that they are pressed fully into position and lubricate the rubber bush with a little liquid detergent to ease installation.

6 Refitting the shock absorber to the vehicle is the reverse sequence to removal.

7 Rear coil spring – removal and refitting

1 Jack up the rear of the vehicle and support it on axle stands positioned clear of the rear suspension trailing arms (see "*Jacking and vehicle support*").

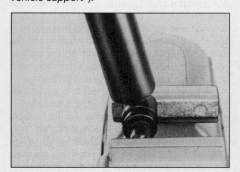

6.5 Using a vice to press in new shock absorber bushes

2 Place a jack beneath the trailing arm and raise the arm slightly.

3 Undo and remove the nut and bolt securing the shock absorber lower mounting to the trailing arm. Release the mounting and pivot the shock absorber clear of the arm.

4 Slowly lower the jack and trailing arm until all the tension is released from the spring. Now pull the trailing arm down and lift out the spring, lower packing and upper spring plate **(see illustration)**. On some models it may be necessary to remove the driveshaft inner joint from the differential as described in Section 2 to allow the trailing arm to be lowered sufficiently.

5 The springs are colour coded by means of paint marks to indicate their load group and vehicle application. The number of paint marks indicates the load group and the colour of the marks denotes the vehicle to which they are fitted. Only springs of the same load group may be fitted to one axle. As with shock absorbers, it is good practice to renew the springs in pairs if they have seen long service.

6 Refitting the rear coil spring is the reverse sequence to removal. Make sure that the locating contours, in the lower packing, seat correctly in the trailing arm and that the end of the spring engages in the contour. The upper spring plate should be turned so that the end of the spring locates in the depression.

8 Rear trailing arm – removal and refitting

1 Jack up the rear of the vehicle and support it on axle stands placed well clear of the trailing arms (see "*Jacking and vehicle support*"). Remove the rear roadwheel.

2 Refer to Section 2 and remove the driveshaft.

3 Using a brake hose clamp or self-locking grips with their jaws suitably protected, clamp

the rear flexible brake hose located just in front of the trailing arm. This will prevent loss of hydraulic fluid during subsequent operations.

4 Clean off the area around the flexible brake hose to metal brake pipe union at the bracket on the trailing arm. Unscrew the brake pipe union, lift away the retaining clip and withdraw the hose. Plug the end of the hose to prevent dirt ingress.

5 Wipe the area around the metal brake pipe to wheel cylinder union at the rear of the brake backplate. Unscrew the union nut and withdraw the pipe from the cylinder. Release the pipe from the retaining clip on the trailing arm and lift off the metal pipe.

6 Undo and remove the four bolts securing the wheel bearing housing and brake assembly to the trailing arm. Release the handbrake cable from the support clip on the underside of the arm and lower the housing and brake assembly to the ground.

7 Refer to Section 7 and remove the rear coil spring.

8 Mark the locations of the trailing arm retaining bolts in the mounting brackets as a guide to refitting. The mounting brackets have elongated slots to provide for rear suspension adjustment and if the original positions are not marked the settings will be lost.

9 Undo and remove the trailing arm retaining nuts, bolts and washers and lever the arm out of its mountings. Note that the outer retaining bolt has a protective cap over the bolt head which must first be removed.

10 Now withdraw the arm from under the vehicle.

11 If necessary the rubber mounting bushes can be removed by drawing them out with a large diameter tube, suitable packing washers and a long bolt or stud and nut. New bushes are fitted in the same way making sure they are liberally lubricated with liquid detergent to ease installation.

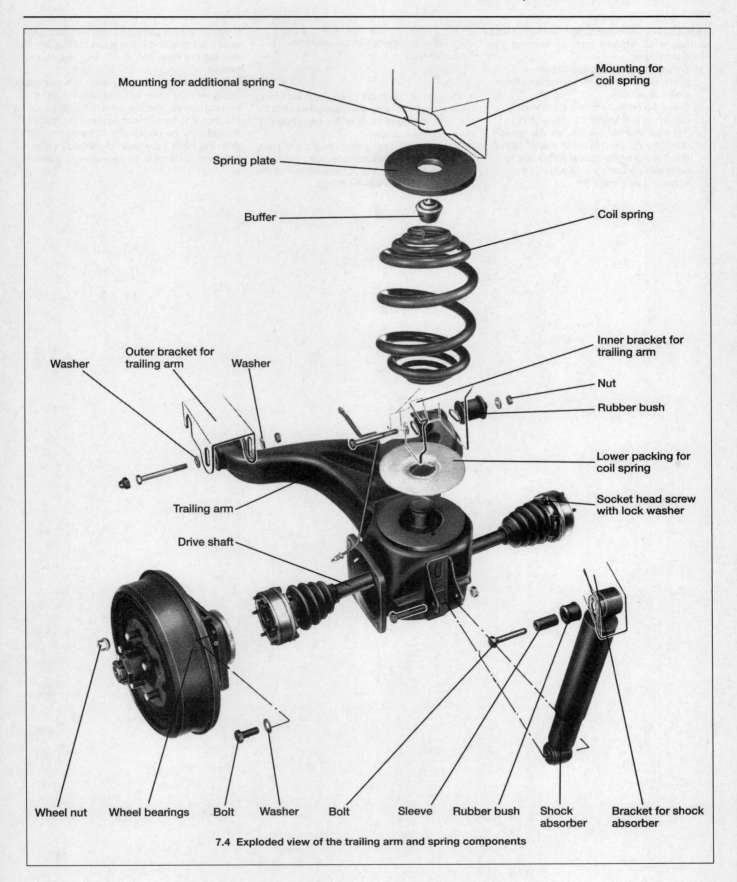

Mounting for additional spring

Mounting for coil spring

Spring plate

Buffer

Coil spring

Outer bracket for trailing arm

Washer

Washer

Inner bracket for trailing arm

Nut

Rubber bush

Lower packing for coil spring

Trailing arm

Socket head screw with lock washer

Drive shaft

Wheel nut

Wheel bearings

Bolt

Washer

Bolt

Sleeve

Rubber bush

Shock absorber

Bracket for shock absorber

7.4 Exploded view of the trailing arm and spring components

12 Refitting the trailing arm is the reverse sequence to removal bearing in mind the following points:

a) *Ensure that all nuts and bolts are tightened to the specified torque settings where applicable*

b) *Bleed the brake hydraulic system as described in Chapter 10 after refitting*

c) *It is advisable to have the rear suspension geometry checked by a VW dealer even if the location of the trailing arm retaining bolts was accurately marked before removal (see Section 9)*

9 Rear suspension geometry – general

1 The rear suspension trailing arm mounting brackets are provided with elongated slots for the retaining bolts to allow for adjustment of the suspension angles.

2 The outer bracket incorporates a vertical slot for camber adjustment and the inner bracket a horizontal slot for adjustment of the rear wheel alignment (toe setting).

3 Adjustment is carried out by slackening the retaining bolts and moving the trailing arm in the desired direction to achieve the correct setting.

4 Due to the need for special gauges and equipment to carry out this adjustment it is recommended that the vehicle be taken to a VW dealer to have the work done. Adjustment should only be necessary if the trailing arm retaining bolts have been disturbed or if rear tyre wear appears to be excessive or uneven.

Chapter 9
Front suspension and steering

Contents

Degrees of difficulty

Easy, suitable for novice with little experience	**Fairly easy,** suitable for beginner with some experience	**Fairly difficult,** suitable for competent DIY mechanic 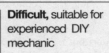	**Difficult,** suitable for experienced DIY mechanic 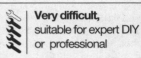	**Very difficult,** suitable for expert DIY or professional

Specifications

Front suspension

Type	Independent by upper and lower suspension arms, coil springs, telescopic shock absorbers, radius rods and anti-roll bar

Steering gear

Type	Rack and pinion with relay unit and connecting shaft; power assistance on some models

Steering wheel turns (lock-to-lock):
Without power assistance	3.75
With power assistance	Information not available at time of writing
Turning circle	9083 mm (357.6 in) between kerbs

Front suspension geometry (unladen)

Camber	0° ± 30'
Castor	7° 15' ± 15'
Castor – maximum difference side to side	1°
Toe setting	20' ± 30' (2.0 ± 3.5 mm / 0.08 ± 0.14 in) toe-in

Torque wrench settings

	Nm	lbf ft
Front suspension		
Upper wishbone to body	75	55
Lower track control arm to body	90	66
Shock absorber upper mounting	25	18
Shock absorber lower mounting	150	111
Upper balljoint to wishbone	55	40
Upper balljoint to steering knuckle*	110	81
Lower balljoint to adaptor*	110	81
Adaptor to track control arm	65	48
Radius rod to body bracket	100	74
Radius rod to track control arm (later models only)	180	133
Anti-roll bar link to radius rod or track control arm	30	22
Anti-roll bar to body	20	15
Tie-rod balljoint to steering knuckle	30	22
Brake caliper to steering knuckle	160	118

Torque wrench settings (continued)

Steering

	Nm	lbf ft
Steering box to body*	25	18
Power steering box fluid unions (banjo bolts)	20	15
Relay unit to body	25	18
Two arm flange to flexible coupling disc*	20	15
Two arm flange to column, connecting shaft, or pinion*	20	15
Steering wheel to column	50	37
Steering column to body	25	18
Tie-rod inner joint to rack	70	52
Tie-rod balljoint to steering knuckle	30	22
Tie-rod balljoint locknut	50	37
Power steering pump fluid unions (banjo bolts)	40	30
Power steering pump-to-bracket bolts	20	15
Power steering pump pivot nut	35	26
Power steering pump pulley bolts	20	15

Always use new self-locking nuts

1 General description

The front suspension is of the independent type incorporating upper and lower suspension arms, coil springs, telescopic shock absorbers, radius rods and an anti-roll bar **(see illustrations)**.

The upper suspension arm or wishbone is attached to the vehicle at its inner end by rubber bushes and a spindle which incorporates eccentric washers for camber adjustment. At its outer end the wishbone is attached to the steering knuckle by a balljoint.

The lower suspension arm or track control arm pivots at its inner end on a rubber bush and is attached at its outer end to the steering knuckle by an adaptor and balljoint. Fore and aft movement of the track control arm is controlled by a radius rod which is adjustable to provide for alterations of the castor angle. An anti-roll bar interconnects each track control arm to reduce body roll when cornering.

Attached to the steering knuckle is the disc brake caliper and the one-piece hub and disc assembly incorporating the front wheel bearings.

The steering gear is of the rack and pinion type with adjustable tie-rods to cater for alterations to the front wheel toe setting. Movements of the steering wheel are transmitted to the steering gear via an upper and lower column, relay unit and connecting shaft. Three flexible couplings and a safety coupling are used to connect the upper and lower columns and connecting shaft to the relay unit and steering gear. In the event of a frontal impact the upper and lower steering columns are designed to separate at the safety coupling, thus reducing the risk of injury to the driver.

Power-assisted steering is available on some models. Assistance is provided hydraulically, the pressure being generated by an engine-driven pump.

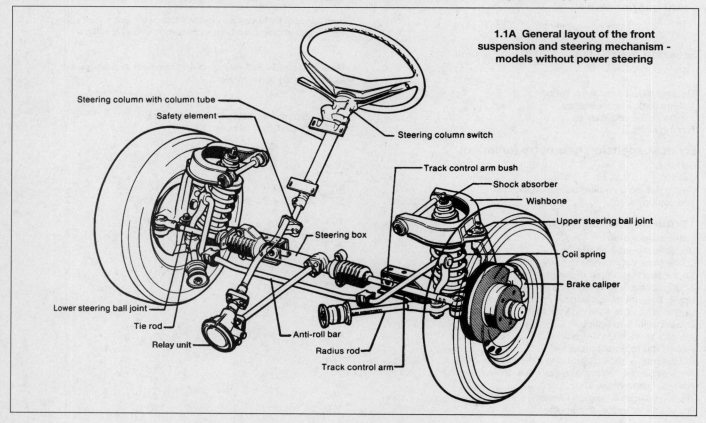

1.1A General layout of the front suspension and steering mechanism - models without power steering

Steering column with column tube
Safety element
Steering column switch
Track control arm bush
Shock absorber
Wishbone
Upper steering ball joint
Coil spring
Steering box
Brake caliper
Lower steering ball joint
Tie rod
Relay unit
Anti-roll bar
Radius rod
Track control arm

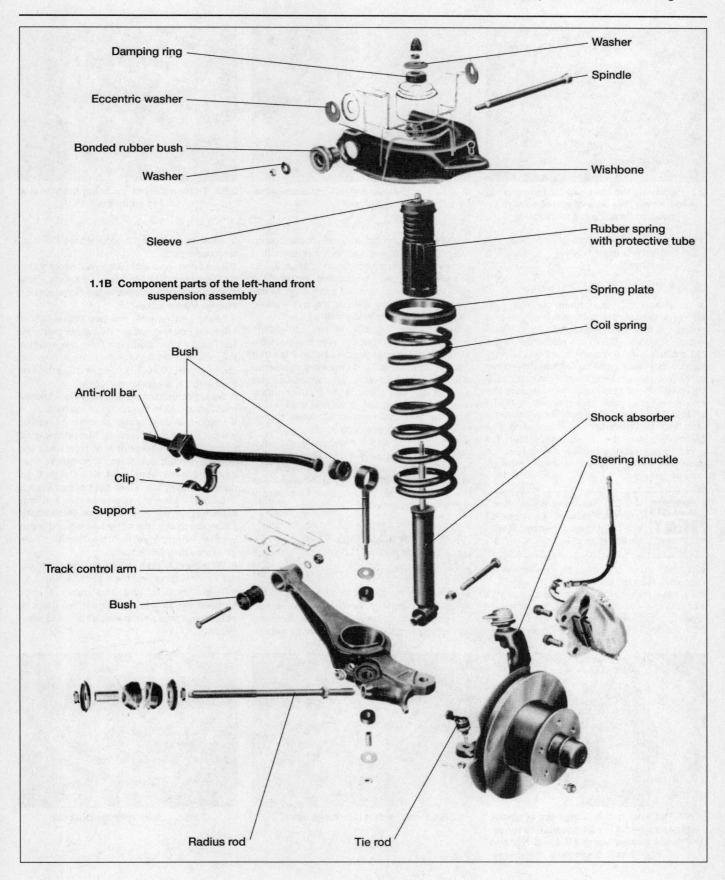

Damping ring

Washer

Spindle

Eccentric washer

Bonded rubber bush

Washer

Wishbone

Sleeve

Rubber spring
with protective tube

**1.1B Component parts of the left-hand front
suspension assembly**

Spring plate

Coil spring

Bush

Anti-roll bar

Shock absorber

Steering knuckle

Clip

Support

Track control arm

Bush

Radius rod

Tie rod

2.3 Removing the dust cap for hub bearing adjustment. This type of wheel does not need to be removed for access

2.4 Tap up the peening which secures the hub nut

2.5A Tighten the nut, spinning the wheel at the same time

2 Front hub bearings – adjustment

1 To check the adjustment of the hub bearings, jack up the front of the vehicle and support it on axle stands (see *Jacking and vehicle support*). Grasp the roadwheel at the '12 o'clock' and '6 o'clock' positions and try to rock it. Watch carefully for any movement in the suspension balljoints which can easily be mistaken for hub movement. Repeat the check with the roadwheel grasped at the '3 o'clock' and '9 o'clock' positions, this time watching for movement in the tie-rod end balljoints. Spin the wheel and listen for grinding or rumbling noises; if these do not disappear after adjustment, new bearings may be required.

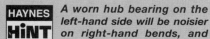
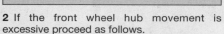
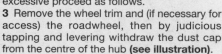

HAYNES HiNT *A worn hub bearing on the left-hand side will be noisier on right-hand bends, and vice versa.*

2 If the front wheel hub movement is excessive proceed as follows.
3 Remove the wheel trim and (if necessary for access) the roadwheel, then by judicious tapping and levering withdraw the dust cap from the centre of the hub **(see illustration)**.

4 Using a small punch or screwdriver, tap up the peening (the indented section) that secures the hub retaining nut to the groove in the stub axle **(see illustration)**. **Note:** *If the hub nut has been peened more than twice, obtain and fit a new hub nut before proceeding with the adjustment.*
5 Tighten the hub nut, at the same time spinning the hub, until it is only just possible to move the thrust washer behind the nut using a screwdriver and finger pressure **(see illustrations)**. Several attempts may be needed to get this right. If the nut is overtightened, slacken it off and start again. Spin the hub again and check that it turns freely with just a trace of play.
6 Peen the nut into the groove in the stub axle using a hammer and a small punch, then refit the dust cap and (if removed) the roadwheel **(see illustrations)**. Finally lower the vehicle to the ground and if necessary tighten the wheel bolts.

3 Front hub bearings – removal and refitting

1 Remove the wheel trim and slacken the wheel bolts. Jack up the front of the vehicle and support it on axle stands (see *Jacking and vehicle support*). Remove the roadwheel.

2 Refer to Chapter 10 and remove the front disc brake pads.
3 Undo and remove the large nut securing the upper balljoint to the steering knuckle and then release the flexible brake hose support bracket from the ball-pin.
4 Undo and remove the two brake caliper retaining bolts, withdraw the caliper complete with brake hose and pipe from the steering knuckle and tie it up out of the way using string or wire. Avoid placing undue strain on the flexible hose and brake pipe.
5 By judicious tapping and levering withdraw the dust cap from the centre of the hub.
6 Using a small punch or screwdriver, tap up the peening that secures the hub retaining nut to the groove in the stub axle. Now undo and remove the hub nut. **Note:** *If the hub nut has been peened more than twice it will be necessary to obtain a new nut before refitting.*
7 Carefully slide the complete hub and disc assembly off the stub axle **(see illustration)**. Take care to hold the outer bearing and thrust washer in place as the hub is withdrawn, otherwise they will fall out.
8 With the hub assembly on the bench, lift out the thrust washer and the outer bearing.
9 Turn the hub over and using a large screwdriver as a lever, extract the inner oil seal. Note that a new seal must be used when refitting.

2.5B The front hub bearings are correctly adjusted when it is just possible to move the thrust washer using a screwdriver and finger pressure

2.6A Peen the nut into the groove . . .

2.6B . . . then refit the dust cap

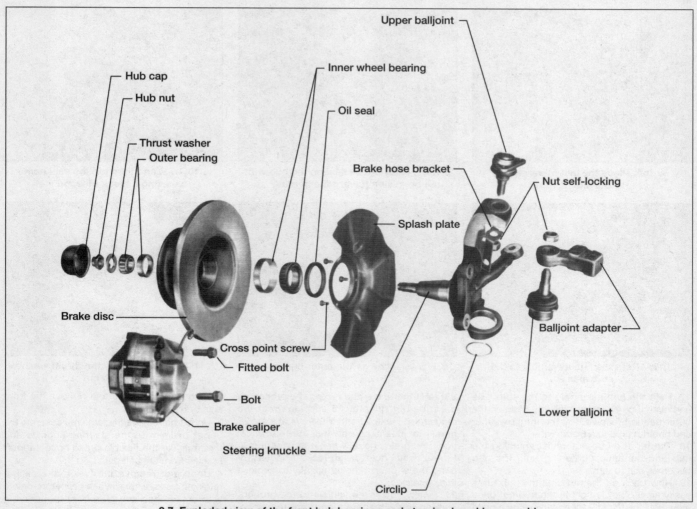

3.7 Exploded view of the front hub bearings and steering knuckle assembly

10 Lift out the inner bearing and then support the hub assembly on blocks of wood. Using a tapered drift inserted through the centre of the hub, drive out the outer bearing outer race. Now turn the hub over again and remove the inner bearing outer race in the same way **(see illustration)**.

11 Thoroughly wash all the parts in paraffin and wipe dry using a lint free cloth.

12 Inspect the bearing rollers and their outer races for signs of rusting, pitting, scoring or overheating and if evident obtain a new set of bearings.

13 Inspect the oil seal journal face of the stub axle for signs of damage or grooving. Any slight grooving may be polished out with fine emery tape, but if the grooving is very bad a new steering knuckle assembly will be required. On later models the oil seal journal ring is manufactured as a separate component and pressed onto the stub axle. In this case it will only be necessary to renew the ring and not the complete steering knuckle in the event of damage or grooving to the journal face. Note that models with renewable oil seal

journal rings are also equipped with modified oil seals. Bear this in mind when ordering new parts.

14 To reassemble the bearings, carefully press or drive the new outer races into position using a tube or large socket of suitable diameter. Make sure that they are fitted with their larger diameters facing outward and driven fully home until they contact the register in the hub.

15 Pack the space between the bearings in the hub and also the bearings themselves with multi-purpose grease **(see illustration)**.

16 Place the inner bearing in position in the hub. Fill the space between the two sealing lips of a new oil seal with grease and lay the seal on the hub with the open face toward the bearing. Using a block of wood tap the seal into position until it is flush with the hub flange **(see illustrations)**.

3.10 Remove the hub inner bearing outer race with a drift inserted through the centre of the hub

3.15 Pack the space between the bearings in the hub with multi-purpose grease

3.16A Place the inner bearing in position . . .

3.16B . . . lay the oil seal on the hub with the open side toward the bearing . . .

3.16C . . . and then tap the seal home using a block of wood

3.17A Refit the hub assembly to the stub axle . . .

3.17B . . . slide on the outer bearing . . .

3.17C . . . followed by the thrust washer and hub nut

17 Refit the hub assembly to the stub axle and push it on as far as it will go. Slide on the outer bearing followed by the thrust washer and hub nut **(see illustrations)**.

18 Tighten the hub nut whilst spinning the hub and continue tightening until the hub becomes stiff to turn.

19 Now back off the nut until the hub turns easily again. Slowly tighten the hub nut once more until the thrust washer can just be moved using a screwdriver and finger pressure.

20 Peen the flange of the hub nut into the groove in the stub axle and then refit the dust cap **(see illustration)**.

21 Place the brake caliper over the disc and refit the two retaining bolts. Tighten the bolts to the specified torque.

22 Engage the brake flexible hose support bracket with the upper balljoint and refit the retaining nut. Tighten the nut to the specified torque.

23 Refit the brake pads using the procedure described in Chapter 10 and then refit the roadwheel. Make sure that there is at least 25 mm (1 in) clearance between the roadwheel and the brake hose when the steering is turned to full right or left lock. If necessary bend the support bracket slightly to achieve this clearance.

24 Finally, lower the vehicle to the ground. Tighten the wheel bolts and refit the wheel trim.

4 Steering knuckle –
removal and refitting

1 Remove the wheel trim and slacken the wheel bolts. Jack up the front of the vehicle and support it on axle stands (see "*Jacking and vehicle support*"). Remove the roadwheel.

2 Refer to Chapter 10 and remove the front disc brake pads.

3 Undo and remove the large nut securing the upper balljoint to the steering knuckle and then release the flexible brake hose support bracket from the ball-pin.

4 Undo and remove the two brake caliper retaining bolts, withdraw the caliper complete with brake hose and pipe from the steering knuckle and tie it up out of the way using string or wire. Avoid placing any excessive strain on the flexible hose or brake pipe.

5 Extract the split pin and then undo and remove the nut securing the steering tie-rod balljoint to the steering knuckle arm. Release the balljoint tapered shank from the steering knuckle using a universal balljoint separator.

6 Undo and remove the three bolts and locknuts securing the lower balljoint adaptor to the track control arm **(see illustration)**.

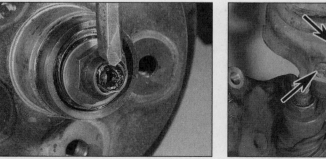

3.20 The hub nut is retained by peening the flange into the groove in the stub axle

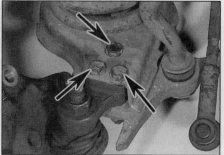

4.6 Steering knuckle lower balljoint adaptor retaining bolts (arrowed)

4.7 Steering knuckle upper balljoint secured to wishbone with two socket-headed bolts (arrowed)

5.2 Removing the brake disc splash plate from the steering knuckle

5.3 Using a hammer and steel block to free the upper balljoint shank from the steering knuckle

5.5 Using VW special tool to remove adaptor from lower balljoint

7 Using a suitable key, undo and remove the two socket-headed bolts securing the upper balljoint to the upper wishbone **(see illustration)**.

8 If working on the left-hand side knuckle, release the retaining ring and withdraw the speedometer cable from the rubber sleeve in the knuckle.

9 Lift up the upper wishbone slightly to release it from the balljoint, then withdraw the steering knuckle assembly complete with hub and balljoints from the front suspension.

10 If it is wished to completely dismantle the steering knuckle, the hub assembly and the balljoints may be removed using the procedures described in the appropriate Sections of this Chapter.

11 Refitting the steering knuckle is the reverse sequence to removal, bearing in mind the following points:

a) *Tighten all retaining nuts and bolts to the specified torque*

b) *Fit a spring washer under the head of each lower balljoint adaptor retaining bolt if one is not already fitted. If a washer is not used the bolt heads may become embedded in the track control arm when fully tightened*

c) *If the left-hand steering knuckle was removed, a new rubber sleeve for the speedometer cable must be fitted and pushed in as far as possible using a suitable tool. Smear the speedometer cable with jointing compound before inserting it in the rubber sleeve*

d) *After refitting ensure that there is at least*

5.7 Using a press and VW special tools to remove the lower balljoint from the steering knuckle

25 mm (1 in) clearance between the roadwheel and the brake flexible hose when the steering is turned to full right or left lock. If necessary bend the support bracket slightly to achieve this clearance

e) *Always use a new split pin to secure the tie-rod balljoint retaining nut*

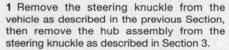

5 Steering knuckle balljoints – removal and refitting

1 Remove the steering knuckle from the vehicle as described in the previous Section, then remove the hub assembly from the steering knuckle as described in Section 3.

2 With the steering knuckle on the bench, undo and remove the three screws and lift off the brake disc splash plate **(see illustration)**.

3 To remove the upper balljoint, undo and remove the retaining nut; a new nut must be used on reassembly. Release the balljoint tapered shank from the steering knuckle using VW tool No 267A or equivalent. If this tool cannot be obtained it may be possible to shock the taper free by striking the steering knuckle flange with a medium hammer whilst resting the knuckle on a solid steel or iron block **(see illustration)**. Once the taper is released the balljoint can be lifted away.

4 Removal of the lower balljoint is a little more difficult. A press will be required and also in this case VW tool 267A (or a proprietary equivalent) is essential. The procedure is as follows.

5 First undo and remove the nut securing the balljoint to the balljoint adaptor. Again, a new nut must be used on reassembly. Using tool 267A, release the adaptor from the tapered shank of the balljoint **(see illustration)**.

6 Using a small screwdriver extract the circlip from its groove in the lower body of the balljoint.

7 Support the flange of the steering knuckle on the press bed using suitable tubing or the VW tools **(see illustration)**. Now press the joint out of the knuckle.

8 With the balljoints removed, inspect the rubber boots for damage or deterioration and check the joints for excessive free play. Individual parts are not available separately,

therefore if the rubber boot is damaged or the joint is worn a complete balljoint must be obtained.

9 Refitting the balljoints is basically the reverse of the removal sequence. In the case of the lower balljoint make sure that it is fitted with the flat side of the shoulder towards the stub axle. Press the joint fully home and ensure that the circlip seats fully into its groove. Do not tighten the balljoint retaining nuts until the steering knuckle has been refitted, otherwise the rubber boot may be damaged.

10 Refit the hub assembly and steering knuckle as described in Sections 3 and 4 respectively.

6 Radius rod – removal and refitting

1 Jack up the front of the vehicle and support it on axle stands (see *"Jacking and vehicle support"*).

Early models (up to chassis no 24 FH 019 682)

2 Undo and remove the nut securing the anti-roll bar connecting link to the radius rod. Lift off the lower shouldered washer and rubber damping ring.

3 Undo and remove the outer nut securing the radius rod to the body mounting bracket **(see illustration)**. Take care not to disturb the position of the inner nut otherwise the castor angle setting will be disturbed **(see illustration)**.

6.3A Radius rod outer retaining nut, shouldered washer and rubber bush

6.3B The radius rod inner nut must not be disturbed otherwise the castor angle will be affected

Lift off the large shouldered washer and the rubber bush.

4 Undo and remove the three nuts securing the radius rod to the track control arm. Pull the radius rod down to release it from the anti-roll bar connecting link and then withdraw it rearwards out of the front mounting bracket. **Note:** *If the radius rod is to be renewed or if it is necessary to remove the remaining front mounting nut, mark its position on the radius rod before doing so. This can then be used as a guide to its approximate position when refitting.*

Later models

5 Measure and note the distance from the radius rod inner nut to the end of the threaded section **(see illustration)**.

6 Remove the radius rod outer nut. Screw the inner nut away from the body mounting bracket as far as possible.

7 Unscrew the radius rod from the track control arm, then withdraw it from the front mounting bracket.

All models

8 Recover the steel sleeves, washers and bushes from the front of the radius rod and the anti-roll bar link attachment.

9 Refitting the radius rod is the reverse sequence to removal bearing in mind the following points:

a) *Renew the front mounting rubber bushes and anti-roll bar connecting link damping rings if they show signs of deterioration or compression damage*

7.2 Anti-roll bar connecting link to radius rod mounting (arrowed)

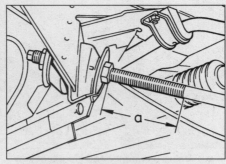

6.5 Measure the distance (a) from the radius rod inner nut to the end of the threaded section

b) *All shouldered washers must be fitted with their shoulders facing away from the appropriate rubber bush or damping ring*

c) *Tighten all retaining nuts and bolts to the specified torque*

d) *If a new radius rod has been fitted or if the position of the front mounting inner nut has been altered the front suspension geometry and wheel alignment should be checked by a VW dealer (see Section 22)*

7 Anti-roll bar – removal and refitting

1 Remove the wheel trim and slacken the wheel bolts. Jack up the front of the vehicle and support it on axle stands (see "*Jacking and vehicle support*"). Remove the roadwheel.

2 Undo and remove the nuts securing the two anti-roll bar connecting links to the radius rods or track control arms. Lift off the shouldered washers and the lower rubber damping rings **(see illustration)**.

3 Swivel the anti-roll bar upwards to release the connecting links. Recover the steel sleeve, upper damping ring and shouldered washer from each link.

4 Undo and remove the two nuts and bolts each side securing the anti-roll bar mounting clips to the chassis members **(see illustration)**. Rotate the anti-roll bar to clear the steering tie-rod and withdraw the bar from under the front of the vehicle.

7.4 Anti-roll bar to chassis member mounting

5 With the anti-roll bar removed, slip off the two split mounting bushes from the centre of the bar and the two connecting links from each end.

6 Inspect the bushes and connecting link damping rings for deterioration of the rubber and renew as necessary.

7 Refitting the anti-roll bar is the reverse sequence to removal, bearing in mind the following points:

a) *The connecting link shouldered washers must be fitted with their shoulders facing away from the damping rings*

b) *Tighten all retaining nuts and bolts to the specified torque*

8 Track control arm – removal and refitting

1 Begin by removing the radius rod using the procedure described in Section 6. On later models also release the anti-roll bar link from the track control arm as described in Section 7.

2 Extract the split pin and undo and remove the nut securing the steering tie-rod balljoint to the steering knuckle arm. Release the balljoint tapered shank from the steering knuckle using a universal balljoint separator.

3 Place a jack beneath the track control arm and raise the arm slightly.

4 Undo and remove the long through-bolt and nut securing the shock absorber lower mounting to the track control arm. Use a long tapered drift or suitable round bar to tap the bolt out of its location in the arm.

5 Using a suitable key, undo and remove the two socket-headed bolts securing the steering knuckle upper balljoint to the wishbone.

6 Support the steering knuckle and hub assembly to avoid straining the flexible brake hose or speedometer cable (where applicable). Now slowly lower the jack beneath the track control arm until all tension is released from the coil spring.

7 Undo and remove the nut, bolt and spring washer securing the track control arm inner mounting to the chassis member. Using a stout screwdriver, lever the arm out of its mounting location **(see illustration)**.

8.7 Track control arm inner mounting

8 Lower the jack fully and then draw the track control arm towards the centre of the vehicle until it is clear of the lower balljoint adaptor which locates in the centre of the arm. Now lift away the track control arm and take out the coil spring complete with upper spring plate.
9 Temporarily refit the steering knuckle upper balljoint to the wishbone using the two socket-headed bolts.
10 With the track control arm removed, carefully inspect the inner mounting for signs of damage or deterioration of the rubber. If renewal is necessary, the mounting may be removed using tubes of suitable diameter and a press or wide opening vice. Coat the new mounting with liquid detergent to aid refitting.
11 Refitting the track control arm is the reverse sequence to removal, bearing in mind the following points:
 a) When refitting the coil spring ensure that the upper spring plate is in position and that the straight end of the spring is at the bottom, correctly engaged in the depression in the track control arm
 b) Tighten all retaining nuts and bolts to the specified torque where applicable and use a new split pin to secure the tie-rod balljoint nut

9 Upper wishbone – removal and refitting

1 Remove the wheel trim and slacken the wheel bolts. Jack up the front of the vehicle and support it on axle stands (see "Jacking and vehicle support"). Remove the roadwheel.
2 Using a suitable key, undo and remove the two socket-headed bolts securing the steering knuckle upper balljoint to the wishbone (see illustration). Lift the wishbone slightly and carefully move the steering knuckle to one side.
3 Undo and remove the wishbone spindle retaining nut and washer and recover the eccentric washer. Now slide out the spindle and recover the second eccentric washer.
4 Ease the wishbone out of its mounting location and remove it from the vehicle.
5 Inspect the bonded rubber bushes in the wishbone and renew them if they show signs of damage or deterioration. If renewal of the bushes is necessary this work must be carried out by a VW dealer. The bush casings are spot welded in position to prevent them turning in the wishbone. Before the bushes can be removed the spot welds must be carefully ground off allowing the bushes to be pressed out. After refitting, the new bushes must also be spot welded in place.
6 To refit the wishbone, position it over its mounting location and then slide one of the eccentric washers onto the spindle. Install the spindle ensuring that the flat side is vertical and facing toward the centre of the vehicle. Position the eccentric washer with the larger space downwards.

9.2 Upper wishbone to balljoint retaining bolts (A) and spindle retaining nut (B)

7 Fit the second eccentric washer, also with the larger space downwards, followed by the plain washer and retaining nut. Tighten the nut to the specified torque.
8 Position the steering knuckle upper balljoint in the hole in the wishbone and secure with the two socket headed bolts. Again observe the correct torque setting.
9 Refit the roadwheel and lower the vehicle to the ground. Tighten the wheel bolts and refit the wheel trim.
10 It will be necessary to have the front suspension geometry and wheel alignment checked by a VW dealer (see Section 22). The two eccentric washers determine the suspension camber angle setting and this must always be reset if the position of the washers is disturbed.

10 Front shock absorber – removal and refitting

1 Remove the wheel trim and slacken the wheel bolts. Jack up the front of the vehicle and support it on axle stands (see "Jacking and vehicle support"). Remove the roadwheel.
2 Place a jack beneath the track control arm, but clear of the shock absorber lower mounting, and then raise the arm slightly.
3 Undo and remove the shock absorber upper domed retaining nut followed by the locknut. Lift off the washer and rubber damping ring (see illustration).

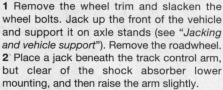
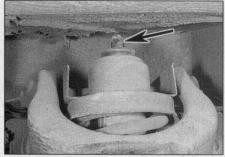
10.3 Shock absorber upper domed retaining nut, locknut, washer and damping ring assembly (arrowed)

4 Now undo and remove the long through-bolt and nut securing the shock absorber to the track control arm (see illustration).
5 Withdraw the shock absorber and rubber spring down through the centre of the track control arm and remove it from the vehicle.
6 With the unit removed, hold it in an upright position and fully extend and compress it several times. The shock absorber should operate with a smooth even pressure, free from dead areas, over the whole stroke. If this is not the case the shock absorber must be renewed. It must also be renewed if there is any damage or deterioration of the chrome on the piston rod or if there is evidence of excessive fluid loss. Shock absorbers may be renewed individually if they become defective early in their service life. It is advisable to renew them in pairs if they have been in service for more than 30 000 miles (48 000 km). There are quite a number of different types of shock absorbers available for Transporter models and their derivatives, and care must be taken to ensure that compatible types are fitted.
7 Refitting the shock absorber to the vehicle is the reverse sequence to removal. Ensure that the mounting nuts and bolts are tightened to the specified torque.

11 Coil spring – removal and refitting

1 Removal of the front coil spring necessitates removal of the track control arm also, and details of both these operations will be found in Section 8.

12 Steering tie-rod balljoint – removal and refitting

1 Remove the wheel trim and slacken the wheel bolts. Jack up the front of the vehicle and support it on axle stands (see "Jacking and vehicle support"). Remove the roadwheel.
2 Slacken the locknut that secures the steering tie-rod to the balljoint by an eighth of a turn only.

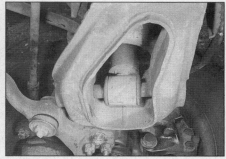
10.4 Shock absorber lower mounting bolt and nut accessible from either side of the track control arm

12.3A Remove the split pin and locknut . . .

12.3B . . . then release the tie-rod balljoint using a universal balljoint separator

13.3 Steering box pinion flange to coupling disc retaining bolts (arrowed)

3 Extract the split pin and then undo and remove the nut securing the balljoint to the steering knuckle arm. Release the balljoint tapered shank from the steering knuckle using a universal balljoint separator **(see illustrations)**.
4 The balljoint can now be unscrewed from the steering tie-rod.
5 Refitting is the reverse sequence to removal. If the position of the locknut on the tie-rod was only disturbed by an eighth of a turn as described, then after refitting, the front wheel alignment should still be approximately correct. It is advisable however to have the setting checked accurately as soon as possible (see Section 22).
6 Make sure that the balljoint locknut and

retaining nut are tightened to the specified torque and in the case of the retaining nut, aligned to the next split pin hole. Always use a new split pin to secure the nut.

13 Steering box –
removal, inspection and refitting

Models without power steering

1 Remove the wheel trim and slacken the wheel bolts. Jack up the front of the vehicle and support it on axle stands (see *"Jacking and vehicle support"*). Remove the roadwheels.

13.4 Steering box to crossmember retaining bolts (arrowed)

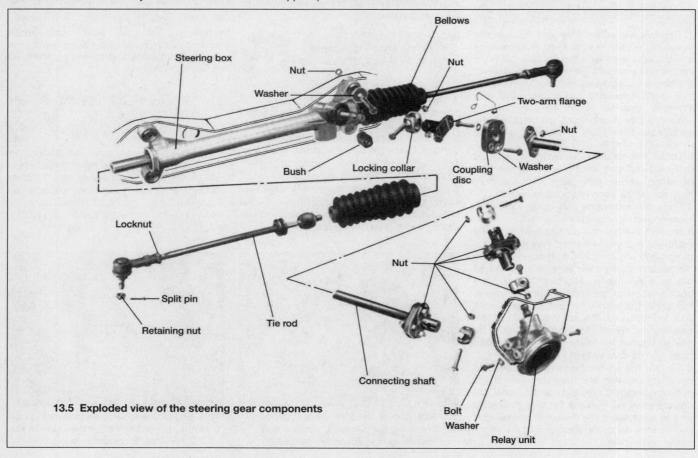

13.5 Exploded view of the steering gear components

2 Extract the split pin and then undo and remove the nut securing the right-hand steering tie-rod balljoint to the steering knuckle arm. Release the balljoint tapered shank from the steering knuckle using a universal balljoint separator. Now repeat this procedure for the left-hand tie-rod balljoint.

3 Undo and remove the two bolts and locknuts securing the flange of the pinion shaft to the steering box flexible coupling disc **(see illustration)**.

4 Undo and remove the four nuts, bolts and washers securing the steering box to the chassis crossmember **(see illustration)**. Lower the box to the ground and withdraw it from under the vehicle.

5 The rack and pinion steering box is non-adjustable and apart from the tie-rods and rubber bellows, cannot be dismantled for repair or overhaul. Should the steering box become damaged or excessively worn it will be necessary to obtain a factory exchange unit from a VW dealer **(see illustration)**.

6 Inspect the four rubber mounting bushes for damage or deterioration and renew as necessary. The bushes may be removed using a press or wide opening vice and a suitable mandrel and tube. The new bushes are fitted in the same way ensuring that the flat sides of the bushes are vertical with the steering box held in its fitted position. Lubricate the bushes in liquid detergent to aid refitting.

7 The removal and refitting of the rubber bellows and tie-rods are described in the following Sections.

8 Refitting the steering box is the reverse sequence to removal. Ensure that all retaining nuts and bolts are tightened to the specified torque and use new split pins in the tie-rod balljoint nuts.

Models with power steering

9 The procedure is as described above, but additionally the power steering fluid pressure and return lines must be disconnected from the pinion valve body. Be prepared for fluid spillage when doing this and plug or cap open unions to keep dirt out.

10 The power steering gear can be overhauled but this is beyond the scope of the home mechanic. Either have the overhaul carried out by a specialist or obtain a new or reconditioned unit.

11 After refitting the power steering gear, top up the fluid and bleed the system as described in "Weekly checks".

14 Steering tie-rod –
removal and refitting

1 Begin by removing the steering box from the vehicle as described in the previous Section.

2 Count the number of exposed threads on the end of the tie-rod and make a note of this figure. Now slacken the locknut securing the balljoint to the tie-rod and unscrew the balljoint, followed by the nut.

3 Release the wire clips securing the rubber bellows to the tie-rod and steering box and then slide off the bellows. New bellows should be used when reassembling unless the old ones are in perfect condition.

4 Clamp the tie-rod in a vice. Using a small punch, tap back the flange of the tie-rod inner joint at the point where it is peened into the groove in the end of the rack **(see illustration)**.

5 Using a large spanner engaged with the flats on the inner joint, unscrew the joint and tie-rod assembly from the rack.

6 Before refitting, obtain a tin of steering gear grease from a VW dealer and liberally lubricate the teeth of the rack and the tie-rod inner joint. Do not use any other type of grease in the steering box.

7 Refit the tie-rod onto the end of the rack and tighten the inner joint to the specified torque. Peen the flange of the joint into the groove in the rack to lock the assembly in place.

8 Slide the rubber bellows over the tie-rod and into position over the end of the steering box. Secure the bellows with new retaining clips, or alternatively use soft iron wire.

9 Refit the tie-rod balljoint and locknut and position them so that when the locknut is tightened against the balljoint, the same number of threads are exposed as was previously noted.

10 The steering box can now be refitted to the vehicle as described in the previous Section. After refitting it will be necessary to have the front wheel alignment checked and if necessary reset by a VW dealer (see Section 22).

15 Steering box rubber bellows
– removal and refitting

1 Begin by removing the steering box from the vehicle as described in Section 13.

2 Count the number of exposed threads on the steering tie-rod and make a note of this figure. Now slacken the locknut securing the balljoint to the tie-rod and then unscrew the balljoint, followed by the nut.

3 Release the wire clips securing the bellows to the tie-rod and steering box and then slide off the bellows.

4 Before refitting the new bellows obtain a tin of steering gear grease from a VW dealer and

14.4 The steering tie-rod inner joint flange is peened into a groove in the rack

liberally lubricate the teeth of the rack and the tie-rod inner joint. Do not use any other type of grease in the steering box.

5 Slide the new rubber bellows over the tie-rod and into position over the end of the steering box. Secure the bellows with new retaining clips or alternatively use soft iron wire.

6 Refit the tie-rod balljoint and locknut and position them so that when the locknut is tightened against the balljoint, the same number of threads are exposed as was previously noted.

7 The steering box can now be refitted to the vehicle as described in Section 13. After refitting it will be necessary to have the front wheel alignment checked and if necessary reset by a VW dealer (see Section 22).

16 Steering relay unit –
removal and refitting

1 Jack up the front of the vehicle and support it on axle stands (see "Jacking and vehicle support").

2 From inside the cab, slide up the rubber boot at the base of the steering column to expose the flexible coupling **(see illustration)**. Undo and remove the two nuts and bolts securing the two-arm flange of the relay unit to the coupling disc.

3 From underneath the front of the vehicle undo and remove the two bolts securing the relay unit lower two-arm flange to the flexible coupling disc at the forward end of the connecting shaft **(see illustration)**.

16.2 Steering column to relay unit flexible coupling

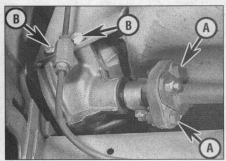

16.3 Relay unit two-arm flange to flexible coupling retaining bolts (A) and left-hand side mounting bolts (B)

16.4 Relay unit right-hand side mounting bolts (arrowed)

4 Undo and remove the four bolts securing the relay unit to its body mounting bracket **(see illustration)**. Manipulate the relay unit to clear the brackets and chassis member and remove the unit from under the vehicle.

5 The relay unit cannot be dismantled for repair or overhaul but it can be lubricated using special steering gear grease, obtainable from a VW dealer. Lubrication is only necessary if the unit exhibits tight areas or becomes stiff to turn.

6 If it is necessary to remove the two-arm flanges from the splined shafts, mark their positions before removal and refit them in the same place.

7 Refitting the relay unit is the reverse sequence to removal. Tighten all retaining nuts and bolts to the specified torque.

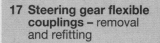
17 Steering gear flexible couplings – removal and refitting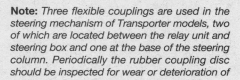

Note: *Three flexible couplings are used in the steering mechanism of Transporter models, two of which are located between the relay unit and steering box and one at the base of the steering column. Periodically the rubber coupling disc should be inspected for wear or deterioration of*

18.2 Carefully prise up the horn push and disconnect the wiring terminals to gain access to the steering wheel retaining nut

the rubber and renewed if at all suspect. The removal and refitting procedure is the same for all three couplings and is as follows.

1 Undo and remove the four nuts and bolts securing the coupling disc to each of the two-armed flanges and lift out the disc, with steel plate where fitted. (On later models the coupling at the base of the steering column may be secured by rivets instead of by nuts and bolts. In this case it will be necessary to remove the coupling and flanges together by undoing the clamp nuts and bolts.)

2 Carefully inspect the coupling disc for splits, cracks, swelling or other deformity of the rubber and renew the disc if any of these conditions are present.

3 If it is necessary to remove the two-arm flanges from their splined shafts, mark their positions on the shafts accurately first, so that they may be refitted in the same place. If this is not done the actual steering of the vehicle will not be affected, but the steering wheel spokes will no longer be horizontal when the vehicle is travelling in a straight line. This will also affect the cancelling of the turn signal indicators.

4 Refitting the steering gear flexible couplings is the reverse sequence to removal, bearing in mind the previously mentioned points. Ensure also that the retaining bolts and nuts are tightened to the specified torque.

18 Steering wheel – removal and refitting

1 Disconnect the battery earth terminal.
2 Carefully prise up the horn push cap from the centre of the steering wheel and disconnect the two wiring terminals **(see illustration)**.
3 Using a suitable socket, undo and remove the nut securing the steering wheel to the upper column.
4 Accurately mark the position of the steering wheel in relation to the upper column using a dab of quick drying paint.
5 Strike the underside of the steering wheel spokes using the palm of one hand until the wheel is released from the column. Hold the wheel with your other hand while doing this to prevent the steering wheel flying off.
6 Refitting is the reverse sequence to removal. Make sure that the previously made marks are aligned and tighten the retaining nut to the specified torque.

19 Steering column – removal and refitting

1 Disconnect the battery earth terminal.
2 Undo and remove the two screws securing the steering column upper and lower cowls to the column. Lift off the cowls, noting that an internal clip is also used to retain the lower cowl to the column **(see illustration)**.
3 Disconnect the wiring harness connectors at the ignition/starter switch and multi-function switch. Place the harnesses to one side.
4 At the base of the steering column, slide up the rubber boot to expose the flexible coupling. Undo and remove the locking collar clamp bolt and nut which secure the splined end of the lower column in the two-arm flange of the coupling.

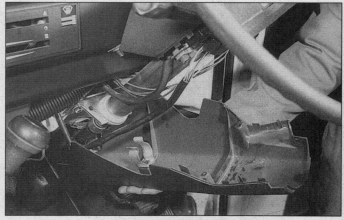

19.2 Removing the steering column cowls

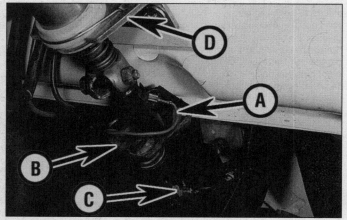

19.5 Steering column safety coupling and lower mounting

A   *Earth lead*
B   *Safety coupling*
C   *Lower column*

D   *Column tube lower mounting bracket*

5 Now disconnect the earth lead that connects the two components of the safety coupling **(see illustration)**.

6 Slide the lower column upwards to disengage its lower end from the flexible coupling and its upper end from the safety coupling. Place the lower column to one side.

7 Centre-punch the heads of the two shear bolts that secure the upper column to the facia. Drill a hole in the centre of each bolt and remove them using a stud extractor. Alternatively, file a slot in their exposed shanks and try unscrewing them with a screwdriver. It may even be possible to free them using a pair of self-locking grips. It will be necessary to use new shear bolts when refitting.

8 Release the wire retaining clip securing the plastic ring to the lower mounting bracket and lift the column assembly away **(see illustration)**.

9 Refitting the steering column is the reverse sequence to removal, bearing in mind the following points:

a) *When refitting the lower column ensure that the roadwheels are in the straight-ahead position, with the steering wheel spokes horizontal, before engaging the lower column with the flexible coupling flange*

b) *Ensure that a gap of 2 to 4 mm (0.08 to 0.16 in) exists between the steering wheel and multi-function switch before tightening the shear bolts. Ensure that the prongs of the lower column flange are fully seated in the safety coupling when taking this measurement*

c) *After setting the steering wheel clearance as described above, tighten the shear bolts until the heads break off*

d) *Tighten all remaining nuts and bolts to the specified torque where applicable*

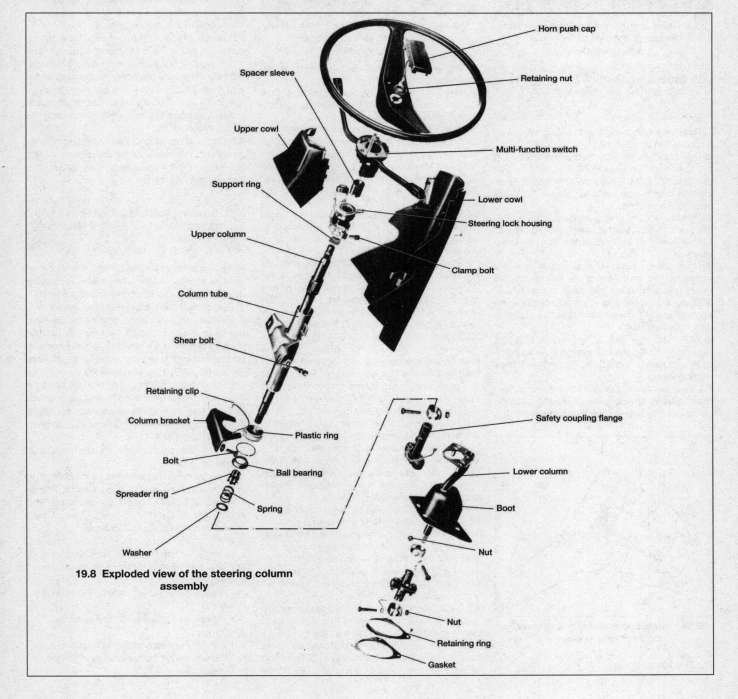

19.8 Exploded view of the steering column assembly

20.6 Using a universal balljoint separator to clamp the two parts of the safety coupling

20 Steering column – dismantling and reassembly

1 Begin by removing the steering wheel as described in Section 18.
2 Undo and remove the two screws securing the upper and lower steering column cowls to the column. Lift off the cowls, noting that an internal clip is also used to secure the lower cowl to the column.
3 Disconnect the wiring harness connectors at the ignition/starter switch and multi-function switch and place the harnesses to one side.
4 Undo and remove the three screws securing the multi-function switch to the steering lock housing and lift off the switch.
5 Using a suitable key undo and remove the socket-headed pinch-bolt from the steering lock housing clamp.
6 With the aid of a universal balljoint separator, clamp the two parts of the steering column safety coupling together **(see illustration)**.
7 Using a conventional two-legged puller, draw off the steering lock housing and the upper column sleeve **(see illustration)**.

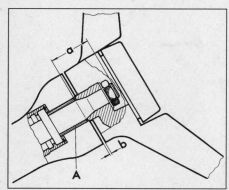

20.18 Correct positioning of the steering column spacer sleeve

A Sleeve
a = 41.5 mm (1.63 in)
b = 2 to 4 mm
(0.8 to 0.16 in)

20.7 Removing the steering lock housing and column sleeve using a two-legged puller

8 Remove the balljoint separator from the safety coupling.
9 Refer to Section 19, paragraphs 4 to 8 inclusive, and remove the steering column assembly from the vehicle.
10 With the column assembly on the bench, undo and remove the locking collar clamp bolt that secures the safety coupling two-arm flange to the upper column. Mark the position of the flange on the column using a dab of quick-drying paint and then slide off the flange.
11 Withdraw the washer, spring, spreader ring and bearing from the end of the upper column. Now slide the upper column out of the top of the column tube.
12 Check the upper column and column tube for straightness by rolling them along a flat surface. Also check for roughness of the support bearings in the steering lock housing and at the base of the column tube. Renew any defective components as necessary.
13 Begin reassembly by inserting the upper column into the column tube. Refit the bearing, spreader ring, spring and washer followed by the two-arm flange. Ensure that the previously made marks on the flange and column are aligned and then secure the flange with the locking collar and clamp bolt.
14 Place the steering column in position in the vehicle and secure the plastic ring at the base of the column to the lower mounting using the wire retaining clip. Now attach the upper mounting to the facia using two new shear bolts. Tighten the shear bolts finger-tight only at this stage.
15 Set the roadwheels to the straight-ahead position and then refit the lower column. Tighten the locking collar clamp bolt on the flexible coupling to the specified torque and then refit the rubber boot and earth lead.
16 Using the balljoint separator, clamp the two parts of the safety coupling together as was done during dismantling.
17 Slide the steering lock housing over the top of the column, ensuring that the support ring is in place beneath the bearing.
18 Fit the spacer sleeve with the notched side toward the lock housing and tap it on using a tube of suitable diameter. The sleeve

must be positioned so that its edge is 41.5 mm (1.63 in) from the end of the upper column **(see illustration)**. Now refit and tighten the lock housing pinch-bolt.
19 Refit the multi-function switch assembly and secure it to the lock housing using the three screws.
20 Reconnect the wiring harness connectors to the multi-function switch and ignition switch.
21 Refit the steering wheel with the spokes horizontal and secure with the retaining nut, tightened to the specified torque. Reconnect the horn push cap wires and refit the cap to the centre of the steering wheel.
22 Move the steering column tube up or down slightly, within the limits of the elongated holes in the mounting brackets, until the clearance between the steering wheel and multi-function switch is between 2 and 4 mm (0.08 and 0.16 in). When the clearance is correct, tighten the two shear bolts until the heads break off.
23 Refit the upper and lower steering column cowls and then remove the balljoint separator from the safety coupling. Reconnect the battery earth terminal.

21 Power-assisted steering pump – removal and refitting

Note: *Depending on equipment fitted, it may be necessary to remove other accessory drivebelt(s) for access to the steering pump.*
1 Disconnect the battery negative lead.
2 Slacken the bolts which secure the steering pump to the mounting brackets. Swing the pump towards the engine to release tension on the drivebelt and remove the drivebelt from the pump pulley **(see illustration)**.
3 Clean around the fluid union banjo bolts on the pump. Remove the bolts and recover the copper washers. Be prepared for fluid spillage. Cover the open banjo unions to keep fluid in and dirt out.
4 Unbolt the pump from its brackets and remove it.
5 If the pump is suspected of being defective, professional advice should be sought. Repair kits are available, but high-pressure test equipment is needed to verify the correct operation of the pump afterwards.
6 Refitting is a reversal of the removal procedure, noting the following points:
 a) *Use new copper washers on the banjo unions*
 b) *Adjust the drivebelt tension (see Chapter 1)*
 c) *Tighten all fastenings to the specified torque*
 d) *Top up the power steering fluid and bleed the system on completion (see "Weekly checks")*

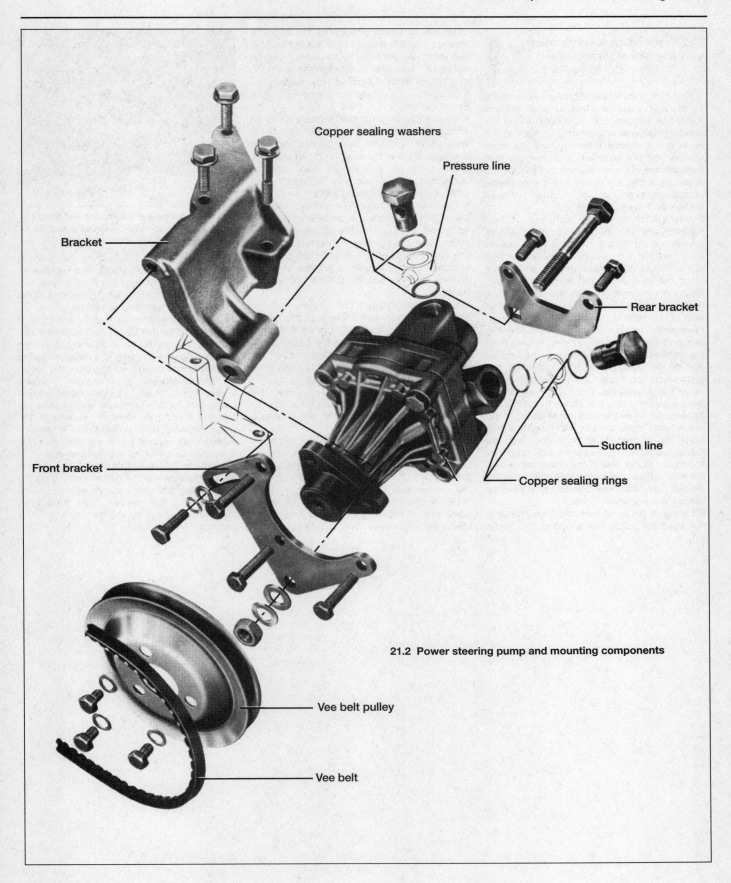

Copper sealing washers

Pressure line

Bracket

Rear bracket

Front bracket

Suction line

Copper sealing rings

21.2 Power steering pump and mounting components

Vee belt pulley

Vee belt

22 Front suspension geometry and wheel alignment – checking and adjustment

1 Accurate front wheel alignment is essential to provide positive steering and prevent excessive tyre wear. Before considering the steering/suspension geometry, check that the tyres are correctly inflated, that the front wheels are not buckled, and that the hub bearings are not worn or incorrectly adjusted. Also check that the steering and suspension components are in good order, without slackness or wear at the joints.

2 Suspension geometry consists of four factors: *Camber* is the angle at which the front wheels are set from the vertical when viewed from the front of the vehicle. 'Positive camber' is the amount (in degrees) that the wheels are tilted outward at the top from the vertical. *Castor* is the angle between the steering axis and a vertical line when viewed from each side of the vehicle. 'Positive castor' is when the steering axis is inclined rearward. *Steering axis inclination* is the angle (when viewed from the front of the vehicle) between the vertical and an imaginary line drawn through the centres of the upper wishbone and track control arm balljoints. *Front wheel alignment (or toe setting)* is the amount by which the distance between the front inside edges of the roadwheels (measured at hub height) differs from the diametrically opposite distance measured between the rear inside edges of the front roadwheels. If the measurement at the front edges is less than that at the rear the wheels are said to toe-in; the reverse condition is known as toe-out.

3 Owing to the need for special gauges, it is not normally within the scope of the home mechanic to check and adjust any of these settings with the exception of the front wheel alignment. Where suitable equipment can be obtained, however, adjustments can be carried out in the following way, setting the tolerances to those given in the Specifications.

4 Before carrying out any measurements or adjustments, position the unladen vehicle on level ground, tyres correctly inflated and front roadwheels set in the straight-ahead position. Make sure all suspension and steering components are securely attached and without wear in the moving parts.

5 *Camber adjustment:* The camber angle is adjusted by altering the position of the two eccentric washers on the upper wishbone inner mounting spindle. To do this, slacken the spindle retaining nut and then turn the spindle with a spanner or socket until the correct angle is obtained. Now tighten the retaining nut.

6 *Castor adjustment:* The castor angle is adjusted by altering the length of the radius rod by means of the two nuts on the body mounting bracket. Note that the castor angle also influences the camber and front wheel alignment and these must be checked after making any alteration to the castor.

7 *Front wheel alignment:* To check the alignment a simple gauge can be made up from a length of tubing or bar and having a bolt and locknut at one end.

8 Use this gauge to measure the distance between the two inner wheel rims at hub height and at the front of the roadwheels.

9 Push or pull the vehicle forward to rotate the roadwheels by 180° (half a turn) then measure the distance between the inner wheel rims at hub height, but this time at the rear of the roadwheels. This last measurement

22.11 Front wheel alignment adjusted by turning both tie-rods by equal amounts in the desired direction

should differ from the first by the amount stated in the Specifications and represents the correct toe setting of the front wheels.

10 Where the front wheel alignment is found to be incorrect, proceed as follows.

11 Slacken the locknuts that secure each of the steering tie-rod balljoints to the tie-rods. Turn each tie-rod by equal amounts, not more than one quarter of a turn at a time, clockwise (viewed from the side) to decrease the toe-in or anti-clockwise to increase it **(see illustration)**. Push or pull the vehicle backwards for one complete revolution of the roadwheel and then move it forwards by the same amount. Now recheck the alignment setting as described previously and continue this procedure until the setting is correct.

12 Tighten the tie-rod balljoint locknuts and then make sure that the rubber bellows on the steering box have not become twisted due to movement of the tie-rods. If so, straighten them, otherwise they will be damaged in a very short time.

Chapter 10
Braking system

Contents

Degrees of difficulty

Easy, suitable for novice with little experience	**Fairly easy,** suitable for beginner with some experience	**Fairly difficult,** suitable for competent DIY mechanic	**Difficult,** suitable for experienced DIY mechanic	**Very difficult,** suitable for expert DIY or professional

Specifications

System type .... Dual-circuit hydraulic, servo-assisted, with discs at the front and drums at the rear. Brake pressure regulator in rear hydraulic circuit. Cable operated handbrake.

Front brakes

Type .... Disc with Girling or Teves calipers
Disc diameter:
  Models with fixed caliper .... 278.0 mm (10.95 in)
  Models with sliding caliper .... 258.0 mm (10.16 in)
Disc thickness (new):
  Models with fixed caliper .... 13.0 mm (0.512 in)
  Models with sliding caliper .... 15.0 mm (0.591 in)
Minimum disc thickness after machining:
  Models with fixed caliper .... 11.0 mm (0.433 in)
  Models with sliding caliper .... 13.0 mm (0.512 in)
Caliper piston diameter:
  Models with fixed caliper .... 54.0 mm (2.127 in)
  Models with sliding caliper .... 60.0 mm (2.362 in)
Minimum brake pad lining thickness (all models) .... 2.0 mm (0.08 in)

Rear brakes

Type .... Single leading shoe drum
Drum internal diameter .... 252.0 mm (9.92 in)
Maximum drum internal diameter after machining .... 253.5 mm (10.0 in)
Wheel cylinder piston diameter .... 23.81 mm (0.938 in)
Brake shoe lining thickness:
  Standard .... 6.0 mm (0.24 in)
  Oversize .... 6.5 mm (0.26 in)
Minimum brake shoe lining thickness .... 2.5 mm (0.10 in)

Master cylinder

Type .... Teves or Bendix tandem
Bore diameter .... 23.81 mm (0.938 in)

Vacuum servo unit

Type . . . . 228.6 mm (9.0 in) single diaphragm
Boost factor 2.4
Pushrod length . . . . 111.5 mm (4.393 in)

Torque wrench settings

	Nm	lbf ft
Brake caliper to steering knuckle:		
Fixed caliper	160	118
Sliding caliper	270	199
Sliding caliper guide pin bolts	35	26
Wheel cylinder to backplate	20	15
Brake shoe lower support to backplate	65	48
Master cylinder to pedal bracket or servo	15	11
Servo to pedal bracket	15	11
Roadwheel retaining nuts and bolts	170	125
ABS speed sensors	10	7

1 General description

The braking system is of the dual-circuit hydraulic type with disc brakes at the front and drum brakes at the rear. The system is servo-assisted. The dual-circuit layout is split on a front-to-rear basis whereby the primary hydraulic circuit operates the front brakes and the secondary circuit operates the rear brakes, from a tandem master cylinder. Under normal conditions both circuits operate in unison; however, in the event of hydraulic failure in one circuit, full braking force will still be available at two wheels. A brake pressure regulator is incorporated in the rear brake hydraulic circuit. This device regulates the pressure applied to each rear brake and reduces the possibility of the rear wheels locking under heavy braking.

The front disc brakes are operated either by twin-piston fixed brake calipers or (on some later models) by single-piston sliding calipers.

At the rear, leading and trailing brake shoes are operated by twin-piston wheel cylinders and are self-adjusted by footbrake application.

An anti-lock braking system (ABS) is available as an optional extra on some models. This system is described in Section 25.

The cable-operated handbrake provides an independent mechanical means of rear brake application.

Note: *When servicing any part of the braking system, work carefully and methodically; also observe scrupulous cleanliness when working on the hydraulic system. Always renew components (in axle sets if applicable) if in doubt about their condition. Use only good quality replacement parts - either genuine VW parts or parts from a reputable source. Note the warnings given in 'Safety First' at the beginning of the manual and at relevant points in this Chapter concerning the dangers of asbestos dust and hydraulic fluid.*

2 Front brake pads – inspection and renewal

⚠️ **Warning: The dust created by brake lining wear may contain asbestos, which is a health hazard. Never blow it out with compressed air, and take care not to inhale or swallow it. An approved filtering mask should be worn when working on the braking system. Do not use petroleum-based solvents to clean brake parts; use brake cleaner or methylated spirit only.**

⚠️ **Warning: Hydraulic fluid is poisonous; wash off immediately and thoroughly in case of skin contact, and seek immediate medical advice if fluid is swallowed or gets into the eyes. Certain types of hydraulic fluid are flammable; take the same precautions**

as if handling petrol. Hydraulic fluid is also an effective paint stripper and will attack plastics; wash off spillages at once using copious quantities of fresh water. Finally, the fluid is hygroscopic (it absorbs moisture from the air) - old fluid may be contaminated and unfit for further use. When topping-up or renewing the fluid, ensure that it comes from a freshly-opened sealed container.

1 Jack up the front of the vehicle and support it on axle stands (see *"Jacking and vehicle support"*). Remove both front road wheels.

Models with twin-piston fixed calipers

2 Either Girling or Teves brake calipers are fitted. Both types are similar in construction, the main differences being the type of brake pad retaining pins used to secure the pads in position in the brake caliper.
3 On models fitted with Teves calipers, the retaining pins are removed by tapping them inwards towards the car, using a thin punch **(see illustration)**. To remove the retaining pins on Girling calipers, withdraw the spring clips and tap the pins outwards, away from the car, using a thin punch.
4 With the retaining pins removed, lift off the spreader spring plate and then withdraw the brake pads one at a time from the caliper. If they are initially tight, use a screwdriver inserted in the slot on the brake pad and lever against the edge of the caliper. Lift out the anti-rattle shims, if not already removed with the pads **(see illustrations)**.

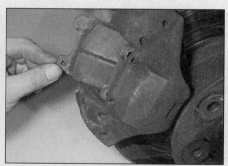
2.4A Withdraw the brake pad . . .

2.4B . . . and the anti-rattle shim

2.3 Driving out a retaining pin - Teves caliper

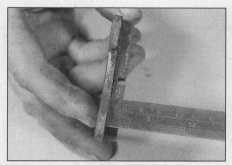

2.5 Measuring the thickness of the friction material on a brake pad

2.8 Retract the caliper pistons using a flat bar as a lever

2.9A Fit the brake pads . . .

2.9B . . . and anti-rattle shims

2.9C On Teves calipers the notches in the anti-rattle shims engage with the recesses (arrowed) in the pistons

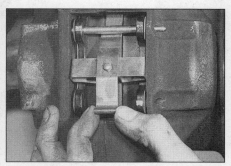

2.10A Refit the spreader spring plate . . .

5 Inspect the thickness of the brake pad friction material **(see illustration)**. If the thickness of the brake pad friction material is less than specified, the pads must be renewed. The pads must also be renewed if there is any sign of oil or brake fluid contamination of the friction material, or if any heavy scoring or cracking is visible on the pad face.

6 When renewing the brake pads, they should always be renewed as a complete set (4 pads); uneven braking or pulling to one side may otherwise occur.

7 With the pads removed, carefully inspect the surface of the brake disc. Concentric scores up to 0.4 mm (0.015 in) are acceptable; however, if deeper scores are found, the brake disc must either be skimmed or preferably renewed (see Section 5).

8 To refit the pads, first ensure that the brake caliper pistons and pad seating areas are clean and free from dust and corrosion. Using a flat bar as a lever, gently push the caliper pistons back into their cylinders as far as they will go **(see illustration)**. This operation will cause a quantity of brake fluid to be returned to the master cylinder via the hydraulic pipes. Place absorbent rags around the master cylinder reservoir to collect any fluid that may overflow, or preferably, drain off a small quantity of fluid from the reservoir before retracting the caliper pistons.

9 Fit the new brake pads and anti-rattle shims into their locations in the caliper. On Teves calipers the notches on the anti-rattle shims engage the recesses in the piston **(see illustrations)**. On Girling calipers the arrows on the anti-rattle shims point upward.

10 Place the spreader spring plate in position and refit the retaining pins, and spring clips, where fitted **(see illustrations)**.

Models with single-piston sliding calipers

11 Remove the lower guide pin bolt, holding the guide pin with a spanner to stop it turning **(see illustration)**. A new bolt will be needed for reassembly.

12 Swing the caliper upwards and remove the pads **(see illustration)**.

13 Inspect the brake disc for wear or damage - see paragraph 7.

14 Inspect the caliper and caliper bracket for signs of hydraulic fluid leaks, corrosion or other damage. If the guide pins or their protective sleeves are damaged, renew the caliper bracket. Uneven brake pad wear may be caused by the caliper failing to slide on the bracket.

15 Push the caliper piston back into its bore using a flat bar. Be prepared for the fluid level in the master cylinder to rise - see paragraph 8.

2.10B . . . followed by the retaining pins (arrowed)

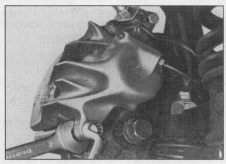

2.11 Removing the lower guide pin bolt - Girling sliding caliper

2.12 Swing the caliper upwards and remove the pads

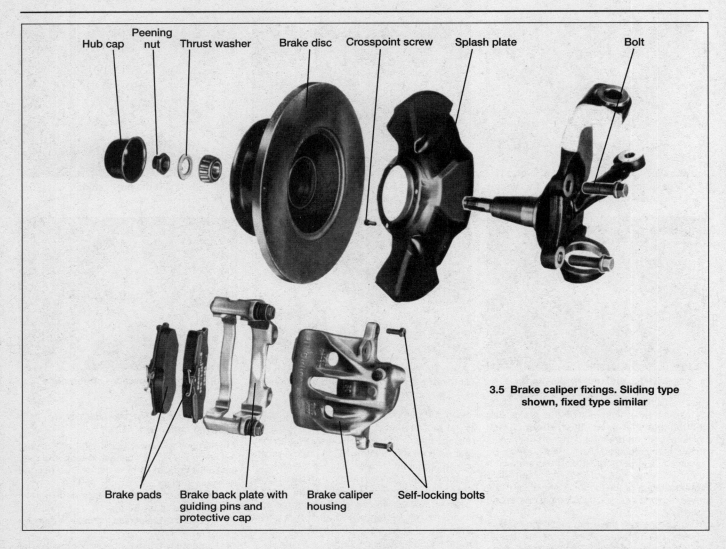

Hub cap   Peening nut   Thrust washer   Brake disc   Crosspoint screw   Splash plate   Bolt

Brake pads   Brake back plate with guiding pins and protective cap   Brake caliper housing   Self-locking bolts

3.5 Brake caliper fixings. Sliding type shown, fixed type similar

16 Fit the new pads to their locations in the caliper bracket, friction side towards the disc.
17 Swing the caliper downwards over the pads. Fit the new lower guide pin bolt and tighten it to the specified torque, holding the guide pin with a spanner to stop it turning.

All models

18 With the brake pads correctly fitted, fully

3.6 Removing the brake caliper from the steering knuckle and disc

depress the brake pedal several times to bring the caliper pistons into contact with the brake pads.
19 Check the brake fluid level in the master cylinder reservoir and top up as necessary (see "Weekly checks").
20 Refit the roadwheels and lower the car to the ground.
Caution: New brake pads should be bedded in slowly over a period of approximately 120 miles (200 km). During this time, avoid unnecessary panic stops or prolonged heavy brake applications.

3 Front brake caliper – removal and refitting

Note: Refer to the warnings at the beginning of Section 2 before starting work.
1 Jack up the front of the vehicle and support it on axle stands (see "Jacking and vehicle support"). Remove the appropriate front roadwheel.

2 Remove the brake pads as described in Section 2 and mark them on their backing plates so that they can be refitted in their original positions. Store the pads face up to avoid contamination of the friction material.
3 Using a brake hose clamp or self-locking wrench with protected jaws, clamp the flexible brake hydraulic hose. This will prevent loss of brake fluid during subsequent operations.
4 Wipe clean the area around the brake pipe or flexible hose to caliper union nut, unscrew the nut and carefully withdraw the pipe from the caliper. Plug the pipe and caliper to prevent dirt entry.
5 Undo and remove the two bolts securing the caliper to the steering knuckle, noting that on fixed calipers the upper bolt is a shouldered type and that on some calipers a shim is fitted between the caliper and steering knuckle at the upper bolt location **(see illustration)**.
6 With the bolts removed, withdraw the caliper from the steering knuckle and disc **(see illustration)**.

7 Refitting is the reverse sequence to removal, bearing in mind the following points:

a) *Tighten the caliper retaining bolts to the specified torque*
b) *Refit the brake pads as described in Section 2*
c) *Bleed the hydraulic system as described in Section 15. If precautions described to prevent brake fluid loss were taken, it should only be necessary to bleed the caliper being worked on*

4 Front brake caliper – overhaul

1 Remove the caliper as described in the previous Section.

Models with twin-piston fixed calipers

2 Using a screwdriver, extract the rubber dust cover around the caliper pistons. If working on the Girling caliper, first remove the dust cover retaining ring **(see illustrations)**.
3 Place a thin flat block of wood over one piston and hold the block and piston in place, using a small G-clamp.
4 The unclamped piston may now be forced out of the caliper, using a compressed air jet or the nozzle of a car foot pump held firmly against the brake pipe union.

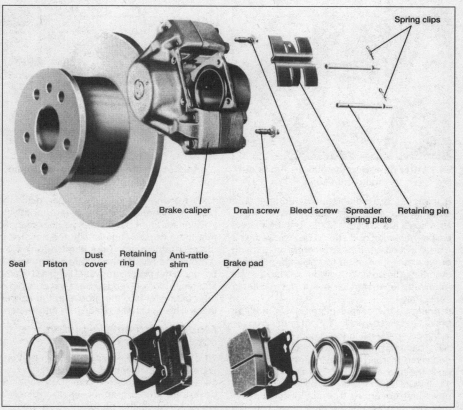

4.2A Exploded view of the Girling twin-piston front brake caliper

Caution: Be careful! The piston may be ejected with some force.
5 With the first piston removed, use a block of wood and the G-clamp to seal off the cylinder opening on the caliper, and repeat the above procedure to remove the remaining piston.
6 Thoroughly clean the caliper and pistons, using clean brake fluid or methylated spirit. *Under no circumstances should the two halves of the caliper be separated.*
7 With all components thoroughly cleaned, the two piston seals can be removed using a thin blunt instrument such as a plastic knitting needle **(see illustration)**.

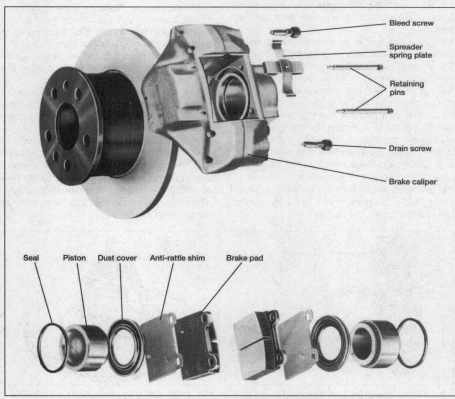

4.2B Exploded view of the Teves twin-piston front brake caliper

4.2C Extract the caliper piston dust cover with a screwdriver

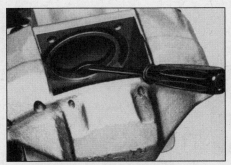

4.7 After removing the pistons, hook out the piston seals

8 Inspect the dismantled components carefully for corrosion, scratches or wear. New seals are available in the form of a brake caliper repair kit, and should be renewed as a matter of course. If severe corrosion, scoring or wear is apparent on the pistons or caliper cylinders, the complete caliper will have to be renewed, as these parts are not available separately.

9 Immerse the caliper piston seals in clean brake fluid and carefully fit them to the grooves in the cylinders, using the fingers only.

10 Coat the pistons with clean brake fluid and insert them in their cylinder bores. Do not push the pistons fully home at this stage.

11 If working on the Girling caliper, locate the new dust covers in the piston and caliper grooves then secure the dust cover with the retaining ring (see illustration). The pistons should now be pushed fully into their bores.

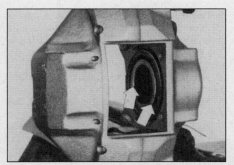

4.12 Use the brake pad anti-rattle shims to position the piston recesses (arrowed) correctly – Teves caliper

4.11 Locate the new dust covers in the piston grooves

12 If working on the Teves caliper, place the brake pad anti-rattle shims temporarily in position and turn the pistons as necessary so that the recesses engage with the notches in the anti-rattle shims (see illustration). Now remove the shims and locate the new dust covers in the piston grooves. Using a G-clamp and small block of wood, press the outer lip of the dust cover into the groove in the caliper, this will also push the piston fully into its bore.

Models with single-piston sliding calipers

13 Remove the remaining guide pin bolt and separate the caliper from its bracket.

14 Remove the piston from the caliper as described in paragraph 4, using a block of wood to catch the piston as it is ejected. Remove the dust seal.

15 Remove the piston seal from the caliper bore, using a blunt object such as a knitting needle.

16 Clean the caliper and piston, using clean brake fluid, brake cleaner or methylated spirit.

17 Inspect the caliper and piston for corrosion, scoring or other damage. Renew the caliper if damage is evident; otherwise, obtain new seals for use when reassembling.

18 Clean and inspect the caliper bracket, paying particular attention to the guide pins and their protective sleeves. Renew the bracket if damage is evident. The new bracket is supplied with the correct quantity of grease already applied to the guide pins.

19 Immerse the caliper piston seal in clean brake fluid and carefully fit it to the groove in the cylinder, using the fingers only.

20 Fit the new dust seal to the piston (see illustration). Coat the piston with clean brake fluid.

21 Fit the lip of the dust seal into its groove in the cylinder, then push the piston into the bore (see illustration).

22 Refit the caliper to the bracket and secure it with a new upper guide pin bolt, tightened to the specified torque.

All models

23 The caliper may now be refitted as described in Section 3.

5   Front brake disc –
inspection, removal and refitting

Note: The disc is an integral part of the front hub assembly and is removed complete with wheel bearings as described in Chapter 9. With the assembly removed from the stub axle a detailed inspection can be carried out as follows.

1 Carefully inspect the surface of the disc. Concentric scores up to 0.4 mm (0.015 in) deep are acceptable. Small surface cracks and some discolouration due to localised surface heating are to be expected. However, if the disc is severely grooved, it must be skimmed until flat or preferably renewed. If the disc is to be skimmed an equal amount of metal must be removed from both sides and the disc thickness must not be reduced below the specified minimum. Note: In order to maintain uniform braking, both front discs must exhibit the same surface characteristics with respect to depth of grooving and surface finish. For this reason any machining should be carried out on both discs and if renewal is necessary the discs should be renewed in pairs.

2 If the discs are in a satisfactory condition, remove any surface corrosion by tapping the circumference of the disc lightly with a small hammer.

3 On models with ABS, it will be necessary to transfer the trigger wheel if a new disc is to be fitted. Pull the wheel off the old disc using a three-legged puller and press it on to the new disc until it contacts the stop (see illustration).

4 Refitting the disc and hub assembly is described in Chapter 9.

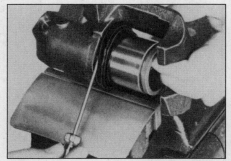

4.20 Dust seal correctly fitted to piston - Girling sliding caliper

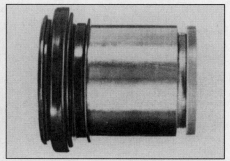

4.21 Fitting the dust seal lip into the groove in the cylinder - Girling sliding caliper

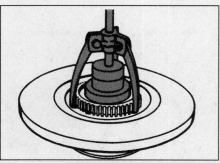

5.3 Pulling the trigger wheel off a brake disc - models with ABS

6 Rear brake shoes and drum – inspection and renewal

Note: *Two inspection holes are provided on each rear brake backplate and after removal of the plugs the lining thicknesses can be observed through the holes. This must be regarded purely as a quick check as only one part of the brake shoe can be viewed and it is not possible to inspect the lining condition, only its thickness. To carry out a thorough inspection the brake drum must be removed as follows. Refer to the warnings at the beginning of Section 2 before starting work.*

1 Jack up the rear of the car and support it on axle stands (see *"Jacking and vehicle support"*). Remove both rear roadwheels, then release the handbrake.

2 Undo the two small bolts securing the brake drum to the rear wheel hub and withdraw the drum. Tap the circumference of the drum with a hide or plastic mallet if it is tight. If the drum cannot be removed due to it binding on the brake shoes, slacken off the brake shoe adjuster as follows.

3 Extract the plug from the rear of the brake backplate, just below the wheel cylinder. Insert a cranked screwdriver or other suitable tool through the hole in the backplate and engage it with the serrated adjuster wheel. When viewed from the rear of the vehicle the adjuster wheel on the left-hand brake assembly should be turned anti-clockwise to slacken off the brake shoes. The adjuster wheel on the right-hand brake assembly should be turned clockwise.

4 With the adjusters slackened, it should now be possible to remove the drum as described in paragraph 2. If, however, the drum is still binding on the brake shoes, slacken the handbrake cable by unscrewing the adjusting nut at the cable equalizer (see Section 17). Now remove the drum as described in paragraph 2.

5 With the drum removed, wipe the dust from the drum, brake shoes, wheel cylinder and backplate using a damp cloth. *Take great care not to inhale the dust as it is injurious to health.* Seal the cloth in a plastic bag for disposal.

6 Measure the brake shoe lining thickness. If the thickness of any of the linings is less than the specified minimum, all four shoes must be renewed. The shoes must also be renewed if any are contaminated with brake fluid or grease, or show signs of cracking, glazing or deep scoring. If contamination is evident the cause must be traced and rectified before fitting new brake shoes.

7 Also examine the internal braking surface of the brake drum for scoring or cracks. The drums may be skimmed to remove minor surface irregularities providing the maximum specified internal diameter is not exceeded. If the drum is severely scored, renewal is

necessary. If the drum can be salvaged by skimming, it will be necessary to fit brake shoes with oversize linings. These are thicker than standard to compensate for the increased internal diameter of the drum.

8 If the brake shoes are in a satisfactory condition proceed to paragraph 26; if removal is necessary, proceed as follows.

9 First make a careful note of the location and fitted direction of the various springs and linkages as an aid to refitting **(see illustration)**.

10 Using pliers, release the operating spring from the adjusting lever on the leading brake shoe **(see illustration)**.

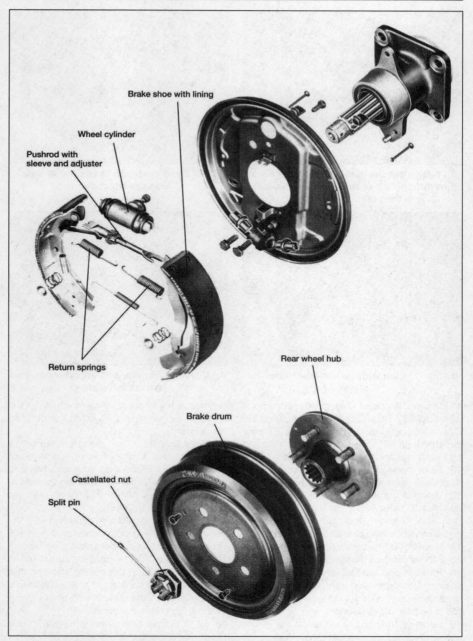

Brake shoe with lining

Wheel cylinder

Pushrod with sleeve and adjuster

Return springs

Rear wheel hub

Brake drum

Castellated nut

Split pin

6.9 Exploded view of the rear brake assembly and related components

6.10 Release the operating spring from the adjusting lever

6.11 Depress the steady spring cups and turn through 90° to remove, while holding the pin from behind

6.12 Ease the brake shoes out of their lower pivot locations

6.13A Rotate the serrated adjuster wheel so that the self-adjust mechanism is fully retracted . . .

6.13B . . . then withdraw the self-adjuster sleeve

6.14 Now lift out the self-adjuster pushrod and adjuster wheel

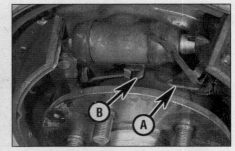

6.15A Release the leading shoe upper return spring (A) from the lug on the backplate (B)

11 Depress the brake shoe steady spring cups whilst holding the steady spring pins, from the rear of the backplate, with your finger. Turn the cups through 90° then remove them, followed by the springs and pins (see illustration).

12 Ease the leading and trailing shoes from their lower pivot locations (see illustration).

13 Using a screwdriver, back off fully the serrated adjuster wheel, lift the upper part of the leading shoe and withdraw the self-adjuster sleeve (see illustrations).

14 Now lift out the self-adjuster pushrod and adjuster wheel (see illustration).

15 Release the leading shoe upper return spring from the lug on the backplate, disengage the lower return spring and lift off the shoe (see illustrations).

16 Release the trailing shoe upper return spring from the lug on the backplate,

disengage the handbrake cable end from the brake shoe lever, and lift off the shoe (see illustration).

17 Prior to installation, clean off the brake backplate with a rag, and apply a trace of silicone grease to the shoe contact areas and pivots (see illustration), and to the threads of the self-adjuster pushrod. Ensure that the serrated wheel turns easily.

18 Engage the handbrake cable end with the lever on the trailing brake shoe and hold the shoe in position on the backplate.

19 Locate the coiled end of the upper return spring in the hole in the trailing shoe so that the spring coil is behind the brake shoe web. Using pliers, pull the straight end of the spring over the lug on the backplate.

20 Fit the lower return spring to both brake shoes ensuring that the spring is positioned

behind the brake shoe webs.

21 Fit the upper return spring to the leading brake shoe using the same procedure as for the trailing shoe.

22 With the adjuster wheel wound down to the end of the thread on the adjuster pushrod, locate the forked end of the pushrod against the trailing shoe and handbrake lever. The longer projection on the fork must face the backplate.

23 Ease the leading shoe out at the top and slip the self-adjuster sleeve over the pushrod, then engage its forked end with the adjusting lever.

24 Refit the steady spring pins through the holes in the backplate and brake shoes. Hold the pins, refit the steady springs and cups then turn the cups through 90° to lock them on the pins.

6.15B Disengage the lower return spring and lift off the shoe

6.16 Release the trailing shoe return springs, disengage the handbrake cable and lift off the shoe

6.17 Apply a trace of silicone grease to the brake shoe contact areas (arrowed) before refitting the shoes

25 Refit the operating spring to the adjusting lever and leading shoe with the straight end towards the adjusting lever.

26 Before refitting the brake drum it is necessary to provide an initial, manual adjustment of the brake shoes. To do this measure the internal diameter of the brake drum and then subtract 1.5 mm (0.06 in) from this dimension. The result is the dimension to which the brake shoes must be set before refitting the drum. Centralise the shoes on the backplate then turn the serrated adjuster wheel as necessary until the correct setting is obtained **(see illustration)**.

27 Refit the brake drum to the wheel hub and secure the drum with the two retaining bolts.

28 Depress the footbrake several times to operate the self-adjusting mechanism then refit the access plugs to the backplate.

29 If it was necessary to slacken the handbrake cable to remove the drum, adjust the cable as described in Section 17.

30 Finally, refit the roadwheel and lower the vehicle to the ground.

7 Rear wheel cylinder – removal and refitting

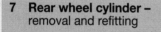

Note: *Refer to the warnings at the beginning of Section 2 before starting work.*

1 Begin by removing the appropriate rear brake drum as described in Section 6, paragraphs 1 to 4.

2 Using a brake hose clamp or self-locking wrench with protected jaws, clamp the flexible hydraulic brake hose located at the front of the rear suspension trailing arm. This will minimise loss of brake fluid during subsequent operations.

3 Wipe clean the area around the brake backplate and wheel cylinder. Unscrew the brake hydraulic pipe union at the rear of the wheel cylinder and carefully ease out the pipe. Plug or tape over the pipe end to prevent dirt entry.

4 Undo and remove the bleed screw at the rear of the wheel cylinder and the single bolt securing the cylinder to the backplate.

5 Apply the handbrake fully to move the brake shoes away from their locations in the wheel cylinder pistons. If necessary ease the shoes away further, using a screwdriver as a lever, and then withdraw the cylinder from the backplate.

6 To refit the wheel cylinder, place it in position on the backplate and engage the brake pipe and union. Screw in the union nut two or three turns to ensure the thread has started.

7 Refit the wheel cylinder retaining bolt and the bleed screw then fully tighten the bolt, bleed screw and brake pipe union nut.

8 Release the handbrake and engage the brake shoes with the wheel cylinder pistons.

9 Refit the brake drum as described in Section 6, paragraphs 26 to 27.

6.26 Set the brake shoes so that dimension 'a' equals the internal diameter of the drum less 1.5 mm (0.06 in) before refitting the drum

10 Remove the brake hose clamp. Bleed the hydraulic system as described in Section 15. If the precautions described were taken to prevent brake fluid loss, it should only be necessary to bleed the brake being worked on.

11 Refit the roadwheel and lower the vehicle to the ground.

8 Rear wheel cylinder – overhaul

Note: *Refer to the warnings at the beginning of Section 2 before starting work.*

1 Remove the wheel cylinder as described in the previous Section.

2 With the cylinder on the bench, withdraw the dust covers from the ends of the pistons and cylinder body.

3 Withdraw the pistons and piston spring, then remove the rubber seals from the pistons **(see illustration)**.

4 Thoroughly clean all the components in methylated spirits or clean brake fluid, and dry with a lint free rag.

5 Carefully examine the surfaces of the pistons and cylinder bore for wear, score marks or corrosion and, if evident, renew the complete wheel cylinder. If the components are in a satisfactory condition, obtain a repair kit consisting of new seals and dust covers.

6 Dip the new seals and pistons in clean brake fluid and assemble the components wet, as follows.

7 Using your fingers, fit the new seals to the pistons with their sealing lips facing inwards.

8 Lubricate the cylinder bore with clean brake fluid and insert one of the pistons, followed by the spring then the second piston.

9 Place the dust covers over the pistons and cylinder edges then refit the assembled wheel cylinder to the vehicle as described in the previous Section.

9 Rear brake backplate – removal and refitting

Note: *Refer to the warnings at the beginning of Section 2 before starting work.*

1 The backplate is removed in conjunction with the rear wheel bearing housing and details of this procedure will be found in Chapter 8.

10 Master cylinder – removal and refitting

Note: *Refer to the warnings at the beginning of Section 2 before starting work.*

1 To gain access to the master cylinder, refer to Chapter 12 and remove the instrument panel.

2 Remove the master cylinder filler cap and draw off as much brake fluid as possible from the reservoir using a clean syringe.

3 Place some absorbent rags beneath the master cylinder to catch any fluid that may drip out after the pipe unions are undone.

4 Unscrew the two brake pipe union nuts **(see illustration)**, and carefully withdraw the pipes from the master cylinder. Immediately plug or tape over the pipe ends and cylinder orifices to prevent further loss of fluid and dirt entry.

5 Using a screwdriver if necessary, ease the clutch master cylinder fluid supply hose from its union on the side of the reservoir. Plug or tape over the union and hose after removal.

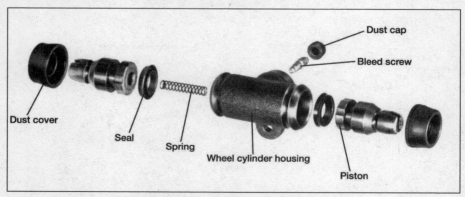

8.3 Exploded view of the rear wheel cylinder

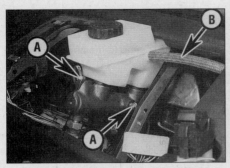

10.4 Brake pipe union nuts (A) and clutch fluid supply hose (B) on the master cylinder

10.7A Remove the master cylinder from its location . . .

10.7B . . . and recover the O-ring seal

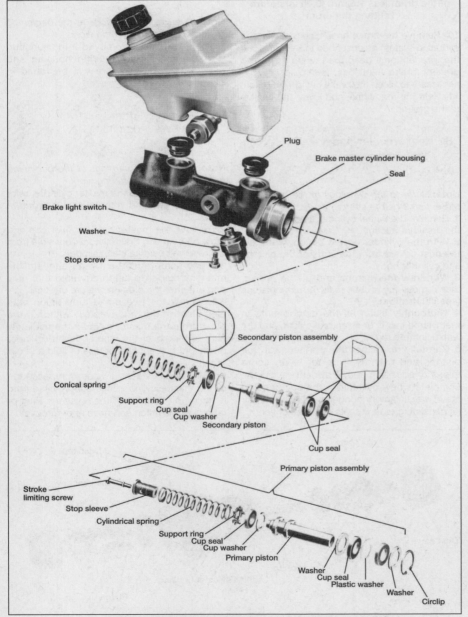

11.2A Exploded view of the Teves master cylinder

Plug

Brake master cylinder housing

Seal

Brake light switch

Washer

Stop screw

Conical spring

Secondary piston assembly

Support ring

Cup seal

Cup washer

Secondary piston

Cup seal

Primary piston assembly

Stroke limiting screw

Stop sleeve

Cylindrical spring

Support ring

Cup seal

Cup washer

Primary piston

Washer

Cup seal

Plastic washer

Washer

Circlip

6 Make a note of their locations. Disconnect the wires at the brake light switch and, if fitted, at the brake failure warning light switch on the master cylinder body.

7 Undo the two nuts securing the master cylinder to the pedal bracket or servo unit and withdraw the cylinder from its location. Remove the O-ring seal from the end of the cylinder (see illustrations).

8 Refitting the master cylinder is the reverse sequence to removal. Bleed the brake and clutch hydraulic systems after fitting as described in Section 15 of this Chapter and Chapter 6 respectively.

11 Master cylinder – overhaul

Note: Refer to the warnings at the beginning of Section 2 before starting work.

1 Begin by removing the master cylinder from the vehicle as described in the previous Section.

2 With the cylinder on the bench undo and remove the brake light switch and, where fitted, the brake failure warning light switch (see illustrations).

3 Support the master cylinder body and carefully lever off the reservoir using a screwdriver. Remove the two rubber sealing plugs from the reservoir ports (see illustrations).

4 Undo and remove the secondary piston stop screw with its washer from the base of the cylinder body (see illustration).

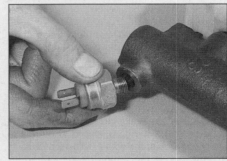

11.2B Remove the brake light switch

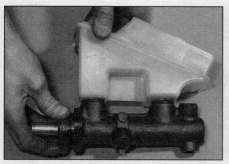

11.3A Carefully lever off the reservoir . . .

11.3B . . . then remove the two rubber sealing plugs

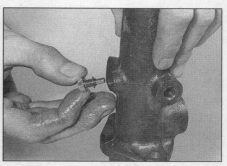

11.4 Remove the secondary piston stop screw with its washer

5 With the cylinder supported in a vice, push the primary piston down slightly and remove the retaining circlip from its groove in the cylinder bore **(see illustration)**.

6 Withdraw the primary piston slightly and slide off the assembly of two metal washers, two cup seals and plastic washer. Now remove the primary piston from the cylinder bore **(see illustrations)**.

7 Tap the master cylinder on a block of wood to eject the secondary piston from the cylinder bore then withdraw the secondary piston assembly **(see illustration)**.

8 Starting with the primary piston, hold the spring in compression and unscrew the stroke limiting screw. Remove the screw followed by the stop sleeve, cylindrical spring and support ring. Do not allow the cylindrical spring to become interchanged with the conical spring on the secondary piston.

11.5 Using circlip pliers to remove the primary piston retaining circlip

9 Withdraw the cup seal and washer from the primary piston.

10 Turning to the secondary piston, withdraw the conical spring and support ring, followed by the cup seal and washer from the inner end of the piston.

11 At the axle end, hook off the two cup seals using a blunt screwdriver, noting the different directions of fitting of the two seals.

12 Thoroughly clean the cylinder and the two pistons in methylated spirit or clean brake fluid then dry with a lint free cloth.

13 Carefully examine the cylinder bore and the surfaces of the two pistons for signs of scoring, wear ridges and corrosion. In order that the seals may adequately maintain hydraulic fluid pressure, the condition of the pistons and cylinder bore must be perfect. If in any doubt whatsoever about the condition of the components, renew the complete master cylinder.

 If a brake hydraulic seal has failed because of rust or corrosion, simply renewing the seal is unlikely to prove a satisfactory solution. Renew the complete assembly if in doubt.

14 If the cylinder and pistons are in a satisfactory condition, a new set of seals must be obtained before reassembly. These are available in the form of a master cylinder repair kit, obtainable from VW dealers or brake and clutch factors.

15 Thoroughly lubricate all the parts in clean brake fluid and assemble them wet, as follows.

16 Using your fingers only, fit the two cup seals to the secondary piston noting that the sealing edge of the innermost seal faces the piston spring and the sealing edge of the outer seal faces away from the spring.

17 Now fit the washer, cup seal, support ring and conical spring to the other end of the secondary piston. The sealing edge of the cup seal must face the spring.

18 Fit the washer and cup seal to the inner end of the primary piston, with the sealing edge of the cup seal towards the spring.

19 Slide on the support ring, cylindrical spring and stop sleeve, compress the spring and fit the stroke limiting screw. Tighten the screw securely.

20 At the other end of the primary piston, fit the assembly of metal washer, cup seal, plastic washer, cup seal and remaining metal washer. The sealing edges of both cup seals face the spring.

21 Thoroughly lubricate the cylinder bore and secondary piston assembly using clean brake fluid then carefully insert the secondary piston into the cylinder bore, spring end first. Take care not to allow the edges of the cup seals to fold over.

22 Using a thin blunt rod, push the secondary piston down to compress the spring then refit the stop screw with its washer. Tighten the screw securely.

11.6A Slide off the cup seals, metal and plastic washers . . .

11.6B . . . then withdraw the primary piston

11.7 Tap the cylinder on a block of wood to eject the secondary piston, then withdraw it from the cylinder bore

13.3 Brake pressure regulator retaining nuts (arrowed)

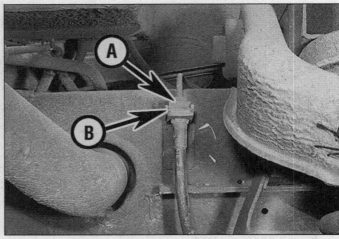

14.7 Front brake hose pipe union nut (A) and hose retaining clip (B)

23 Lubricate the primary piston with clean brake fluid and insert this assembly into the cylinder bore, spring end first.

24 Push the piston down and refit the retaining circlip to its groove in the cylinder bore.

25 Fit the two new rubber sealing plugs to the reservoir ports in the cylinder and push the reservoir firmly into place.

26 Refit the brake light switch and where applicable the warning light switch to the cylinder body. Tighten the switches securely.

27 The assembled master cylinder can now be refitted as described in the previous Section.

12 Brake pressure regulator – description

A brake pressure regulator, which controls hydraulic fluid pressure applied to the rear brakes, is mounted on the right-hand front chassis member just in front of the steering gear.

The purpose of the regulator is to prevent the rear wheels locking under heavy braking when the vehicle is lightly loaded.

The regulator consists of a steel ball in an inclined chamber and two spring-loaded subsidiary pistons which act as pressure reducers. When braking occurs, the ball is thrown forward and depending on the rate of deceleration and the angle up which it has to roll (affected by the attitude of the vehicle), it shuts off the direct fluid flow to the rear wheel cylinders. Pressure is then directed to two intermediate pistons of different diameter which effectively reduce the output pressure to the rear brakes.

Testing of the valve is not possible without the use of special equipment and if the valve is suspect, testing should be left to a VW dealer.

In the event of the valve being proved faulty it must be renewed as a complete assembly; parts are not available separately.

13 Brake pressure regulator – removal and refitting

Note: Refer to the warnings at the beginning of Section 2 before starting work.

1 Jack up the front of the vehicle and support it on axle stands (see "*Jacking and vehicle support*").

2 Wipe clean the area around the brake pipe unions on top of the regulator and unscrew the pipe union nuts. Carefully withdraw the pipes and then quickly plug their ends to prevent further loss of fluid.

3 Undo the two nuts and bolts securing the regulator to the chassis member, withdraw the regulator and recover the distance sleeves **(see illustration)**.

4 Refitting is the reverse sequence to removal, bearing in mind the following points:
 a) *Ensure that the distance sleeves are fitted between the regulator and chassis member*
 b) *Ensure that the heads of the bolts securing the two halves of the regulator body together face the front of the vehicle*
 c) *Bleed the rear brakes as described in Section 15 after fitting the regulator*

14 Hydraulic pipes and hoses – inspection, removal and refitting

Note: Refer to the warnings at the beginning of Section 2 before starting work.

1 At the intervals given in Chapter 1, carefully examine all the brake pipes, hoses, hose connections and pipe unions.

2 First check for signs of leakage at the pipe unions. Then examine the flexible hoses for signs of cracking, chafing and fraying.

3 The brake pipes must be examined carefully and methodically. They must be cleaned off and checked for signs of dents, corrosion or other damage. Corrosion should be scraped off, and, if the depth of pitting is significant, the pipes renewed. This is particularly likely in those areas underneath the vehicle body where the pipes are exposed and unprotected.

4 If any section of pipe or hose is to be removed, first unscrew the master cylinder reservoir filler cap and place a piece of polythene over the filler neck. Secure the polythene with an elastic band ensuring that an airtight seal is obtained. This will minimise brake fluid loss when the pipe or hose is removed.

5 Brake pipe removal is usually quite straightforward. The union nuts at each end are undone, the pipe and union pulled out and the centre section of the pipe removed from the body clips. Where the union nuts are exposed to the full force of the weather they can sometimes be quite tight. As only an open-ended or split ring spanner can be used, burring of the flats on the nuts is not uncommon when attempting to undo them. For this reason a self-locking wrench is often the only way to separate a stubborn union.

6 To remove a flexible hose, wipe the unions and bracket free of dirt and undo the union nut from the brake pipe end(s).

7 Next extract the hose retaining clips and lift the ends of the hose out of its brackets **(see illustration)**.

8 Brake pipes can be obtained individually, or in sets, from most accessory shops or garages with the end flares and union nuts in place. The pipe is then bent to shape, using the old pipe as a guide, and is ready for fitting.

9 Refitting the pipes and hoses is a reverse of the removal sequence. Make sure that the hoses are not kinked when in position and also make sure that the brake pipes are securely supported in their clips. After refitting, remove the polythene from the reservoir and bleed the brake hydraulic system, as described in Section 15.

15 Hydraulic system –
bleeding

Note: *Refer to the warnings at the beginning of Section 2 before starting work.*

General

1 Any hydraulic system will only function correctly once all the air has been removed from the components and circuit; this is achieved by bleeding the system.

2 During the bleeding procedure, add only clean, fresh hydraulic fluid of the recommended type; never use old fluid, nor re-use any which has already been bled from the system. Ensure that sufficient fresh fluid is available before starting work.

3 If there is any possibility of the wrong fluid being in the system, the brake components and circuit must be flushed completely with uncontaminated, correct fluid, and new seals should be fitted to the various components.

4 If hydraulic fluid has been lost from the system (or if air has entered) because of a leak, ensure that the fault is cured before proceeding further.

5 Park the vehicle on level ground, switch off the engine and select first or reverse gear, then chock the wheels and release the handbrake.

6 Check that all pipes and hoses are secure, that the pipe unions are tight, and that the bleed screws are closed. Clean any dirt from around the bleed screws.

7 Unscrew the master cylinder reservoir cap, and top the master cylinder reservoir up to the "MAX" level line; refit the cap loosely, and remember to maintain the fluid level at least above the "MIN" level line throughout the procedure, to avoid the risk of further air entering the system.

8 There are a number of one-man, do-it-yourself brake bleeding kits currently available from motor accessory shops. It is recommended that one of these kits is used whenever possible, as they greatly simplify the bleeding operation, and also reduce the risk of expelled air and fluid being drawn back into the system. If such a kit is not available, the basic (two-man) method must be used, which is described in detail below.

9 If a kit is to be used, prepare the vehicle as described previously, and follow the kit manufacturer's instructions, as the procedures may vary slightly according to the type being used; generally, they will be as outlined below.

10 Whichever method is used, the same sequence must be followed (paragraphs 11 and 12) to ensure the removal of all air from the system.

Bleeding sequence

11 If the system has been only partially disconnected, and suitable precautions were taken to minimise fluid loss, it should only be necessary to bleed that part of the system (ie. the primary or secondary circuit).

12 If the complete system is to be bled, then it should be done working in the following sequence:

   a) Right-hand rear brake.
   b) Left-hand rear brake.
   c) Right-hand front brake.
   d) Left-hand front brake.

Bleeding - basic (two-man) method

13 Collect a clean glass jar, a suitable length of plastic or rubber tubing which is a tight fit over the bleed screw, and a ring spanner to fit the bleed screw. The help of an assistant will also be required.

14 Remove the dust cap from the first screw in the sequence. Fit the spanner and tube to the screw, place the other end of the tube in the jar, and pour in sufficient fluid to cover the end of the tube.

15 Ensure that the master cylinder reservoir fluid level is maintained at least above the "MIN" level line throughout the procedure.

16 Have the assistant fully depress the brake pedal several times to build up pressure, then maintain it on the final stroke.

17 While pedal pressure is maintained, unscrew the bleed screw (approximately one turn) and allow the fluid and air to flow into the jar. The assistant should maintain pedal pressure, following it down to the floor if necessary, and should not release it until instructed to do so. When the flow stops, tighten the bleed screw again; the pedal should then be released slowly, and the reservoir fluid level checked and topped-up.

18 Repeat the steps given in paragraphs 16 and 17 until the fluid emerging from the bleed screw is free from air bubbles. If the master cylinder has been drained and refilled, and air is being bled from the first screw in the sequence, allow approximately five seconds between cycles for the master cylinder passages to refill.

19 When no more air bubbles appear, tighten the bleed screw securely, remove the tube and spanner, and refit the dust cap. Do not overtighten the bleed screw.

20 Repeat the procedure on the remaining screws in the sequence, until all air is removed from the system and the brake pedal feels firm again.

Bleeding - using a one-way valve kit

21 As their name implies, these kits consist of a length of tubing with a one-way valve fitted, to prevent expelled air and fluid being drawn back into the system; some kits include a translucent container, which can be positioned so that the air bubbles can be more easily seen flowing from the end of the tube.

22 The kit is connected to the bleed screw, which is then opened **(see illustration)**. The user returns to the driver's seat, depresses the brake pedal with a smooth, steady stroke, then slowly releases it; this is repeated until the expelled fluid is clear of air bubbles.

23 These kits simplify work so much that it is easy to forget the master cylinder reservoir fluid level; ensure that this is maintained at least above the "MIN" level line at all times, or air will be drawn into the system.

Bleeding - using a pressure bleeding kit

24 These kits are usually operated by the reservoir of pressurised air contained in the spare tyre, noting that it will probably be necessary to reduce the pressure to less than normal; refer to the instructions supplied with the kit.

25 By connecting a pressurised, fluid-filled container to the master cylinder reservoir, bleeding can be carried out simply by opening each screw in turn (in the specified sequence) and allowing the fluid to flow out until no more air bubbles can be seen in the expelled fluid.

26 This method has the advantage that the large reservoir of fluid provides an additional safeguard against air being drawn into the system during bleeding.

27 Pressure bleeding is particularly effective when bleeding "difficult" systems, or when bleeding the complete system at the time of routine fluid renewal.

All methods

28 When bleeding is complete and firm pedal feel is restored, wash off any spilt fluid, tighten the bleed screws securely, and refit their dust caps.

29 Check the hydraulic fluid level, and top-up if necessary (see *"Weekly checks"*).

30 Discard any hydraulic fluid that has been bled from the system; it will not be fit for re-use. Bear in mind that this fluid may be flammable.

31 Check the feel of the brake pedal. If it feels at all spongy, air must still be present in the system, and further bleeding is required. Failure to bleed satisfactorily after a reasonable repetition of the bleeding procedure may be due to worn master cylinder seals.

15.22 Brake bleeding kit connected to front brake caliper

16 Brake fluid – renewal

1 Owing to its hygroscopic nature, the brake fluid used in the hydraulic system will gradually absorb moisture from the air. This will, over a period of time, lower the boiling point of the fluid to such an extent that under conditions of prolonged heavy braking the fluid will boil. If this occurs the brakes will become virtually inoperative. Additionally the moisture in the fluid can cause corrosion of the cylinder bores and pistons in the master cylinder, calipers and wheel cylinders, leading to seal failure or seizure of the pistons. For these reasons it is important to renew the fluid in the system at the recommended service intervals using the following procedure (see Chapter 1).

2 To drain the old fluid, obtain a suitable length of plastic or rubber tubing and a large receptacle.

3 Clean the area around the bleed screws on the rear wheel cylinders and remove the dust covers over the bleed screws.

4 Connect the tube to one of the bleed screws and place its other end in the receptacle.

5 Open the bleed screw at least one full turn and pump the brake pedal until fluid ceases to flow from the tube. Close the bleed screw,

transfer the tube to the other rear brake and repeat the procedure.

6 Carry out the same operations at the front, but note that on some models there are two bleed screws on each caliper. In this case the lower screw is used for draining and the upper screw is used for bleeding.

7 When all the old fluid has been drained, refill the master cylinder reservoir with clean fresh fluid of the specified type, up to the "MAX" mark.

8 Initially prime the system prior to bleeding by opening all four bleed screws. Allow the fluid to slowly trickle through the system, then close each bleed screw as soon as fluid appears. Keep the reservoir topped up during this operation.

9 The system can now be bled in the normal way as described in Section 15. Note that it may also be necessary to bleed the clutch hydraulic system, which obtains its fluid from the brake master cylinder reservoir.

17 Handbrake – adjustment

Note: *The handbrake will normally be kept in correct adjustment by the self-adjusting action of the rear brake shoes. If however the cable has been disconnected or renewed, or if the travel of the lever becomes excessive owing to*

17.4 Handbrake adjusting nut (arrowed) on the primary cable

cable stretch, the following operations should be carried out:

1 Jack up the rear of the vehicle and support it on axle stands (see *"Jacking and vehicle support"*). Release the handbrake.

2 Apply the footbrake firmly three or four times to ensure full movement of the self-adjust mechanism on the rear brake shoes. This is particularly important if the brake drums have recently been removed.

3 Apply the handbrake sharply then release it to equalise the cable loads. Now reapply the handbrake to the second notch of the ratchet.

4 From under the vehicle, turn the adjusting nut whilst holding the primary cable **(see illustration)** until the brake shoes are just dragging on the drums.

5 Operate the handbrake and check that the rear wheels are locked between the second and fourth notches of the ratchet and are free to turn without binding when the handbrake is released.

6 When the adjustment is correct, lower the vehicle to the ground.

18 Handbrake cables – removal and refitting

1 Jack up the rear of the vehicle and support it on axle stands (see *"Jacking and vehicle support"*). Release the handbrake.

Front (primary) cable

2 From inside the cab, lift up the carpet or rubber mat then slide the handbrake lever boot up the handle **(see illustration)**.

3 Extract the circlip and withdraw the clevis pin securing the end of the cable to the handbrake lever.

4 Release the rubber boot from its location in the floor pan and push the boot and cable end through the aperture in the floor.

5 From underneath the vehicle undo the adjusting nut and withdraw the other end of the cable from the equaliser.

6 Release the cable guide from its support clip and pull the cable through the circular grommet on the underbody.

7 Slide the rubber boot off the cable then withdraw the cable from under the vehicle.

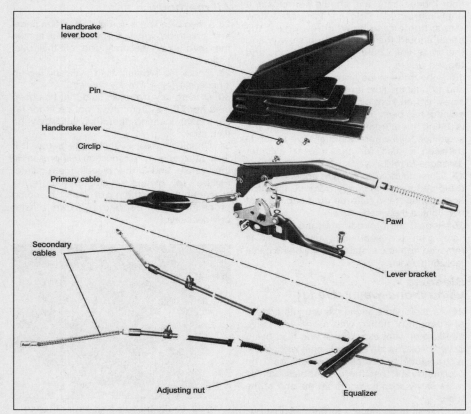

Handbrake lever boot

Pin

Handbrake lever

Circlip

Primary cable

Secondary cables

Pawl

Lever bracket

Adjusting nut

Equalizer

18.2 Exploded view of the handbrake cables and lever components

8 Refitting is the reverse sequence to removal, but adjust the handbrake as described in Section 17 after refitting.

Rear (secondary) cables

9 Slacken the adjusting nut on the primary cable then slip the secondary cable end out of the elongated slot on the cable equaliser.
10 Refer to Section 6 and remove the brake drum.
11 Unhook the cable end from the brake shoe lever then push the cable and guide out of the backplate.
12 Release the cable retaining clips and supports from their locations on the underbody and suspension arms then withdraw the cable from under the vehicle.
13 Refitting the cable is the reverse sequence to removal, bearing in mind the following points:
a) Refit the brake drum (see Section 6)
b) After fitting the cable, adjust the handbrake (see Section 17), before lowering the vehicle to the ground

19.4 Handbrake lever retaining bolts (arrowed)

19 Handbrake lever – removal and refitting

1 From inside the cab, lift up the carpet or rubber mat then slide the handbrake lever boot up the handle.

2 Extract the circlip then withdraw the clevis pin securing the primary handbrake cable to the lever.
3 Where fitted, disconnect the handbrake warning light wires at the switch on the lever.
4 Undo the two bolts securing the handbrake lever to the floor **(see illustration)** and withdraw the assembly from inside the cab.
5 Refitting is the reverse sequence to removal.

20 Handbrake lever – dismantling and reassembly

1 Remove the handbrake lever from the vehicle as described in the previous Section.
2 Undo the retaining screw and lift off the warning light switch (where fitted).
3 Unscrew the push button from the end of the lever then withdraw the spring and spring seat.
4 Extract the circlip and withdraw the clevis pin securing the lever to the mounting bracket. Lift off the lever.
5 Extract the circlip and withdraw the clevis pin securing the pawl to the lever. Lift out the pawl and operating rod.
6 Examine the components for signs of wear, paying close attention to the pawl and ratchet. Also check for any elongation of the clevis pin holes. Renew any worn parts as necessary.
7 Lubricate the pawl, ratchet and clevis pins with multi-purpose grease then reassemble the handbrake using the reverse of the dismantling procedure.

21 Footbrake pedal – removal and refitting

1 Begin by removing the instrument panel as described in Chapter 12, and the facia panel as described in Chapter 11.
2 Remove the clutch master cylinder as described in Chapter 6, and the brake master cylinder as described in Section 10 of this Chapter.
3 Carefully prise out the vacuum hose elbow connector from the grommet on the servo front face, using a screwdriver **(see illustrations)**.

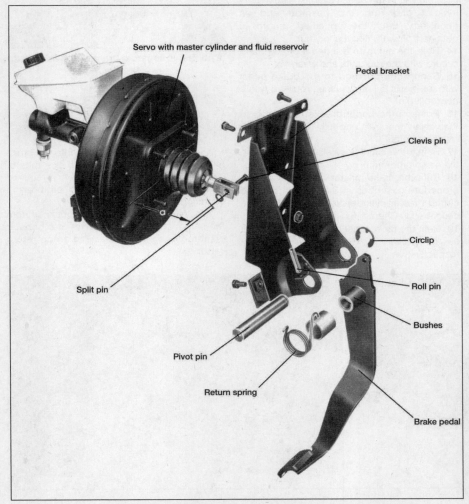

21.3A Exploded view of the brake pedal and pedal bracket assembly

a = Specified servo unit pushrod length

21.3B Removing the vacuum hose elbow connector from the servo grommet

21.4A Undo the four pedal bracket retaining bolts (right-hand pair arrowed) . . .

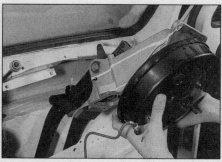

21.4B . . . then lift out the bracket assembly complete with pedals and servo

21.5 Servo pushrod clevis pin, washer and retaining split pin (arrowed)

4 Undo the four bolts securing the pedal bracket assembly to the front bulkhead. Lift the bracket complete with pedals and servo upwards and out of its bulkhead location **(see illustrations)**.
5 Extract the split pin and washer then withdraw the clevis pin securing the servo pushrod to the brake pedal **(see illustration)**.
6 Undo the four nuts and washers and withdraw the servo from the pedal bracket **(see illustration)**.
7 Remove the clutch pedal return spring with pliers and release the brake pedal return spring using a screwdriver.
8 Extract the circlip securing the pedal pivot shaft in position **(see illustration)** then tap the shaft out of the bracket using a drift. The brake and clutch pedals can now be lifted out.
9 The bushes in the pedals can be removed by driving them out using a drift of suitable diameter. Press in new bushes using a vice. Renew the pedal pivot shaft if there are signs of scoring or wear ridges.
10 Lubricate the pedal bushes and pivot shaft with multi-purpose grease then place the pedals and brake pedal return spring in position.
11 Refit the pivot shaft ensuring that the roll pin in the end of the shaft locates in the groove in the pedal bracket **(see illustration)**.

Secure the shaft with the retaining circlip.
12 Locate the brake pedal return spring over the pedal and refit the clutch pedal return spring.
13 Before refitting the servo, check the servo pushrod length by measuring the distance from the servo mounting face to the centre of the pushrod clevis pin hole. If the dimension is not as given in the Specifications, slacken the locknut and turn the pushrod end as necessary until the specified length is obtained. Now tighten the locknut.
14 Refit the servo to the pedal bracket and secure with the four nuts and washers.
15 Secure the pushrod to the brake pedal with the clevis pin and washer, retained with a new split pin.
16 Position the pedal bracket assembly in the vehicle then refit and fully tighten the four retaining bolts.
17 Refit the vacuum hose elbow connector to the servo grommet.
18 Refit the brake master cylinder using the procedure described in Section 10, and the clutch master cylinder using the procedure described in Chapter 6.
19 Refit the facia panel and instrument panel as described in Chapters 11 and 12 respectively.

21.6 Servo to pedal bracket retaining nuts (arrowed)

22 Vacuum servo unit – description

A vacuum servo unit is fitted into the brake hydraulic circuit in series with the master cylinder. The servo reduces the effort required to operate the brakes under all braking conditions.
The unit operates by vacuum obtained from the inlet manifold and consists of a booster diaphragm, control valve, and a non-return valve.

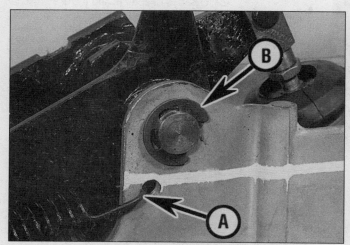

21.8 Clutch pedal return spring (A) and pedal pivot shaft retaining circlip (B)

21.11 The pedal pivot shaft roll pin must engage with the bracket groove

24.3 Servo vacuum hose non-return valve (arrowed)

The servo unit and hydraulic master cylinder are connected together so that the servo unit piston rod acts as the master cylinder pushrod. The driver's braking effort is transmitted through another pushrod to the servo unit piston and its built-in control system. The servo unit piston does not fit tightly into the cylinder, but has a strong diaphragm to keep its edges in constant contact with the cylinder wall, so assuring an airtight seal between the two parts. The forward chamber is held under vacuum conditions created in the inlet manifold of the engine and, during periods when the brake pedal is not in use, the controls open a passage to the rear chamber so placing it under vacuum conditions as well. When the brake pedal is depressed, the vacuum passage to the rear chamber is cut off and the chamber opened to atmospheric pressure. The consequent rush of air pushes the servo piston forward in the vacuum chamber and operates the main pushrod to the master cylinder.

The controls are designed so that assistance is given under all conditions and, when the brakes are not required, vacuum in the rear chamber is established when the brake pedal is released. All air from the atmosphere entering the rear chamber is passed through a small air filter.

23 Vacuum servo unit – removal and refitting

1 The servo unit and brake master cylinder are located together behind the instrument panel. The servo is removed in conjunction with the brake and clutch pedals and pedal bracket, and full details will be found in Section 21, paragraphs 1 to 6 and 13 to 19.

24 Vacuum servo unit – testing

1 With the engine switched off depress the footbrake several times and then hold it down. Start the engine and, as this is done, there

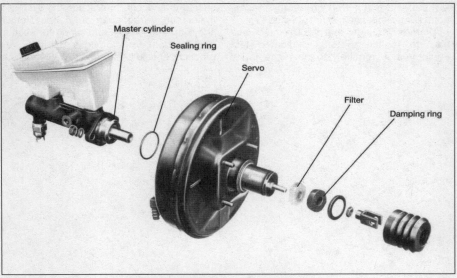

24.4 Vacuum servo unit components

should be a noticeable 'give' in the brake pedal.

2 Allow the engine to run for at least two minutes and then switch it off. If the brake pedal is now depressed again, a slight hiss should be noticeable from the unit when the pedal is depressed. After about four or five applications no further hissing will be heard and the pedal will feel considerably firmer.

3 If the servo does not function as described, check the vacuum hose and all unions for leaks and check the operation of the non-return valve. To do this disconnect the vacuum hose from the connector on the inlet manifold or air intake housing. Slacken the hose clamp and withdraw the non-return valve from the vacuum hose **(see illustration)**. Check that it is only possible to blow through

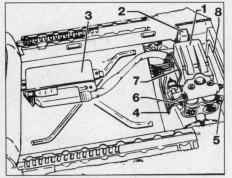

25.1 ABS hydraulic unit (1) located under the driver's seat

2 *Relay*
3 *Electronic control unit*
4 *From master cylinder*
5 *To pressure regulator*
6 *To front left caliper*
7 *To front right caliper*
8 *To rear brakes*

the valve in the direction of the arrow stamped on the body. Renew the valve if faulty.

4 If no leaks were found in the vacuum hose and the non-return valve is operating correctly, renew the servo air filter. To do this the servo must be removed as described in Section 21. Once this has been done, withdraw the rubber boot surrounding the servo pushrod, slacken the locknut and unscrew the clevis end from the pushrod. Hook out the seal, damping ring and air filter and renew these components **(see illustration)**. Reassemble, then refit the servo as described in Section 21, ensuring that the pushrod length is accurately adjusted as described.

5 If the servo is still inoperative, renewal will be necessary. It is not possible to dismantle the servo for repairs as it is a sealed unit and parts are not available separately.

25 Anti-lock braking system (ABS) – general information

An anti-lock braking system (ABS) is available as an optional extra on later models. The system monitors the rate of rotation of each roadwheel. If during braking the speed of one or more wheels drops rapidly, indicating that wheel locking is taking place, the system reduces the brake hydraulic pressure to that wheel until traction is regained. The main components of the system are a hydraulic unit and an electronic control unit, both located under the driver's seat **(see illustration)**. Wheel speed is monitored by four sensors, one per wheel, which respond to the passage of teeth on a trigger wheel attached to the brake disc or rear wheel bearing. An instrument panel warning lamp alerts the driver to any malfunction.

If the ABS is not working for any reason, normal brake operation is not affected.

There is very little that the DIY mechanic can do to the system. Dedicated test equipment is required to diagnose faults should they occur. In practice the system is maintenance-free apart from occasionally checking the sensors and wiring for security and freedom from obvious damage. Any problems should be referred to a VW dealer or other qualified specialist.

Always disconnect the battery earth lead before undertaking any work involving the ABS.

Chapter 11
Bodywork

Contents

Degrees of difficulty

Easy, suitable for novice with little experience	Fairly easy, suitable for beginner with some experience	Fairly difficult, suitable for competent DIY mechanic	Difficult, suitable for experienced DIY mechanic	Very difficult, suitable for expert DIY or professional

1 General description

The bodyshell is of conventional welded steel unitary construction available in a number of versions according to vehicle application and territory of export. In addition an extensive list of optional body, interior and exterior equipment is available to suit each version.

Owing to the large number of vehicle arrangements available, the contents of this Chapter cover manufacturers' standard equipment only.

2 Maintenance – bodywork and underframe

The general condition of a vehicle's bodywork is the one thing that significantly affects its value. Maintenance is easy but needs to be regular. Neglect, particularly after minor damage, can lead quickly to further deterioration and costly repair bills. It is important also to keep watch on those parts of the vehicle not immediately visible, for instance the underbody, inside all the wheel arches and the lower part of the engine compartment.

The basic maintenance routine for the bodywork is washing - preferably with a lot of water, from a hose. This will remove all the loose solids which may have stuck to the vehicle. It is important to flush these off in such a way as to prevent grit from scratching the finish. The wheel arches and underbody need washing in the same way to remove any accumulated mud which will retain moisture and tend to encourage rust, particularly in winter when it is essential that any salt (from that put down on the roads) is washed off. Paradoxically enough, the best time to clean the underbody and wheel arches is in wet weather when the mud is thoroughly wet and soft. In very wet weather the underbody is usually cleaned automatically of large accumulations; this is therefore a good time for inspection.

If the vehicle is very dirty, especially underneath or in the engine compartment, it is tempting to use one of the pressure washers or steam cleaners available on garage forecourts. Whilst these are quick and effective, especially for the removal of the accumulation of oily grime which sometimes is allowed to become thick in certain areas, their usage does have some disadvantages. If caked-on dirt is simply blasted off the paintwork, its finish soon becomes scratched and dull and the pressure can allow water to penetrate door and window seals and the lock

mechanisms. If the full force of such a jet is directed at the vehicle's underbody, the wax-based protective coating can easily be damaged and water (with whatever cleaning solvent is used) could be forced into crevices or components that it would not normally reach. Similarly, if such equipment is used to clean the engine compartment, water can be forced into the components of the fuel and electrical systems and the protective coating can be removed that is applied to many small components during manufacture; this may therefore actually promote corrosion (especially inside electrical connectors) and initiate engine problems or other electrical faults. Also, if the jet is pointed directly at any of the oil seals, water can be forced past the seal lips and into the engine or transmission. Great care is required, therefore, if such equipment is used and, in general, regular cleaning by such methods should be avoided. A much better solution in the long term is just to flush away as much loose dirt as possible using a hose alone, even if this leaves the engine compartment looking dirty. If an oil leak has developed, or if any other accumulation of oil or grease is to be removed, there are excellent grease solvents available which can be brush applied. The dirt can then be simply hosed off. Take care to replace the wax-based protective coat, if this was affected by the solvent. Normal washing of the bodywork is best carried out using cold or warm water with a proprietary car shampoo. Tar spots can be removed by using white spirit, followed by soapy water to remove all traces of spirit. Try to keep water out of the bonnet air intakes and check afterwards that the heater air inlet box drain tube is clear so that any water has drained out of the box.

After washing the paintwork, wipe off with a chamois leather to give an unspotted clear finish. A coat of clear protective wax polish will give added protection against chemical pollutants in the air. If the paintwork sheen has dulled or oxidised, use a cleaner/polisher combination to restore the brilliance of the shine. This requires a little effort, but such dulling is usually caused because regular washing has been neglected. Care needs to be taken with metallic paintwork, as special non-abrasive cleaner/polisher is required to avoid damage to the finish. Brightwork should be treated in the same way as paintwork. Windscreens and windows can be kept clear of the smeary film which often appears, by the use of a proprietary glass cleaner. Never use any form of wax or other body or chromium polish on glass.

On models with a sliding roof, check periodically that the drain tubes are clear and that the rear drain pipes fit into their grommets correctly **(see illustration)**. The valves should be removed from the front drain tubes before cleaning; the rear pipes are accessible through the ventilators. A thin flexible wire, such as curtain wire or an old speedometer cable inner, is ideal for cleaning the drain tubes.

3 Maintenance – upholstery and carpets

Mats and carpets should be brushed or vacuum cleaned regularly to keep them free of grit. If they are badly stained remove them from the vehicle for scrubbing or sponging and make quite sure they are dry before refitting.

Fabric-trimmed seats and interior trim panels can be kept clean by wiping with a damp cloth and a proprietary fabric cleaner. If they do become stained (which can be more apparent on light coloured upholstery) use a little liquid detergent and a soft nail brush to scour the grime out of the grain of the material. Keep the headlining clean in the same way as the upholstery.

When using liquid cleaners of any sort inside the vehicle, do not over-wet the surfaces being cleaned. Excessive damp could get into the seams and padded interior causing stains, offensive odours or even rot. If the inside of the vehicle gets wet accidentally it is worthwhile taking some trouble to dry it out properly, particularly where carpets are involved. *Do not leave oil or electric heaters inside the vehicle for this purpose.*

4 Minor body damage – repair

Repair of minor scratches in bodywork

If the scratch is very superficial and does not penetrate to the metal of the bodywork, repair is very simple. Lightly rub the area of the scratch with a paintwork renovator or a very fine cutting paste to remove loose paint from the scratch and to clear the surrounding bodywork of wax polish. Rinse the area with clean water.

Apply touch-up paint to the scratch using a fine paint brush. Continue to apply fine layers of paint until the surface of the paint in the scratch is level with the surrounding paintwork. Allow the new paint at least two weeks to harden, then blend it into the surrounding paintwork by rubbing the scratch area with a paintwork renovator or very fine cutting paste. Finally, apply wax polish.

Where the scratch has penetrated right through to the metal of the bodywork, causing the metal to rust, a different repair technique is required. Remove any loose rust from the bottom of the scratch with a penknife, then apply rust inhibiting paint to prevent the formation of rust in the future. Using a rubber or nylon applicator, fill the scratch with bodystopper paste. If required, this paste can be mixed with cellulose thinners to provide a very thin paste which is ideal for filling narrow scratches. Before the stopper-paste in the scratch hardens, wrap a piece of smooth cotton rag around the top of a finger. Dip the finger in cellulose thinners and quickly sweep it across the surface of the stopper-paste in the scratch. This will ensure that the surface of the stopper-paste is slightly hollowed. The scratch can now be painted over as described earlier in this Section.

Repair of dents in bodywork

When deep denting of the vehicle's bodywork has taken place, the first task is to pull the dent out, until the affected bodywork almost attains its original shape. There is little point in trying to restore the original shape completely, as the metal in the damaged area will have stretched on impact and cannot be

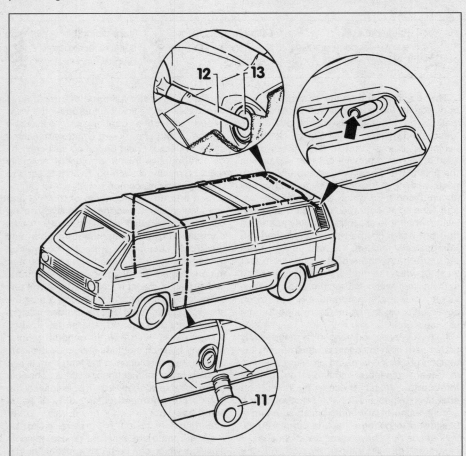

2.5 Location of sliding roof drain tubes

11 Valve   12 Rear drain pipe   13 Grommet

reshaped fully to its original contour. It is better to bring the level of the dent up to a point which is about 3 mm below the level of the surrounding bodywork. In cases where the dent is very shallow anyway, it is not worth trying to pull it out at all. If the underside of the dent is accessible, it can be hammered out gently from behind, using a mallet with a wooden or plastic head. Whilst doing this, hold a suitable block of wood firmly against the outside of the panel to absorb the impact from the hammer blows and thus prevent a large area of the bodywork from being "belled-out".

Should the dent be in a section of the bodywork which has a double skin or some other factor making it inaccessible from behind, a different technique is called for. Drill several small holes through the metal inside the area - particularly in the deeper section. Then screw long self-tapping screws into the holes just sufficiently for them to gain a good purchase in the metal. Now the dent can be pulled out by pulling on the protruding heads of the screws with a pair of pliers.

The next stage of the repair is the removal of the paint from the damaged area and from an inch or so of the surrounding sound bodywork. This is accomplished most easily by using a wire brush or abrasive pad on a power drill, although it can be done just as effectively by hand using sheets of abrasive paper. To complete the preparation for filling, score the surface of the bare metal with a screwdriver or the tang of a file, or alternatively, drill small holes in the affected area. This will provide a really good key for the filler paste. To complete the repair see the Section on filling and respraying.

Repair of rust holes or gashes in bodywork

Remove all paint from the affected area and from an inch or so of the surrounding sound bodywork, using an abrasive pad or a wire brush on a power drill. If these are not available a few sheets of abrasive paper will do the job most effectively. With the paint removed you will be able to judge the severity of the corrosion and therefore decide whether to renew the whole panel (if this is possible) or to repair the affected area. New body panels are not as expensive as most people think and it is often quicker and more satisfactory to fit a new panel than to attempt to repair large areas of corrosion.

Remove all fittings from the affected area except those which will act as a guide to the original shape of the damaged bodywork (eg headlamp shells etc). Then, using tin snips or a hacksaw blade, remove all loose metal and any other metal badly affected by corrosion. Hammer the edges of the hole inwards in order to create a slight depression for the filler paste.

Wire brush the affected area to remove the powdery rust from the surface of the remaining metal. Paint the affected area with rust inhibiting paint. If the back of the rusted area is accessible, treat this also.

Before filling can take place it will be necessary to block the hole in some way. This can be achieved by the use of aluminium or plastic mesh, or aluminium tape.

Aluminium or plastic mesh or glass-fibre matting is probably the best material to use for a large hole. Cut a piece to the approximate size and shape of the hole to be filled, then position it in the hole so that its edges are below the level of the surrounding bodywork. It can be retained in position by several blobs of filler paste around its periphery.

Aluminium tape should be used for small or very narrow holes. Pull a piece off the roll and trim it to the approximate size and shape required, then pull off the backing paper (if used) and stick the tape over the hole. The tape can be overlapped if the thickness of one piece is insufficient. Burnish down the edges of the tape with the handle of a screwdriver or similar, to ensure that the tape is securely attached to the metal underneath.

Bodywork repairs - filling and respraying

Before using this Section, see the Sections on dent, deep scratch, rust holes and gash repairs.

Many types of bodyfiller are available, but generally speaking those proprietary kits are best for this type of repair which contain a tin of filler paste and a tube of resin hardener. A wide, flexible plastic or nylon applicator will be found invaluable for imparting a smooth and well contoured finish to the surface of the filler.

Mix up a little filler on a clean piece of card or board. Measure the hardener carefully (following the maker's instructions on the pack) otherwise the filler will set too rapidly or too slowly. Using the applicator, apply the filler paste to the prepared area. Draw the applicator across the surface of the filler to achieve the correct contour and to level the surface. As soon as a contour that approximates to the correct one is achieved, stop working the paste. If you carry on too long the paste will become sticky and begin to pick-up on the applicator. Continue to add thin layers of filler paste at twenty minute intervals until the level of the filler is just proud of the surrounding bodywork.

Once the filler has hardened, excess can be removed using a metal plane or file. From then on, progressively finer grades of abrasive paper should be used, starting with a 40 grade production paper and finishing with a 400 grade wet-and-dry paper. Always wrap the abrasive paper around a flat rubber, cork, or wooden block - otherwise the surface of the filler will not be completely flat. During the smoothing of the filler surface the wet-and-dry paper should be periodically rinsed in water. This will ensure that a very smooth finish is imparted to the filler at the final stage.

At this stage, the dent should be surrounded by a ring of bare metal, which in turn should be encircled by the finely feathered edge of the good paintwork. Rinse the repair area with clean water, until all of the dust produced by the rubbing-down operation has gone.

Spray the whole area with a light coat of primer. This will show up any imperfections in the surface of the filler. Repair these imperfections with fresh filler paste or bodystopper and once more smooth the surface with abrasive paper. If bodystopper is used, it can be mixed with cellulose thinners to form a really thin paste which is ideal for filling small holes. Repeat this spray and repair procedure until you are satisfied that the surface of the filler and the feathered edge of the paintwork are perfect. Clean the repair area with clean water and allow to dry fully.

The repair area is now ready for final spraying. Paint spraying must be carried out in a warm, dry, windless and dust free atmosphere. This condition can be created artificially if you have access to a large indoor working area, but if you are forced to work in the open, you will have to pick your day very carefully. If you are working indoors, dousing the floor in the work area with water will help to settle the dust which would otherwise be in the atmosphere. If the repair area is confined to one body panel, mask off the surrounding panels; this will help to minimise the effects of a slight mis-match in paint colours. Bodywork fittings (eg chrome strips, door handles etc) will also need to be masked off. Use genuine masking tape and several thicknesses of newspaper for the masking operations.

Before commencing to spray, agitate the aerosol can thoroughly, then spray a test area (an old tin, or similar) until the technique is mastered. Cover the repair area with a thick coat of primer; the thickness should be built up using several thin layers of paint rather than one thick one. Using 400 grade wet-and-dry paper, rub down the surface of the primer until it is really smooth. While doing this, the work area should be thoroughly doused with water and the wet-and-dry paper periodically rinsed in water. Allow to dry before spraying on more paint.

Spray on the top coat, again building up the thickness by using several thin layers of paint. Start spraying in the centre of the repair area and then, with a side-to-side motion, work outwards until the whole repair area and about 50 mm of the surrounding original paintwork is covered. Remove all masking material 10 to 15 minutes after spraying on the final coat of paint.

Allow the new paint at least two weeks to harden, then, using a paintwork renovator or very fine cutting paste, blend the edges of the paint into the existing paintwork. Finally, apply wax polish.

Plastic components

With the use of more and more plastic body components by the vehicle manufacturers (eg bumpers, spoilers and in some cases major body panels), rectification of more serious

8.2 Remove the caps on the bumper extensions . . .

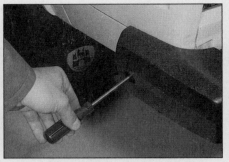

8.3 . . . to gain access to the retaining screw

8.4 Disengage the catches and remove the extensions

damage to such items has become a matter of either entrusting repair work to a specialist in this field, or renewing complete components. Repair of such damage by the DIY owner is not really feasible owing to the cost of the equipment and materials required for effecting such repairs. The basic technique involves making a groove along the line of the crack in the plastic using a rotary burr in a power drill. The damaged part is then welded back together by using a hot air gun to heat up and fuse a plastic filler rod into the groove. Any excess plastic is then removed and the area rubbed down to a smooth finish. It is important that a filler rod of the correct plastic is used, as body components can be made of a variety of different types (eg polycarbonate, ABS, polypropylene).

Damage of a less serious nature (abrasions, minor cracks etc) can be repaired by the DIY owner using a two-part epoxy filler repair material. Once mixed in equal proportions, this is used in similar fashion to the bodywork filler used on metal panels. The filler is usually cured in twenty to thirty minutes, ready for sanding and painting.

If the owner is renewing a complete component himself, or if he has repaired it with epoxy filler, he will be left with the problem of finding a suitable paint for finishing which is compatible with the type of plastic used. At one time the use of a universal paint was not possible owing to the complex range of plastics encountered in body component applications. Standard paints, generally speaking, will not bond satisfactorily to plastic or rubber. However, it is now possible to

obtain a plastic body parts finishing kit which consists of a pre-primer treatment, a primer and coloured top coat. Full instructions are normally supplied with a kit but basically, the method of use is to first apply the pre-primer to the component concerned and allow it to dry for up to 30 minutes. Then the primer is applied and left to dry for about an hour before finally applying the special coloured top coat. The result is a correctly-coloured component where the paint will flex with the plastic or rubber, a property that standard paint does not normally possess.

5 Major body damage – repair

Where serious damage has occurred or large areas need renewal owing to neglect, it means certainly that completely new sections or panels will need welding in and this is best left to professionals. If the damage is due to impact it will also be necessary to completely check the alignment of the bodyshell structure. Due to the principle of construction the strength and shape of the whole can be affected by damage to a part. In such instances the services of a VW agent with specialist checking jigs are essential. If a frame is left misaligned it is first of all dangerous as the vehicle will not handle properly and secondly uneven stresses will be imposed on the steering, engine and transmission causing abnormal wear or complete failure. Tyre wear may be excessive.

6 Maintenance – hinges and locks

1 At regular intervals oil the hinges of the doors, tailgate and all other hinged panels as applicable with a drop or two of light oil.
2 At the same time lightly lubricate all the lock assemblies and striker plates. Do not however lubricate the steering lock.

7 Door rattles – tracing and rectification

1 Check first that the door is not loose at the hinges, and that the latch is holding the door firmly in position. Check also that the door lines up with the aperture in the body. If the door is out of alignment, adjust it, as described in the relevant Sections of this Chapter.
2 If the latch is holding the door in the correct position, but the latch still rattles, the lock mechanism is worn and should be renewed.
3 Other rattles from the door could be caused by wear in the window operating mechanism, interior lock mechanism, or loose glass channels.

8 Bumpers – removal and refitting

1 The removal and refitting procedures for both front and rear bumpers is identical and is as follows.
2 Prise out the small caps on the side of the bumper wrap around extensions **(see illustration)**.
3 Undo the retaining screw securing the extensions to the body **(see illustration)**.
4 Disengage the retaining catches and remove the extensions from the main bumper **(see illustration)**.
5 Release the caps over the bumper retaining bolts, undo the bolts and lift off the bumper **(see illustrations)**.
6 Refitting is the reverse sequence to removal.

8.5A Release the caps over the bumper retaining bolts . . .

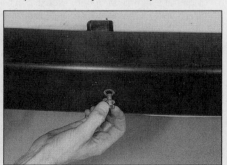

8.5B . . . and remove the bolts

9.1 Front grille panel quick release retainer

9.2 Removing the front grille

9.4 Removing a lower grille securing screw

9 Front grille panels – removal and refitting

Upper panel

1 Turn the three quick release retainers along the top edge of the grille through 90° to release (see illustration).

2 Tip the grille out of the top then lift it up to disengage the lower locating tags (see illustration).

3 Refitting is the reverse sequence to removal.

Lower panel

4 Remove the five securing screws and lift out the panel (see illustration).

5 Refitting is the reverse sequence to removal.

10 Tailgate – removal, refitting and adjustment

All models except pick-up

1 Disconnect the battery negative terminal.

2 Open the tailgate and disconnect the wiring to the heated rear window. Unscrew the earth lead and pull the wiring out of the tailgate.

3 Support the tailgate in the open position with the help of an assistant or with a stout length of wood.

4 Extract the circlips and washers then slip the tailgate support struts off their mounting pegs on the body (see illustrations).

5 Mark the outline of the hinge positions on the body with a soft pencil. Have an assistant support the tailgate then undo the four hinge retaining bolts using a suitable Allen key.

6 Carefully lift the tailgate away.

7 Refitting the tailgate is the reverse sequence to removal ensuring that the hinges are aligned with the previously made alignment marks.

8 If it is necessary, reposition the tailgate within the body aperture, this is done by moving the tailgate sideways or up and down accordingly, with the hinge retaining bolts slack. For the tailgate to open properly there must be a gap of 11 to 13 mm (0.43 to 0.51 in) between the tailgate top edge and the body.

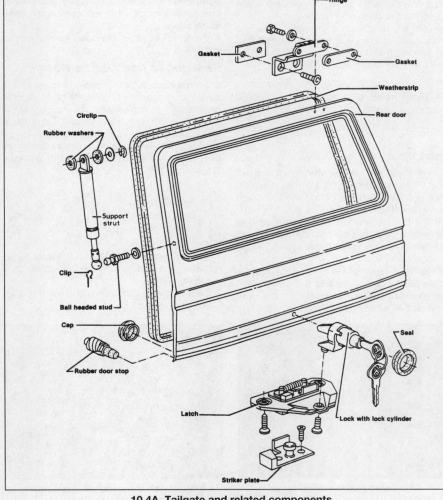

10.4A Tailgate and related components

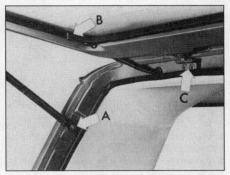

10.4B Tailgate removal

A Support strut mounting peg
B Wiring connection
C Hinge retaining bolts

14.1 Lift back the trim capping to gain access to the window crank handle retaining screw

14.2 The upper and lower door handle screws are located behind the trim caps

14.3 Release the finger plate for access to the escutcheon retaining screw

The rubber buffers should be screwed in or out as required so that the tailgate is flush with the body.

9 Adjust the position of the striker plate so that the tailgate shuts and locks without slamming.

Pick-up

10 The tailgate and the drop side flaps are removed in the same way. First remove the circlips from the hinge pins.

11 Have an assistant support the tailgate or drop side flap. Drive out the hinge pins and remove the tailgate or flap.

12 The lower compartment doors are removed by unbolting their hinges from the body.

13 Refitting is a reversal of the removal procedure.

11 Tailgate support strut – removal and refitting

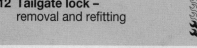

1 Open the tailgate and support it in the open position using a stout length of wood or with the help of an assistant.

2 Extract the retaining wire clip and carefully prise the ball end of the strut piston off the tailgate peg.

3 Extract the circlip and washers then slip the other end of the strut off the body peg. Lift away the strut.

4 Refitting is the reverse sequence to removal.

12 Tailgate lock – removal and refitting

1 With the tailgate open, undo the three screws securing the lock assembly and lock cylinder to the tailgate.

2 Withdraw the lock assembly followed by the lock cylinder.

3 Refitting is the reverse sequence to removal, but apply a little thread locking compound to the screw which retains the lock cylinder.

13 Windscreen and rear window – removal and refitting

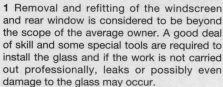

1 Removal and refitting of the windscreen and rear window is considered to be beyond the scope of the average owner. A good deal of skill and some special tools are required to install the glass and if the work is not carried out professionally, leaks or possibly even damage to the glass may occur.

2 If you are unfortunate enough to have a windscreen shatter, it is recommended that you entrust the renewal to a VW dealer or windscreen replacement specialist.

14 Door inner trim panels – removal and refitting

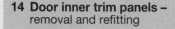

Front door

1 On models without electric windows, lift back the trim capping, undo the retaining screw and carefully prise off the window crank handle **(see illustration)**.

2 At the top and bottom of the door closing grip handle, prise out the trim caps and undo the retaining screws **(see illustration)**. Lift off the handle.

3 Release the remote control door handle finger plate to gain access to the escutcheon retaining screw **(see illustration)**. Undo the screw and lift off the escutcheon.

4 If an armrest is fitted, undo the two screws and withdraw the armrest from the door.

5 Starting at the upper rear corner, release the trim panel retaining buttons by carefully levering between the panel and door with a screwdriver or flat bar. With all the buttons released, lift off the panel **(see illustration)**. On models with electric windows, disconnect the window operating switch.

6 To gain access to the door internal components, carefully pull back the plastic condensation barrier, as necessary **(see illustration)**.

7 Refitting is the reverse sequence to removal.

Passenger and sliding door

8 The procedure for trim panel removal on the passenger doors and sliding door (as applicable) is essentially the same as the procedure for the front doors. On certain versions additional self-tapping screws are used to retain the panel, but minor differences such as this will be obvious after a visual inspection.

15 Front door – removal, refitting and adjustment

1 Carefully mark the outline of the door hinge retaining bolt washers on the body pillar as a guide to refitting.

2 Extract the circlip then withdraw the door check strap retaining pin.

14.5 Inner trim panel removal

14.6 Pull back the condensation barrier to reach the door components

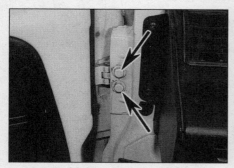

15.3 Front door hinge retaining bolts (arrowed)

15.4 An Allen key is needed for the striker retaining bolts

3 Support the door on blocks and have an assistant steady it, then undo the four hinge retaining bolts **(see illustration)**. Carefully lift away the door.

4 Refitting is the reverse sequence to removal. Adjust the position of the door as necessary so that there is a uniform gap all round before tightening the hinge retaining bolts. Adjust the striker plate so that the door closes fully without slamming **(see illustration)**. Up and down and side to side movement is possible at both hinges and at the striker plate to cater for adjustment.

16 Front door lock components – removal and refitting

Note: *For models with central locking, also see Section 23.*

1 Remove the inner trim panel as described in Section 14.

2 Undo the two bolts securing the remote control handle to the door and disconnect the handle from the lock pull rod **(see illustration)**.

3 Carefully pull the door rubber seal away around the door lock and undo the screw securing the exterior handle to the lock and door **(see illustration)**.

4 Pivot the handle outwards then release the lug at the other end of the handle from its location **(see illustration)**.

5 Using an Allen key, undo the two socket-headed retaining bolts securing the lock to the door. Pull the lock outwards to disengage the locking lever from the sleeve on the locking rod. Now withdraw the lock assembly complete with remote control pullrod **(see illustration)**.

6 Refitting is the reverse sequence to removal, but ensure that the locking rod sleeve engages with the locking lever as the lock is fitted **(see illustration)**. Apply a little thread locking compound to the lock, exterior handle and remote control handle retaining screws before fitting.

17 Front door glass and regulator – removal and refitting

1 Remove the inner trim panel as described in Section 14 for access to the door glass and associated components **(see illustration)**.

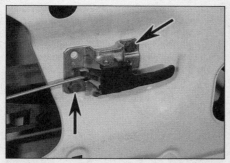

16.2 Remote control handle retaining bolts (arrowed)

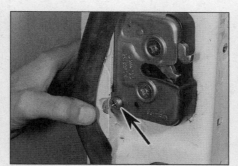

16.3 Outer handle retaining screw (arrowed)

16.4 Removing the outer handle from the door

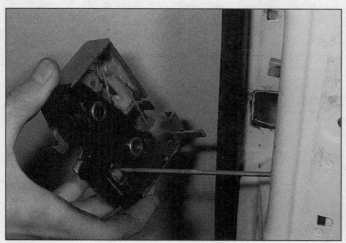

16.5 Removing the door lock

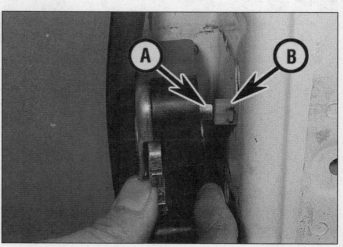

16.6 The door lock locking finger (A) must engage with the locking sleeve (B) as the lock is fitted

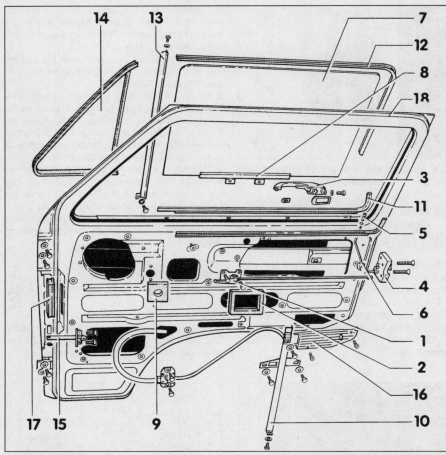

17.1 Front door components

1	Inner handle and pullrod	9	Gasket
2	Seal	10	Window lifter mechanism
3	Outer handle	11	Seals
4	Lock	12	Runner
5	Knob	13	Front guide runner
6	Locking rod and sleeve	14	Quarter window
7	Window	15	Check strap
8	Window lifting channel	16	Ventilator
		17	Air duct seal
		18	Door seal

Models without electric windows

2 Lower the window glass and undo the two bolts securing the regulator slide to the window frame **(see illustration)**.

3 Push the window upwards and wedge it in the raised position.

4 Undo the two bolts securing the regulator slide to the door frame **(see illustrations)**.

5 Lift off the foam rubber seal around the regulator crank spindle and undo the two bolts securing the regulator crank to the door **(see illustration)**.

6 Carefully bend back the metal tag supporting the regulator rack loop then manipulate the regulator assembly out of the door aperture.

7 Lift up the rubber seal directly above the front guide channel and undo the guide upper retaining bolt **(see illustration)**.

8 Undo the front guide channel lower retaining bolt **(see illustration)**. Pull the guide down and remove it from the door aperture.

17.2 Regulator slide to window frame retaining bolts (arrowed)

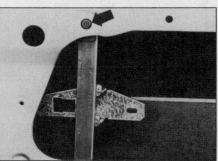

17.4A Window regulator slide upper retaining bolt (arrowed)

17.4B Window regulator slide lower retaining bolt (arrowed)

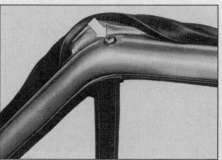

17.5 Window regulator retaining bolts (arrowed) and supporting tag (5)

17.7 Front guide channel upper retaining bolt (arrowed)

17.8 Front guide channel lower retaining bolt (arrowed)

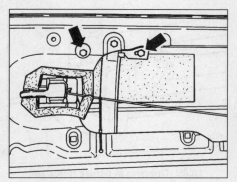

17.14 Regulator slide to window frame retaining bolts (arrowed) - models with electric windows

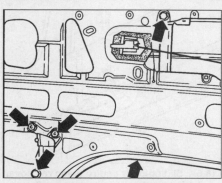

17.18 Regulator securing nuts and bolts (arrowed) - models with electric windows

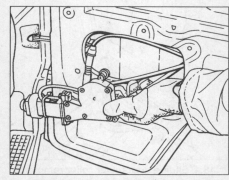

17.19 Removing the electric window regulator mechanism from the door

9 Lower the window glass carefully to the bottom of the door.
10 Release the inner and outer window slot seals by carefully prising them free.
11 Move the corner window rearward and remove it from the door.
12 The window glass can now be carefully lifted upwards and out of the door.
13 Refitting is the reverse sequence to removal. Before tightening the window frame

to regulator slide retaining bolts, raise the window fully to centralise it in the channels. The glass can then be lowered slightly and the bolts tightened through the access hole.

Models with electric windows

14 Temporarily refit the window operating switch. Lower the window glass and undo the two bolts securing the regulator slide to the window frame **(see illustration)**. If the regulator motor is not working (and assuming that it is the motor and not its power supply which is defective), it will be necessary to cut the regulator cables in order to lower the glass.
15 Disconnect the battery earth lead.
16 Push the window glass upwards and wedge it in the raised position.
17 Cut the cable tie which secures the regulator motor wiring harness to the door frame.
18 Remove the three bolts and two nuts which secure the regulator assembly to the door frame **(see illustration)**.
19 Manoeuvre the regulator assembly out of the door aperture **(see illustration)**. This is a fiddly business; it is necessary to withdraw

the motor part way, then turn it over in order to allow the cables to pass through the aperture. Wear protective gloves and be careful not to damage the cable guides.
20 The window glass can now be removed as described earlier in this Section (paragraph 7 onwards).
21 Refitting is a reversal of the removal procedure. Check the operation of the window before refitting the trim panel.

18 Sliding door – removal and refitting

Early models (up to 1984)

1 Undo the retaining screw securing the centre guide rail cover in position at the rear **(see illustration)**. With the door open, remove the screw securing the guide rail cover at the front **(see illustration)**. The guide rail cover must now be carefully tapped upward using a hammer and plastic drift to release it from the upper U-shaped rail into which it is passed.
2 With the guide rail cover removed and with the help of an assistant, slide the door back until the hinge guide and link can be released from the opening in the centre guide rail **(see illustration)**.
3 Pivot the door outwards at the rear, slide it back fully and lift the door to release the upper sliding block from its guide **(see illustration)**.

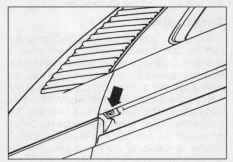

18.1A Sliding door centre guide rail cover rear retaining screw (arrowed)

18.1B Sliding door centre guide rail cover front retaining screw (arrowed) - early models

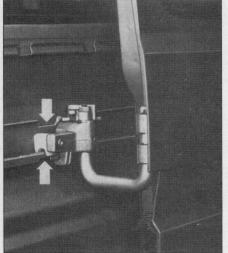

18.2 Opening in centre guide rail (arrowed) for hinge guide and link removal - early models

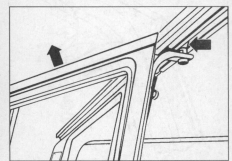

18.3 Pivot the sliding door outwards and back to release the upper sliding block

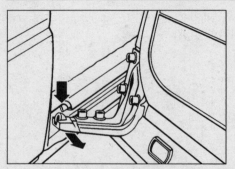

18.4 Sliding door lower roller removal

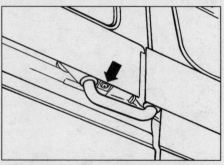

18.6A Sliding door centre guide rail cover front retaining screw (arrowed) - later models

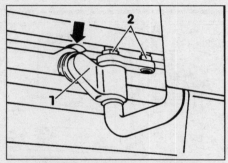

18.6B Opening in centre guide rail (arrowed) - later models

1 Roller carrier 2 Upper rollers

4 Pivot the door outwards as necessary and slip the lower roller out of the guide rail opening **(see illustration)**.

5 Refitting is the reverse sequence to removal. Open and close the door several times to check its operation after refitting and check the fit of the door in the closed position.

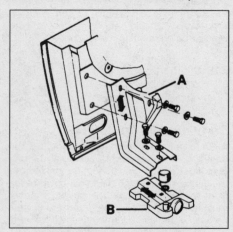

19.2 Sliding door roller arm (A) and guide assembly (B) retaining bolt and adjustment details

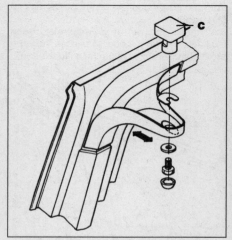

19.4 Sliding door upper guide block (C) adjustment details

Carry out the adjustments described in Section 19 if necessary.

Later models (1985 on)

6 The procedure is the same as that just described for early models, but note the detail differences shown **(see illustrations)**.

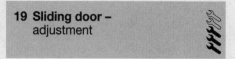

19 Sliding door – adjustment

1 The sliding door should be adjusted to give a uniform gap all round with the door closed, and a flush fit in relation to the adjacent body panels. The guides and rollers and the striker plate can be individually adjusted to achieve this after removing the centre guide rail cover as described in Section 18.

Lower roller guide

2 If the front end of the door is not in alignment slacken the bolts securing the roller arm to the door and move the door up or down as necessary. Tighten the bolts when the correct position is obtained **(see illustration)**.

19.5A Sliding door striker plate adjustment details - early models

3 Slacken the bolts securing the guide assembly to the roller arm and move the front of the door in or out as necessary. Tighten the bolts when the correct position is obtained.

Upper guide block

4 If the top of the door is not aligned with the outer panel, prise off the protective cap, slacken the guide block retaining bolt and move the door in or out as required. When the correct position is achieved, tighten the bolt and refit the cap **(see illustration)**.

Striker plate

5 To adjust the fit of the door, horizontal and vertical adjustment of the striker plate is provided. On early models, slacken the socket headed retaining bolts using an Allen key and reposition the striker plate as necessary. Tighten the bolts fully after adjustment **(see illustration)**. On later models, slacken the striker pin itself **(see illustration)**. On all models, if the position of the striker plate is moved appreciably the hinge link will also require adjustment.

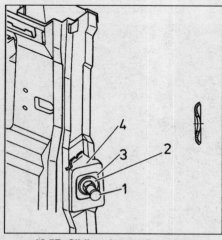

19.5B Sliding door striker plate adjustment details - later models

1 Striker pin
2 Spring retainer (sectional detail also shown)
3 Reference lines
4 Bracket

19.6 Sliding door remote control striker plate (arrowed)

Remote control striker plate

6 Using an Allen key, slacken the two remote control striker plate retaining bolts **(see illustration)**.

7 Close the door from the inside to centralise the striker plate, hold the plate in this position and open the door again. Tighten the bolts without moving the striker plate position.

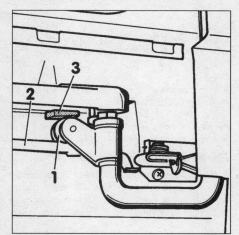

19.10 Position the roller (1) on the guide rail (2) by using a wooden or plastic wedge (3)

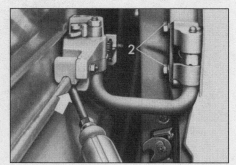

19.11 With the sliding door open tighten the retaining bolts (2). On early models, hold the roller central at the point arrowed

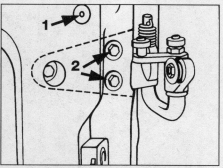

19.9 Hinge link front (1) and rear (2) retaining bolts

8 If, after adjustment, it is still not possible to easily lock the door from the outside using the key, and from the inside using the locking lever, then the striker plate should be moved out by placing packing pieces behind it. Up to two packing pieces may be used which are available from VW parts stockists.

Hinge link

9 Slacken the hinge link rear retaining bolts **(see illustration)** then close the door from the outside. Check the gap at the front and rear of the door and if necessary slacken the hinge link front retaining bolt and correct the door

position. Tighten the front retaining bolt only at this stage.

10 Close the door. On early models, lever the hinge guide and link down using a screwdriver until the roller is located in the centre of the guide rail. On later models, position the roller on the guide rail by driving in a small wooden or plastic wedge **(see illustration)**.

11 Carefully open the sliding door while supporting it at the rear. Hold the door in this position and tighten the rear retaining bolts **(see illustration)**. On later models, remove the wooden or plastic wedge on completion.

20 Sliding door locks – removal and refitting

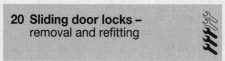

1 Remove the inner trim panel from the sliding door, referring to the procedure in Section 14 as a guide.

Remote control lock components

2 With the door open undo the retaining screw and pull the inner door handle off its spindle **(see illustration)**.

3 Undo the retaining screw and withdraw the outer handle with seal, escutcheon and spacer washer from the lock.

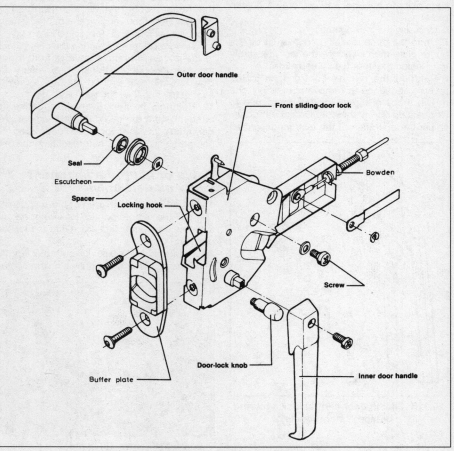

20.2 Exploded view of the sliding door lock components

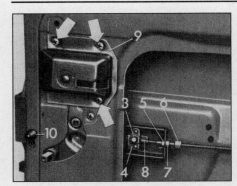

**20.4 Sliding door lock removal -
early type shown**

3 Circlip
4 Lock lever peg
5 Cable locknut
6 Adjusting nut
7 Cable locknut
8 Bowden cable
9 Door latch plate
10 Locking knob

4 Extract the circlip securing the Bowden
cable or pullrod to the peg on the lock lever
and slip off the pullrod or cable end. Where a
Bowden cable is used slacken the locknut
securing the cable to the lock bracket and
unscrew the cable as necessary so that it can
be slipped out of the bracket (see
illustration).
5 Undo the three screws securing the door
latch plate to the door and withdraw the latch
plate.
6 Unscrew the locking knob.
7 Undo the three retaining screws, lift off the
buffer plate then withdraw the lock assembly
from inside the door (see illustration).
8 Refitting the remote control lock is the
reverse sequence to removal, but apply one
or two drops of thread locking compound to
all retaining screw threads. On early models,
adjust the operation of the lock as described

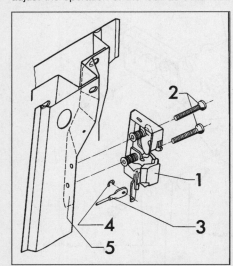

**20.11B Sliding door central lock securing
details - later models**

1 Lock
2 Securing
   screws
3 Pullrod
4 Circlip
5 Door

**20.7 Sliding door lock buffer plate (11),
door lock (12) and retaining screws
(arrowed) - early type shown**

in paragraph 13 onwards before refitting the
trim panel.

Central lock components

9 Pull the remote control lock inner handle to
throw the central lock latch into the locked
position.
10 Release the Bowden cable or pullrod from
the remote control lock as described in
paragraph 4, then remove the cable from its
support cushions and door panel clip.
11 Undo the screws securing the central lock
to the door and remove the lock from inside
the door (see illustrations). If necessary the
Bowden cable or pullrod may be removed
after extracting the retaining clip.
12 Refitting is the reverse sequence to
removal, but on early models adjust the
operation of the lock as described in
paragraph 13 onwards before refitting the trim
panel.

Cable or pullrod adjustment (early models only)

13 To adjust the Bowden cable or pullrod,
first pull the remote control lock inner handle
to throw the central lock latch into the locked
position.
14 Using an M4 screw of suitable length,
push the screw into the drilling in the central

**20.14 M4 screw (16) in place in central
lock drilling (17) prior to adjustment**

**20.11A Sliding door central lock (13) and
retaining screws (arrowed) - early models**

lock and screw it into the operating lever (see
illustration).
15 Slacken the Bowden cable or the
threaded sleeve of the pullrod, then adjust the
cable or rod length so that the remote control
lock operating rod just contacts its stop (see
illustration). Tighten the cable or rod locknuts
in this position, then remove the M4 locating
screw.
16 Check the operation of the door and its fit
in the body aperture and if necessary carry
out the adjustments described in Section 19.
17 Refit the inner trim panel after completing
the adjustments.

21 Sliding door hinge link – removal, overhaul and refitting

1 Remove the sliding door from the vehicle as
described in Section 18.
2 Remove the inner trim panel, undo the three
hinge link retaining bolts and withdraw the
assembly from inside the door.

Early models (up to 1984)

3 Carefully examine the hinge link assembly
for wear, particularly around the roller, guide,
locking lever and cam. Certain parts are
available separately and if wear has taken

**20.15 Sliding door Bowden cable
adjustment**

3 Circlip
4 Lock lever peg
5 Cable locknut
6 Adjusting nut
7 Cable locknut
8 Bowden cable
18 Operating rod
   stop

21.3 Exploded view of the sliding door hinge link assembly - early models

1 Housing	14 Nut
2 Seal	15 Cam
3 Spring attachment	16 Spring washer
4 Pin	17 Nut
5 Hinge link	18 Washer
6 Spring	19 Lower locking
7 Circlip	lever
8 Hinge mounting	20 Spacer
9 Roller	21 Spring
10 Stud	22 Upper locking
11 Screw	lever
12 Guide	23 Stud
13 Spring washer	24 Circlip

place the assembly can be dismantled as follows for the new parts to be fitted **(see illustration)**.

4 Extract the small circlip and withdraw the housing and spring from the hinge link.

5 Withdraw the spring attachment from the spring after tapping out the pin.

6 If the guide requires renewal, file or grind off the retaining rivet and remove the guide. Note that a new guide is supplied with a retaining nut, bolt and washer in place of the rivet.

7 Remove the roller from the mounting by pressing out the retaining pin.

8 Extract the locking lever pin circlip, press the pin out of the housing and recover the locking levers, springs, spacers and washers noting the fitted direction of all the parts.

9 Finally undo the nut and washer and withdraw the operating cam.

Later models (1985 on)

10 On later models the hinge link assembly has fewer parts **(see illustration)**. Dismantling is relatively straightforward, the hinge end of the assembly being released by driving out the cotter pin and the roller end by removing the circlips and nuts.

All models

11 Renew any worn parts and then reassemble the unit using the reverse sequence to removal. Lubricate all moving parts and contact areas with a light smear of multi-purpose grease.

21.10 Exploded view of the sliding door hinge link assembly - later models

1 Hinge	11 Nut
2 Seal	12 Washer
3 Spring	13 Roller
4 Seal	14 Roller carrier
5 Seal	15 Seal
6 Seal	16 Guide lever
7 Seal	17 Nut
8 Cotter pin	18 Bearing
9 Link	19 Circlips
10 Seal	

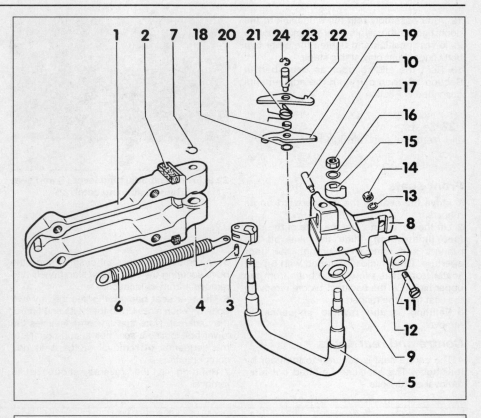

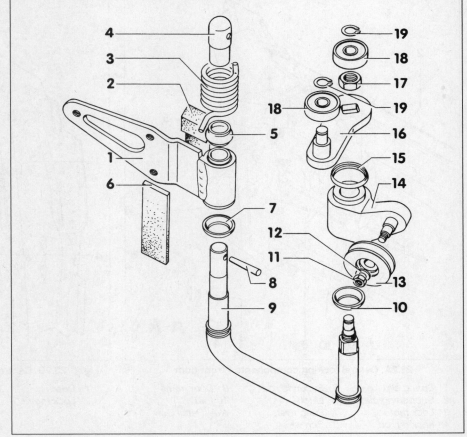

12 After assembly refit the hinge link to the door, tighten the single front retaining bolt in its lowest position and tighten the other two bolts finger tight only at this stage.

13 Refit the sliding door as described in Section 18, then carry out the adjustments described in Section 19.

22 Seats –
removal and refitting

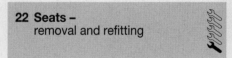

Front seats

1 Move the seat all the way forward on its runners.

2 Lift the small catch on the side of the seat (see illustration). Slide the seat off the runners and remove it through the door aperture. On vehicles equipped with a two-seater front seat, remove the bolts from the upper hinge on the backrest before removing the seat from the runners.

3 Refitting is the reverse sequence to removal.

Centre and rear seats

4 The centre seat is secured to the floor by four bolts. The seat can be lifted out after removal of the bolts.

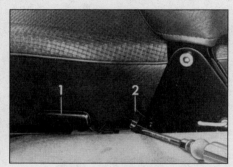

22.2 Front seat adjusting lever (1) and seat runner retaining catch (2)

5 To remove the rear seat cushion undo the bolts securing the seat to the side panels and remove it from its location.

6 The rear seat backrest is secured by two bolts on each side. Undo the bolts and lift out the backrest. Note that on some vehicles the lower bolt is also a seat belt anchorage. Note the sequence of removal of the seat belt components.

7 Refitting is the reverse sequence to removal.

23 Central locking system –
general information

1 A central locking system is available as an option on most models from 1986.

2 Access to the locking system motors is gained by removing the appropriate door trim panel. Details of the motor fastenings and connections are as shown (see illustrations).

3 The front door and sliding door lock motors may be removed with or without their supporting plates. The lock motors are screwed to the supporting plates; the plates themselves are secured by rivets which must be drilled out for removal. Use new blind rivets when refitting.

24 Sunroof panel –
removal and refitting

1 Open the sunroof slightly.

2 Release the five clips securing the trim panel at the front edge of the sunroof (see illustration).

3 Push the trim panel to the rear as far as the stop.

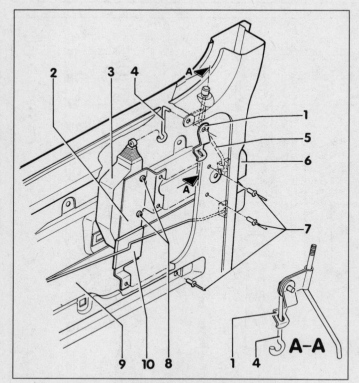

23.2A Central locking components - front door

1 Spring clip	*5 Securing rod*	*9 Door frame*
2 Supporting plate	*6 Latch*	*10 Pad*
3 Lock motor	*7 Blind rivets*	*A-A Detail view*
4 Locking rod	*8 Screws*	

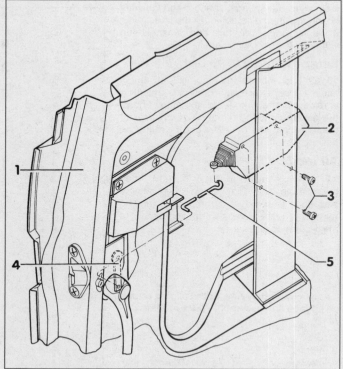

23.2B Central locking components - sliding door

1 Door	*3 Screws*	*5 Locking rod*
2 Lock motor	*4 Lock lever*	

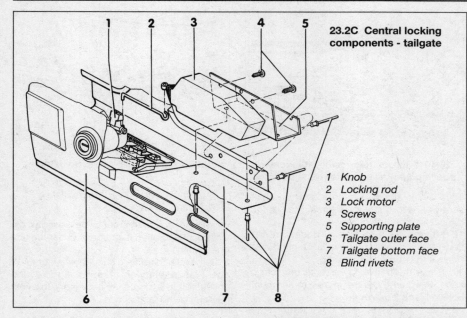

23.2C Central locking
components - tailgate

1 Knob
2 Locking rod
3 Lock motor
4 Screws
5 Supporting plate
6 Tailgate outer face
7 Tailgate bottom face
8 Blind rivets

4 Pull the sunroof panel forward but stop before the lifter is activated.
5 Pull the leaf spring to the centre, then pull the crank out of its support **(see illustration)**.
6 Undo the two screws securing the panel to the front guide.
7 Lift the panel at the front, then lift out the panel at the rear through the openings in the guide rail **(see illustration)**.
8 Refitting is the reverse sequence to removal.

25 Sunroof trim panel – removal and refitting

1 Remove the sunroof panel as described in Section 24.
2 Remove the drive handle, slacken the two handle plate retaining screws by approximately six turns then detach the cables from the drivegear **(see illustration)**.

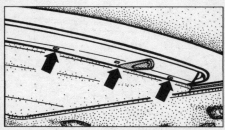

24.2 Sunroof trim panel front edge clips (arrowed)

3 Remove the guide block, move the guide plate forward and slide it out of the rail **(see illustration)**.
4 Move the cable guides forward and slide them out of the rail **(see illustration)**.
5 Remove all the rail securing screws on one side.
6 Push the rail to the rear and lift it together with the trim panel.
7 Push the rail to the outside slightly and remove the trim panel.
8 Refitting is the reverse sequence to removal.

26 Sunroof panel – adjustment

1 Refer to Section 24 and carry out the operations described in paragraphs 1 to 3.

Front height alignment

2 Slacken the two screws securing the panel to the front guide **(see illustration)**.

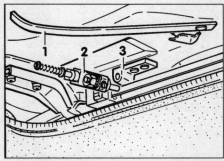

24.5 Sunroof panel leaf spring (1), crank (2) and crank support (3)

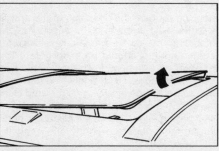

24.7 Lift the sunroof panel up at the front then out through the guide rail openings at the rear

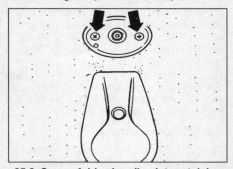

25.2 Sunroof drive handle plate retaining screws (arrowed)

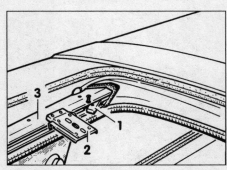

25.3 Sunroof guide block (1), guide plate (2) and guide rail (3)

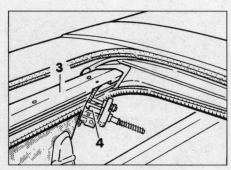

25.4 Sunroof guide rail (3) and cable guide (4)

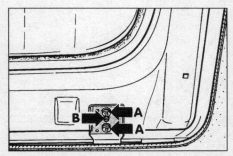

26.2 Sunroof front guide retaining screws (A) and front height alignment adjusting screw (B)

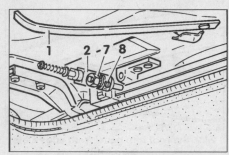

26.6 Sunroof rear height alignment

1 Leaf spring   *7 Pin retaining nut*
2 Crank assembly   *8 Retaining screw*

3 Turn the small adjusting screw, located between the two retaining screws, until the panel is in alignment.
4 Tighten the retaining screws.

Rear height alignment

5 Lower the sunroof panel at the rear.
6 Swing the leaf spring to the centre then withdraw the crank from its support (see illustration).
7 Slacken the retaining nut and the screw in the side of the crank.
8 Move the pin in the crank slot as necessary to achieve the correct alignment then tighten the screw and retaining nut.
9 Refit the crank to its support, close the sunroof and check the alignment.

Guide plate adjustment

10 The guide plate should always be adjusted after adjustment of the rear height alignment. Adjustment is carried out with the panel closed and the guide plates located above the slot in the rails (see illustration).
11 Lower the panel and slacken the two guide plate retaining screws.
12 Turn the adjusting screw in the guide plate until all the play between the guide plate and rail is eliminated then tighten the retaining screws (see illustration).

Parallel adjustment

13 Turn the drive handle approximately two turns anti-clockwise to lower the panel at the rear.
14 Remove the handle and the cover plate.

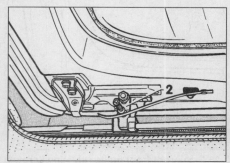

26.17 Sunroof cranks (2) positioned vertically during panel parallel adjustment

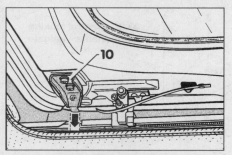

26.10 Sunroof guide plate (10) located above guide rail slot prior to adjustment

15 Slacken the two handle plate retaining screws approximately six turns, then detach the cables from the drivegear.
16 Move the sunroof panel back and forth several times in its guide rails by hand, then move it forward up to the stop.
17 Press the panel upwards at the rear by hand, then turn both the cranks to an upright position (see illustration).
18 Temporarily refit the drive handle then turn the drive to the right, to its stop.
19 Lubricate the cables with multi-purpose grease and refit them to their locations.
20 Refit the cover plate and the drive handle with the handle positioned so that it rests in its recess when the panel is closed.

27 Pop-up and hinged roofs – inspection

1 The most important points to check on the opening roof are the condition of the special weather seal strips and the security of the mounting bracket screws. If any sealing strip comes adrift it should be fixed before it is trapped and damaged. The main roof seal strip incorporates steel clips which may have lost some of their tension. Pull the strip clear, squeeze the clips together and then push the seal back on. See that all the pivot pins of the support brackets are lightly oiled and the slotted runners thinly greased.
2 The fabric parts should be wiped clean without the use of detergents and should never be folded and left damp. Whenever

28.2 Removing the heater control trim panel

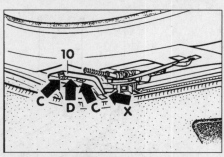

26.12 Sunroof guide plate adjustment

C Guide plate   *X Guide rail*
*   retaining screws*   *10 Guide plate*
D Adjusting screw

conditions require the roof to be closed whilst wet be sure to open it and dry it out at the first opportunity.
3 Removal and refitting should be left to a VW agent as a number of special tools and considerable expertise is necessary to avoid damage to the fabric parts.

28 Facia – removal and refitting

1 Remove the instrument panel as described in Chapter 12 and the steering column as described in Chapter 9.
2 Pull off the heater and ventilator operating levers then carefully prise off the heater control trim panel (see illustration).
3 Undo the four retaining screws and remove the glovebox.
4 From behind the facia detach the fresh air outlet hoses at the ventilators.
5 Undo the screws securing the facia top edge below the windscreen and the side screws securing the facia to the pillars (see illustration). Undo the heater control retaining screws.
6 Pull the facia away from its location and when sufficient clearance exists, remove any additional optional equipment or accessories as applicable.
7 Remove the facia through the front door opening.
8 Refitting is the reverse sequence to removal.

28.5 Facia to pillar retaining screws (arrowed)

Chapter 12
Electrical system

Contents

Degrees of difficulty

Easy, suitable for novice with little experience		Fairly easy, suitable for beginner with some experience		Fairly difficult, suitable for competent DIY mechanic		Difficult, suitable for experienced DIY mechanic		Very difficult, suitable for expert DIY or professional	

Specifications

System type .... 12 volt, negative earth

Fuses (typical) - models up to 1985

Fuse	Circuits protected	Rating (A)
1	Left-hand tail light, parking light and side marker lamp	8
2	Right-hand tail light, parking light and side marker lamp, number plate lamps, foglamps	8
3	Left-hand dipped beam	8
4	Right-hand dipped beam	8
5	Left-hand main beam, main beam warning lamp	8
6	Right-hand main beam	8
7	Radiator fan	8
8	Interior lights, brake lights, cigarette lighter	8
9	Hazard flasher system, radio	16
10	Windscreen wipers and washer pump, heater blower	16
11	Direction indicators	8
12	Horn	8

Additional line fuses located to the right of the fusebox protect the following circuits (where fitted):

Heated rear window	8
Rear foglights	8
Rear wiper	8
Auxiliary heater main fuse	16
Auxiliary heater overheating protection	8

Additional line fuse in engine compartment:

Reversing lights	8

Fuses (typical) - 1986 and later models

Fuse	Circuits protected	Rating (A)
1	Radiator fan	30
2	Brake lights	10
3	Interior lights, clock, cigarette lighter, radio	15
4	Hazard warning lights	15
5	Spare	
6	Foglamps	15
7	Left-hand tail and sidelamps	10
8	Right-hand tail and sidelamps	10
9	Right-hand main beam	10
10	Left-hand main beam	10
11	Windscreen wipe/wash switch	15
12	Electric windows, air conditioning, rear wiper	20
13	Heater blower	20
14	Heated rear window, lighting switch illumination	20
15	Reversing lights	10
16	Horn	15
17	Windscreen wiper motor	10
18	Braking system warning lamp, heated seat	10 or 20
19	Direction indicators	10
20	Number plate lamp, headlamp washer	10
21	Left-hand dipped beam	10
22	Right-hand dipped beam	10

Additional fuses under right-hand rear seat:

	Reading light	8
	Luggage area lights	8

Additional fuses above main fusebox:

	Instrument lighting	10
	Rear foglight	10
	Auxiliary heater overheating protection	10
	Auxiliary heater main fuse	20
	Central locking	20
	Electric windows	20

Torque wrench settings

	Nm	lbf ft
Windscreen wiper spindle retaining nuts	8	6
Windscreen wiper arm retaining nuts	5	4

1 General information

Warning: Before carrying out any work on the electrical system, read through the precautions given in 'Safety First!' at the beginning of this manual and in Chapter 5A.

The electrical system is of the 12 volt negative earth type. Power for the lights and all electrical accessories is supplied by a lead-acid battery which is charged by the alternator.

This Chapter covers repair and service procedures for the various electrical components not associated with the engine. Information on the battery, alternator and starter motor can be found in Chapter 5A.

2 Electrical fault-finding – general information

Note: *Refer to the precautions given in 'Safety first!' and in Chapter 5A before starting work. The following tests relate to testing of the main electrical circuits, and should not be used to test delicate electronic circuits (such as engine management systems, anti-lock braking systems, etc.), particularly where an electronic control module is used.*

General

1 A typical electrical circuit consists of an electrical component, any switches, relays, motors, fuses, fusible links or circuit breakers related to that component, and the wiring and connectors that link the component to both the battery and the chassis. To help to pinpoint a problem in an electrical circuit, wiring diagrams are included at the end of this manual.

2 Before attempting to diagnose an electrical fault, first study the appropriate wiring diagram to obtain a complete understanding of the components included in the particular circuit concerned. The possible sources of a fault can be narrowed down by noting if other components related to the circuit are operating properly. If several components or circuits fail at one time, the problem is likely to be related to a shared fuse or earth connection.

3 Electrical problems often stem from simple causes, such as loose or corroded connections, a faulty earth connection, a blown fuse, a melted fusible link, or a faulty relay (refer to Section 3 for details of testing relays). Visually inspect the condition of all fuses, wires and connections in a problem circuit before testing the components. Use the wiring diagrams to determine which terminal connections will need to be checked, to pinpoint the trouble-spot.

4 The basic tools required for electrical fault-finding include a circuit tester or voltmeter (a 12-volt bulb with a set of test leads can also be used for certain tests); a self-powered test light (sometimes known as a continuity tester); an ohmmeter (to measure resistance); a battery and set of test leads; and a jumper wire, preferably with a circuit breaker or fuse incorporated, which can be used to bypass suspect wires or electrical components. Before attempting to locate a problem with test instruments, use the wiring diagram to determine where to make the connections.

5 To find the source of an intermittent wiring fault (usually due to a poor or dirty connection, or damaged wiring insulation), a 'wiggle' test can be performed on the wiring. This involves wiggling the wiring by hand to see if the fault occurs as the wiring is moved. It should be possible to narrow down the source of the fault to a particular section of wiring. This method of testing can be used in conjunction with any of the tests described in the following sub-Sections.

6 Apart from problems due to poor connections, two basic types of fault can occur in an electrical circuit - open-circuit, or short-circuit.

7 Open-circuit faults are caused by a break somewhere in the circuit, which prevents current from flowing. An open-circuit fault will prevent a component from working, but will not cause the relevant circuit fuse to blow.

8 Short-circuit faults are caused by a 'short' somewhere in the circuit, which allows the current flowing in the circuit to 'escape' along an alternative route, usually to earth. Short-circuit faults are normally caused by a breakdown in wiring insulation, which allows a feed wire to touch either another wire, or an earthed component such as the bodyshell. A short-circuit fault will normally cause the relevant circuit fuse to blow.

Finding an open-circuit

9 To check for an open-circuit, connect one lead of a circuit tester or voltmeter to either the negative battery terminal or a known good earth.

10 Connect the other lead to a connector in the circuit being tested, preferably nearest to the battery or fuse.

11 Switch on the circuit, remembering that some circuits are live only when the ignition switch is moved to a particular position.

12 If voltage is present (indicated either by the tester bulb lighting or a voltmeter reading, as applicable), this means that the section of the circuit between the relevant connector and the battery is problem-free.

13 Continue to check the remainder of the circuit in the same fashion.

14 When a point is reached at which no voltage is present, the problem must lie between that point and the previous test point with voltage. Most problems can be traced to a broken, corroded or loose connection.

Finding a short-circuit

15 To check for a short-circuit, first disconnect the load (s), from the circuit (loads are the components that draw current from a circuit, such as bulbs, motors, heating elements, etc.).

16 Remove the relevant fuse from the circuit, and connect a circuit tester or voltmeter to the fuse connections.

17 Switch on the circuit, remembering that some circuits are live only when the ignition switch is moved to a particular position.

18 If voltage is present (indicated either by the tester bulb lighting or a voltmeter reading, as applicable), this means that there is a short-circuit.

19 If no voltage is present, but the fuse still blows with the load(s) connected, this indicates an internal fault in the load(s).

Finding an earth fault

20 The battery negative terminal is connected to 'earth' - the metal of the engine/transmission and the car body - and most systems are wired so that they only receive a positive feed, the current returning through the metal of the car body. This means that the component mounting and the body form part of that circuit. Loose or corroded mountings can therefore cause a range of electrical faults, ranging from total failure of a circuit, to a puzzling partial fault. In particular, lights may shine dimly (especially when another circuit sharing the same earth point is in operation), motors (e.g. wiper motors or the radiator cooling fan motor) may run slowly, and the operation of one circuit may have an apparently unrelated effect on another. Note that on many vehicles, earth straps are used between certain components, such as the engine/transmission and the body, usually where there is no metal-to-metal contact between components due to flexible rubber mountings, etc.

21 To check whether a component is properly earthed, disconnect the battery, and connect one lead of an ohmmeter to a known good earth point. Connect the other lead to the wire or earth connection being tested. The resistance reading should be zero; if not, check the connection as follows.

22 If an earth connection is thought to be faulty, dismantle the connection, and clean back to bare metal both the bodyshell and the wire terminal or the component earth connection mating surface. Be careful to remove all traces of dirt and corrosion, then use a knife to trim away any paint, so that a clean metal-to-metal joint is made. On reassembly, tighten the joint fasteners securely; if a wire terminal is being refitted, use serrated washers between the terminal and the bodyshell, to ensure a clean and secure connection. When the connection is re-made, prevent the onset of corrosion in the future by applying a coat of petroleum jelly or silicone-based grease. Alternatively, (at regular intervals) spray on a proprietary ignition sealer or a water-dispersant lubricant.

3.1 Fusebox with retaining screws (arrowed) - early type

3 Fuses and relays – general information

Fuses

1 The fusebox is situated below the facia on the left-hand side **(see illustration)**. To gain access to the fuses simply lift off the transparent plastic cover. The fuse numbers are shown on the cover and information on the circuits they protect is given in the Specifications.

2 Early models (up to 1985) use ceramic fuses; later models use 'blade' fuses. Each fuse is colour coded and has its rating stamped on it. To remove a fuse, ease it carefully out of its locating contacts. A pair of special tweezers for removing blade fuses is provided in the later type fusebox.

3 A blown fuse can be recognised by the wire in the centre having melted. Before renewing a blown fuse, trace and rectify the cause and always use a fuse of the correct value. Never substitute a fuse of a higher rating or use such things as a piece of wire, metal foil or a pin to act as a makeshift fuse as more serious damage or even fire may result.

4 In addition to the fuses in the main fusebox, line fuses are found in various locations (see Specifications) to protect optional or territory-specific equipment.

Relays

5 A relay is an electrically-operated switch. The most common automotive use for relays is to switch high currents at a distance, so avoiding the need for long runs of heavy cable and heavy-duty switches. The direction indicator/hazard warning flasher unit is also a type of relay.

6 The relays are of the plug-in type and are situated on top of the main fusebox. To gain access to the relays, undo the fusebox retaining screw(s) and lower the fusebox **(see illustration)**. The relays can now be simply pulled out.

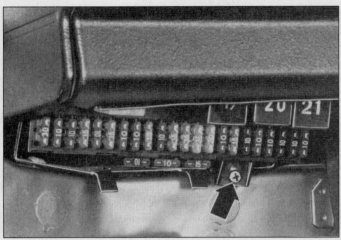

3.6 Fusebox retaining screw (arrowed) - later type

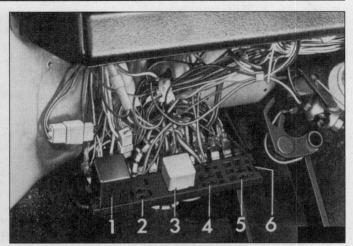

3.7A Relay locations on the fusebox (6) - early type

1 Flasher unit   4 Foglamp
2 For ambulance light   5 Wiper delay
3 X-contact (load reduction)

7 On early models five relay positions are provided in the fusebox; later models have provision for 18. The number of relays actually used varies according to vehicle specification **(see illustrations)**.

8 If a system controlled by a relay becomes inoperative, and the relay is suspect, operate the system: if the relay is functioning it should be possible to hear it click as it is energised. If this is the case, the fault probably lies with the other components of the system. If the relay is not being energised then it is not receiving a switching voltage, or the relay itself is faulty.

4 Direction indicator and hazard flasher system – fault finding

1 Should the direction indicators become faulty in operation, check the bulbs for security and make sure that the contact surfaces are not corroded. If one bulb blows or is making a poor connection due to corrosion, either the system will not flash on that side of the car, or it will flash abnormally quickly.

3.7B Relay and auxiliary fuse locations - later type. Not all items are fitted to all models

1 Spare   10 Wiper delay
2 Spare   11 Rear wash-wipe
3 Low coolant   12 Flasher unit
  warning   13 Headlight washer
4 Spare   14 Spare
5 Cooling fan   15 Rear foglamp fuse
6 Horn   16 Instrument lighting
7 Foglamp   fuse
8 X-contact (load   17 Spare
  reduction)   18 Spare
9 Not used

Location	Relay designation	Production control number	Remarks
1			vacant
2			vacant
3	Switch unit for coolant shortage indicator	43	
4			vacant
5	Relay for radiator fan	24	
6	Relay for dual tone horn	53	
7	Relay for fog light	15	

7.2 Lifting off the instrument panel cover

7.3 Removing the instrument panel plastic cover

7.4 Instrument panel switch removal

2 If the indicators operate in one direction and not the other, the fault is likely to be in the bulbs or wiring to the bulbs. If the system will not operate in either direction, operate the hazard flashers. If these function, check for a blown direction indicator fuse. If the fuse is satisfactory, the fault is likely to lie with the flasher unit.

3 If it is noticed that operation of the direction indicators is affected by the brake lights, the fault is due to a bad earth connection in the rear light cluster wiring.

5 Door pillar switches – removal and refitting

1 Disconnect the battery negative terminal.
2 Undo the retaining screw and withdraw the switch.
3 Disconnect the wiring terminal and remove the switch.
4 Refitting is the reverse sequence to removal.

6 Steering column switches – removal and refitting

1 Removal and refitting of the steering column switches is covered as part of the steering column dismantling procedure. Refer to Chapter 9.

7 Instrument panel switches – removal and refitting

1 Disconnect the battery negative terminal.
2 Remove the instrument panel cover by lifting up at the two recesses nearest the windscreen. Disengage the rear catches and lift off the cover (**see illustration**).
3 Take out the protective plastic cover over the instrument panel to provide greater access (**see illustration**).
4 Disconnect the wiring plugs from the rear of the relevant switch, depress the catches on the side and withdraw the switch from the instrument panel (**see illustration**).
5 Refitting the switches and instrument panel cover is the reverse sequence to removal.

8 Instrument panel illumination bulbs – renewal

1 Carry out the operations described in paragraphs 1 to 3 of the previous Section.
2 The panel illumination bulbholders can now be removed by carefully turning them 90° anti-clockwise (**see illustrations**).
3 The panel illumination bulbs are a push fit in their holders.
4 Refitting is the reverse sequence to removal.

9 Instrument panel – removal and refitting

1 Carry out the operations described in paragraphs 1 to 3 of Section 7.
2 Disconnect the wiring plugs from the rear of the instrument panel switches.
3 Disconnect the speedometer cable and the instrument panel wiring multi-plug connector.
4 Undo the screws securing the instrument panel to the facia, then lift the panel up and out of its location (**see illustration**).
5 Refitting is the reverse sequence to removal. Make sure that the speedometer cable is properly engaged.

10 Instrument panel – dismantling and reassembly

1 Remove the instrument panel from the vehicle as described in the previous Section.
2 Undo the screws securing the warning lamp casing mounting plate and lever the plate off carefully (**see illustrations**).
3 The panel warning lamp bulb or light emitting diodes (LED) can now be removed by easing back the printed circuit and withdrawing the bulb/LEDs from their terminals. The bulb, where fitted, is coloured blue, all the LEDs are coloured red, yellow or green. The LEDs are

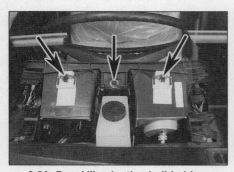

8.2A Panel illumination bulbholders (arrowed)

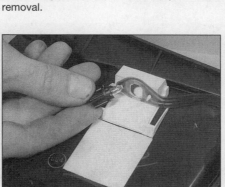

8.2B Removing a panel illumination bulbholder and bulb

9.4 Instrument panel retaining screws (arrowed)

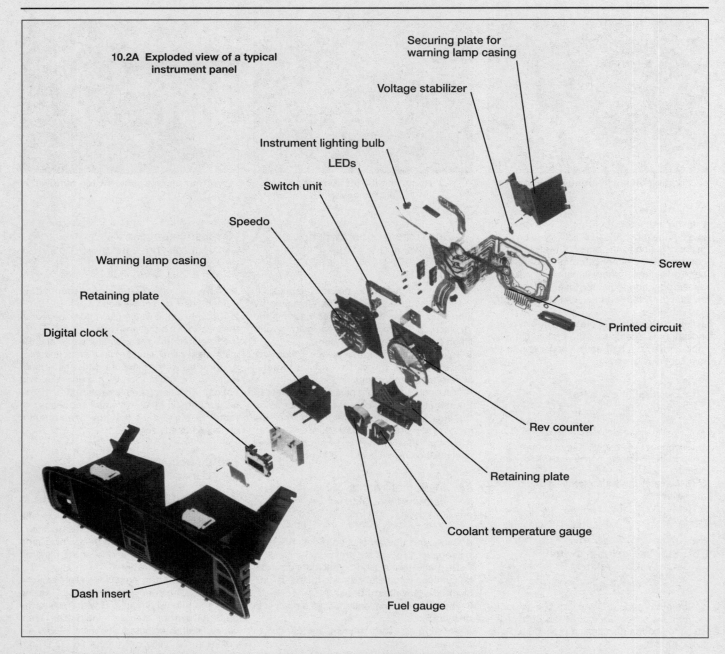

10.2A Exploded view of a typical instrument panel

Securing plate for warning lamp casing

Voltage stabilizer

Instrument lighting bulb

LEDs

Switch unit

Speedo

Warning lamp casing

Retaining plate

Digital clock

Screw

Printed circuit

Rev counter

Retaining plate

Coolant temperature gauge

Fuel gauge

Dash insert

10.2B Ease off the mounting plate carefully to avoid damaging the printed circuit

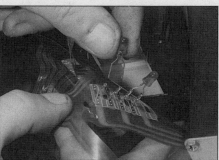

10.3A Renewing the instrument panel warning LEDs

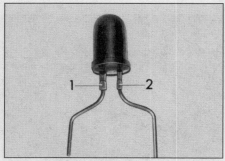

10.3B LED negative terminal (1) and positive terminal (2)

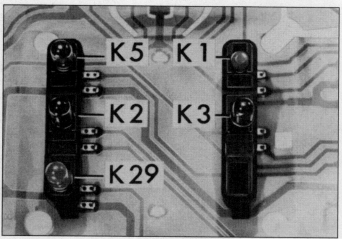

10.3C LED and bulb terminal positioning in the printed circuit

K1 *Blue bulb - high beam*
K2 *Red LED - alternator*
K3 *Red LED - oil pressure*
K5 *Green LED - direction indicator*
K29 *Not petrol models*

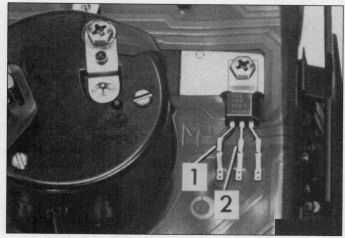

10.4 Voltage stabilizer location on instrument panel

1 *Positive terminal*
2 *Earth terminal*

polarity conscious and must be fitted into their terminals correctly. The negative terminal of the LED is slightly wider than the positive terminal, and must engage in the corresponding negative terminal of the printed circuit when refitting **(see illustrations)**.

4 Undo the retaining screw and slide the voltage stabilizer out of its printed circuit connections **(see illustration)**.

5 Undo the nuts, screws, terminals and tags as applicable, then carefully lift off the printed circuit.

6 Undo the four screws securing the speedometer and remove the instrument from the panel.

7 Undo the four screws securing the fuel gauge baseplate and withdraw the baseplate from the panel. Remove the fuel gauge from the panel.

8 If a conventional clock is fitted, undo the retaining screws and withdraw the clock, then remove the retaining plate and fuel gauge from the clock face **(see illustration)**.

9 On models with a digital clock, remove the securing screws and the bulb holder **(see illustration)**. Unplug the connector and remove the clock.

10 If necessary the warning lamp casing can be removed after undoing the retaining screws.

11 Reassembly of the instrument panel is the reverse sequence to dismantling.

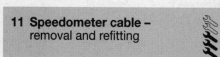

11 Speedometer cable – removal and refitting

1 Disconnect the battery negative terminal.

2 Jack up the front of the vehicle and support it on axle stands (see "*Jacking and vehicle support*"). Remove the spare wheel.

3 From inside the cab, remove the instrument

10.8 Conventional clock terminal mounting

1 *Printed circuit earth*
2 *Printed circuit positive*

panel cover by lifting up at the two recesses nearest the windscreen. Disengage the rear catches and lift off the cover.

4 Release the cable from the rear of the speedometer by squeezing the retaining clip and pulling the cable out **(see illustration)**.

5 Working under the vehicle, release the cable from the retaining clips and cable ties and unscrew the cable clip retaining nut.

11.4 Speedometer cable retaining clip (arrowed)

10.9 Digital clock securing screws (arrowed) and illumination bulb (A)

6 When applicable, unscrew the cable at its connections to the EGR/oxygen sensor mileage recorder (not UK vehicles).

7 Remove the left-hand wheel trim and extract the small circlip securing the cable to the hub cap, then withdraw the cable from the steering knuckle **(see illustrations)**.

8 Draw the cable down and out of the cab and remove it from under the vehicle.

11.7A Speedometer cable retaining circlip (arrowed)

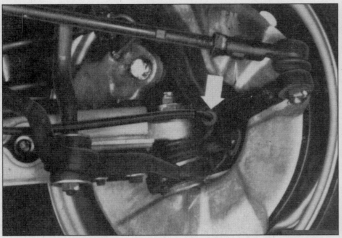

11.7B Speedometer cable rubber sleeve location (arrowed) in steering knuckle

11.9A If there are marks on the speedometer cable, they must be positioned on either side of the cable clip (arrowed)

9 Refitting is the reverse sequence to removal, bearing in mind the following points:

a) Renew the rubber sleeve in the steering knuckle before refitting the cable, ensuring that the sleeve is fitted flush with the edge of the hole in the knuckle

b) Ensure that the marks on the cable are positioned on either side of the cable clip. If there is no mark, position the cable as shown (see illustration).

c) Route the cable so that it is free of tension and without acute bends

d) Seal the cable end at the hub cap with a rubber sealing compound to prevent water entry

12 Horn – fault finding

1 The horn is under the front of the vehicle bolted to the frame (see illustration).
2 The wires connected to it are the earth wire, which is connected, via the steering column, to the horn button and then to earth when the button is pressed, and the live feed wire which is connected directly to the fusebox.

12.1 Horn location under front of vehicle

3 If the horn refuses to function at all, first check the fuse. Next check the earth circuit, testing first from the horn earth terminal, then from the flexible coupling on the steering column, and finally prise out the horn button and disconnect the wire from it and check continuity back to the horn earth terminal. The horn button contacts may be dirty or bent. Check these and clean if necessary. Check the potential at the positive terminal. It should be 12 volts. If the two circuits are correct then the horn itself is at fault.
4 As a last resort, if an adjusting screw is fitted, the sealing compound on the back which covers the adjusting screw should be chipped away and the screw turned clockwise 1/4 turn at a time. If this produces no noise then the horn should be renewed.

13 Bulbs – renewal

Caution: Don't touch the glass envelope of a halogen bulb with your fingers - the grease from your skin could blacken the glass and shorten the bulb life. If the bulb is accidentally touched, clean it with methylated spirit.

Headlamp

1 Either sealed beam or bulb type headlamps may be fitted. The bulb renewal procedure is the same for both types.
2 Remove the front upper grille panel by turning the quick release fasteners along the top edge 90° anti-clockwise. Lift the grille up, tip it forward and remove.
3 Undo the three or four small securing screws around the headlamp retaining ring and lift off the ring (see illustrations).
4 On models with sealed beam units, disconnect the wiring plug at the rear of the headlamp and remove the unit from the car.

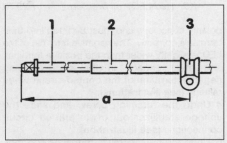

11.9B If there are no marks on the speedometer cable, position the cable so that 'a' = 740 mm

1 Cable   3 Clip
2 Sleeve

Fit the new headlamp unit using the reverse of the removal sequence.
5 On models with bulb units, disconnect the wiring plugs from the headlamp and sidelamp bulbs (see illustrations).
6 Lift off the rubber cap and release the bulb by either turning the retaining ring anti-clockwise (see illustration) if standard bulbs are fitted, or by pivoting back the hinged retaining clip if halogen headlamps are fitted.
7 The bulb can now be lifted out of the lens unit (see illustration). Remember not to touch the bulb glass with your fingers.
8 Fitting the new bulb is the reverse sequence to removal. Make sure that the locating tags on the bulb rim engage with the recesses in the reflector unit.

Sidelamp

9 On models with bulb type headlamps, remove the headlamp assembly as described in paragraphs 2 to 5.
10 Turn the sidelamp bulbholder anti-clockwise to remove it from the headlamp, then remove the bulb by turning it anti-clockwise to remove it from the holder (see illustrations).

13.3A Exploded view of twin headlamp assembly fitted to some later models

Support frame

Vertical adjustment screw

Lateral adjustment screw

Screw

Pivot

Adjusting screw

Cap with connections

Halogen bulb
• 12 V/55 W

Retaining spring

Cap

Halogen bulb
55 W/60 W (H 4)

Side light holder

High beam headlight

Side light bulb
12 V/4 W

Headlight

13.3B Removing the headlamp retaining ring screws

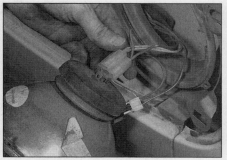

13.5A Disconnecting the wiring plugs from the headlamp. . .

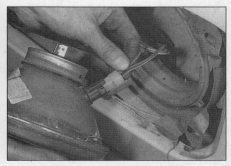

13.5B . . . and sidelamp bulbs

13.6 The standard headlamp bulb is held by a retaining ring

13.7 Headlamp bulb removal

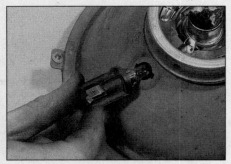

13.10A Removing the sidelamp bulbholder from the lens unit. . .

13.10B . . . and the bulb from the holder

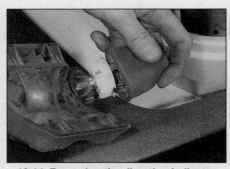

13.14 Removing the direction indicator bulbholder

13.17A Undo the four screws . . .

11 Refitting is the reverse sequence to removal.
12 On models with sealed beam headlamps the sidelamp is incorporated in the direction indicator lens assembly. Removal is described in the following paragraphs.

Front direction indicators

13 Undo the retaining screws and withdraw the lens unit.
14 Lift up the rubber boot, press the spring clip inwards and remove the bulbholder **(see illustration)**.
15 Turn the bulb anti-clockwise to remove it from the holder.
16 Refitting is the reverse sequence to removal.

Rear lamp cluster

17 Undo the four retaining screws and withdraw the lens unit **(see illustrations)**.
18 Press the two side lugs together and lift out the bulb plate **(see illustration)**.
19 Remove the relevant bulb by turning anti-clockwise **(see illustration)**.
20 Refitting is the reverse sequence to removal.

Side marker lamp (when fitted)

21 Undo the two screws and withdraw the lens assembly.
22 Pull back the rubber boot, release the spring clip and take out the bulbholder **(see illustration)**.
23 Turn the bulb anti-clockwise to remove it from the holder.

24 Refitting is the reverse sequence to removal.

Number plate lamp

25 Undo the retaining screws and withdraw the lens and the bulbholder **(see illustration)**.
26 Turn the bulb anti-clockwise to remove it from the holder.
27 Refitting is the reverse sequence to removal.

Interior light

28 Depress the retaining clip on the left-hand side of the lens using a screwdriver then withdraw the lens and bulb assembly **(see illustration)**.
29 Withdraw the bulb from its contacts.
30 Refitting is the reverse sequence to removal.

13.17B . . . and withdraw the lens unit

13.18 Lift out the bulb plate . . .

13.19 . . . and renew the bulbs as necessary

13.22 Side marker lamp bulbholder spring
clip (arrowed)

13.25 Number plate lens and bulbholder

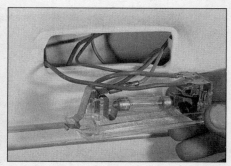

13.28 Depress the retaining clip to remove
the interior light assembly

14.6A Headlamp aim adjusting screws (arrowed) -
models with round headlamps

14.6B Headlamp aim adjusting screws (arrowed) -
models with square headlamps

A   Lateral setting   B   Vertical setting

14 Headlamp aim – adjustment

1 The headlamp beam adjustment is most
important, not only for your own safety but for
that of other road users as well. Accurate
beam alignment can only be obtained using
optical beam setting equipment and you
should regard any adjustments made without
such equipment as purely temporary.
2 To make a temporary adjustment, position
the vehicle on level ground about 3 metres
(10ft) in front of a vertical wall or a piece of
board secured vertically. The wall or board
should be square to the centre-line of the
vehicle and the vehicle should be normally
laden. Check that the tyre pressures are
correct.
3 Draw a vertical line on the board or card in
line with the vehicle centreline.
4 Bounce the vehicle on its suspension
several times to ensure correct levelling and
then accurately measure the height between
the ground and the centre of the headlamps.
5 Draw a horizontal line across the wall or

board at the same height as the headlamp
centres and on this line mark a cross on either
side of the centre line at the same distance
apart as the headlamp centres.
6 Now locate the adjusters. On models with
round headlamps there are two, diagonally
opposite each other, on each headlamp. On
models with square headlamps there are four
adjusters per side (see illustrations).
7 Switch the headlamps on to full beam and,
using the adjusters, adjust each headlamp to

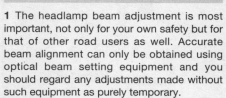

15.4 Wiper arm retaining nut

align the beam to shine just below the
corresponding cross on the wall or board.
8 Bounce the vehicle on its suspension again
to check that the beams return to the correct
position. At the same time check the
operation of the dipswitch to confirm that the
beams dip correctly. Switch off the
headlamps on completion.

15 Wiper blades and arms – removal and refitting

1 To renew a wiper blade, refer to "Weekly
checks" at the beginning of the manual.
2 Before removing a wiper arm make sure
that it is in its parked position having been
switched off by the wiper switch and not the
ignition key.
3 To facilitate re-alignment of the arms on the
screen, stick a length of masking tape on the
glass parallel to the blade before removing the
arm.
4 Lift off the plastic cover and unscrew the
arm retaining nut (see illustration).
5 Pull the arm from the splined driving
spindle.

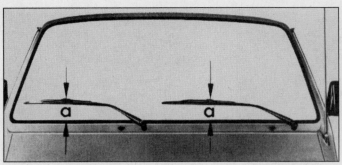

15.6A Correct positioning of windscreen wiper blades in the parked position

a = 70 mm

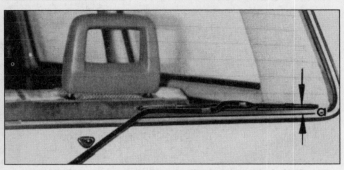

15.6B Correct positioning of tailgate wiper blade in the parked position

a = 27 mm

16.5A Windscreen wiper motor and frame location behind facia

6 Refitting is a reversal of removal; do not overtighten the nut. If tape was not applied to the glass, observe the setting dimensions in the diagram **(see illustrations)**.

16 Windscreen wiper motor and linkage – removal and refitting

1 To gain access to the wiper motor and linkage it will be necessary to remove the facia glovebox as described in Chapter 11, and the instrument panel as described in Section 9 of this Chapter.

2 Remove the wiper arms (see Section 15).
3 Lift off the rubber covers and remove the nuts, spacers and washers from the wiper arm spindles.
4 Disconnect the wiring multi-plug from the wiper motor.
5 Undo the screws securing the wiper frame and auxiliary frame to the body and remove the frame, linkage and motor assembly from the passenger's side **(see illustrations)**.
6 With the assembly removed from the vehicle the motor may be removed as follows.
7 Mark the position of the linkage crank in relation to the motor shaft, undo the retaining nut and remove the crank from the shaft.

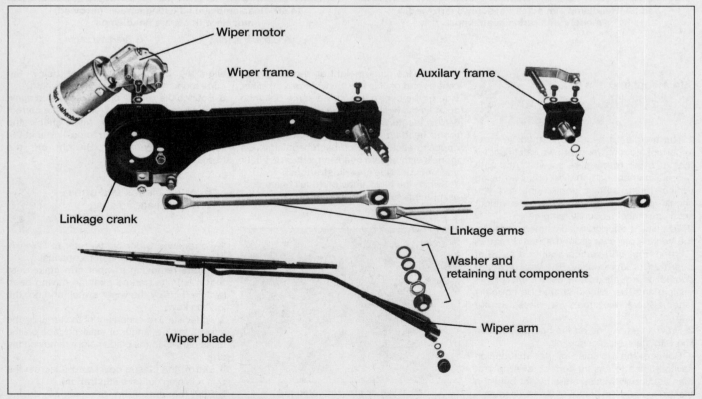

16.5B Exploded view of the windscreen wiper motor and linkage

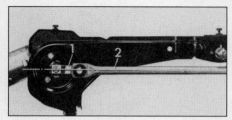

16.10 Correct positioning of crank (1) and linkage arm (2) with wiper motor in park position

8 Undo the three retaining bolts and lift the motor off the frame.

9 To remove the linkage, prise the linkage arms off the spindles, extract the retaining circlips and slide the spindles out of their bushes.

10 Reassembly and refitting is the reverse of the dismantling and removal sequence. Lubricate the spindles with molybdenum disulphide grease before fitting. Ensure that the marks made on the crank and motor shaft are aligned when the crank is fitted or if no marks were made, position the crank as shown with the motor in the parked position **(see illustration)**.

17 Tailgate wiper motor – removal and refitting

1 Disconnect the battery negative lead.

2 Depending on model and equipment, it may be necessary to remove trim panels from inside the tailgate to gain access to the wiper motor **(see illustration)**.

3 Remove the rear wiper arm (Section 15).

4 Remove the four screws which secure the wiper motor bracket **(see illustration)**. Disconnect the multi-plug and remove the motor, bracket and connecting linkage. The motor may then be separated from the bracket and linkage.

5 Before refitting, temporarily reconnect the electrical supply to the motor and allow it to run to its parked position. In this position the angle of the crank arm must be as shown **(see illustration)**. Adjust the fitted position of the crank arm if necessary.

6 The remainder of refitting is a reversal of the removal procedure.

18 Windscreen/tailgate washer system – adjustments and pump renewal

Windscreen washer

1 The windscreen washer system consists of a reservoir located under the footwell on the left-hand side of the cab, an electric pump mounted on the reservoir, two spray nozzles and related plastic tubing **(see illustration)**.

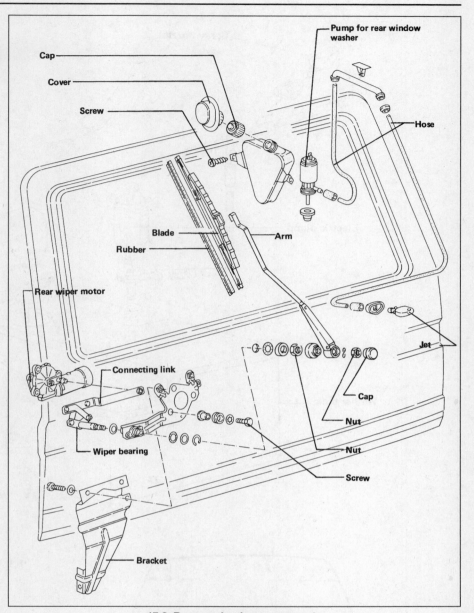

17.2 Rear wash-wipe components

17.4 Rear wiper motor bracket retaining screws (arrowed)

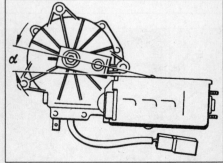

17.5 Rear wiper motor in parked position

$\partial = 8°$

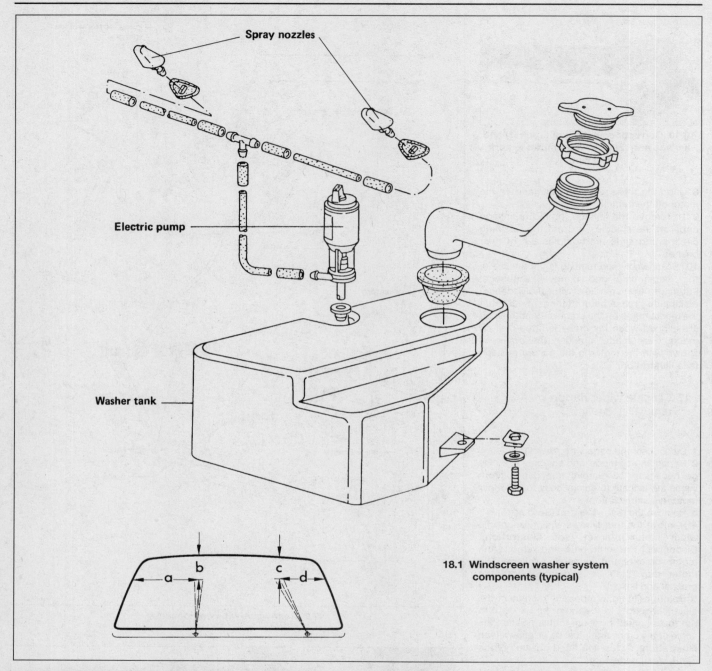

18.1 Windscreen washer system components (typical)

18.2 Windscreen washer reservoir retaining bolts (arrowed)

The system is operated by a switch on the steering column.

2 To remove the reservoir and pump undo the three retaining bolts (see illustration), detach the filler pipe and washer tube, disconnect the pump wiring and remove the reservoir and pump.

3 With the reservoir removed the pump can be carefully withdrawn by prising it out of its retaining rubber grommet.

4 Refitting the reservoir and pump is the reverse sequence to removal.

5 The washer nozzles can be adjusted using a pin and should be set so that the spray of liquid lands on the windscreen in the centre of the arc of each wiper blade.

6 It is recommended that only additives specially prepared for washer systems are used in the fluid reservoir. The use of household detergent or other cleaning agents is likely to damage the pump and rubber components of the system.

7 Never use a cooling system antifreeze in a washer system or the paintwork will be damaged. In very cold weather, a small quantity of methylated spirit may be poured into the fluid to prevent freezing.

Tailgate washer

8 The tailgate washer reservoir and pump are located in the luggage compartment on the right-hand side. There is a single jet located on the rear face of the tailgate.

9 The same remarks apply as were made for the windscreen washer system.

19 Headlamp washer system – general

1 A headlamp washer system is available as an option on some models. The system shares the same reservoir as the windscreen washer (**see illustration**).

2 The same general remarks apply as were made for the windscreen washer system.

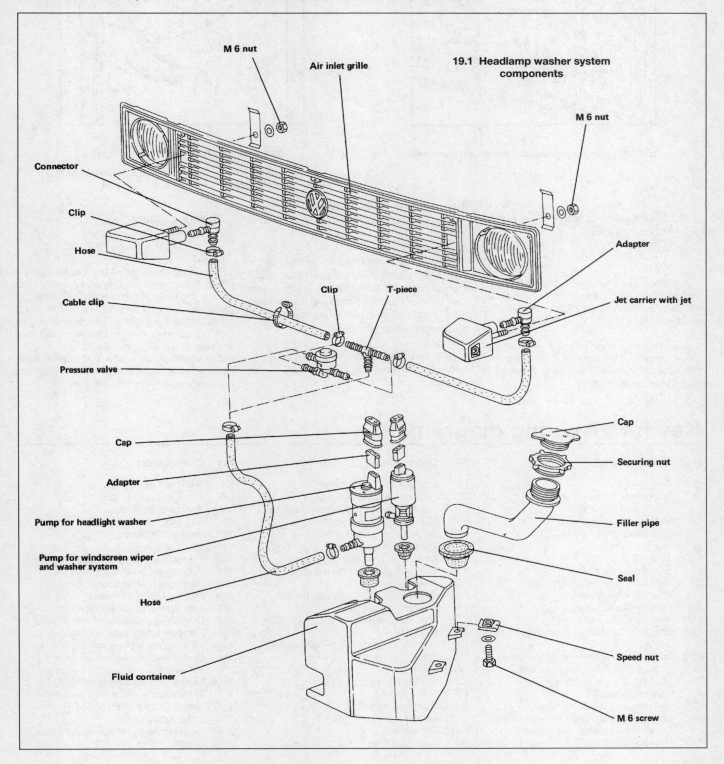

19.1 Headlamp washer system components

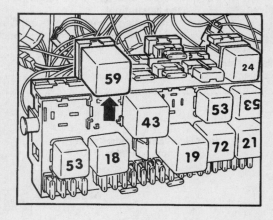

20.2 Heated seat electrical control unit (arrowed)

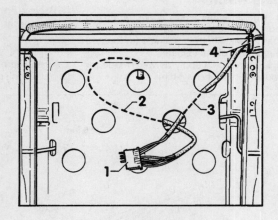

20.4 Heated seat electrical connections

1 Connector	3 To backrest heater
2 To seat heater	4 Cable tie

20 Heated driver's seat – element renewal

1 A heated driver's seat is available as an option on some models. The heating takes place by means of two elements similar to small electric blankets.

2 The heated seat control switch is located in the upper part of the steering column trim. An electrical control unit is located with the other relays **(see illustration)**.

3 If renewal of a heating element is necessary, first disconnect the battery earth lead.

4 Note the locations of the connectors in the multi-plug underneath the seat, then press them out **(see illustration)**. The elements can then be removed after separating the backrest from the seat and taking off the seat or backrest cover, as applicable.

5 Refit by reversing the removal operations, making sure that the new element is not creased.

21 Wiring diagrams – general

The wiring diagrams on the following pages are of the 'current flow' type, in which each circuit is shown schematically, with the live (positive) feed at the top and the earth (negative) at the bottom. The diagrams may look complicated at first sight but in fact they are easy to use with practice.

For reasons of space it has not been possible to include every possible diagram, but only a representative selection.

Key for all wiring diagrams

No	Description	No	Description	No	Description
A	Battery	F5	Luggage boot light switch	H1	Dual tone horn
B	Starter	F7	Door contact switch, rear	J2	Emergency light relay
C	Alternator	F9	Handbrake warning system switch	J4	Dual tone horn relay
C1	Voltage regulator	F18	Radiator fan thermo switch	J5	Fog light relay
D	Ignition/starter switch	F22	Oil pressure switch (0.3 bar)	J6	Voltage stabilizer
E1	Lighting switch	F25	Throttle valve switch	J17	Fuel pump relay
E2	Turn signal switch	F34	Brake fluid level warning contact	J30	Rear window wiper/washer relay
E3	Emergency light switch	F35	Thermoswitch for inlet manifold preheating	J31	Intermittent wash/wipe relay
E4	Headlight dimmer/flasher switch	F66	Coolant shortage indicator switch	J39	Headlight washer system relay
E9	Fresh air blower switch	F88	Pressure switch for PAS	J59	Relief relay for x contact
E15	Heated rear window switch	G	Fuel gauge sender	J81	Inlet manifold preheating relay
E19	Parking light switch	G1	Fuel gauge	J87	DIS (Idling stabilization) switch unit
E20	Instrument/instrument panel lighting control	G2	Coolant temperature gauge sender	J101	Radiator fan 2nd stage relay
		G3	Coolant temperature gauge	J114	Oil pressure monitor control unit
E22	Intermittent windscreen wiper switch	G5	Rev.counter	J120	Switch unit for coolant low level indicator
E23	Foglight and rear foglight switch	G6	Electric fuel pump		
E100	Switch for warm air blower	G7	TDC sender	J140	Control unit for switch-off delay - interior lights, under rear seat, right
F	Brake light switch	G18	Temperature sensor		
F1	Oil pressure switch (0.9 bar)	G19	Air flow meter	J142	Switch unit for idling speed stabilization/Digijet
F2	Door contact switch, front left	G40	Hall sender		
F3	Door contact switch, front right	H	Horn/dual horn	J144	Blocking diode for interior light delay circuit
F4	Reversing light switch				

No	Description
J147	Switch unit for Digijet
J167	Current supply relay for Digijet and idling speed stabilization control units
K	Dash insert
K1	Main beam warning lamp
K2	Generator warning lamp
K3	Oil pressure warning lamp
K5	Turn signal warning lamp
K6	Emergency light system warning lamp
K7	Dual circuit brake and handbrake warning lamp
K10	Heated rear window warning lamp
K17	Fog light warning lamp
K28	Warning lamp for coolant temperature/coolant shortage
L1	Twin filament bulb, left
L2	Twin filament bulb, right
L8	Clock light bulb
L9	Lighting switch light bulb
L10	Instrument panel insert light bulb
L13	Main beam headlight bulb, left
L14	Main beam headlight bulb, right
L16	Fresh air controls light bulb
L20	Rear fog light bulb
L22	Fog light bulb, left
L23	Fog light bulb, right
L28	Cigarette lighter light bulb
L38	Cigarette lighter light bulb, rear right
L39	Heated rear window switch bulb
L48	Ashtray lighting bulb, rear left
L49	Ashtray lighting bulb, rear right
L50	Bulb for warm air blower switch light
M1	Side light bulb, left
M2	Tail light bulb, right
M3	Side light bulb, right
M4	Tail light bulb, left
M5	Turn signal bulb, front left
M6	Turn signal bulb, rear left
M7	Turn signal bulb, front right
M8	Turn signal bulb, rear right
M9	Brake light bulb, left
M10	Brake light bulb, right
M16	Reversing light bulb, left
M17	Reversing light bulb, right
N	Ignition coil
N1	Automatic choke, left
N3	By-pass air cut-off valve
N23	Series resistance for fresh air blower
N30	Injector, cylinder 1
N31	Injector, cylinder 2
N32	Injector, cylinder 3

No	Description
N33	Injector, cylinder 4
N41	TCI control unit
N47	Fan run on serious resistance
N51	Heater element for inlet manifold preheating
N52	Heater element for throttle channel heating/carburettor
N71	Control valve for idling speed stabilization
N72	Series resistance for warm air blower
N79	Heater element (crankcase breather)
O	Ignition distributor
P	Spark plug connector
Q	Spark plugs
R	Connection for radio
S24	Micro-temperature fuse for warm air blower
S27	Separate fuse for rear fog light
S42	Separate fuse for radiator fan
S47	Fuse for reading lamp, under rear seat, right
S48	Fuse for cigarette lighter, under rear seat, right
S50	Fuse, terminal 58b, on fusebox/relay plate
S51	Fuse, engine compartment junction box
T1	Single connector, engine compartment junction box
T1a	Single connector, engine compartment junction box
T1b	Single connector, engine compartment, left
T1c	Single connector, behind dash panel
T1d	Single connector, engine compartment junction box
T1e	Single connector, engine compartment centre
T1f	Single connector, engine compartment centre
T1g	Single connector, engine compartment, left
T1h	Single connector, under rear seat, right
T2	2-pin connector, near dual tone horn
T2a	2-pin connector, behind upper air outlet trim, left
T2b	2-pin connector, behind upper air outlet trim, right
T2c	2-pin connector, behind dash panel
T2d	2-pin connector, A pillar upper left
T2e	2-pin connector, in tailgate

No	Description
T2f	2-pin connector, behind dash panel
T2g	2-pin connector, engine compartment junction box
T2h	2-pin connector, under rear seat, centre
T2i	2-pin connector, engine compartment junction box
T2j	2-pin connector, behind relay plate
T2m	2-pin connector, in relay unit
T2x	2-pin connector, engine compartment, centre
T3	3-pin connector, generator
T3a	3-pin connector, behind C pillar trim
T3b	3-pin connector, behind dash panel
T3c	3-pin connector, under rear seat, right
T3d	3-pin connector, under rear seat, right
T3e	3-pin connector, under rear seat, right
T3f	3-pin connector, behind RH side trim panel
T3g	3-pin connector, on generator
T4	4-pin connector, behind dash panel
T4a	4-pin connector, underneath rear seat
T7	7-pin connector, engine compartment junction box
T7a	7-pin connector, engine compartment junction box
T14	14-pin connector, dash panel insert
U1	Cigarette lighter
U7	Cigarette lighter, rear right
V	Windscreen wiper motor
V1	Rear wiper motor
V2	Fresh air blower
V5	Windscreen washer pump
V7	Radiator fan
V11	Headlight washer pump
V13	Rear window washer pump
V47	Warm air blower
W	Interior light, driver
W3	Luggage boot light, right
W11	Reading lamp, rear left
W13	Reading lamp, front passenger
W14	Illuminated make-up mirror, passenger
W18	Luggage boot light, left
W21	Reading lamp, rear right with switch-off delay
W22	Reading lamp behind driver's seat
W23	Sill panel light with switch-off delay
W24	Reading lamp, pull-out table
X	Number plate light
Y2	Digital clock
Z1	Heated rear window

Earth connections

No	Description
1	Earthing strap, battery to body
2	Earthing strap, gearbox to body
7	Earth wire via steering gear
9	Earth point on tailgate, right
10	Earth point, next to relay plate
11	Earth point in tailgate, left
12	Earth point, front crossmember/left

No	Description
13	Earth point next to rear water container, right
14	Earth point, under rear seat, right
15	Earth point, engine compartment, underneath coil
18	Earth point on longitudinal member, near fuel pump
19	Earth point in engine compartment, on cylinder head, left

No	Description
20	Earth connection, dash panel wiring loom
21	Threaded connection, terminal 30, engine compartment junction box
22	Positive (+) connection, terminal 58b, dash panel wiring loom
23	Positive(+) connection in Digijet wiring loom

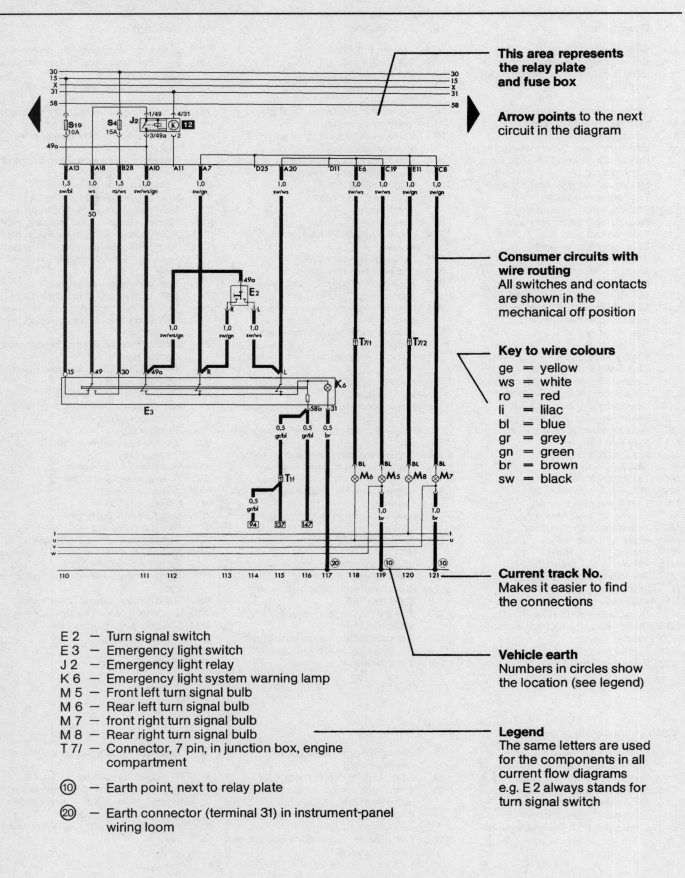

This area represents
the relay plate
and fuse box

Arrow points to the next
circuit in the diagram

Consumer circuits with
wire routing
All switches and contacts
are shown in the
mechanical off position

Key to wire colours
ge = yellow
ws = white
ro = red
li = lilac
bl = blue
gr = grey
gn = green
br = brown
sw = black

Current track No.
Makes it easier to find
the connections

Vehicle earth
Numbers in circles show
the location (see legend)

Legend
The same letters are used
for the components in all
current flow diagrams
e.g. E 2 always stands for
turn signal switch

E 2 — Turn signal switch
E 3 — Emergency light switch
J 2 — Emergency light relay
K 6 — Emergency light system warning lamp
M 5 — Front left turn signal bulb
M 6 — Rear left turn signal bulb
M 7 — front right turn signal bulb
M 8 — Rear right turn signal bulb
T 7/ — Connector, 7 pin, in junction box, engine
          compartment

⑩ — Earth point, next to relay plate

⑳ — Earth connector (terminal 31) in instrument-panel
          wiring loom

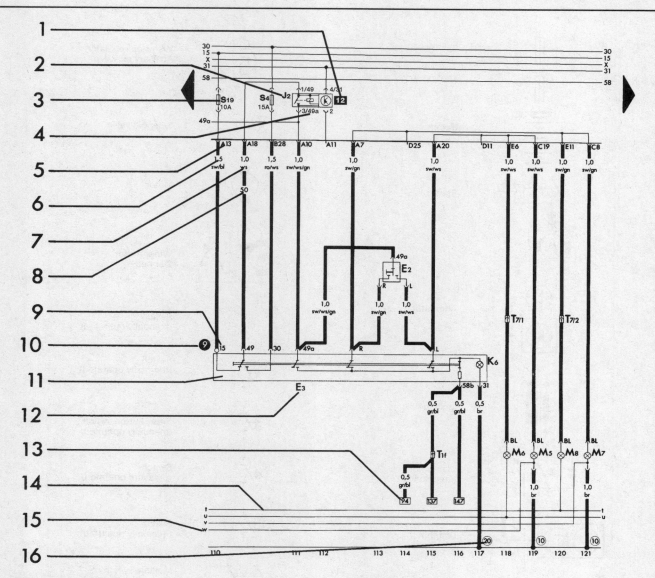

1 Relay location number
Indicatesthe relay location on the relay plate

2 Designation of relay/control unit on the relay plate
In the legend you will see what the part is called

3 Designation of a fuse
e.g. Fuse number 19 (10 amps) on fuse box

4 Designation of connectors on relay plate
Shows the individual contacts in a multi-pin connector
e.g.   3/49a
        3 = contact 3 at location 12 on relay plate
        49a = contact 49a on relay/control plate

5 Designation of connectors on relay plate
Shows wiring of multi-pin or single connectors
e.g. A13 = multi-pin connector A, contact 13

6 Wire cross-section
in mm²

7 Wire colour
Abbreviations are explained in colour key next to current flow diagram

8 Identification no. printed on white coloured wires
For identification purposes with several white wires in a wiring loom

9 Terminal
with the designation which appears on the actual component

10 Test point for fault finding programme
The number in the black circle is to be found in an illustration or in a current flow diagram for the fault finding programme

11 Symbol
for emergency lights switch

12 Part designation
Using the legend you can identify the part referred to

13 Numbers in square
Shows in which track the wire is continued

14 Internal connections (thin lines)
These connections are not to be found in the form of wires. Internal connections are, however, current-carrying connections. They make it possible to trace the flow of current inside components and wiring looms

15 Letters
Indicate connections to next part of diagram

16 Designation of earth
Location of vehicle earth is indicated in legend

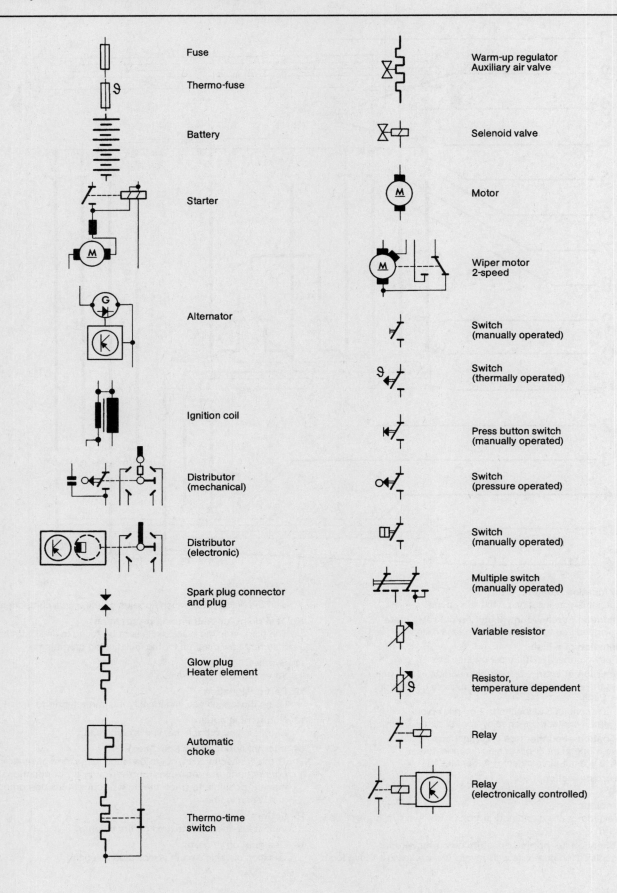

Fuse

Thermo-fuse

Battery

Starter

Alternator

Ignition coil

Distributor
(mechanical)

Distributor
(electronic)

Spark plug connector
and plug

Glow plug
Heater element

Automatic
choke

Thermo-time
switch

Warm-up regulator
Auxiliary air valve

Selenoid valve

Motor

Wiper motor
2-speed

Switch
(manually operated)

Switch
(thermally operated)

Press button switch
(manually operated)

Switch
(pressure operated)

Switch
(manually operated)

Multiple switch
(manually operated)

Variable resistor

Resistor,
temperature dependent

Relay

Relay
(electronically controlled)

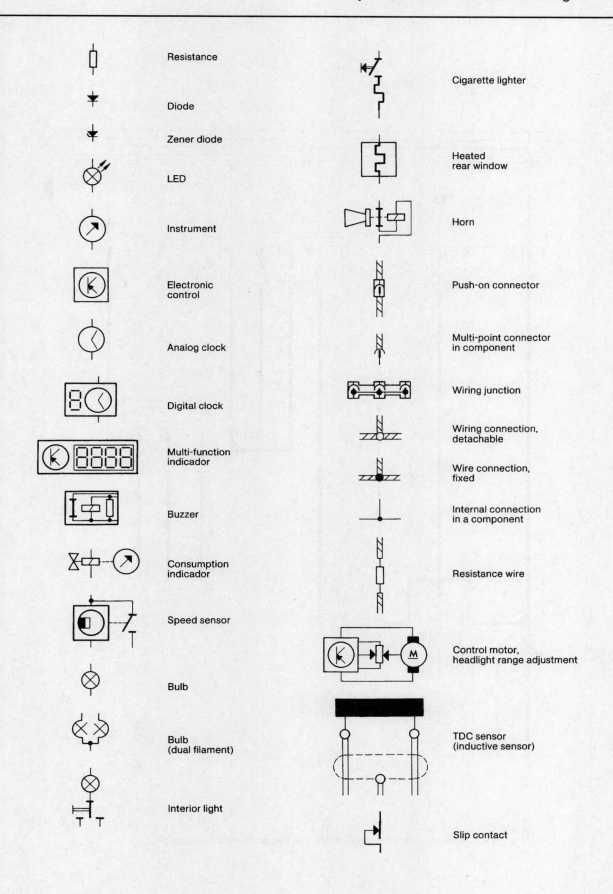

Resistance

Diode

Zener diode

LED

Instrument

Electronic
control

Analog clock

Digital clock

Multi-function
indicador

Buzzer

Consumption
indicador

Speed sensor

Bulb

Bulb
(dual filament)

Interior light

Cigarette lighter

Heated
rear window

Horn

Push-on connector

Multi-point connector
in component

Wiring junction

Wiring connection,
detachable

Wire connection,
fixed

Internal connection
in a component

Resistance wire

Control motor,
headlight range adjustment

TDC sensor
(inductive sensor)

Slip contact

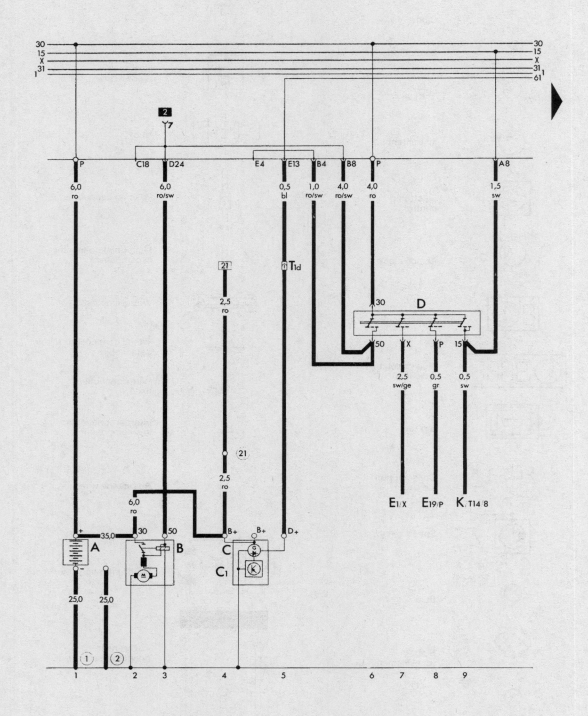

Battery, starter and alternator (1.9 litre carburettor engine only)

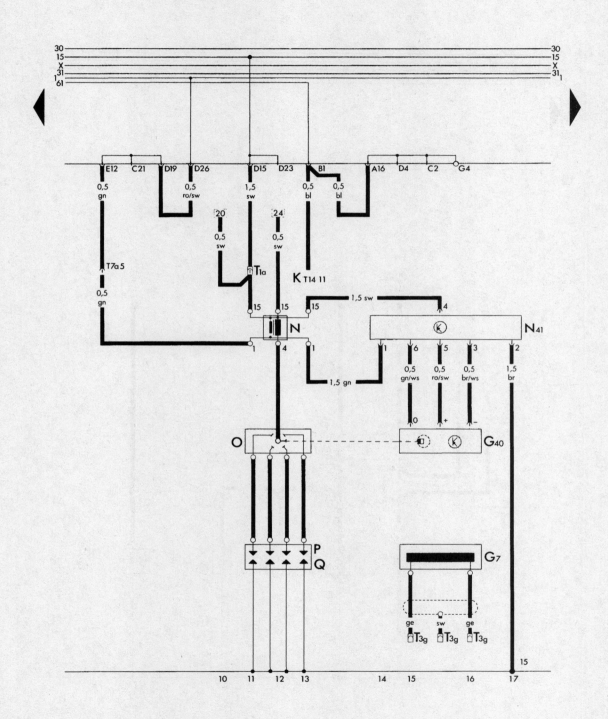

Ignition system (1.9 litre carburettor engine only)

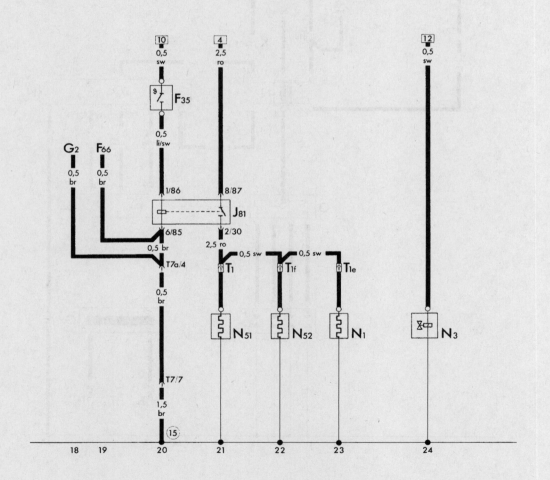

Manifold and carburettor heating, autochoke and by-pass air cut-off (1.9 litre carburettor engine only)

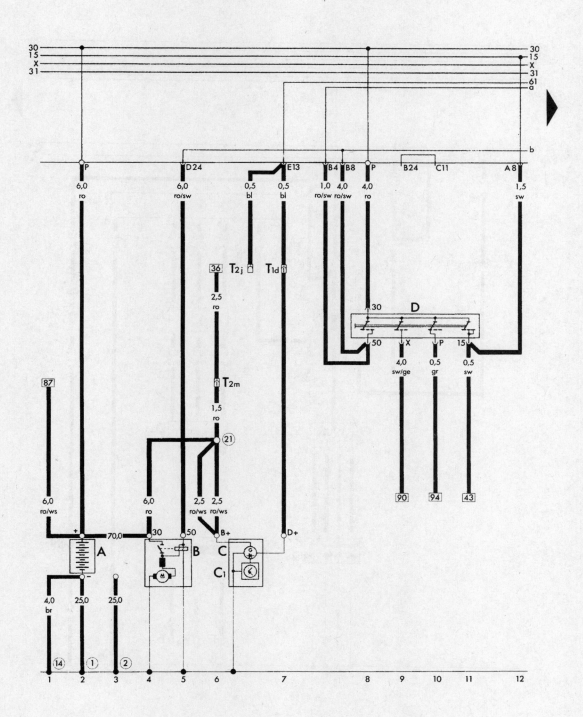

Typical battery, starter, alternator

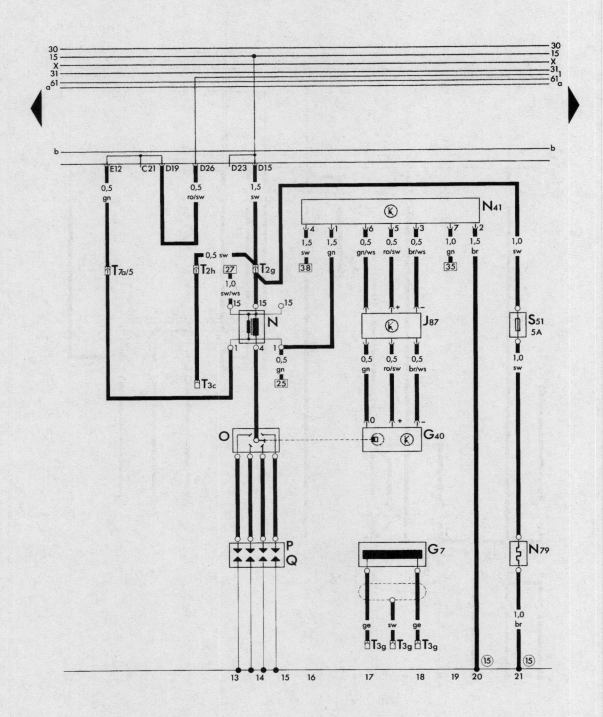

Typical ignition system, electric heating for crankcase breather

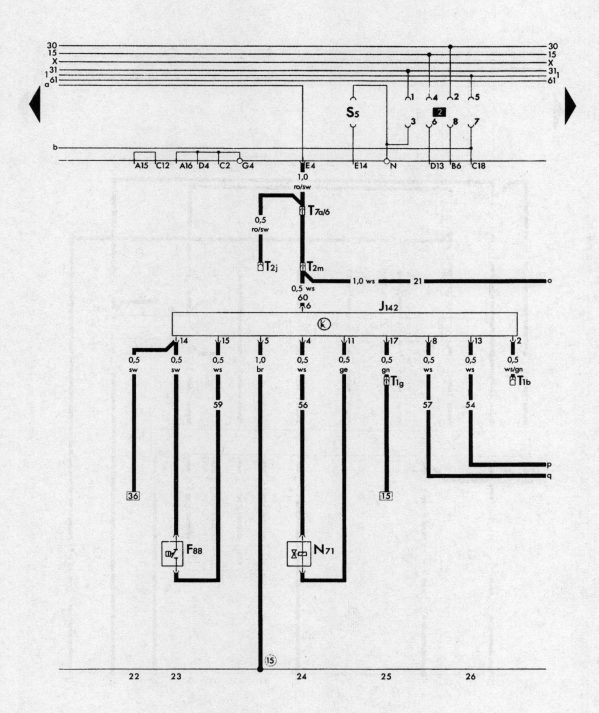

Typical idling speed stabilization

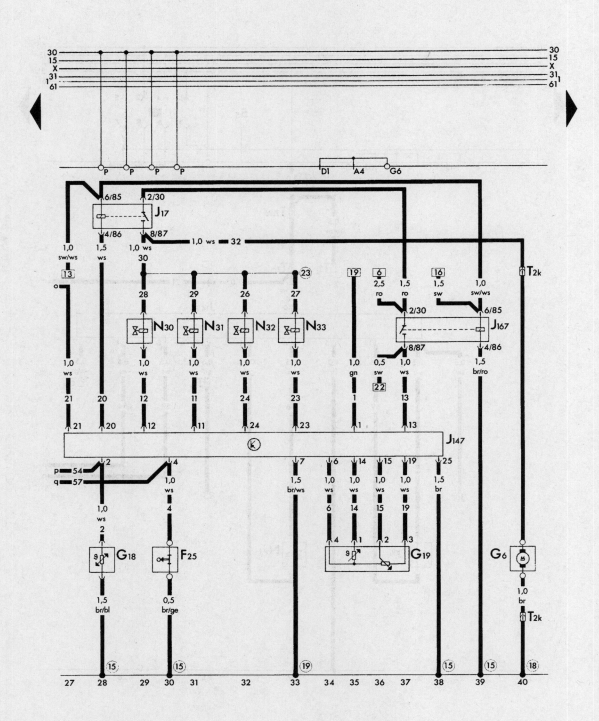

Digital fuel injection system (Digijet)

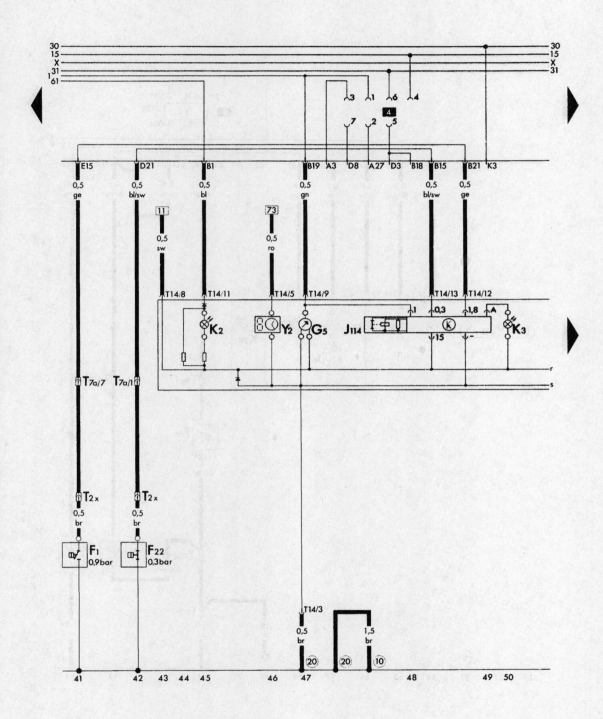

Typical dash panel insert, optical and acoustic oil pressure warning

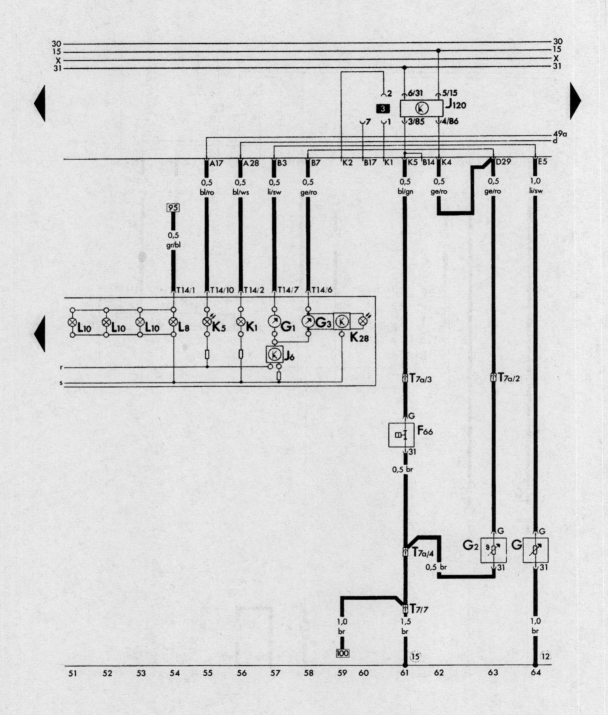

Typical dash panel insert, coolant temperature and coolant shortage indicators

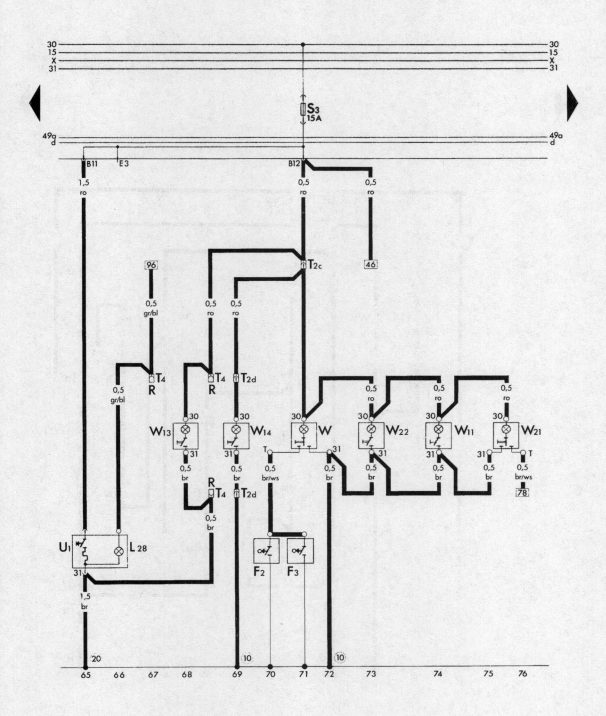

Typical cigarette lighter, radio, interior light, reading lamp

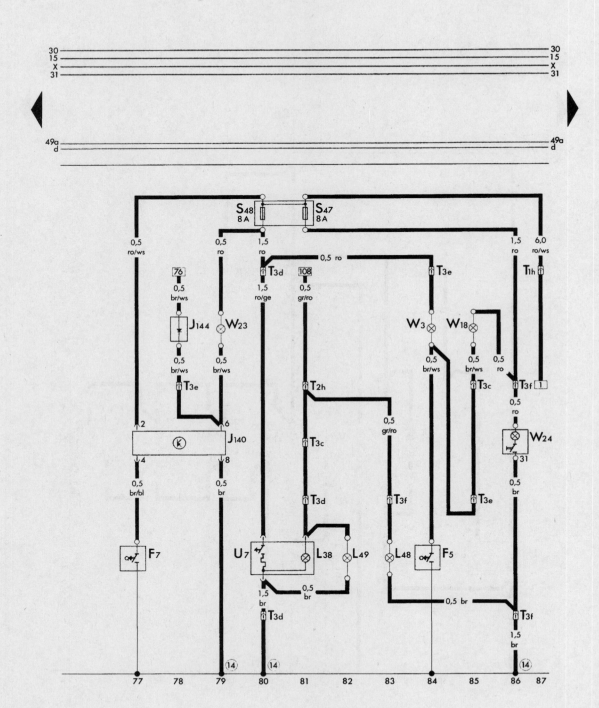

Typical interior light, luggage boot light

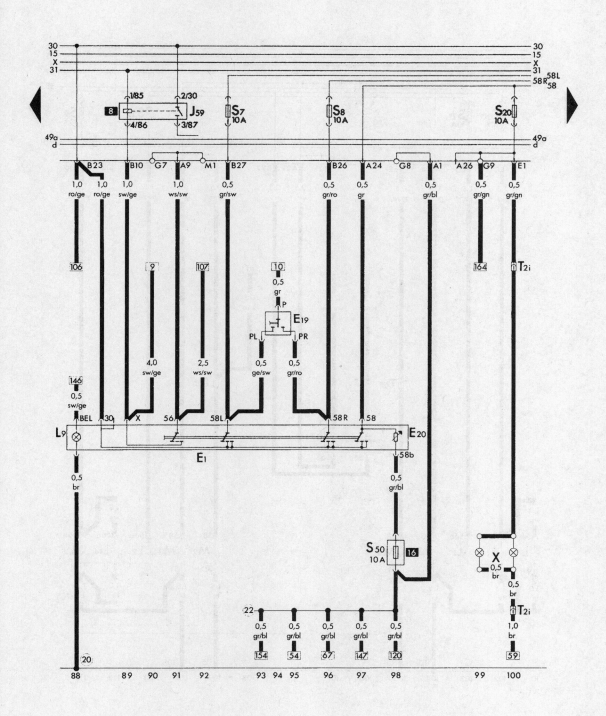

Typical lighting switch, number plate light

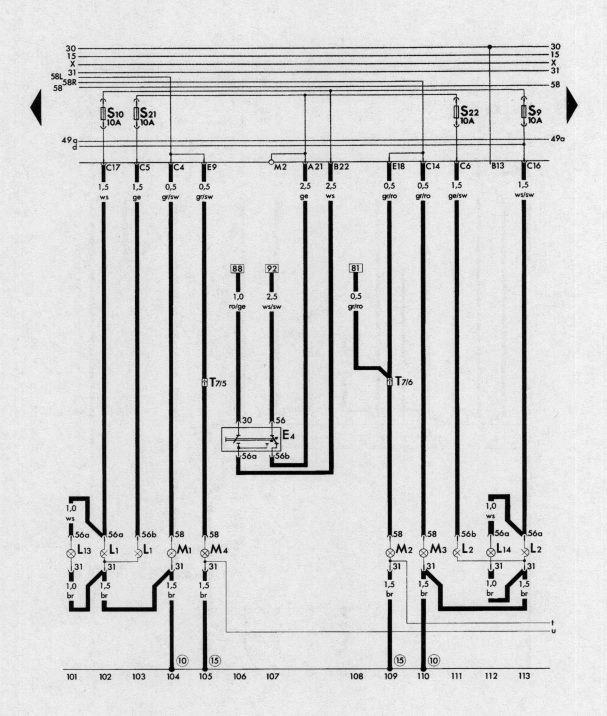

Typical headlights, tail lights, headlight dimmer/flasher switch

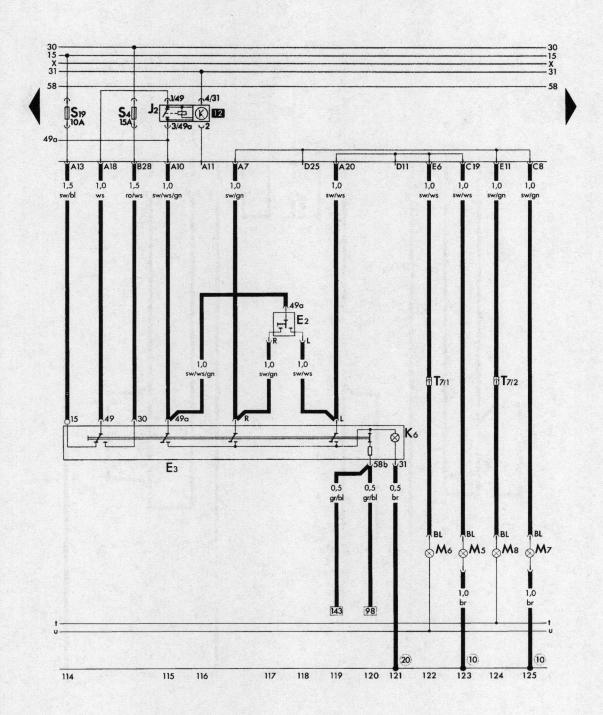

Typical turn signals and emergency light systems

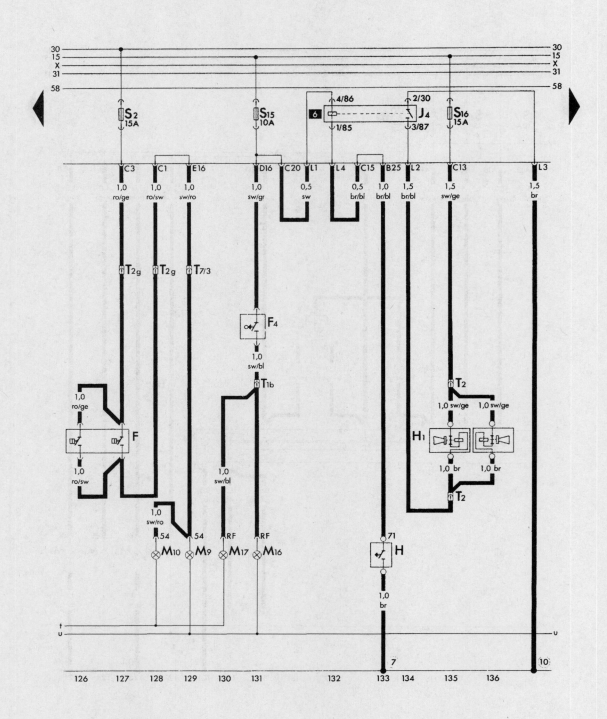

Typical brake lights, reversing light, dual tone horn system

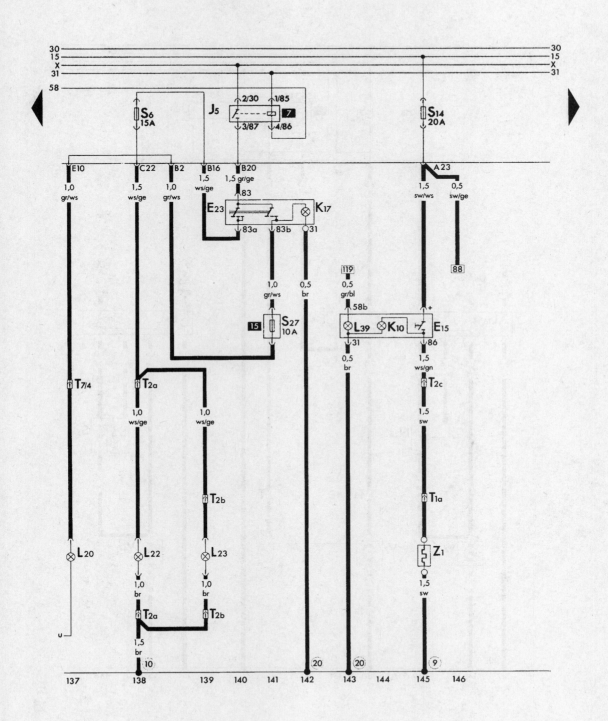

Typical front and rear foglights, heated rear window

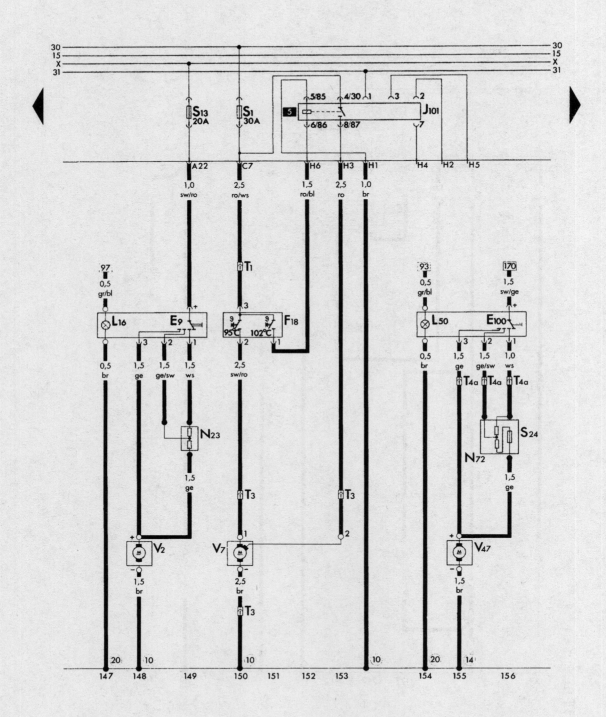

Typical fresh air blower, radiator fan, warm air blower

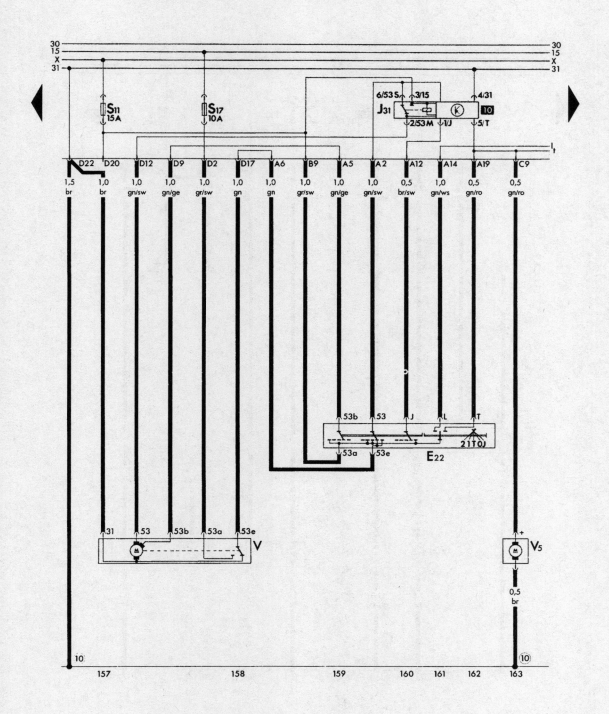

Typical windscreen wiper/washer system

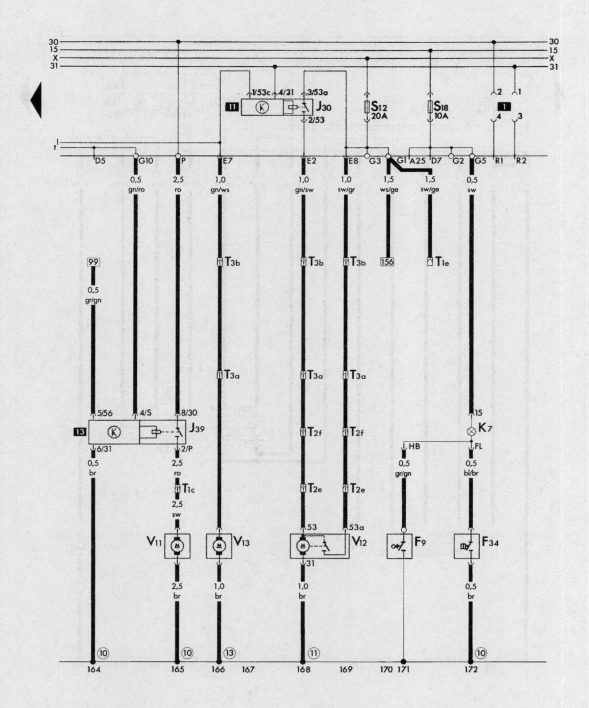

Typical headlight washer system, rear window wiper/washer system, handbrake and brake fluid warning

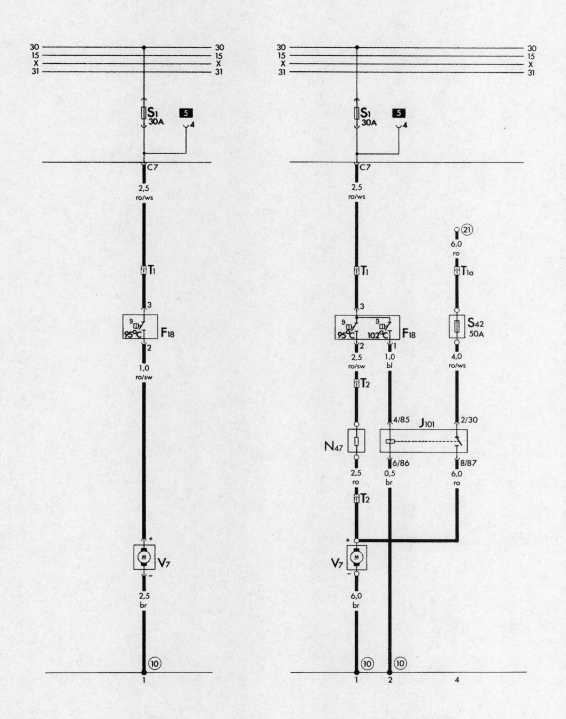

Typical radiator fan

Notes

Reference REF•1

Dimensions and Weights

Note: *All figures are approximate, and may vary according to model. Refer to manufacturer's data for exact figures.*

Dimensions
Overall length	4570 mm
Overall width:	
Except Pick-up	1845 mm
Standard Pick-up	1870 mm
Pick-up with large platform	2000 mm
Overall height:	
Pick-up	1930 mm
Caravelle, Combi L	1950 mm
Combi	1960 mm
Van	1965 mm
High-roofed Combi	2360 mm
High-roofed Van	2365 mm
Wheelbase	2460 mm
Track:	
Front	1583 mm
Rear	1570 mm
Ground clearance	190 mm

Weights
Kerb weight (depending on model and equipment)	1395 to 1570 kg
Gross vehicle weight	2390 to 2600 kg (see type designation plate on door pillar)

Conversion factors

Length (distance)

Inches (in)	x 25.4	=	Millimetres (mm)	x 0.0394 =	Inches (in)
Feet (ft)	x 0.305	=	Metres (m)	x 3.281 =	Feet (ft)
Miles	x 1.609	=	Kilometres (km)	x 0.621 =	Miles

Volume (capacity)

Cubic inches (cu in; in^3)	x 16.387	=	Cubic centimetres (cc; cm^3)	x 0.061 =	Cubic inches (cu in; in^3)
Imperial pints (Imp pt)	x 0.568	=	Litres (l)	x 1.76 =	Imperial pints (Imp pt)
Imperial quarts (Imp qt)	x 1.137	=	Litres (l)	x 0.88 =	Imperial quarts (Imp qt)
Imperial quarts (Imp qt)	x 1.201	=	US quarts (US qt)	x 0.833 =	Imperial quarts (Imp qt)
US quarts (US qt)	x 0.946	=	Litres (l)	x 1.057 =	US quarts (US qt)
Imperial gallons (Imp gal)	x 4.546	=	Litres (l)	x 0.22 =	Imperial gallons (Imp gal)
Imperial gallons (Imp gal)	x 1.201	=	US gallons (US gal)	x 0.833 =	Imperial gallons (Imp gal)
US gallons (US gal)	x 3.785	=	Litres (l)	x 0.264 =	US gallons (US gal)

Mass (weight)

Ounces (oz)	x 28.35	=	Grams (g)	x 0.035 =	Ounces (oz)
Pounds (lb)	x 0.454	=	Kilograms (kg)	x 2.205 =	Pounds (lb)

Force

Ounces-force (ozf; oz)	x 0.278	=	Newtons (N)	x 3.6 =	Ounces-force (ozf; oz)
Pounds-force (lbf; lb)	x 4.448	=	Newtons (N)	x 0.225 =	Pounds-force (lbf; lb)
Newtons (N)	x 0.1	=	Kilograms-force (kgf; kg)	x 9.81 =	Newtons (N)

Pressure

Pounds-force per square inch (psi; lbf/in^2; lb/in^2)	x 0.070	=	Kilograms-force per square centimetre (kgf/cm^2; kg/cm^2)	x 14.223 =	Pounds-force per square inch (psi; lbf/in^2; lb/in^2)
Pounds-force per square inch (psi; lbf/in^2; lb/in^2)	x 0.068	=	Atmospheres (atm)	x 14.696 =	Pounds-force per square inch (psi; lbf/in^2; lb/in^2)
Pounds-force per square inch (psi; lbf/in^2; lb/in^2)	x 0.069	=	Bars	x 14.5 =	Pounds-force per square inch (psi; lbf/in^2; lb/in^2)
Pounds-force per square inch (psi; lbf/in^2; lb/in^2)	x 6.895	=	Kilopascals (kPa)	x 0.145 =	Pounds-force per square inch (psi; lbf/in^2; lb/in^2)
Kilopascals (kPa)	x 0.01	=	Kilograms-force per square centimetre (kgf/cm^2; kg/cm^2)	x 98.1 =	Kilopascals (kPa)
Millibar (mbar)	x 100	=	Pascals (Pa)	x 0.01 =	Millibar (mbar)
Millibar (mbar)	x 0.0145	=	Pounds-force per square inch (psi; lbf/in^2; lb/in^2)	x 68.947 =	Millibar (mbar)
Millibar (mbar)	x 0.75	=	Millimetres of mercury (mmHg)	x 1.333 =	Millibar (mbar)
Millibar (mbar)	x 0.401	=	Inches of water (inH$_2$O)	x 2.491 =	Millibar (mbar)
Millimetres of mercury (mmHg)	x 0.535	=	Inches of water (inH$_2$O)	x 1.868 =	Millimetres of mercury (mmHg)
Inches of water (inH$_2$O)	x 0.036	=	Pounds-force per square inch (psi; lbf/in^2; lb/in^2)	x 27.68 =	Inches of water (inH$_2$O)

Torque (moment of force)

Pounds-force inches (lbf in; lb in)	x 1.152	=	Kilograms-force centimetre (kgf cm; kg cm)	x 0.868 =	Pounds-force inches (lbf in; lb in)
Pounds-force inches (lbf in; lb in)	x 0.113	=	Newton metres (Nm)	x 8.85 =	Pounds-force inches (lbf in; lb in)
Pounds-force inches (lbf in; lb in)	x 0.083	=	Pounds-force feet (lbf ft; lb ft)	x 12 =	Pounds-force inches (lbf in; lb in)
Pounds-force feet (lbf ft; lb ft)	x 0.138	=	Kilograms-force metres (kgf m; kg m)	x 7.233 =	Pounds-force feet (lbf ft; lb ft)
Pounds-force feet (lbf ft; lb ft)	x 1.356	=	Newton metres (Nm)	x 0.738 =	Pounds-force feet (lbf ft; lb ft)
Newton metres (Nm)	x 0.102	=	Kilograms-force metres (kgf m; kg m)	x 9.804 =	Newton metres (Nm)

Power

Horsepower (hp)	x 745.7	=	Watts (W)	x 0.0013 =	Horsepower (hp)

Velocity (speed)

Miles per hour (miles/hr; mph)	x 1.609	=	Kilometres per hour (km/hr; kph)	x 0.621 =	Miles per hour (miles/hr; mph)

Fuel consumption*

Miles per gallon (mpg)	x 0.354	=	Kilometres per litre (km/l)	x 2.825 =	Miles per gallon (mpg)

Temperature

Degrees Fahrenheit = (°C x 1.8) + 32   Degrees Celsius (Degrees Centigrade; °C) = (°F - 32) x 0.56

It is common practice to convert from miles per gallon (mpg) to litres/100 kilometres (l/100km), where mpg x l/100 km = 282

Spare parts are available from many sources, including maker's appointed garages, accessory shops, and motor factors. To be sure of obtaining the correct parts, it may sometimes be necessary to quote the vehicle identification number. If possible, it can also be useful to take the old parts along for positive identification. Items such as starter motors and alternators may be available under a service exchange scheme - any parts returned should always be clean.

Our advice regarding spare part sources is as follows.

Officially-appointed garages

This is the best source of parts which are peculiar to your vehicle, and are not otherwise generally available (eg badges, interior trim, certain body panels, etc). It is also the only place at which you should buy parts if the vehicle is still under warranty.

Accessory shops

These are very good places to buy materials and components needed for maintenance (oil, air and fuel filters, spark plugs, light bulbs, drivebelts, oils and greases, brake pads, touch-up paint, etc). Parts like this sold by a reputable shop are of the same standard as those used by the manufacturer.

Motor factors

Good factors will stock all the more important components which wear out comparatively quickly and can sometimes supply individual components needed for the overhaul of a larger assembly. They may also handle work such as cylinder block reboring, crankshaft regrinding and balancing, etc.

Tyre and exhaust specialists

These outlets may be independent or part

of a local or national chain. They frequently offer competitive prices compared with a main dealer or local garage, but it pays to get several quotes before making a decision. Also ask what 'extras' may be added to the quote - for instance, fitting a new valve and balancing the wheel are both often charged on top of the price of a new tyre.

Other sources

Beware of parts or materials obtained from market stalls, car boot sales or similar outlets. Such items are not invariably sub-standard, but there is little chance of compensation if they do prove unsatisfactory. In the case of safety-critical components such as brake pads there is the risk not only of financial loss but also of an accident causing injury or death.

Vehicle Identification

Modifications are a continuing and unpublicised process in vehicle manufacture, quite apart from major model changes. Spare parts manuals and lists are compiled upon a numerical basis, the individual vehicle identification numbers being essential to correct identification of the component concerned.

When ordering spare parts, always give as much information as possible. Quote the vehicle model, year of manufacture, body and engine numbers as appropriate.

The *vehicle identification number* is located on a plate attached to the right-hand front door pillar **(see illustration)**.

The *chassis number* is stamped underneath the vehicle on the front crossmember **(see illustration)**.

The *engine number* is stamped on the block behind the vee belt pulley **(see illustration)**.

The vehicle identification number is located on a plate attached to the right-hand front door pillar

The chassis number is stamped underneath the vehicle on the front crossmember

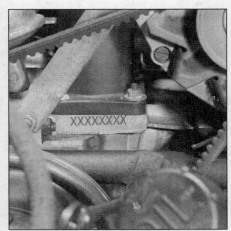

The engine number is stamped on the block behind the vee belt pulley

Whenever servicing, repair or overhaul work is carried out on the car or its components, observe the following procedures and instructions. This will assist in carrying out the operation efficiently and to a professional standard of workmanship.

Joint mating faces and gaskets

When separating components at their mating faces, never insert screwdrivers or similar implements into the joint between the faces in order to prise them apart. This can cause severe damage which results in oil leaks, coolant leaks, etc upon reassembly. Separation is usually achieved by tapping along the joint with a soft-faced hammer in order to break the seal. However, note that this method may not be suitable where dowels are used for component location.

Where a gasket is used between the mating faces of two components, a new one must be fitted on reassembly; fit it dry unless otherwise stated in the repair procedure. Make sure that the mating faces are clean and dry, with all traces of old gasket removed. When cleaning a joint face, use a tool which is unlikely to score or damage the face, and remove any burrs or nicks with an oilstone or fine file.

Make sure that tapped holes are cleaned with a pipe cleaner, and keep them free of jointing compound, if this is being used, unless specifically instructed otherwise.

Ensure that all orifices, channels or pipes are clear, and blow through them, preferably using compressed air.

Oil seals

Oil seals can be removed by levering them out with a wide flat-bladed screwdriver or similar implement. Alternatively, a number of self-tapping screws may be screwed into the seal, and these used as a purchase for pliers or some similar device in order to pull the seal free.

Whenever an oil seal is removed from its working location, either individually or as part of an assembly, it should be renewed.

The very fine sealing lip of the seal is easily damaged, and will not seal if the surface it contacts is not completely clean and free from scratches, nicks or grooves. If the original sealing surface of the component cannot be restored, and the manufacturer has not made provision for slight relocation of the seal relative to the sealing surface, the component should be renewed.

Protect the lips of the seal from any surface which may damage them in the course of fitting. Use tape or a conical sleeve where possible. Lubricate the seal lips with oil before fitting and, on dual-lipped seals, fill the space between the lips with grease.

Unless otherwise stated, oil seals must be fitted with their sealing lips toward the lubricant to be sealed.

Use a tubular drift or block of wood of the appropriate size to install the seal and, if the seal housing is shouldered, drive the seal down to the shoulder. If the seal housing is unshouldered, the seal should be fitted with its face flush with the housing top face (unless otherwise instructed).

Screw threads and fastenings

Seized nuts, bolts and screws are quite a common occurrence where corrosion has set in, and the use of penetrating oil or releasing fluid will often overcome this problem if the offending item is soaked for a while before attempting to release it. The use of an impact driver may also provide a means of releasing such stubborn fastening devices, when used in conjunction with the appropriate screwdriver bit or socket. If none of these methods works, it may be necessary to resort to the careful application of heat, or the use of a hacksaw or nut splitter device.

Studs are usually removed by locking two nuts together on the threaded part, and then using a spanner on the lower nut to unscrew the stud. Studs or bolts which have broken off below the surface of the component in which they are mounted can sometimes be removed using a stud extractor. Always ensure that a blind tapped hole is completely free from oil, grease, water or other fluid before installing the bolt or stud. Failure to do this could cause the housing to crack due to the hydraulic action of the bolt or stud as it is screwed in.

When tightening a castellated nut to accept a split pin, tighten the nut to the specified torque, where applicable, and then tighten further to the next split pin hole. Never slacken the nut to align the split pin hole, unless stated in the repair procedure.

When checking or retightening a nut or bolt to a specified torque setting, slacken the nut or bolt by a quarter of a turn, and then retighten to the specified setting. However, this should not be attempted where angular tightening has been used.

For some screw fastenings, notably cylinder head bolts or nuts, torque wrench settings are no longer specified for the latter stages of tightening, "angle-tightening" being called up instead. Typically, a fairly low torque wrench setting will be applied to the bolts/nuts in the correct sequence, followed by one or more stages of tightening through specified angles.

Locknuts, locktabs and washers

Any fastening which will rotate against a component or housing during tightening should always have a washer between it and the relevant component or housing.

Spring or split washers should always be renewed when they are used to lock a critical component such as a big-end bearing retaining bolt or nut. Locktabs which are folded over to retain a nut or bolt should always be renewed.

Self-locking nuts can be re-used in non-critical areas, providing resistance can be felt when the locking portion passes over the bolt or stud thread. However, it should be noted that self-locking stiffnuts tend to lose their effectiveness after long periods of use, and should then be renewed as a matter of course.

Split pins must always be replaced with new ones of the correct size for the hole.

When thread-locking compound is found on the threads of a fastener which is to be re-used, it should be cleaned off with a wire brush and solvent, and fresh compound applied on reassembly.

Special tools

Some repair procedures in this manual entail the use of special tools such as a press, two or three-legged pullers, spring compressors, etc. Wherever possible, suitable readily-available alternatives to the manufacturer's special tools are described, and are shown in use. In some instances, where no alternative is possible, it has been necessary to resort to the use of a manufacturer's tool, and this has been done for reasons of safety as well as the efficient completion of the repair operation. Unless you are highly-skilled and have a thorough understanding of the procedures described, never attempt to bypass the use of any special tool when the procedure described specifies its use. Not only is there a very great risk of personal injury, but expensive damage could be caused to the components involved.

Environmental considerations

When disposing of used engine oil, brake fluid, antifreeze, etc, give due consideration to any detrimental environmental effects. Do not, for instance, pour any of the above liquids down drains into the general sewage system, or onto the ground to soak away. Many local council refuse tips provide a facility for waste oil disposal, as do some garages. If none of these facilities are available, consult your local Environmental Health Department, or the National Rivers Authority, for further advice.

With the universal tightening-up of legislation regarding the emission of environmentally-harmful substances from motor vehicles, most vehicles have tamperproof devices fitted to the main adjustment points of the fuel system. These devices are primarily designed to prevent unqualified persons from adjusting the fuel/air mixture, with the chance of a consequent increase in toxic emissions. If such devices are found during servicing or overhaul, they should, wherever possible, be renewed or refitted in accordance with the manufacturer's requirements or current legislation.

OIL CARE
FOLLOW THE CODE
OIL BANK LINE
0800 66 33 66
www.oilbankline.org.uk

Note: It is antisocial and illegal to dump oil down the drain. To find the location of your local oil recycling bank, call this number free.

The jack supplied with the vehicle tool kit should only be used for changing the roadwheels - see *"Wheel changing"*. When carrying out any other kind of work, raise the vehicle using a hydraulic (or "trolley") jack, and always supplement the jack with axle stands positioned under the vehicle jacking points **(see illustration)**.

When using a hydraulic jack or axle stands, always position the jack head or axle stand head under one of the relevant jacking points.

To raise the front of the vehicle, remove the engine undertray and position the jack head below the centre of the front axle crossmember. Do not jack the vehicle under the sump or any of the steering or suspension components.

To raise the rear of the vehicle, position the jack head under the rear axle final drive casing, but use a block of wood between the jack head and the casing.

The jack supplied with the vehicle locates in the jacking points on the underside of the sills. Ensure that the jack head is correctly engaged before attempting to raise the vehicle.

Never work under, around or near a raised vehicle unless it is adequately supported in at least two places.

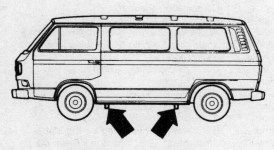

Vehicle jacking points

Radio/cassette Anti-theft System precautions

Many modern radio/cassette units are equipped with a built-in security code, to deter thieves. If the power source to the unit is cut, the anti-theft system will activate. Even if the power source is immediately reconnected, the radio/ cassette unit will not function until the correct security code has been entered.

Therefore, if you do not know the correct security code for the radio/cassette unit **do not** disconnect either of the battery terminals, or remove the radio/cassette unit from the vehicle.

To enter the correct security code, follow the instructions provided with the radio/cassette player handbook.

If an incorrect code is entered, the unit will become locked, and cannot be operated. If this happens, or if the security code is lost or forgotten, seek the advice of the equipment manufacturer or supplier.

Introduction

A selection of good tools is a fundamental requirement for anyone contemplating the maintenance and repair of a motor vehicle. For the owner who does not possess any, their purchase will prove a considerable expense, offsetting some of the savings made by doing-it-yourself. However, provided that the tools purchased meet the relevant national safety standards and are of good quality, they will last for many years and prove an extremely worthwhile investment.

To help the average owner to decide which tools are needed to carry out the various tasks detailed in this manual, we have compiled three lists of tools under the following headings: *Maintenance and minor repair, Repair and overhaul,* and *Special.* Newcomers to practical mechanics should start off with the *Maintenance and minor repair* tool kit, and confine themselves to the simpler jobs around the vehicle. Then, as confidence and experience grow, more difficult tasks can be undertaken, with extra tools being purchased as, and when, they are needed. In this way, a *Maintenance and minor repair* tool kit can be built up into a *Repair and overhaul* tool kit over a considerable period of time, without any major cash outlays. The experienced do-it-yourselfer will have a tool kit good enough for most repair and overhaul procedures, and will add tools from the *Special* category when it is felt that the expense is justified by the amount of use to which these tools will be put.

Maintenance and minor repair tool kit

The tools given in this list should be considered as a minimum requirement if routine maintenance, servicing and minor repair operations are to be undertaken. We recommend the purchase of combination spanners (ring one end, open-ended the other); although more expensive than open-ended ones, they do give the advantages of both types of spanner.

- ☐ *Combination spanners:*
  Metric - 8 to 19 mm inclusive
- ☐ *Adjustable spanner - 35 mm jaw (approx.)*
- ☐ *Spark plug spanner (with rubber insert) - petrol models*
- ☐ *Spark plug gap adjustment tool - petrol models*
- ☐ *Set of feeler gauges*
- ☐ *Brake bleed nipple spanner*
- ☐ *Screwdrivers:*
  Flat blade - 100 mm long x 6 mm dia
  Cross blade - 100 mm long x 6 mm dia
  Torx - various sizes (not all vehicles)
- ☐ *Combination pliers*
- ☐ *Hacksaw (junior)*
- ☐ *Tyre pump*
- ☐ *Tyre pressure gauge*
- ☐ *Oil can*
- ☐ *Oil filter removal tool*
- ☐ *Fine emery cloth*
- ☐ *Wire brush (small)*
- ☐ *Funnel (medium size)*
- ☐ *Sump drain plug key (not all vehicles)*

Repair and overhaul tool kit

These tools are virtually essential for anyone undertaking any major repairs to a motor vehicle, and are additional to those given in the *Maintenance and minor repair* list. Included in this list is a comprehensive set of sockets. Although these are expensive, they will be found invaluable as they are so versatile - particularly if various drives are included in the set. We recommend the half-inch square-drive type, as this can be used with most proprietary torque wrenches.

The tools in this list will sometimes need to be supplemented by tools from the *Special* list:

- ☐ *Sockets (or box spanners) to cover range in previous list (including Torx sockets)*
- ☐ *Reversible ratchet drive (for use with sockets)*
- ☐ *Extension piece, 250 mm (for use with sockets)*
- ☐ *Universal joint (for use with sockets)*
- ☐ *Flexible handle or sliding T "breaker bar" (for use with sockets)*
- ☐ *Torque wrench (for use with sockets)*
- ☐ *Self-locking grips*
- ☐ *Ball pein hammer*
- ☐ *Soft-faced mallet (plastic or rubber)*
- ☐ *Screwdrivers:*
  Flat blade - long & sturdy, short (chubby), and narrow (electrician's) types
  Cross blade – long & sturdy, and short (chubby) types
- ☐ *Pliers:*
  Long-nosed
  Side cutters (electrician's)
  Circlip (internal and external)
- ☐ *Cold chisel - 25 mm*
- ☐ *Scriber*
- ☐ *Scraper*
- ☐ *Centre-punch*
- ☐ *Pin punch*
- ☐ *Hacksaw*
- ☐ *Brake hose clamp*
- ☐ *Brake/clutch bleeding kit*
- ☐ *Selection of twist drills*
- ☐ *Steel rule/straight-edge*
- ☐ *Allen keys (inc. splined/Torx type)*
- ☐ *Selection of files*
- ☐ *Wire brush*
- ☐ *Axle stands*
- ☐ *Jack (strong trolley or hydraulic type)*
- ☐ *Light with extension lead*
- ☐ *Universal electrical multi-meter*

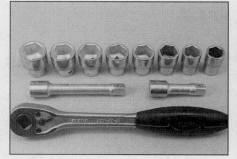

Sockets and reversible ratchet drive

Brake bleeding kit

Torx key, socket and bit

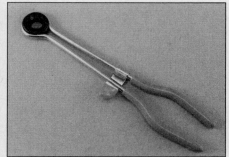

Hose clamp

Angular-tightening gauge

Special tools

The tools in this list are those which are not used regularly, are expensive to buy, or which need to be used in accordance with their manufacturers' instructions. Unless relatively difficult mechanical jobs are undertaken frequently, it will not be economic to buy many of these tools. Where this is the case, you could consider clubbing together with friends (or joining a motorists' club) to make a joint purchase, or borrowing the tools against a deposit from a local garage or tool hire specialist. It is worth noting that many of the larger DIY superstores now carry a large range of special tools for hire at modest rates.

The following list contains only those tools and instruments freely available to the public, and not those special tools produced by the vehicle manufacturer specifically for its dealer network. You will find occasional references to these manufacturers' special tools in the text of this manual. Generally, an alternative method of doing the job without the vehicle manufacturers' special tool is given. However, sometimes there is no alternative to using them. Where this is the case and the relevant tool cannot be bought or borrowed, you will have to entrust the work to a dealer.

- ☐ Angular-tightening gauge
- ☐ Valve spring compressor
- ☐ Valve grinding tool
- ☐ Piston ring compressor
- ☐ Piston ring removal/installation tool
- ☐ Cylinder bore hone
- ☐ Balljoint separator
- ☐ Coil spring compressors (where applicable)
- ☐ Two/three-legged hub and bearing puller
- ☐ Impact screwdriver
- ☐ Micrometer and/or vernier calipers
- ☐ Dial gauge
- ☐ Stroboscopic timing light
- ☐ Dwell angle meter/tachometer
- ☐ Fault code reader
- ☐ Cylinder compression gauge
- ☐ Hand-operated vacuum pump and gauge
- ☐ Clutch plate alignment set
- ☐ Brake shoe steady spring cup removal tool
- ☐ Bush and bearing removal/installation set
- ☐ Stud extractors
- ☐ Tap and die set
- ☐ Lifting tackle
- ☐ Trolley jack

Buying tools

Reputable motor accessory shops and superstores often offer excellent quality tools at discount prices, so it pays to shop around.

Remember, you don't have to buy the most expensive items on the shelf, but it is always advisable to steer clear of the very cheap tools. Beware of 'bargains' offered on market stalls or at car boot sales. There are plenty of good tools around at reasonable prices, but always aim to purchase items which meet the relevant national safety standards. If in doubt, ask the proprietor or manager of the shop for advice before making a purchase.

Care and maintenance of tools

Having purchased a reasonable tool kit, it is necessary to keep the tools in a clean and serviceable condition. After use, always wipe off any dirt, grease and metal particles using a clean, dry cloth, before putting the tools away. Never leave them lying around after they have been used. A simple tool rack on the garage or workshop wall for items such as screwdrivers and pliers is a good idea. Store all normal spanners and sockets in a metal box. Any measuring instruments, gauges, meters, etc, must be carefully stored where they cannot be damaged or become rusty.

Take a little care when tools are used. Hammer heads inevitably become marked, and screwdrivers lose the keen edge on their blades from time to time. A little timely attention with emery cloth or a file will soon restore items like this to a good finish.

Working facilities

Not to be forgotten when discussing tools is the workshop itself. If anything more than routine maintenance is to be carried out, a suitable working area becomes essential.

It is appreciated that many an owner-mechanic is forced by circumstances to remove an engine or similar item without the benefit of a garage or workshop. Having done this, any repairs should always be done under the cover of a roof.

Wherever possible, any dismantling should be done on a clean, flat workbench or table at a suitable working height.

Any workbench needs a vice; one with a jaw opening of 100 mm is suitable for most jobs. As mentioned previously, some clean dry storage space is also required for tools, as well as for any lubricants, cleaning fluids, touch-up paints etc, which become necessary.

Another item which may be required, and which has a much more general usage, is an electric drill with a chuck capacity of at least 8 mm. This, together with a good range of twist drills, is virtually essential for fitting accessories.

Last, but not least, always keep a supply of old newspapers and clean, lint-free rags available, and try to keep any working area as clean as possible.

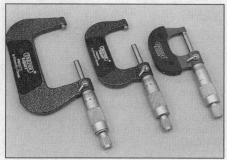

Micrometers

Dial test indicator ("dial gauge")

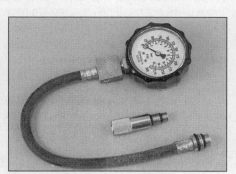

Strap wrench

Fault code reader

Compression tester

This is a guide to getting your vehicle through the MOT test. Obviously it will not be possible to examine the vehicle to the same standard as the professional MOT tester. However, working through the following checks will enable you to identify any problem areas before submitting the vehicle for the test.

Where a testable component is in borderline condition, the tester has discretion in deciding whether to pass or fail it. The basis of such discretion is whether the tester would be happy for a close relative or friend to use the vehicle with the component in that condition. If the vehicle presented is clean and evidently well cared for, the tester may be more inclined to pass a borderline component than if the vehicle is scruffy and apparently neglected.

It has only been possible to summarise the test requirements here, based on the regulations in force at the time of printing. Test standards are becoming increasingly stringent, although there are some exemptions for older vehicles.

An assistant will be needed to help carry out some of these checks.

The checks have been sub-divided into four categories, as follows:

1 Checks carried out **FROM THE DRIVER'S SEAT**

2 Checks carried out **WITH THE VEHICLE ON THE GROUND**

3 Checks carried out **WITH THE VEHICLE RAISED AND THE WHEELS FREE TO TURN**

4 Checks carried out on **YOUR VEHICLE'S EXHAUST EMISSION SYSTEM**

---

1 Checks carried out **FROM THE DRIVER'S SEAT**

Handbrake

☐ Test the operation of the handbrake. Excessive travel (too many clicks) indicates incorrect brake or cable adjustment.

☐ Check that the handbrake cannot be released by tapping the lever sideways. Check the security of the lever mountings.

Footbrake

☐ Depress the brake pedal and check that it does not creep down to the floor, indicating a master cylinder fault. Release the pedal, wait a few seconds, then depress it again. If the pedal travels nearly to the floor before firm resistance is felt, brake adjustment or repair is necessary. If the pedal feels spongy, there is air in the hydraulic system which must be removed by bleeding.

☐ Check that the brake pedal is secure and in good condition. Check also for signs of fluid leaks on the pedal, floor or carpets, which would indicate failed seals in the brake master cylinder.

☐ Check the servo unit (when applicable) by operating the brake pedal several times, then keeping the pedal depressed and starting the engine. As the engine starts, the pedal will move down slightly. If not, the vacuum hose or the servo itself may be faulty.

Steering wheel and column

☐ Examine the steering wheel for fractures or looseness of the hub, spokes or rim.

☐ Move the steering wheel from side to side and then up and down. Check that the steering wheel is not loose on the column, indicating wear or a loose retaining nut. Continue moving the steering wheel as before, but also turn it slightly from left to right.

☐ Check that the steering wheel is not loose on the column, and that there is no abnormal

movement of the steering wheel, indicating wear in the column support bearings or couplings.

Windscreen, mirrors and sunvisor

☐ The windscreen must be free of cracks or other significant damage within the driver's field of view. (Small stone chips are acceptable.) Rear view mirrors must be secure, intact, and capable of being adjusted.

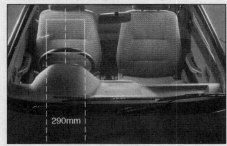

☐ The driver's sunvisor must be capable of being stored in the "up" position.

Seat belts and seats

Note: *The following checks are applicable to all seat belts, front and rear.*

☐ Examine the webbing of all the belts (including rear belts if fitted) for cuts, serious fraying or deterioration. Fasten and unfasten each belt to check the buckles. If applicable, check the retracting mechanism. Check the security of all seat belt mountings accessible from inside the vehicle.

☐ Seat belts with pre-tensioners, once activated, have a "flag" or similar showing on the seat belt stalk. This, in itself, is not a reason for test failure.

☐ The front seats themselves must be securely attached and the backrests must lock in the upright position.

Doors

☐ Both front doors must be able to be opened and closed from outside and inside, and must latch securely when closed.

2 Checks carried out WITH THE VEHICLE ON THE GROUND

Vehicle identification

☐ Number plates must be in good condition, secure and legible, with letters and numbers correctly spaced – spacing at (A) should be at least twice that at (B).

☐ The VIN plate and/or homologation plate must be legible.

Electrical equipment

☐ Switch on the ignition and check the operation of the horn.

☐ Check the windscreen washers and wipers, examining the wiper blades; renew damaged or perished blades. Also check the operation of the stop-lights.

☐ Check the operation of the sidelights and number plate lights. The lenses and reflectors must be secure, clean and undamaged.

☐ Check the operation and alignment of the headlights. The headlight reflectors must not be tarnished and the lenses must be undamaged.

☐ Switch on the ignition and check the operation of the direction indicators (including the instrument panel tell-tale) and the hazard warning lights. Operation of the sidelights and stop-lights must not affect the indicators - if it does, the cause is usually a bad earth at the rear light cluster.

☐ Check the operation of the rear foglight(s), including the warning light on the instrument panel or in the switch.

☐ The ABS warning light must illuminate in accordance with the manufacturers' design. For most vehicles, the ABS warning light should illuminate when the ignition is switched on, and (if the system is operating properly) extinguish after a few seconds. Refer to the owner's handbook.

Footbrake

☐ Examine the master cylinder, brake pipes and servo unit for leaks, loose mountings, corrosion or other damage.

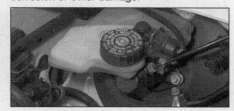

☐ The fluid reservoir must be secure and the fluid level must be between the upper (A) and lower (B) markings.

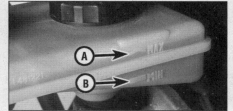

☐ Inspect both front brake flexible hoses for cracks or deterioration of the rubber. Turn the steering from lock to lock, and ensure that the hoses do not contact the wheel, tyre, or any part of the steering or suspension mechanism. With the brake pedal firmly depressed, check the hoses for bulges or leaks under pressure.

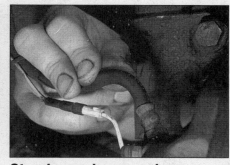

Steering and suspension

☐ Have your assistant turn the steering wheel from side to side slightly, up to the point where the steering gear just begins to transmit this movement to the roadwheels. Check for excessive free play between the steering wheel and the steering gear, indicating wear or insecurity of the steering column joints, the column-to-steering gear coupling, or the steering gear itself.

☐ Have your assistant turn the steering wheel more vigorously in each direction, so that the roadwheels just begin to turn. As this is done, examine all the steering joints, linkages, fittings and attachments. Renew any component that shows signs of wear or damage. On vehicles with power steering, check the security and condition of the steering pump, drivebelt and hoses.

☐ Check that the vehicle is standing level, and at approximately the correct ride height.

Shock absorbers

☐ Depress each corner of the vehicle in turn, then release it. The vehicle should rise and then settle in its normal position. If the vehicle continues to rise and fall, the shock absorber is defective. A shock absorber which has seized will also cause the vehicle to fail.

Exhaust system

☐ Start the engine. With your assistant holding a rag over the tailpipe, check the entire system for leaks. Repair or renew leaking sections.

3 Checks carried out **WITH THE VEHICLE RAISED AND THE WHEELS FREE TO TURN**

Jack up the front and rear of the vehicle, and securely support it on axle stands. Position the stands clear of the suspension assemblies. Ensure that the wheels are clear of the ground and that the steering can be turned from lock to lock.

Steering mechanism

☐ Have your assistant turn the steering from lock to lock. Check that the steering turns smoothly, and that no part of the steering mechanism, including a wheel or tyre, fouls any brake hose or pipe or any part of the body structure.
☐ Examine the steering rack rubber gaiters for damage or insecurity of the retaining clips. If power steering is fitted, check for signs of damage or leakage of the fluid hoses, pipes or connections. Also check for excessive stiffness or binding of the steering, a missing split pin or locking device, or severe corrosion of the body structure within 30 cm of any steering component attachment point.

Front and rear suspension and wheel bearings

☐ Starting at the front right-hand side, grasp the roadwheel at the 3 o'clock and 9 o'clock positions and rock gently but firmly. Check for free play or insecurity at the wheel bearings, suspension balljoints, or suspension mountings, pivots and attachments.
☐ Now grasp the wheel at the 12 o'clock and 6 o'clock positions and repeat the previous inspection. Spin the wheel, and check for roughness or tightness of the front wheel bearing.

☐ If excess free play is suspected at a component pivot point, this can be confirmed by using a large screwdriver or similar tool and levering between the mounting and the component attachment. This will confirm whether the wear is in the pivot bush, its retaining bolt, or in the mounting itself (the bolt holes can often become elongated).

☐ Carry out all the above checks at the other front wheel, and then at both rear wheels.

Springs and shock absorbers

☐ Examine the suspension struts (when applicable) for serious fluid leakage, corrosion, or damage to the casing. Also check the security of the mounting points.
☐ If coil springs are fitted, check that the spring ends locate in their seats, and that the spring is not corroded, cracked or broken.
☐ If leaf springs are fitted, check that all leaves are intact, that the axle is securely attached to each spring, and that there is no deterioration of the spring eye mountings, bushes, and shackles.

☐ The same general checks apply to vehicles fitted with other suspension types, such as torsion bars, hydraulic displacer units, etc. Ensure that all mountings and attachments are secure, that there are no signs of excessive wear, corrosion or damage, and (on hydraulic types) that there are no fluid leaks or damaged pipes.
☐ Inspect the shock absorbers for signs of serious fluid leakage. Check for wear of the mounting bushes or attachments, or damage to the body of the unit.

Driveshafts (fwd vehicles only)

☐ Rotate each front wheel in turn and inspect the constant velocity joint gaiters for splits or damage. Also check that each driveshaft is straight and undamaged.

Braking system

☐ If possible without dismantling, check brake pad wear and disc condition. Ensure that the friction lining material has not worn excessively, (A) and that the discs are not fractured, pitted, scored or badly worn (B).

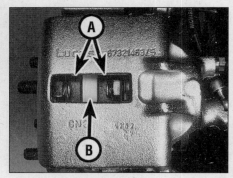

☐ Examine all the rigid brake pipes underneath the vehicle, and the flexible hose(s) at the rear. Look for corrosion, chafing or insecurity of the pipes, and for signs of bulging under pressure, chafing, splits or deterioration of the flexible hoses.
☐ Look for signs of fluid leaks at the brake calipers or on the brake backplates. Repair or renew leaking components.
☐ Slowly spin each wheel, while your assistant depresses and releases the footbrake. Ensure that each brake is operating and does not bind when the pedal is released.

☐ Examine the handbrake mechanism, checking for frayed or broken cables, excessive corrosion, or wear or insecurity of the linkage. Check that the mechanism works on each relevant wheel, and releases fully, without binding.

☐ It is not possible to test brake efficiency without special equipment, but a road test can be carried out later to check that the vehicle pulls up in a straight line.

Fuel and exhaust systems

☐ Inspect the fuel tank (including the filler cap), fuel pipes, hoses and unions. All components must be secure and free from leaks.

☐ Examine the exhaust system over its entire length, checking for any damaged, broken or missing mountings, security of the retaining clamps and rust or corrosion.

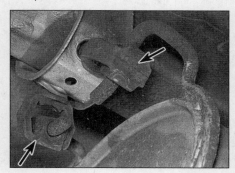

Wheels and tyres

☐ Examine the sidewalls and tread area of each tyre in turn. Check for cuts, tears, lumps, bulges, separation of the tread, and exposure of the ply or cord due to wear or damage. Check that the tyre bead is correctly seated on the wheel rim, that the valve is sound and properly seated, and that the wheel is not distorted or damaged.

☐ Check that the tyres are of the correct size for the vehicle, that they are of the same size and type on each axle, and that the pressures are correct.

☐ Check the tyre tread depth. The legal minimum at the time of writing is 1.6 mm over at least three-quarters of the tread width. Abnormal tread wear may indicate incorrect front wheel alignment.

Body corrosion

☐ Check the condition of the entire vehicle structure for signs of corrosion in load-bearing areas. (These include chassis box sections, side sills, cross-members, pillars, and all suspension, steering, braking system and seat belt mountings and anchorages.) Any corrosion which has seriously reduced the thickness of a load-bearing area is likely to cause the vehicle to fail. In this case professional repairs are likely to be needed.

☐ Damage or corrosion which causes sharp or otherwise dangerous edges to be exposed will also cause the vehicle to fail.

4 Checks carried out on YOUR VEHICLE'S EXHAUST EMISSION SYSTEM

Petrol models

☐ Have the engine at normal operating temperature, and make sure that it is in good tune (ignition system in good order, air filter element clean, etc).

☐ Before any measurements are carried out, raise the engine speed to around 2500 rpm, and hold it at this speed for 20 seconds. Allow the engine speed to return to idle, and watch for smoke emissions from the exhaust tailpipe. If the idle speed is obviously much too high, or if dense blue or clearly-visible black smoke comes from the tailpipe for more than 5 seconds, the vehicle will fail. As a rule of thumb, blue smoke signifies oil being burnt (engine wear) while black smoke signifies unburnt fuel (dirty air cleaner element, or other carburettor or fuel system fault).

☐ An exhaust gas analyser capable of measuring carbon monoxide (CO) and hydrocarbons (HC) is now needed. If such an instrument cannot be hired or borrowed, a local garage may agree to perform the check for a small fee.

CO emissions (mixture)

☐ At the time of writing, for vehicles first used between 1st August 1975 and 31st July 1986 (P to C registration), the CO level must not exceed 4.5% by volume. For vehicles first used between 1st August 1986 and 31st July 1992 (D to J registration), the CO level must not exceed 3.5% by volume. Vehicles first

used after 1st August 1992 (K registration) must conform to the manufacturer's specification. The MOT tester has access to a DOT database or emissions handbook, which lists the CO and HC limits for each make and model of vehicle. The CO level is measured with the engine at idle speed, and at "fast idle". The following limits are given as a general guide:

At idle speed -
    CO level no more than 0.5%
At "fast idle" (2500 to 3000 rpm) -
    CO level no more than 0.3%
    (Minimum oil temperature 60°C)

☐ If the CO level cannot be reduced far enough to pass the test (and the fuel and ignition systems are otherwise in good condition) then the carburettor is badly worn, or there is some problem in the fuel injection system or catalytic converter (as applicable).

HC emissions

☐ With the CO within limits, HC emissions for vehicles first used between 1st August 1975 and 31st July 1992 (P to J registration) must not exceed 1200 ppm. Vehicles first used after 1st August 1992 (K registration) must conform to the manufacturer's specification. The MOT tester has access to a DOT database or emissions handbook, which lists the CO and HC limits for each make and model of vehicle. The HC level is measured with the engine at "fast idle". The following is given as a general guide:

At "fast idle" (2500 to 3000 rpm) -
    HC level no more than 200 ppm
    (Minimum oil temperature 60°C)

☐ Excessive HC emissions are caused by incomplete combustion, the causes of which can include oil being burnt, mechanical wear and ignition/fuel system malfunction.

Diesel models

☐ The only emission test applicable to Diesel engines is the measuring of exhaust smoke density. The test involves accelerating the engine several times to its maximum unloaded speed.

Note: *It is of the utmost importance that the engine timing belt is in good condition before the test is carried out.*

☐ The limits for Diesel engine exhaust smoke, introduced in September 1995 are:
Vehicles first used before 1st August 1979:
    Exempt from metered smoke testing, but must not emit "dense blue or clearly visible black smoke for a period of more than 5 seconds at idle" or "dense blue or clearly visible black smoke during acceleration which would obscure the view of other road users".
Non-turbocharged vehicles first used after 1st August 1979: 2.5m-1
Turbocharged vehicles first used after 1st August 1979: 3.0m-1

☐ Excessive smoke can be caused by a dirty air cleaner element. Otherwise, professional advice may be needed to find the cause.

Fault finding

Engine

- [ ] Engine fails to rotate when attempting to start
- [ ] Engine rotates but will not start
- [ ] Engine difficult to start when cold
- [ ] Engine difficult to start when hot
- [ ] Starter motor noisy or excessively-rough in engagement
- [ ] Engine starts but stops immediately
- [ ] Engine idles erratically
- [ ] Engine misfires at idle speed
- [ ] Engine misfires throughout the driving speed range
- [ ] Engine hesitates on acceleration
- [ ] Engine stalls
- [ ] Engine lacks power
- [ ] Engine backfires
- [ ] Oil pressure warning light illuminated with engine running
- [ ] Engine runs-on after switching off
- [ ] Engine noises

Cooling system

- [ ] Overheating
- [ ] Overcooling
- [ ] External coolant leakage
- [ ] Internal coolant leakage
- [ ] Corrosion

Fuel and exhaust systems

- [ ] Excessive fuel consumption
- [ ] Fuel leakage and/or fuel odour
- [ ] Excessive noise or fumes from exhaust system

Clutch

- [ ] Pedal travels to floor - no pressure or very little resistance
- [ ] Clutch fails to disengage (unable to select gears)
- [ ] Clutch slips (engine speed increases with no increase in vehicle speed)
- [ ] Judder as clutch is engaged
- [ ] Noise when depressing or releasing clutch pedal

Manual transmission

- [ ] Noisy in neutral with engine running
- [ ] Noisy in one particular gear
- [ ] Difficulty engaging gears
- [ ] Jumps out of gear
- [ ] Vibration and noise in all gears
- [ ] Lubricant leaks

Automatic transmission

- [ ] Fluid leakage
- [ ] Transmission fluid brown, or has burned smell
- [ ] General gear selection problems
- [ ] Transmission will not downshift (kickdown) with accelerator pedal fully depressed
- [ ] Engine will not start in any gear, or starts in gears other than Park or Neutral
- [ ] Transmission slips, is noisy, or has no drive in forward or reverse gears

Driveshafts

- [ ] Vibration when accelerating or decelerating
- [ ] Noise (knocking or clicking) when accelerating or decelerating

Braking system

- [ ] Vehicle pulls to one side under braking
- [ ] Noise (grinding or high-pitched squeal) when brakes applied
- [ ] Excessive brake pedal travel
- [ ] Brake pedal feels spongy when depressed
- [ ] Excessive brake pedal effort required to stop vehicle
- [ ] Judder felt through brake pedal or steering wheel when braking
- [ ] Brakes binding
- [ ] Rear wheels locking under normal braking

Suspension and steering systems

- [ ] Vehicle pulls to one side
- [ ] Wheel wobble and vibration
- [ ] Excessive pitching and/or rolling around corners, or during braking
- [ ] Wandering or general instability
- [ ] Excessively-stiff steering
- [ ] Excessive play in steering
- [ ] Lack of power assistance (when applicable)
- [ ] Tyre wear excessive

Electrical system

- [ ] Battery will not hold a charge for more than a few days
- [ ] Ignition/no-charge warning light remains illuminated with engine running
- [ ] Ignition/no-charge warning light fails to come on
- [ ] Lights inoperative
- [ ] Instrument readings inaccurate or erratic
- [ ] Horn inoperative, or unsatisfactory in operation
- [ ] Windscreen/tailgate wipers inoperative, or unsatisfactory in operation
- [ ] Windscreen/tailgate washers inoperative, or unsatisfactory in operation
- [ ] Electric windows inoperative, or unsatisfactory in operation
- [ ] Central locking system inoperative, or unsatisfactory in operation

Introduction

The vehicle owner who does his or her own maintenance according to the recommended service schedules should not have to use this section of the manual very often. Modern component reliability is such that, provided those items subject to wear or deterioration are inspected or renewed at the specified intervals, sudden failure is comparatively rare. Faults do not usually just happen as a result of sudden failure, but develop over a period of time. Major mechanical failures in particular are usually preceded by characteristic symptoms over hundreds or even thousands of miles. Those components which do occasionally fail without warning are often small and easily carried in the vehicle.

With any fault-finding, the first step is to decide where to begin investigations. Sometimes this is obvious, but on other occasions, a little detective work will be necessary. The owner who makes half a dozen haphazard adjustments or replacements may be successful in curing a fault (or its symptoms), but will be none the wiser if the fault recurs, and ultimately may have spent more time and money than was necessary. A calm and logical approach will be found to be more satisfactory in the long run. Always take into account any warning signs or abnormalities that may have been noticed in the period preceding the fault - power loss, high or low gauge readings, unusual smells, etc - and remember that failure of components such as fuses or spark plugs may only be pointers to some underlying fault.

The pages which follow provide an easy reference guide to the more common problems which may occur during the operation of the vehicle. These problems and their possible causes are grouped under headings denoting various components or systems, such as Engine, Cooling system, etc. The Chapter and/or Section which deals with the problem is also shown in brackets. Whatever the fault, certain basic principles apply. These are as follows:

Verify the fault. This is simply a matter of being sure that you know what the symptoms are before starting work. This is particularly important if you are investigating a fault for someone else, who may not have described it very accurately.

Don't overlook the obvious. For example, if the vehicle won't start, is there petrol in the tank? (Don't take anyone else's word on this particular point, and don't trust the fuel gauge either!) If an electrical fault is indicated, look for loose or broken wires before digging out the test gear.

Cure the disease, not the symptom. Substituting a flat battery with a fully-charged one will get you off the hard shoulder, but if the underlying cause is not attended to, the new battery will go the same way. Similarly, changing oil-fouled spark plugs for a new set will get you moving again, but remember that the reason for the fouling (if it wasn't simply an incorrect grade of plug) will have to be established and corrected.

Don't take anything for granted. Particularly, don't forget that a "new" component may itself be defective (especially if it's been rattling around in the boot for months), and don't leave components out of a fault diagnosis sequence just because they are new or recently fitted. When you do finally diagnose a difficult fault, you'll probably realise that all the evidence was there from the start.

Engine

Engine fails to rotate when attempting to start
- [ ] Battery terminal connections loose or corroded ("*Weekly checks*").
- [ ] Battery discharged or faulty (Chapter 5A).
- [ ] Broken, loose or disconnected wiring in the starting circuit (Chapter 5A).
- [ ] Defective starter solenoid or switch (Chapter 5A).
- [ ] Defective starter motor (Chapter 5A).
- [ ] Starter pinion or flywheel ring gear teeth loose or broken (Chapter 2 or 5A).
- [ ] Automatic transmission not in Park/Neutral position, or selector lever position sensor faulty (Chapter 7B).

Engine rotates but will not start
- [ ] Fuel tank empty.
- [ ] Battery discharged (engine rotates slowly) (Chapter 5A).
- [ ] Battery terminal connections loose or corroded ("*Weekly checks*").
- [ ] Ignition components damp or damaged (Chapters 1 and 5B).
- [ ] Broken, loose or disconnected wiring in the ignition circuit (Chapters 1 and 5B).
- [ ] Worn, faulty or incorrectly-gapped spark plugs (Chapter 1).
- [ ] Low cylinder compressions (Chapter 2A).
- [ ] Major mechanical failure (Chapter 2A or 2B).

Engine difficult to start when cold
- [ ] Battery discharged (Chapter 5A).
- [ ] Battery terminal connections loose or corroded ("*Weekly checks*").
- [ ] Worn, faulty or incorrectly-gapped spark plugs (Chapter 1).
- [ ] Other ignition system fault (Chapters 1 and 5B).
- [ ] Fuel injection system fault (Chapter 4B).
- [ ] Low cylinder compressions (Chapter 2A).

Engine difficult to start when hot
- [ ] Air filter element dirty or clogged (Chapter 1).
- [ ] Fuel injection system fault (Chapter 4B).
- [ ] Low cylinder compressions (Chapter 2A).

Starter motor noisy or excessively-rough in engagement
- [ ] Starter pinion or flywheel ring gear teeth loose or broken (Chapter 2 or 5A).
- [ ] Starter motor mounting bolts loose or missing (Chapter 5A).
- [ ] Starter motor internal components worn or damaged (Chapter 5A).

Engine starts but stops immediately
- [ ] Loose or faulty electrical connections in the ignition circuit (Chapters 1 and 5B).
- [ ] Fuel injection system fault (Chapter 4B).

Engine idles erratically
- [ ] Fuel injection system fault (Chapter 4B).
- [ ] Air filter element clogged (Chapter 1).
- [ ] Vacuum leak at the inlet manifold or associated hoses (Chapter 4A or 4B).
- [ ] Worn, faulty or incorrectly-gapped spark plugs (Chapter 1).
- [ ] Uneven or low cylinder compressions (Chapter 2A).
- [ ] Camshaft lobes worn (Chapter 2B).
- [ ] Carburettor idle cut-off valve defective or disconnected (Chapter 4A).

Engine misfires at idle speed
- [ ] Worn, faulty or incorrectly-gapped spark plugs (Chapter 1).
- [ ] Faulty spark plug HT leads (Chapter 1).
- [ ] Incorrect ignition timing (Chapter 5B).
- [ ] Fuel injection system fault (Chapter 4B).
- [ ] Vacuum leak at the inlet manifold or associated hoses (Chapter 4A or 4B).
- [ ] Uneven or low cylinder compressions (Chapter 2A).
- [ ] Disconnected, leaking or perished crankcase ventilation hoses (Chapters 1 and 4A or 4B).

Engine misfires throughout the driving speed range
- [ ] Fuel filter choked (Chapter 1).
- [ ] Fuel pump faulty (Chapter 4A or 4B).
- [ ] Fuel tank vent hose blocked or fuel pipes restricted (Chapter 4A).
- [ ] Vacuum leak at the inlet manifold or associated hoses (Chapter 4A or 4B).
- [ ] Worn, faulty or incorrectly-gapped spark plugs (Chapter 1).
- [ ] Faulty spark plug HT leads (Chapter 1).
- [ ] Faulty ignition coil (Chapter 5B).
- [ ] Fuel injection system fault (Chapter 4B).
- [ ] Uneven or low cylinder compressions (Chapter 2A).

Engine hesitates on acceleration
- [ ] Worn, faulty or incorrectly-gapped spark plugs (Chapter 1).
- [ ] Fuel injection system fault (Chapter 4B).
- [ ] Vacuum leak at the inlet manifold or associated hoses (Chapter 4A or 4B).

Engine stalls
- [ ] Fuel injection system fault (Chapter 4B).
- [ ] Vacuum leak at the inlet manifold or associated hoses (Chapter 4A or 4B).
- [ ] Fuel filter choked (Chapter 1).
- [ ] Fuel pump faulty (Chapter 4A or 4B).
- [ ] Fuel tank vent hose blocked or fuel pipes restricted (Chapter 4A).
- [ ] Carburettor idle cut-off valve defective or disconnected (Chapter 4A).

Engine (continued)

Engine lacks power

- ☐ Incorrect ignition timing (Chapter 5B).
- ☐ Fuel injection system fault (Chapter 4B).
- ☐ Fuel filter choked (Chapter 1).
- ☐ Fuel pump faulty (Chapter 4A or 4B).
- ☐ Uneven or low cylinder compressions (Chapter 2A).
- ☐ Worn, faulty or incorrectly-gapped spark plugs (Chapter 1).
- ☐ Vacuum leak at the inlet manifold or associated hoses (Chapter 4A and 4B).
- ☐ Brakes binding (Chapters 1 and 10).
- ☐ Clutch slipping (Chapter 6).
- ☐ Automatic transmission fluid level incorrect (Chapter 1).

Engine backfires

- ☐ Ignition timing incorrect (Chapter 5B).
- ☐ Fuel injection system fault (Chapter 4B).
- ☐ Vacuum leak at the inlet manifold or associated hoses (Chapter 4A or 4B).
- ☐ Exhaust valve(s) burnt.
- ☐ Emission control system fault (Chapter 4A or 4B).

Oil pressure warning light illuminated with engine running

- ☐ Low oil level or incorrect oil grade ("*Weekly checks*").
- ☐ Faulty oil pressure warning light switch (Chapter 2B).
- ☐ Worn engine bearings and/or oil pump (Chapter 2B).
- ☐ Overheating (Chapter 3).
- ☐ Oil pressure relief valve defective (Chapter 2A).
- ☐ Oil pick-up strainer clogged (Chapter 2B).

Engine runs-on after switching off

- ☐ Idle speed excessively high (Chapter 1).
- ☐ Carburettor idle cut-off valve defective (Chapter 4A).
- ☐ Fuel injection system fault (Chapter 4B).
- ☐ Excessive carbon build-up in engine (Chapter 2B).
- ☐ Overheating (Chapter 3).

Engine noises

Pre-ignition (pinking) or knocking during acceleration or under load

- ☐ Ignition timing incorrect (Chapter 5B).
- ☐ Incorrect grade of fuel (Chapter 4A or 4B).
- ☐ Vacuum leak at the inlet manifold or associated hoses (Chapter 4A or 4B).
- ☐ Excessive carbon build-up in engine (Chapter 2B).

Whistling or wheezing noises

- ☐ Leaking inlet manifold hose or gasket (Chapter 4A or 4B).
- ☐ Leaking exhaust joint (Chapters 1, 4A or 4B).
- ☐ Leaking vacuum hose (Chapters 1, 2A, 2B , 4A, 4B and 10).
- ☐ Blowing cylinder head sealing ring (Chapter 2B).

Tapping or rattling noises

- ☐ Hydraulic tappets worn (Chapter 2B).
- ☐ Worn valve gear or camshaft (Chapter 2B).
- ☐ Worn timing gears (Chapter 2B).
- ☐ Ancillary component fault (water pump, alternator, etc) (Chapters 3 and 5A).

Knocking or thumping noises

- ☐ Worn big-end bearings (regular heavy knocking, perhaps less under load) (Chapter 2B).
- ☐ Worn main bearings (rumbling and knocking, perhaps worsening under load) (Chapter 2B).
- ☐ Piston slap (most noticeable when cold) (Chapter 2B).
- ☐ Ancillary component fault (water pump, alternator, etc) (Chapters 3 and 5A).

Cooling system

Overheating

- ☐ Insufficient coolant in system ("*Weekly checks*").
- ☐ Thermostat faulty (Chapter 3).
- ☐ Radiator core blocked or grille restricted (Chapter 3).
- ☐ Radiator electric cooling fan or coolant temperature sensor faulty (Chapter 3).
- ☐ Fuel injection system fault (Chapter 4B).
- ☐ Pressure cap faulty (Chapter 3).
- ☐ Auxiliary drivebelt(s) worn or slipping (Chapter 1).
- ☐ Ignition timing incorrect (Chapter 5B).
- ☐ Inaccurate coolant temperature gauge sender (Chapter 3).
- ☐ Cooling system not correctly refilled (Chapter 1).

Overcooling

- ☐ Thermostat faulty (Chapter 3).
- ☐ Inaccurate coolant temperature gauge sender (Chapter 3).

External coolant leakage

- ☐ Deteriorated or damaged hoses or hose clips (Chapter 1).
- ☐ Radiator core or heater matrix leaking (Chapter 3).
- ☐ Pressure cap faulty (Chapter 3).
- ☐ Water pump leaking (Chapter 3).
- ☐ Boiling due to overheating (Chapter 3).
- ☐ Crankcase water jacket or joint leaking (Chapter 2B).

Internal coolant leakage

- ☐ Leaking cylinder head sealing ring (Chapter 2B).
- ☐ Cracked cylinder head, crankcase or liner (Chapter 2B).

Corrosion

- ☐ Infrequent draining and flushing (Chapter 1).
- ☐ Incorrect antifreeze mixture, or inappropriate antifreeze type ("*Weekly checks*" and Chapter 1).

Fuel and exhaust systems

Excessive fuel consumption
- [ ] Unsympathetic driving style, or adverse conditions.
- [ ] Air filter element dirty or clogged (Chapter 1).
- [ ] Fuel injection system fault (Chapter 4B).
- [ ] Ignition timing incorrect (Chapter 5B).
- [ ] Tyres under-inflated ("*Weekly checks*").

Fuel leakage and/or fuel odour
- [ ] Damaged or corroded fuel tank, pipes or connections (Chapter 1).

Excessive noise or fumes from exhaust system
- [ ] Leaking exhaust system or manifold joints (Chapter 1 or 4A).
- [ ] Leaking, corroded or damaged exhaust system components (Chapter 1 or 4A).
- [ ] Broken mountings, causing body or suspension contact (Chapter 1 or 4A).

Clutch

Pedal travels to floor - no pressure or very little resistance
- [ ] Air in clutch hydraulic system (Chapter 6).
- [ ] Faulty clutch slave cylinder (Chapter 6).
- [ ] Faulty clutch master cylinder (Chapter 6).
- [ ] Broken diaphragm spring in clutch pressure plate (Chapter 6).

Clutch fails to disengage (unable to select gears)
- [ ] Air in clutch hydraulic system (Chapter 6).
- [ ] Faulty clutch slave cylinder (Chapter 6).
- [ ] Faulty clutch master cylinder (Chapter 6).
- [ ] Clutch disc sticking on transmission mainshaft splines (Chapter 6).
- [ ] Clutch disc sticking to flywheel or pressure plate (Chapter 6).
- [ ] Faulty pressure plate assembly (Chapter 6).
- [ ] Clutch release mechanism worn or incorrectly assembled (Chapter 6).

Clutch slips (engine speed increases with no increase in vehicle speed)
- [ ] Clutch disc linings excessively worn (Chapter 6).
- [ ] Clutch disc linings contaminated with oil or grease (Chapter 6).
- [ ] Faulty pressure plate or weak diaphragm spring (Chapter 6).

Judder as clutch is engaged
- [ ] Clutch disc linings contaminated with oil or grease (Chapter 6).
- [ ] Clutch disc linings excessively worn (Chapter 6).
- [ ] Faulty or distorted pressure plate or diaphragm spring (Chapter 6).
- [ ] Worn or loose engine/transmission mountings (Chapter 2A).
- [ ] Clutch disc hub or transmission mainshaft splines worn (Chapter 6).

Noise when depressing or releasing clutch pedal
- [ ] Worn clutch release bearing (Chapter 6).
- [ ] Worn or dry clutch pedal bushes (Chapter 6).
- [ ] Faulty pressure plate assembly (Chapter 6).
- [ ] Pressure plate diaphragm spring broken (Chapter 6).
- [ ] Broken clutch disc cushioning springs (Chapter 6).

Manual transmission

Noisy in neutral with engine running
- [ ] Mainshaft bearings worn (noise apparent with clutch pedal released, but not when depressed) (Chapter 7A).*
- [ ] Clutch release bearing worn (noise apparent with clutch pedal depressed, possibly less when released) (Chapter 6).

Noisy in one particular gear
- [ ] Worn, damaged or chipped gear teeth (Chapter 7A).*
- [ ] Worn bearings (Chapter 7A).*

Difficulty engaging gears
- [ ] Clutch fault (Chapter 6).
- [ ] Oil level too high or incorrect grade (Chapter 1 and "*Weekly checks*").
- [ ] Worn or damaged gear linkage (Chapter 7A).
- [ ] Worn synchroniser assemblies (Chapter 7A).*

Jumps out of gear
- [ ] Worn or damaged gear linkage (Chapter 7A).
- [ ] Worn synchroniser assemblies (Chapter 7A).*
- [ ] Worn selector forks (Chapter 7A).*

Vibration and noise in all gears
- [ ] Lack of oil or incorrect grade (Chapter 1 and "*Weekly checks*").
- [ ] Worn bearings (Chapter 7A).*

Lubricant leaks
- [ ] Leaking driveshaft flange oil seal (Chapter 7A).*
- [ ] Leaking gearchange shaft oil seal (Chapter 7A).*
- [ ] Leaking housing joint (Chapter 7A).*
- [ ] Leaking mainshaft oil seal (Chapter 7A).*

* Although the corrective action necessary to remedy the symptoms described is beyond the scope of the home mechanic, the above information should be helpful in isolating the cause of the condition, so that the owner can communicate clearly with a professional mechanic.

Automatic transmission

Note: *Due to the complexity of the automatic transmission, it is difficult for the home mechanic to properly diagnose and service this unit. For problems other than the following, the vehicle should be taken to a dealer service department or automatic transmission specialist.*

Fluid leakage

☐ To determine the source of a leak, first remove all built-up dirt and grime from the transmission housing and surrounding areas, using a degreasing agent, or by steam-cleaning. Drive the vehicle at low speed, so airflow will not blow the leak far from its source. Raise and support the vehicle, and determine where the leak is coming from. The following are common areas of leakage:
a) *Transmission oil sump (Chapters 1 and 7B).*
b) *Dipstick tube (Chapters 1 and 7B).*
c) *Transmission-to-fluid cooler pipes/unions (Chapter 1 and 7B).*
d) *Transmission oil seals (Chapter 7B).*

Transmission fluid brown, or has burned smell

☐ Transmission fluid level low, or fluid in need of renewal (Chapter 1).

General gear selection problems

☐ Chapter 7B deals with checking and adjusting the selector linkage on automatic transmissions. The following are common problems which may be caused by a poorly-adjusted gear selector or accelerator cable linkage:
a) *Engine starting in gears other than Park or Neutral.*

b) *Indicator on gear selector lever pointing to a gear other than the one actually being used.*
c) *Vehicle moves when in Park or Neutral.*
d) *Poor gear shift quality or erratic gear changes.*
   Refer to Chapter 7B for the selector cable adjustment procedure, and to Chapter 4A for the accelerator cable adjustment procedure.

Transmission will not downshift (kickdown) with accelerator pedal fully depressed

☐ Low transmission fluid level (Chapter 1).
☐ Incorrect accelerator cable adjustment (Chapter 4A).
☐ Incorrect selector cable adjustment (Chapter 7B).

Engine will not start in any gear, or starts in gears other than Park or Neutral

☐ Incorrect selector linkage/starter inhibitor switch adjustment (Chapter 7B).

Transmission slips, is noisy, or has no drive in forward or reverse gears

☐ There are many probable causes for the above problems, but the home mechanic should be concerned with only one possibility - fluid level. Before taking the vehicle to a dealer or transmission specialist, check the fluid level and condition of the fluid as described in Chapter 1. Correct the fluid level as necessary, or change the fluid if needed. If the problem persists, professional help will be necessary.

Driveshafts

Vibration when accelerating or decelerating

☐ Driveshaft flange bolts loose (Chapter 8).
☐ Excessive wear in CV joints (Chapter 8).

Noise (knocking or clicking) when accelerating or decelerating

☐ Driveshaft flange bolts loose (Chapter 8).
☐ Excessive wear in CV joints (Chapter 8).

Braking system

Note: *Before assuming that a brake problem exists, make sure that the tyres are in good condition and correctly inflated, that the front wheel alignment is correct, and that the vehicle is not loaded with weight in an unequal manner. Apart from checking the condition of all pipe and hose connections, any faults occurring on the Anti-lock Braking System (ABS) should be referred to a Volvo dealer for diagnosis.*

Vehicle pulls to one side under braking

☐ Worn, defective, damaged or contaminated front or rear brake pads or shoes on one side (Chapter 10).
☐ Seized or partially-seized caliper or wheel cylinder piston (Chapter 10).
☐ A mixture of brake pad lining materials fitted between sides (Chapter 10).
☐ Brake caliper mounting bolts loose (Chapter 10).
☐ Worn or damaged steering or suspension components (Chapter 8 or 9).

Noise (grinding or high-pitched squeal) when brakes applied

☐ Brake friction lining material worn down to metal backing (Chapter 10).
☐ Corrosion of brake disc or drum (may be apparent after the vehicle has been standing for some time) (Chapter 10).

Excessive brake pedal travel

☐ Faulty master cylinder (Chapter 10).
☐ Air in hydraulic system (Chapter 10).
☐ Rear brake self-adjusting mechanism faulty (Chapter 10).

Brake pedal feels spongy when depressed

☐ Air in hydraulic system (Chapter 10).
☐ Deteriorated flexible rubber brake hoses (Chapter 10).
☐ Master cylinder mounting nuts loose (Chapter 10).
☐ Faulty master cylinder (Chapter 10).

Excessive brake pedal effort required to stop vehicle

☐ Faulty vacuum servo unit (Chapter 10).
☐ Disconnected, damaged or insecure brake servo vacuum hose (Chapter 10).
☐ Primary or secondary hydraulic circuit failure (Chapter 10).
☐ Seized brake caliper piston(s) (Chapter 10).
☐ Brake pads or shoes incorrectly fitted (Chapter 10).
☐ Incorrect grade of brake pads or shoes fitted (Chapter 10).
☐ Brake linings contaminated (Chapter 10).

Braking system (continued)

Judder felt through brake pedal or steering wheel when braking

- [ ] Distorted or damaged brake discs or drums (Chapter 10).
- [ ] Brake linings worn (Chapter 10).
- [ ] Brake caliper mounting bolts loose (Chapter 10).
- [ ] Wear in suspension or steering components or mountings (Chapter 8 or 9).

Brakes binding

- [ ] Seized brake caliper piston(s) (Chapter 10).
- [ ] Faulty self-adjusting mechanism (Chapter 10).
- [ ] Faulty handbrake mechanism (Chapter 10).
- [ ] Faulty master cylinder (Chapter 10).

Rear wheels locking under normal braking

- [ ] Rear brake linings contaminated (Chapter 10).
- [ ] Faulty brake pressure regulator (Chapter 10).

Suspension and steering systems

Note: *Before diagnosing suspension or steering faults, be sure that the trouble is not due to incorrect tyre pressures, mixtures of tyre types, or binding brakes.*

Vehicle pulls to one side

- [ ] Defective tyre ("*Weekly checks*").
- [ ] Excessive wear in suspension or steering components (Chapter 8 or 9).
- [ ] Incorrect front or rear wheel alignment (Chapter 8 or 9).
- [ ] Accident damage to steering or suspension components (Chapter 8 or 9).

Wheel wobble and vibration

- [ ] Front roadwheels out of balance (vibration felt mainly through the steering wheel).
- [ ] Rear roadwheels out of balance (vibration felt throughout the vehicle).
- [ ] Roadwheels damaged or distorted (Chapter 1 and "*Weekly checks*").
- [ ] Faulty or damaged tyre ("*Weekly checks*").
- [ ] Worn steering or suspension joints, bushes or components (Chapter 8 or 9).
- [ ] Roadwheel nuts or bolts loose (Chapter 1).

Excessive pitching and/or rolling around corners, or during braking

- [ ] Defective shock absorbers (Chapter 8 or 9).
- [ ] Broken or weak coil spring and/or suspension component (Chapter 8 or 9).

Wandering or general instability

- [ ] Incorrect wheel alignment (Chapter 8 or 9).
- [ ] Worn steering or suspension joints, bushes or components (Chapter 8 or 9).
- [ ] Roadwheels out of balance.
- [ ] Faulty or damaged tyre ("*Weekly checks*").
- [ ] Roadwheel nuts or bolts loose (Chapter 1).
- [ ] Defective shock absorbers (Chapter 8 or 9).

Excessively-stiff steering

- [ ] Broken or incorrectly adjusted power-assisted steering pump (auxiliary) drivebelt (when applicable) (Chapter 1).
- [ ] Power-assisted steering pump faulty (when applicable) (Chapter 9).
- [ ] Seized tie-rod end balljoint or suspension balljoint (Chapter 9).
- [ ] Incorrect front wheel alignment (Chapter 9).
- [ ] Steering rack or column bent or damaged (Chapter 9).

Excessive play in steering

- [ ] Worn steering linkage joints (Chapter 9).
- [ ] Worn steering tie-rod end balljoints (Chapter 9).
- [ ] Worn rack-and-pinion steering gear (Chapter 9).
- [ ] Worn steering or suspension joints, bushes or components (Chapter 8 or 9).

Lack of power assistance (when applicable)

- [ ] Broken or slipping power-assisted steering pump (auxiliary) drivebelt (Chapter 1).
- [ ] Incorrect power steering fluid level ("*Weekly checks*").
- [ ] Faulty power-assisted steering pump (Chapter 9).
- [ ] Faulty rack-and-pinion steering gear (Chapter 9).

Tyre wear excessive

Tyres worn on inside or outside edges

- [ ] Incorrect camber or castor angles (wear on one edge only) (Chapter 9).
- [ ] Worn steering or suspension joints, bushes or components (Chapter 8 or 9).
- [ ] Excessively-hard cornering.
- [ ] Accident damage.

Tyre treads exhibit feathered edges

- [ ] Incorrect toe setting (Chapter 9).

Tyres worn in centre of tread

- [ ] Tyres over-inflated ("*Weekly checks*").

Tyres worn on inside and outside edges

- [ ] Tyres under-inflated ("*Weekly checks*").

Tyres worn unevenly

- [ ] Tyres out of balance.
- [ ] Wheel bent or damaged.
- [ ] Worn shock absorbers (Chapter 8 or 9).
- [ ] Faulty tyre ("*Weekly checks*").

Electrical system

Note: *For problems associated with the starting system, refer to the faults listed under "Engine" earlier in this Section.*

Battery will not hold a charge for more than a few days

- ☐ Battery defective internally (Chapter 5A).
- ☐ Battery electrolyte level low (Chapter 1).
- ☐ Battery terminal connections loose or corroded ("*Weekly checks*").
- ☐ Auxiliary drivebelt worn or slack (Chapter 1).
- ☐ Alternator or voltage regulator faulty (Chapter 5A).
- ☐ Short-circuit causing continual battery drain (Chapters 5A and 12).

Ignition/no-charge warning light remains illuminated with engine running

- ☐ Auxiliary drivebelt broken, worn, or slack (Chapter 1).
- ☐ Alternator brushes worn, sticking, or dirty (Chapter 5A).
- ☐ Alternator brush springs weak or broken (Chapter 5A).
- ☐ Internal fault in alternator or voltage regulator (Chapter 5A).
- ☐ Broken, disconnected, or loose wiring in charging circuit (Chapter 5A).

Ignition/no-charge warning light fails to come on

- ☐ Warning light bulb blown (Chapter 12).
- ☐ Broken, disconnected, or loose wiring in warning light circuit (Chapter 12).
- ☐ Alternator faulty (Chapter 5A).

Lights inoperative

- ☐ Bulb blown (Chapter 12).
- ☐ Corrosion of bulb or bulbholder contacts (Chapter 12).
- ☐ Blown fuse (Chapter 12).
- ☐ Faulty relay (Chapter 12).
- ☐ Broken, loose, or disconnected wiring (Chapter 12).
- ☐ Faulty switch (Chapter 12).

Instrument readings inaccurate or erratic

Fuel or temperature gauges give no reading

- ☐ Faulty gauge sender unit (Chapters 3 or 4A).
- ☐ Wiring open-circuit (Chapter 12).
- ☐ Faulty gauge (Chapter 12).

Fuel or temperature gauges give continuous maximum reading

- ☐ Faulty gauge sender unit (Chapters 3 or 4A).
- ☐ Wiring short-circuit (Chapter 12).
- ☐ Faulty gauge (Chapter 12).

Horn inoperative, or unsatisfactory in operation

Horn fails to operate

- ☐ Blown fuse (Chapter 12).
- ☐ Connections loose, broken or disconnected (Chapter 12).
- ☐ Faulty horn (Chapter 12).

Horn emits intermittent or unsatisfactory sound

- ☐ Connections loose, broken or disconnected (Chapter 12).
- ☐ Horn mountings loose (Chapter 12).
- ☐ Faulty horn (Chapter 12).

Horn operates all the time

- ☐ Horn push either earthed or stuck down (Chapter 12).
- ☐ Cable connections earthed (Chapter 12).

Windscreen/tailgate wipers inoperative or unsatisfactory in operation

Wipers fail to operate, or operate very slowly

- ☐ Wiper blades stuck to screen, or linkage seized or binding (Chapter 12).
- ☐ Blown fuse (Chapter 12).
- ☐ Cable or cable connections loose, broken or disconnected (Chapter 12).
- ☐ Faulty relay (Chapter 12).
- ☐ Faulty wiper motor (Chapter 12).

Wiper blades sweep over too large or too small an area of the glass

- ☐ Wiper arms incorrectly-positioned or loose on spindles (Chapter 12).
- ☐ Excessive wear of wiper linkage (Chapter 12).
- ☐ Wiper motor or linkage mountings loose or insecure (Chapter 12).

Wiper blades fail to clean the glass effectively

- ☐ Wiper blade rubbers worn or perished ("*Weekly checks*").
- ☐ Wiper arm springs broken, or arm pivots seized (Chapter 12).
- ☐ Insufficient windscreen washer additive ("*Weekly checks*").

Windscreen/tailgate washers inoperative, or unsatisfactory in operation

One or more washer jets inoperative

- ☐ Blocked washer jet.
- ☐ Disconnected, kinked or restricted fluid hose.
- ☐ Insufficient fluid in washer reservoir ("*Weekly checks*").

Washer pump fails to operate

- ☐ Broken or disconnected wiring or connections (Chapter 12).
- ☐ Blown fuse (Chapter 12).
- ☐ Faulty washer switch (Chapter 12).
- ☐ Faulty washer pump (Chapter 12).

Electric windows inoperative, or unsatisfactory in operation

Window glass will only move in one direction

- ☐ Faulty switch (Chapter 12).

Window glass slow to move

- ☐ Regulator seized or damaged, or in need of lubrication (Chapter 11).
- ☐ Door internal components or trim fouling regulator (Chapter 11).
- ☐ Faulty motor (Chapter 11).

Window glass fails to move

- ☐ Incorrectly-adjusted door glass guide channels (Chapter 11).
- ☐ Blown fuse or faulty relay (Chapter 12).
- ☐ Broken or disconnected wiring or connections (Chapter 12).
- ☐ Faulty motor (Chapter 11).

Central locking system inoperative, or unsatisfactory in operation

Complete system failure

- ☐ Blown fuse (Chapter 12).
- ☐ Faulty relay (Chapter 12).
- ☐ Broken or disconnected wiring or connections (Chapter 12).

Latch locks but will not unlock, or unlocks but will not lock

- ☐ Broken or disconnected latch operating rods or levers (Chapter 11).
- ☐ Faulty relay (Chapter 12).

A

ABS (Anti-lock brake system) A system, usually electronically controlled, that senses incipient wheel lockup during braking and relieves hydraulic pressure at wheels that are about to skid.

Air bag An inflatable bag hidden in the steering wheel (driver's side) or the dash or glovebox (passenger side). In a head-on collision, the bags inflate, preventing the driver and front passenger from being thrown forward into the steering wheel or windscreen.

Air cleaner A metal or plastic housing, containing a filter element, which removes dust and dirt from the air being drawn into the engine.

Air filter element The actual filter in an air cleaner system, usually manufactured from pleated paper and requiring renewal at regular intervals.

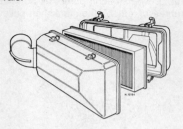

Air filter

Allen key A hexagonal wrench which fits into a recessed hexagonal hole.

Alligator clip A long-nosed spring-loaded metal clip with meshing teeth. Used to make temporary electrical connections.

Alternator A component in the electrical system which converts mechanical energy from a drivebelt into electrical energy to charge the battery and to operate the starting system, ignition system and electrical accessories.

Alternator (exploded view)

Ampere (amp) A unit of measurement for the flow of electric current. One amp is the amount of current produced by one volt acting through a resistance of one ohm.

Anaerobic sealer A substance used to prevent bolts and screws from loosening. Anaerobic means that it does not require oxygen for activation. The Loctite brand is widely used.

Antifreeze A substance (usually ethylene glycol) mixed with water, and added to a vehicle's cooling system, to prevent freezing of the coolant in winter. Antifreeze also contains chemicals to inhibit corrosion and the formation of rust and other deposits that

would tend to clog the radiator and coolant passages and reduce cooling efficiency.

Anti-seize compound A coating that reduces the risk of seizing on fasteners that are subjected to high temperatures, such as exhaust manifold bolts and nuts.

Anti-seize compound

Asbestos A natural fibrous mineral with great heat resistance, commonly used in the composition of brake friction materials. Asbestos is a health hazard and the dust created by brake systems should never be inhaled or ingested.

Axle A shaft on which a wheel revolves, or which revolves with a wheel. Also, a solid beam that connects the two wheels at one end of the vehicle. An axle which also transmits power to the wheels is known as a live axle.

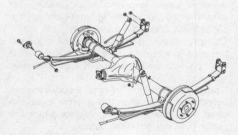

Axle assembly

Axleshaft A single rotating shaft, on either side of the differential, which delivers power from the final drive assembly to the drive wheels. Also called a driveshaft or a halfshaft.

B

Ball bearing An anti-friction bearing consisting of a hardened inner and outer race with hardened steel balls between two races.

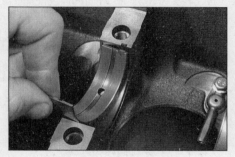

Bearing

Bearing The curved surface on a shaft or in a bore, or the part assembled into either, that permits relative motion between them with minimum wear and friction.

Big-end bearing The bearing in the end of the connecting rod that's attached to the crankshaft.

Bleed nipple A valve on a brake wheel cylinder, caliper or other hydraulic component that is opened to purge the hydraulic system of air. Also called a bleed screw.

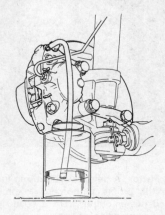

Brake bleeding

Brake bleeding Procedure for removing air from lines of a hydraulic brake system.

Brake disc The component of a disc brake that rotates with the wheels.

Brake drum The component of a drum brake that rotates with the wheels.

Brake linings The friction material which contacts the brake disc or drum to retard the vehicle's speed. The linings are bonded or riveted to the brake pads or shoes.

Brake pads The replaceable friction pads that pinch the brake disc when the brakes are applied. Brake pads consist of a friction material bonded or riveted to a rigid backing plate.

Brake shoe The crescent-shaped carrier to which the brake linings are mounted and which forces the lining against the rotating drum during braking.

Braking systems For more information on braking systems, consult the *Haynes Automotive Brake Manual*.

Breaker bar A long socket wrench handle providing greater leverage.

Bulkhead The insulated partition between the engine and the passenger compartment.

C

Caliper The non-rotating part of a disc-brake assembly that straddles the disc and carries the brake pads. The caliper also contains the hydraulic components that cause the pads to pinch the disc when the brakes are applied. A caliper is also a measuring tool that can be set to measure inside or outside dimensions of an object.

Camshaft A rotating shaft on which a series of cam lobes operate the valve mechanisms. The camshaft may be driven by gears, by sprockets and chain or by sprockets and a belt.

Canister A container in an evaporative emission control system; contains activated charcoal granules to trap vapours from the fuel system.

Canister

Carburettor A device which mixes fuel with air in the proper proportions to provide a desired power output from a spark ignition internal combustion engine.

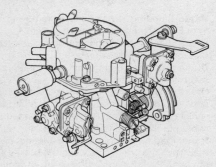

Carburettor

Castellated Resembling the parapets along the top of a castle wall. For example, a castellated balljoint stud nut.

Castellated nut

Castor In wheel alignment, the backward or forward tilt of the steering axis. Castor is positive when the steering axis is inclined rearward at the top.

Catalytic converter A silencer-like device in the exhaust system which converts certain pollutants in the exhaust gases into less harmful substances.

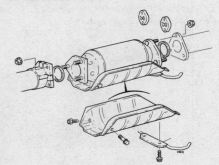

Catalytic converter

Circlip A ring-shaped clip used to prevent endwise movement of cylindrical parts and shafts. An internal circlip is installed in a groove in a housing; an external circlip fits into a groove on the outside of a cylindrical piece such as a shaft.

Clearance The amount of space between two parts. For example, between a piston and a cylinder, between a bearing and a journal, etc.

Coil spring A spiral of elastic steel found in various sizes throughout a vehicle, for example as a springing medium in the suspension and in the valve train.

Compression Reduction in volume, and increase in pressure and temperature, of a gas, caused by squeezing it into a smaller space.

Compression ratio The relationship between cylinder volume when the piston is at top dead centre and cylinder volume when the piston is at bottom dead centre.

Constant velocity (CV) joint A type of universal joint that cancels out vibrations caused by driving power being transmitted through an angle.

Core plug A disc or cup-shaped metal device inserted in a hole in a casting through which core was removed when the casting was formed. Also known as a freeze plug or expansion plug.

Crankcase The lower part of the engine block in which the crankshaft rotates.

Crankshaft The main rotating member, or shaft, running the length of the crankcase, with offset "throws" to which the connecting rods are attached.

Crankshaft assembly

Crocodile clip See Alligator clip

D

Diagnostic code Code numbers obtained by accessing the diagnostic mode of an engine management computer. This code can be used to determine the area in the system where a malfunction may be located.

Disc brake A brake design incorporating a rotating disc onto which brake pads are squeezed. The resulting friction converts the energy of a moving vehicle into heat.

Double-overhead cam (DOHC) An engine that uses two overhead camshafts, usually one for the intake valves and one for the exhaust valves.

Drivebelt(s) The belt(s) used to drive accessories such as the alternator, water pump, power steering pump, air conditioning compressor, etc. off the crankshaft pulley.

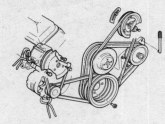

Accessory drivebelts

Driveshaft Any shaft used to transmit motion. Commonly used when referring to the axleshafts on a front wheel drive vehicle.

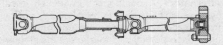

Driveshaft

Drum brake A type of brake using a drum-shaped metal cylinder attached to the inner surface of the wheel. When the brake pedal is pressed, curved brake shoes with friction linings press against the inside of the drum to slow or stop the vehicle.

Drum brake assembly

E

EGR valve A valve used to introduce exhaust gases into the intake air stream.

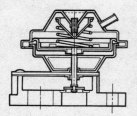

EGR valve

Electronic control unit (ECU) A computer which controls (for instance) ignition and fuel injection systems, or an anti-lock braking system. For more information refer to the *Haynes Automotive Electrical and Electronic Systems Manual*.

Electronic Fuel Injection (EFI) A computer controlled fuel system that distributes fuel through an injector located in each intake port of the engine.

Emergency brake A braking system, independent of the main hydraulic system, that can be used to slow or stop the vehicle if the primary brakes fail, or to hold the vehicle stationary even though the brake pedal isn't depressed. It usually consists of a hand lever that actuates either front or rear brakes mechanically through a series of cables and linkages. Also known as a handbrake or parking brake.

Endfloat The amount of lengthwise movement between two parts. As applied to a crankshaft, the distance that the crankshaft can move forward and back in the cylinder block.

Engine management system (EMS) A computer controlled system which manages the fuel injection and the ignition systems in an integrated fashion.

Exhaust manifold A part with several passages through which exhaust gases leave the engine combustion chambers and enter the exhaust pipe.

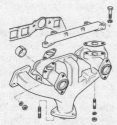

Exhaust manifold

F

Fan clutch A viscous (fluid) drive coupling device which permits variable engine fan speeds in relation to engine speeds.

Feeler blade A thin strip or blade of hardened steel, ground to an exact thickness, used to check or measure clearances between parts.

Feeler blade

Firing order The order in which the engine cylinders fire, or deliver their power strokes, beginning with the number one cylinder.

Flywheel A heavy spinning wheel in which energy is absorbed and stored by means of momentum. On cars, the flywheel is attached to the crankshaft to smooth out firing impulses.

Free play The amount of travel before any action takes place. The "looseness" in a linkage, or an assembly of parts, between the initial application of force and actual movement. For example, the distance the brake pedal moves before the pistons in the master cylinder are actuated.

Fuse An electrical device which protects a circuit against accidental overload. The typical fuse contains a soft piece of metal which is calibrated to melt at a predetermined current flow (expressed as amps) and break the circuit.

Fusible link A circuit protection device consisting of a conductor surrounded by heat-resistant insulation. The conductor is smaller than the wire it protects, so it acts as the weakest link in the circuit. Unlike a blown fuse, a failed fusible link must frequently be cut from the wire for replacement.

G

Gap The distance the spark must travel in jumping from the centre electrode to the side

Adjusting spark plug gap

electrode in a spark plug. Also refers to the spacing between the points in a contact breaker assembly in a conventional points-type ignition, or to the distance between the reluctor or rotor and the pickup coil in an electronic ignition.

Gasket Any thin, soft material - usually cork, cardboard, asbestos or soft metal - installed between two metal surfaces to ensure a good seal. For instance, the cylinder head gasket seals the joint between the block and the cylinder head.

Gasket

Gauge An instrument panel display used to monitor engine conditions. A gauge with a movable pointer on a dial or a fixed scale is an analogue gauge. A gauge with a numerical readout is called a digital gauge.

H

Halfshaft A rotating shaft that transmits power from the final drive unit to a drive wheel, usually when referring to a live rear axle.

Harmonic balancer A device designed to reduce torsion or twisting vibration in the crankshaft. May be incorporated in the crankshaft pulley. Also known as a vibration damper.

Hone An abrasive tool for correcting small irregularities or differences in diameter in an engine cylinder, brake cylinder, etc.

Hydraulic tappet A tappet that utilises hydraulic pressure from the engine's lubrication system to maintain zero clearance (constant contact with both camshaft and valve stem). Automatically adjusts to variation in valve stem length. Hydraulic tappets also reduce valve noise.

I

Ignition timing The moment at which the spark plug fires, usually expressed in the number of crankshaft degrees before the piston reaches the top of its stroke.

Inlet manifold A tube or housing with passages through which flows the air-fuel mixture (carburettor vehicles and vehicles with throttle body injection) or air only (port fuel-injected vehicles) to the port openings in the cylinder head.

J

Jump start Starting the engine of a vehicle with a discharged or weak battery by attaching jump leads from the weak battery to a charged or helper battery.

L

Load Sensing Proportioning Valve (LSPV) A brake hydraulic system control valve that works like a proportioning valve, but also takes into consideration the amount of weight carried by the rear axle.

Locknut A nut used to lock an adjustment nut, or other threaded component, in place. For example, a locknut is employed to keep the adjusting nut on the rocker arm in position.

Lockwasher A form of washer designed to prevent an attaching nut from working loose.

M

MacPherson strut A type of front suspension system devised by Earle MacPherson at Ford of England. In its original form, a simple lateral link with the anti-roll bar creates the lower control arm. A long strut - an integral coil spring and shock absorber - is mounted between the body and the steering knuckle. Many modern so-called MacPherson strut systems use a conventional lower A-arm and don't rely on the anti-roll bar for location.

Multimeter An electrical test instrument with the capability to measure voltage, current and resistance.

N

NOx Oxides of Nitrogen. A common toxic pollutant emitted by petrol and diesel engines at higher temperatures.

O

Ohm The unit of electrical resistance. One volt applied to a resistance of one ohm will produce a current of one amp.

Ohmmeter An instrument for measuring electrical resistance.

O-ring A type of sealing ring made of a special rubber-like material; in use, the O-ring is compressed into a groove to provide the sealing action.

O-ring

Overhead cam (ohc) engine An engine with the camshaft(s) located on top of the cylinder head(s).

Overhead valve (ohv) engine An engine with the valves located in the cylinder head, but with the camshaft located in the engine block.

Oxygen sensor A device installed in the engine exhaust manifold, which senses the oxygen content in the exhaust and converts this information into an electric current. Also called a Lambda sensor.

P

Phillips screw A type of screw head having a cross instead of a slot for a corresponding type of screwdriver.

Plastigage A thin strip of plastic thread, available in different sizes, used for measuring clearances. For example, a strip of Plastigage is laid across a bearing journal. The parts are assembled and dismantled; the width of the crushed strip indicates the clearance between journal and bearing.

Plastigage

Propeller shaft The long hollow tube with universal joints at both ends that carries power from the transmission to the differential on front-engined rear wheel drive vehicles.

Proportioning valve A hydraulic control valve which limits the amount of pressure to the rear brakes during panic stops to prevent wheel lock-up.

R

Rack-and-pinion steering A steering system with a pinion gear on the end of the steering shaft that mates with a rack (think of a geared wheel opened up and laid flat). When the steering wheel is turned, the pinion turns, moving the rack to the left or right. This movement is transmitted through the track rods to the steering arms at the wheels.

Radiator A liquid-to-air heat transfer device designed to reduce the temperature of the coolant in an internal combustion engine cooling system.

Refrigerant Any substance used as a heat transfer agent in an air-conditioning system. R-12 has been the principle refrigerant for many years; recently, however, manufacturers have begun using R-134a, a non-CFC substance that is considered less harmful to the ozone in the upper atmosphere.

Rocker arm A lever arm that rocks on a shaft or pivots on a stud. In an overhead valve engine, the rocker arm converts the upward movement of the pushrod into a downward movement to open a valve.

Rotor In a distributor, the rotating device inside the cap that connects the centre electrode and the outer terminals as it turns, distributing the high voltage from the coil secondary winding to the proper spark plug. Also, that part of an alternator which rotates inside the stator. Also, the rotating assembly of a turbocharger, including the compressor wheel, shaft and turbine wheel.

Runout The amount of wobble (in-and-out movement) of a gear or wheel as it's rotated. The amount a shaft rotates "out-of-true." The out-of-round condition of a rotating part.

S

Sealant A liquid or paste used to prevent leakage at a joint. Sometimes used in conjunction with a gasket.

Sealed beam lamp An older headlight design which integrates the reflector, lens and filaments into a hermetically-sealed one-piece unit. When a filament burns out or the lens cracks, the entire unit is simply replaced.

Serpentine drivebelt A single, long, wide accessory drivebelt that's used on some newer vehicles to drive all the accessories, instead of a series of smaller, shorter belts. Serpentine drivebelts are usually tensioned by an automatic tensioner.

Serpentine drivebelt

Shim Thin spacer, commonly used to adjust the clearance or relative positions between two parts. For example, shims inserted into or under bucket tappets control valve clearances. Clearance is adjusted by changing the thickness of the shim.

Slide hammer A special puller that screws into or hooks onto a component such as a shaft or bearing; a heavy sliding handle on the shaft bottoms against the end of the shaft to knock the component free.

Sprocket A tooth or projection on the periphery of a wheel, shaped to engage with a chain or drivebelt. Commonly used to refer to the sprocket wheel itself.

Starter inhibitor switch On vehicles with an

automatic transmission, a switch that prevents starting if the vehicle is not in Neutral or Park.

Strut See MacPherson strut.

T

Tappet A cylindrical component which transmits motion from the cam to the valve stem, either directly or via a pushrod and rocker arm. Also called a cam follower.

Thermostat A heat-controlled valve that regulates the flow of coolant between the cylinder block and the radiator, so maintaining optimum engine operating temperature. A thermostat is also used in some air cleaners in which the temperature is regulated.

Thrust bearing The bearing in the clutch assembly that is moved in to the release levers by clutch pedal action to disengage the clutch. Also referred to as a release bearing.

Timing belt A toothed belt which drives the camshaft. Serious engine damage may result if it breaks in service.

Timing chain A chain which drives the camshaft.

Toe-in The amount the front wheels are closer together at the front than at the rear. On rear wheel drive vehicles, a slight amount of toe-in is usually specified to keep the front wheels running parallel on the road by offsetting other forces that tend to spread the wheels apart.

Toe-out The amount the front wheels are closer together at the rear than at the front. On front wheel drive vehicles, a slight amount of toe-out is usually specified.

Tools For full information on choosing and using tools, refer to the *Haynes Automotive Tools Manual*.

Tracer A stripe of a second colour applied to a wire insulator to distinguish that wire from another one with the same colour insulator.

Tune-up A process of accurate and careful adjustments and parts replacement to obtain the best possible engine performance.

Turbocharger A centrifugal device, driven by exhaust gases, that pressurises the intake air. Normally used to increase the power output from a given engine displacement, but can also be used primarily to reduce exhaust emissions (as on VW's "Umwelt" Diesel engine).

U

Universal joint or U-joint A double-pivoted connection for transmitting power from a driving to a driven shaft through an angle. A U-joint consists of two Y-shaped yokes and a cross-shaped member called the spider.

V

Valve A device through which the flow of liquid, gas, vacuum, or loose material in bulk may be started, stopped, or regulated by a movable part that opens, shuts, or partially obstructs one or more ports or passageways. A valve is also the movable part of such a device.

Valve clearance The clearance between the valve tip (the end of the valve stem) and the rocker arm or tappet. The valve clearance is measured when the valve is closed.

Vernier caliper A precision measuring instrument that measures inside and outside dimensions. Not quite as accurate as a micrometer, but more convenient.

Viscosity The thickness of a liquid or its resistance to flow.

Volt A unit for expressing electrical "pressure" in a circuit. One volt that will produce a current of one ampere through a resistance of one ohm.

W

Welding Various processes used to join metal items by heating the areas to be joined to a molten state and fusing them together. For more information refer to the *Haynes Automotive Welding Manual*.

Wiring diagram A drawing portraying the components and wires in a vehicle's electrical system, using standardised symbols. For more information refer to the *Haynes Automotive Electrical and Electronic Systems Manual*.

Note: *References throughout this index are in the form - "Chapter number" • "page number"*

Preserving Our Motoring Heritage

< The Model J Duesenberg Derham Tourster. Only eight of these magnificent cars were ever built – this is the only example to be found outside the United States of America

Almost every car you've ever loved, loathed or desired is gathered under one roof at the Haynes Motor Museum. Over 300 immaculately presented cars and motorbikes represent every aspect of our motoring heritage, from elegant reminders of bygone days, such as the superb Model J Duesenberg to curiosities like the bug-eyed BMW Isetta. There are also many old friends and flames. Perhaps you remember the 1959 Ford Popular that you did your courting in? The magnificent 'Red Collection' is a spectacle of classic sports cars including AC, Alfa Romeo, Austin Healey, Ferrari, Lamborghini, Maserati, MG, Riley, Porsche and Triumph.

A Perfect Day Out

Each and every vehicle at the Haynes Motor Museum has played its part in the history and culture of Motoring. Today, they make a wonderful spectacle and a great day out for all the family. Bring the kids, bring Mum and Dad, but above all bring your camera to capture those golden memories for ever. You will also find an impressive array of motoring memorabilia, a comfortable 70 seat video cinema and one of the most extensive transport book shops in Britain. The Pit Stop Cafe serves everything from a cup of tea to wholesome, home-made meals or, if you prefer, you can enjoy the large picnic area nestled in the beautiful rural surroundings of Somerset.

> John Haynes O.B.E., Founder and Chairman of the museum at the wheel of a Haynes Light 12.

< Graham Hill's Lola Cosworth Formula 1 car next to a 1934 Riley Sports.

The Museum is situated on the A359 Yeovil to Frome road at Sparkford, just off the A303 in Somerset. It is about 40 miles south of Bristol, and 25 minutes drive from the M5 intersection at Taunton.
Open 9.30am - 5.30pm (10.00am - 4.00pm Winter) 7 days a week, *except Christmas Day, Boxing Day and New Years Day*
Special rates available for schools, coach parties and outings Charitable Trust No. 292048